Action & Character
according to Aristotle

Kevin L. Flannery, SJ

Action & Character according to Aristotle

The Logic of the Moral Life

The Catholic University of America Press
Washington, D.C.

Copyright © 2013
The Catholic University of America Press
All rights reserved
The paper used in this publication meets the minimum requirements of
American National Standards for Information Science—Permanence
of Paper for Printed Library Materials, ANSI Z39.48-1984.
∞

Library of Congress Cataloging-in-Publication Data
Flannery, Kevin L.
Action and character according to Aristotle : the logic of the moral life /
Kevin L. Flannery, SJ.
    pages cm
Includes bibliographical references and index.
ISBN 978-0-8132-3220-1 (pbk : alk. paper)
1. Aristotle. 2. Ethics. I. Title.
B491.E7F53 2013
171'.3—dc23   2013019468

For my mother

CONTENTS

Introduction ix

1 Logic, Perception, and the Practical Syllogism   1
2 The "Physical" Structure of the Human Act   39
3 Internal Articulation and Force   71
4 The Constituents of Human Action and Ignorance Thereof   110
5 Intelligibility and the Per Se   139
6 Action, Φρόνησις, and Pleasure   173
7 Φρόνησις and the Φρόνιμος   207
8 Some Other Character Types   240
Conclusion   271

APPENDIX 1 On the Text of *Metaph.* ix,6, 1048b18-35   277
APPENDIX 2 *Eudemian Ethics* ii,6-9   280
Bibliography   291
Index of Names   299
Index of Aristotelian Passages Cited   303
Index of Subjects   313

INTRODUCTION

I have tried in this book to get to the bottom of some issues in Aristotle's theory of human action and his philosophical psychology, but my original reason for looking at a good number of these issues in Aristotle was to resolve—or, at least, to shed some light upon—related issues in contemporary ethics and in the interpretation of Thomas Aquinas. It may be useful, therefore, before offering summaries of the arguments of the various chapters, to go briefly into a few (certainly not all) of these background issues so that the reader might understand why some of the more technical discussions that follow are important.

A very general issue has to do with the legitimacy of ethical theory itself, especially when it enters into the kind of detail we find, for instance, in questions six through twenty-one of the *prima secundae* of Aquinas's *Summa theologiae* [ST 1-2.6–21]. Does not Aristotle himself say that we ought not to expect to find in ethics the same sort of precision we find in the harder sciences, such as mathematics? And yet many of the fundamental concepts employed and presented in that section of the *prima secundae* are Aristotelian in origin: the voluntary and the involuntary, the "circumstances" of human acts, intention, the object of the human act—to mention just a few. This seeming inconsistency in Aristotle—and, indeed, in Aquinas, for he appreciates what "the Philosopher" says about ethics' lack of precision but also his close analysis of the structure of human action—is resolvable by attending to the distinction that Aristotle makes in the *Prior analytics* between two levels of discourse: the "perceptual" and the syllogistic; the singular and the universal (syllogistically arranged). As argued in chapter 1, ethical theory has primarily to do with the former: the perceptual or the singular. The entities studied at this level, human acts, resist systematization, and yet they can and ought to be studied in their own right, that is, *as* particular acts. We can identify, for example, the intention with which a person performs an action as distinct from what he does; or we can recognize that seemingly unrelated types of acts (stealing and committing adultery, to use Aristotelian examples) fit together into an intelligible plan of action in a particular instance.

Another background issue has to do with the extent to which the physical might enter into the analysis of a human act (what is sometimes called a "moral act," for which a person might be held responsible). There exist contemporary ethicists, some of them functioning as interpreters of Aquinas, who insist that the physical characteristics of an act can have no bearing upon its moral analysis—that, for instance, the physical structure of the act of crushing a fetus's skull by a medical doctor hoping to save the life of the fetus's mother cannot be taken into consideration when determining whether the doctor's act constitutes the direct killing of an innocent. The present work makes no claims about Aquinas's use of Aristotle in this regard; rather, particularly in chapter 2, its aim is simply to give an account of what Aristotle says in the *Physics* about the structure of (physical) movements. It turns out that, for Aristotle, the analysis of even purely physical movements requires identification of an intelligible structure, irreducible in the final analysis to the physical objects involved in the movement. This involvement of intelligible structure in any movement makes the interface between the physical and the moral quite seamless in Aristotle, since the key to understanding any human act is its intelligible structure (which structure may or may not include reference to physical objects). As a consequence, some of Aristotle's standard examples of physical movements are in fact human acts. Contemporary moralists can make of this what they will, but interpreters of Aquinas will have to deal with the fact that Aquinas wrote a full commentary on the *Physics* in which he appears not at all ill at ease with Aristotle's use of human acts as examples of physical movements.

A third issue is bound up with the interpretation of *Summa theologiae, secunda secundae*, question 64, article 7 [*ST* 2-2.64.7], which is at the core of most every theory of human action that claims a connection with Aquinas. That article, the *locus classicus* for the "principle of double effect," asks whether it is permitted to kill someone in self-defense. Aquinas's answer is complicated. He says that a private person might kill an attacker, provided he does not intend to kill the other in order to defend himself. On the other hand, someone with the proper public authority might legitimately intend to kill a man (although, even in this case, the agent would "refer this to the public good"). Contemporary interpreters of Aquinas have tended to look away from this second part of the argument and toward the first, focusing in upon a remark that Aquinas makes near the beginning of that first part: "Moral acts, however, receive their species according to that which is intended [*intenditur*], not from that which is beside the intention [*praeter intentionem*], since it is per accidens, as is apparent from what was said above." This remark is interpreted as saying that the moral species—indeed, the morality—of an act depends upon what is intended by the agent rather than upon anything else, such as the physical structure of what the agent does.

But this interpretation ignores the back-reference at the end of the sentence: "as is apparent from what was said above." Aquinas is most likely referring to *ST* 2-2.59.2, where he remarks that an act (he is speaking about an act of injustice) "receives its species and name from its per se object and not from its per accidens object"; he goes on immediately to speak of that which is per accidens as "beside the intention [*praeter intentionem*]." (He makes similar remarks at *ST* 2-2.43.3.) So it is apparent that Aquinas's talk in *ST* 2-2.64.7 of that which is intended and that which is beside the intention has as much to do with the identification of types of acts—and giving them names—as it does with the intention of the person who performs an act with that name. His point is not that the moral character of the private self-defender's act comes from what he intends but rather (and simply) that, unlike the public official, he does not intend the death of anyone (that is to say, the attacker) but rather the conservation of his own life: his act is per se an act of self-defense. A person could very well intend to kill and do so morally but only if he has the proper public authority. In this latter case, his act is per se the act of a public official. The moral universe contains a huge variety of such named, per se units of intelligibility.

The per se–per accidens distinction not only enters into the articles mentioned (*ST* 2-2.43.3, 59.2, and 64.7) but absolutely pervades Aquinas's theory of human action. It is important for understanding not only the principle of double effect but the entire theory of which it is a part. The distinction is often misunderstood, however, especially when the expression *per accidens* is coupled with the expression *praeter intentionem*, as in *ST* 2-2.59.2 and 64.7. For all these reasons, it seems like a good idea to study what Aristotle says about the distinction, as is done here especially in chapter 5.

One final word about these background issues (which could easily be added to) and, in particular, about Thomas Aquinas. In writing this book, I have never been concerned with whether my interpretation of Aristotle corresponds to what Aquinas says, for example, in his commentaries on Aristotle or in the *Summa theologiae*. Indeed, I have become aware while working on it that, on certain points (such as the nature of the "circumstances" of human acts), Aquinas's approach and Aristotle's are quite different—although not, I think, utterly incompatible. So, I would hope that the book might be judged as an interpretation of Aristotle and not for anything it might be perceived as saying about Aquinas. Of course, how the book is used is another matter—and I do hope that it might be used by those trying to understand possibly Aristotelian ideas in Thomas Aquinas and in other authors.

I. Chapter Summaries

The movement of this book is roughly from the consideration of singular acts (their nature and their structure) to the consideration of that to which they contribute: ethics itself and the ethical character types, such as the practically wise man (the φρόνιμος) and the incontinent man (the ἀκρατής). Although it has not always been possible—or desirable—to sequester these two considerations one from the other, it can be said that the first four chapters of the book are about the characteristics of human acts considered simply as acts, the remaining four about the ways in which human acts fit into the larger systems known as human lives, which is where the terms 'good' and 'bad' have their primary application. As we shall see, the ethical evaluation of both actions and character types is much bound up with culture. Since this theme pertains not to the analysis of the structure of acts qua acts but is more general, it too is treated primarily in the second half of the book.

In order to enable the reader to perceive the book's structure as it develops, it will be useful at this point to describe in fairly general terms the arguments of the various chapters. (At the beginning of each chapter, I give a more detailed summary of the argument of that chapter.) So then, as already suggested, the basic purpose of chapter 1 ("Logic, Perception, and the Practical Syllogism") is to identify the subject matter of the study that lies before us. What this subject matter is, is, in a sense, obvious: it is individual human acts. It is with these particular entities that the study begins, even if it goes on eventually to consider (among other things) the character types to which they contribute. But there is a mistaken way of understanding human acts that needs to be cleared away in order that this subject matter might come into focus. Since human acts, in order to be human acts, require some degree of deliberation on the part of their agents, a familiar starting point for their consideration has often been the so-called "practical syllogism," which typically describes the means-end path along which a human act is directed. But the term 'syllogism' also calls to mind other terms such as 'premise' and 'conclusion'—if not also the medieval names of syllogistic moods themselves, such as 'Barbara,' 'Celarent,' and 'Darii'—and associating our subject with *these* terms gives the impression that our subject matter is more orderly than it actually is.

The human act has little to do with Aristotle's syllogistic (as presented in the early chapters of the *Prior analytics* [*APr.*]). Genuinely Aristotelian syllogisms—unlike the oft-invoked 'All men are mortal, Socrates is a man, Socrates is a man'—contain no singular terms (such as 'Socrates') but only universal terms ('all men') and particular terms ('some men'), the latter representing subsections of universals but still referring possibly to several individuals. But human acts are singulars. So, my first task is to show that, despite Aristotle's occasional use, when speaking about human acts, of terms that we associate with his syllogistic, the basic subject matter of ethics stands outside the world of the syllogistic—although it is not wholly disconnected from it.

In this regard, I examine first what Aristotle says about the perceptual (understood as the material *from* which a science or other syllogistically organized discipline derives its terms) and its relationship to the syllogistic (understood as the realm of such sciences and organized disciplines themselves). Aristotle sets out the pertinent ideas, among other places, in *APr.*, in connection with a method of proof called ἔκθεσις ("taking out"). This method of proof appears to violate one of Aristotle's basic organizational canons, that a discipline ought not to stray beyond the limits of its proper subject matter—which is, in this case, universal terms. Aristotle argues that, correctly understood, ἔκθεσις does not stray beyond the logical. In the course of defending ἔκθεσις as a logical proof method, he also tells us a good deal about the realm of the perceptual or the strictly practical.

This information in turn gives us guidance as to how the Aristotelian remarks (especially in the *Nicomachean Ethics* [*EN*]) usually associated with the practical syllogism are to be understood. Put briefly, the process or the event that Aristotle depicts in those passages bears little resemblance to what occurs when a person draws a conclusion from premises in a standard syllogism. If it is true that universal terms such as might find their way into an organized discipline play a part in what he says, in those remarks Aristotle is more concerned with the passage *from* that more logical realm *to* the realm of singular human acts. Understanding things in this way, we are able to make better sense of the practical syllogism remarks than does René-Antoine Gauthier (one of the major contemporary commentators on that work).

It needs to be said, however, that, although the realm of the practical is distinct from the realm of the syllogistic, it is not an utterly lawless realm. The major law in force here is the principle of non-contradiction, which (at least as Aristotle understands it) has to do in the first instance with singulars. This principle, as we shall see in subsequent chapters, determines the structure of the entire moral realm: the structure of human acts as heading toward definite objects, for instance, and the structure of the blameless life.

It must also be said that, in a certain sense, the realm of the practical is subject to a sort of science. As we shall see in chapter 7, φρόνησις (the characteristic virtue of the practically wise man or φρόνιμος) is an intellectual virtue and is therefore concerned with universals; but it also has as its subject matter human acts. Only φρόνησις is capable of bringing into proper order this otherwise chaotic and aimless realm of the practical.

Having identified the basic subject matter of ethics as singular human acts, in chapter 2 ("The "physical" structure of the human act") I consider them as movements. This is necessary to do since, as singulars, they might just as well be mere acts of the will, without further articulation. That, however, is not Aristotle's approach, for he recognizes in human acts the type of structure he finds in physical movements. As mentioned above, many of Aristotle's standard examples in the *Physics* [*Phys.*] (whose subject matter is movements) are human acts: walking to Athens, for example, or teaching a student. While certainly never denying that human acts are essentially acts of the will, Aristotle understands willed human acts as having structure that takes their intelligibility—what it is for them to be that which they are—beyond the acts of the will of their agents.

This becomes apparent in a passage in *Phys.* iii where Aristotle asks how many "actualizations" [ἐνέργειαι] there are in an event like teaching. A teacher's act of teaching belongs certainly in some sense to him: *he* teaches; but it also belongs to his student, whose presence is necessary if we are to say that the teacher has taught. Does this mean that there are two actualizations: one in the teacher, the other in the student? But then the two actualizations would be quite separate, and how can we account for the fact that the two—teacher and student—are participants in a single event? So (Aristotle asks rhetorically) maybe there is just one actualization? But that idea bears with it problems as well, for it would entail that in the case before us there is no difference between teaching and learning. Aristotle's solution to this complex of problems is to say that a particular act of teaching and the corresponding experience of learning are indeed two—each has its proper intelligibility—but they are also one, for they are united by a single event, just as the way from Thebes to Athens and the way from Athens to Thebes are different, even while they have in common a particular road—as it happens, Route 3 on the Attic peninsula (as the road is called today). This sounds like a compromise, but actually it is not. Aristotle is identifying units of intelligibility that are really *there*, in particular, the various interlocking lines of intelligibility present in human events such as teaching (or learning).

In pursuit of a deeper understanding of the same ideas and their implications, I also examine in this chapter some other passages in Aristotle. In the last book of *Phys.*, as he is demonstrating the existence of a first unmoved mover, Aristotle discusses the role of types of movement in the organization of the universe itself. The conclusion here—a conclusion that allows him ultimately to conclude that there is a mover that just affects other things and is affected not at all by them—is that the intelligibility of movement depends on there being a whence and a whither for each and every movement. If there were a movement without a proper "finishing spot" (a proper object), the intelligibility of the entire universe would be undermined. This same general theme comes into Aristotle's application, in *Metaphysics* [*Metaph.*] iv,4, of the principle of non-contradiction to practical matters ("Why does a man, who thinks he ought to, walk to Megara and not remain inactive?") and into Aristotle's consideration, in *De anima* [*de An.*] iii,4, of acts, such as seeing and thinking, that are not movements, although they can be understood as structured similarly, with a whence and a whither.

One of the most discussed passages in contemporary Aristotelian studies is found in the back third of *Metaph.* ix,6, where Aristotle draws a distinction between perfect and imperfect actions, that is, between πράξεις properly speaking and κινήσεις (movements). Among the former are seeing and thinking (as in *De an.* iii,4). I discuss this passage since it is clearly relevant to the analysis of human acts as movements but also because the ideas found there will be useful in chapters 5 and 6, where I consider not so much singular human acts as the way in which human acts fit into human lives. My thesis here in chapter 2, however, is just that a perfect action (or πρᾶξις), even though it is quite different from a movement and therefore from the typical human act, encapsulates the intelligibility of human action in a way not done by the typical human act.

Coming into chapter 3 ("Internal articulation and force"), there can remain little room for doubt that, for Aristotle, the general structure of a human act corresponds to that of a physical movement, even when an act itself involves no such movement. But the structure of human acts is even more complicated than this model suggests, since, granted that they always involve the "whence and whither" logical structure of physical movements, this basic unit of intelligibility is overlaid—and sometimes even altered—by many other moral factors. Indeed, the factors are so many that many thinkers, both ancient and modern, have despaired of finding intelligibility anywhere but in the bare act of the will directed toward its object. Aristotle, of course, does not react in this fashion but wades into this sea of factors, never claiming to be able to give a fully scientific account of it all, but also recognizing that it is possible to distinguish one factor from another and so to articulate with precision what a particular person is doing when he performs a particular human act.

In *EN* iii,1, Aristotle identifies two general factors that determine the limits of a man's responsibility for the things he causes: force and ignorance, that is, whether a man has been forced to do that which he does and whether he understands what he does in all its relevant respects. In this third chapter, I examine the first of these general factors. But even just getting to a discussion of this factor entails a good deal of rather labyrinthine taxiing, since presupposed by the remarks on force (and also by those on ignorance) is a theory about the internal articulation of actions, such as allows it to be the case that an action might be forced or beyond an agent's awareness in certain respects but not in others. This theory is found not in the *Nicomachean Ethics* but in some very difficult and debated chapters—chapters 6 through 9—in the second book of the *Eudemian Ethics* [*EE*]. So, the first four sections of my third chapter are an exposition of the argumentation of these chapters, showing that they are meant primarily to distinguish the voluntariness of a human act itself from the voluntariness (or involuntariness) attaching to its particular aspects.

The main difficulty in interpreting *EE* ii, 6–9 is determining why Aristotle says many of the things he says there. The first section of the argument (*EE* ii,6) contains remarks about the relationship between mathematical principles and their consequences, making the point that, when the principles alter, so also do the consequences. Aristotle clearly wants to connect this phenomenon with the relationship between a man and his acts, but it is not immediately apparent what that connection might be, for the realm of human action is contingent, that of mathematics necessary. In the next section of *EE* ii (basically, *EE* ii,7), Aristotle puts together a sort of demonstration by elimination, by means of which he intends to arrive at a definition of the voluntary. He says that the defining characteristic must be one of just three things: 'that which is according to appetite,' 'that which is according to choice,' and 'that which is according to thought.' He then proceeds to eliminate the first two candidates by means of a painstaking consideration of a series of sophistic arguments having to do with the continent man (the ἐγκρατής) and the incontinent man (the ἀκρατής) and with virtue and vice. He identifies a number of contradictions in these arguments, contradictions which apparently lead him to opt in the end (that is, at the beginning of *EE* ii,9) for the third candidate, 'that which is according to thought.'

But before actually announcing this result, another even more elaborate argument intervenes (comprising most of *EE* ii,8), having to do with force and, at least initially, with its bearing upon ethical types such as experience internal conflict between reason and appetite. An example of such a type would be the incontinent man. In this argument, Aristotle offers an explanation of why some thinkers tend toward a simplistic understanding of force, declaring a whole act forced the second they see in it some forced aspect. The problem, says Aristotle, is that such thinkers are assimilating the type of force that affects human acts to the force that affects both inanimate things and animals without reason. He then changes tack, moving away from conflicted character types (such as the incontinent man), considering now individuals in whom there is no such psychological conflict. In this context, he discusses the particular actions of people who are, for instance, forced to perform disgraceful acts in order to save the lives of family members. The thing that is puzzling in all of this is that the arguments presented here in *EE* ii,8, especially before the change of tack, are apparently intended to resolve the contradictions identified in *EE* ii,7. They seem also to do this successfully, and yet *EE* ii,9 begins, as already mentioned, by stating that, since the first two candidates as defining characteristic of the voluntary have been *eliminated*, that leaves only the third. The reader is left wondering why Aristotle went to the effort of resolving the problems inherent in the candidates that he would eventually just eliminate.

I argue in this chapter that Aristotle engages in this very convoluted argumentation because he is interested ultimately in showing that, although individual actions must be regarded as themselves voluntary, once this is established, there is still philosophical work to do. In the interest of giving a full analysis of the human act, it is important to recognize that individual acts are articulated—have an internal structure—and that this articulation is dependent upon such factors as force. The sophistic puzzles presented in *EE* ii,7 (that is, the arguments that finish in contradictions) serve to identify factors that have a bearing upon the action of certain conflicted character types considered as such; but, once Aristotle changes tack in *EE* ii,8 in order to discuss characters in whom there is no conflict between reason and appetite, all of his attention is upon the internal articulation of individual acts. Also part of this strategy are the remarks in *EE* ii,6 drawing a parallel between mathematical principles and man as principle of his own acts. Aristotle recognizes that man is free to do what he wills (his actions are "up to him"), but the necessary connection between his acts of will (involving as they do both appetite and reason) and the human acts he performs entails that those acts be as internally articulated as their principles (the corresponding acts of will).

In chapter 4 ("The Constituents of Human Action and Ignorance Thereof"), I discuss the second general factor determining the limits of a man's responsibility for the things he causes: ignorance of an act's "circumstances"—which are the members of a list, given in *EN* iii,1, that includes such things as 'what instrument the agent is using' and 'what the agent is doing.' Mention of this latter ('what the agent is doing') strongly suggests that the traditional term 'circumstance' might not be the best for referring to members of the list. The term—which does not appear in Aristotle's account—obscures the idea that the things to which it refers are essential components of acts: they in no way "stand around" (*circum-stant*) the acts themselves. In this chapter, I argue for calling members of the list not 'circumstances' but 'constituents.' Accordingly, from now on in this Introduction, I will refer to members of the list as 'constituents.'

Although the constituents are definitely positive aspects of an act, it is easier to grasp their positive contribution by considering an agent's occasional ignorance of them. We grasp, for instance, what it means to say that knowing the instrument is a constituent of one's action the moment it is explained that not knowing that a cup contains poison changes the moral significance of giving the cup to another. But it is important to bear in mind that the constituents are essentially things of which an agent *is* aware. If an agent is unaware of a constituent, provided this ignorance is not culpable ignorance, that aspect of his act is excluded from it as far as ethics is concerned. But this is just to say that that aspect is excluded from the human act as such, since human acts contain only things for which one is responsible. So, the constituents are essentially positive things—more easily identified, however, by speaking of their shadow counterparts.

Although *EN* iii,1 contains the fullest list and, in certain respects, the most complete account of the constituents, the parallel passage in *EE* ii,9 brings out some points left (at best) implicit in *EN* iii,1. I have already alluded to one of these points. In *EE* ii,9 Aristotle discusses with more precision and completeness than elsewhere the types of ignorance that might make an act—or an aspect of an act—involuntary. I examine this issue in this fourth chapter, showing that Aristotle recognizes that exonerating ignorance includes more than just ignorance of constituents, for it includes also ignorance of the moral law, provided that such ignorance is not due to negligence.

This understanding is connected, indeed, with the argument of chapter 3 (of the present work), since the crucial question is always, what has truly caused the act to have the internal characteristics it has (or has not)? If the cause is ultimately the will of the agent, as in the case of negligence, then the ignorance is not exonerating; if, on the other hand, the cause is not the will of the agent, then the ignorance is exonerating. We see here again (as in chapter 3) the necessary connection between the agent's will and the internal structure of the human act he performs, a connection not unlike that between a mathematical principle and its consequences, although having to do with the agent's free engagement in the contingent world of actions that may or may not have their desired effects.

In this fourth chapter, I examine the individual constituents in considerable detail—including textual detail, for the manuscript tradition behind certain remarks about the constituents is in disarray. A summary of this detailed argument can be found at the beginning of that chapter. But here, with a view again to showing why it is important to consider such matters, a brief word about how Aquinas understands the constituents (which he does call 'circumstances') might be in order. Although hampered by both bad Latin translations and a tradition of dodgy interpretation, Aquinas develops what Aristotle says about the constituent in important and insightful ways. To make use of a constituent that appears in no Aristotelian list but is employed by Aquinas—"the where": whether a man steals an object from one place rather than another usually has no bearing upon the moral character of what he does. But it does make a difference to the very nature of his act whether he steals a golden cup from a private home or rather from a temple: the difference is the difference between stealing and sacrilege (or stealing with sacrilege). Aquinas's remarks about such matters bring into relief the strange character of human acts, whose natures can change radically, depending on factors that within other intelligible contexts might be quite peripheral. Because of the importance of such factors in Aquinas and in action theory quite generally, it seems worth our while trying to pin down what Aristotle's constituents are and how he understands them.

With chapter 5 ("Intelligibility and the per se"), whose beginning marks the midpoint of the book, our discourse begins to turn more ethical in the strict sense. Previous chapters have been about the nature and structure of human acts and about the factors that shape them internally. Such factors are important for an act's moral evaluation, but the fact that human acts have such features does not yet tell us how acts are to be evaluated morally. The moral evaluation of an act depends rather upon whether it, in all its constituents, is in accordance with right reason; that is to say, it depends upon whether it heads toward the true good for man.

Key here is the per se–per accidens distinction. As noted above, the Aristotelian way of employing this distinction is not always understood by contemporary authors. They tend to assume that he uses the expressions 'per se' and 'per accidens' to refer always to the same types of relationships, much as standard referring terms refer always to the same types of things. In fact, however, for Aristotle, the per se–per accidens distinction is a tool he uses in order to point to relationships of *various* types. His use of the expression 'per se,' for example, indicates only that he sees *some* type of intelligible relationship between two or more things. It may be a type of relationship which, in another context or with respect to something else, he declares to be lacking in intelligibility (and to be, therefore, per accidens). Aristotle's investigative procedure in any discipline involves searching out pieces of intelligibility. This invariably means distinguishing them from things that do not have intelligibility—at least, of the type just previously identified. This all allows him to treat in a (roughly) scientific manner even ethics, without any pretensions to be constructing a system in which all the elements are related to one another in the compact and necessary manner of wholly apodeictic sciences such as mathematics.

In this chapter, I run through Aristotle's most explicit treatment of the per se (or the καθ' αὐτό) near the beginning of the *Posterior analytics* [*APo.*]. Two important ideas emerge from these remarks: first, that, although *APo.* is about the sciences and therefore deals primarily with theoretical reason, several of the examples that Aristotle employs in this exposition of the per se belong to the practical sphere; secondly, that the per se has to do with lines of intelligibility. The latter becomes evident in Aristotle's use, when speaking of the per se, of linguistically related terms. He speaks, for instance of a "sacrificed thing" dying due to its "being sacrificed." Although not all per se relationships involve such explicit linguistic indications of the intelligible affinity of their *relata*, the per se is always about intelligible affinity of some sort, that is, about lines of intelligibility.

In *EN* v,8, Aristotle says that a constituent is a constituent per se only if the agent is not ignorant of its being a constituent of his own act; otherwise it is a constituent per accidens. This entails that a per se "constituent" of a physical act might not be a per se constituent of the corresponding human act—when, that is, the agent does not know *what* he is doing even though what he does is perfectly intelligible in itself. There is nothing incoherent about this: in either case (the purely physical act or the human act), there is present a line of intelligibility; in ethics, however, we are primarily (although not solely) interested in lines of intelligibility that issue from the will and pertain ultimately to the human good.

Aristotle also says that a man might commit an immoral act with full knowledge of its relevant constituents (so that they would be per se constituents) and yet not be per se the type of person who commits such acts: he may have truly committed parricide but not *be* in the fullest sense a parricide. The full intelligibility (so to speak) of being a parricide would be found only in the person who is wholly given over to killing a parent: he would be a parricide per se. Obviously, this use of the expression 'per se' is quite different from Aristotle's use of the same expression with respect to the constituents of human acts. Failure to appreciate this difference can make certain passages in Aristotle—and also in other authors who take over his technical language—extremely difficult to comprehend.

A related issue has to do with "the end" (one of the constituents). As suggested in chapter 4, this constituent (like all the others) has two faces: the end of the action that in fact comes about and the end that the agent has in mind. The latter is the end per se of the human act. But the action as given species by the end in this second (per se) sense might harbor within itself the per accidens in various ways. There may, for example, be segments of the larger action that are per accidens related to other aspects of the action, as a song and dance routine might be related only per accidens to committing murder, even if the routine is a necessary step in the plot to be rid of the murder victim. Such combinations of the per se and the per accidens are possible because ethics is not obliged, as are the sciences, to eliminate the per accidens (understood as opposed to the per se in the strictly scientific sense).

We find yet another use of the per se–per accidens distinction in a difficult passage in *EN* vii,9, where Aristotle discusses (among other things) the "anomalous ἀκρατής" or the man who, out of weakness, does what he thinks he ought not to do although, because he believes incorrectly that the right thing to do is the wrong thing to do, in doing what he thinks he ought not to do, he in fact does the right thing. Aristotle says that such a man does in fact seek the true good for man per se, even if he does not know what the true good is. This position strikes one as inconsistent with other passages in Aristotle, until one realizes that, when he speaks of the per se in this context, he has in mind the intelligibility of human nature and not the intelligibility of a human act. In other words, in this context he is saying that the *nature* of the anomalous ἀκρατής pursues per se the true good for man. None of this should be interpreted, however, as denying that behaving ethically is indeed a matter of bringing one's actions into line with the true good. The morally upright agent seeks not a merely apparent good but the true good and strives to bring the acts he performs per se into line with the true good.

When speaking of seeking the true good, Aristotle often uses the language of archery: virtuous behavior is a matter of taking aim at and hitting the mean between extremes. Since aiming in archery is always of matter of counterbalancing forces, it involves necessarily a certain imprecision. In *EN* ix,2, Aristotle mentions a number of moral situations in which such aiming, such weighing of factors, is required: a man may need to decide, for instance, whether to ransom his father or rather the person who has ransomed him (the man deciding) in times past. It is impossible to establish fixed rules regarding such situations—although, even here, the practically wise man follows (or pursues) lines of intelligibility. Archery is not about shots in the dark. It must also be acknowledged, however, that, although practical wisdom is very often a tentative enterprise, deciding how to act in some situations is quite straightforward. There are certain actions, says Aristotle in *EN* ii,6—adultery, theft, and murder, for example—that one ought never to perform, since they are per se disordered. This too is part of the intelligibility of the practical realm.

In chapter 6 ("Action, Φρόνησις, and Pleasure"), our perspective continues to open up, that is, to become more general and more ethical. Conceiving acts as aimings opened things up to some extent, especially regarding ends, for an individual agent's posited overall end must be related somehow to the true good for man. But ethics has to do not just with how well a man aims but also with the context within which he takes aim. This more general consideration (context) enters into Aristotle's theory by way of the knowledge that an agent has of what he is bringing about as he brings it about.

In *Metaph.* ix,6 Aristotle insists on the distinction between πράξεις (actions, properly speaking) and κινήσεις (movements). As always, the issue is intelligibility. The intelligibility of a movement, qua movement, comes only at its end: the process of building, for instance, gets its sense from the house that comes at its end. But knowledge that one is building a house and knowledge of how one builds a house are present throughout the process. This is the difference between human "makings" [ποιήσεις] and those of a mere (non-rational) animal. Even if at the end of the latter we find a "house" (a nest, for instance), the making itself is not informed by knowledge of the sort involved in the craft of building. Even human makings, therefore, which are a type of movement, can involve the type of intelligibility that is present throughout the process. This is what allows it to be the case that the individual acts of (for instance) builders hold together as a craft and that the city (the πόλις) holds together as a city. The φρόνιμος, the man who possesses the intellectual virtue of φρόνησις, is especially concerned with this latter knowledge—that is to say, with the practical knowledge of how a city holds together.

One might ask where within a making the intelligibility, of which a human agent might have knowledge, resides. Remarks in *Phys.* viii,5 and *Metaph.* ix,8 suggest that its place is in the first non-extended point from which self-movement emerges. In *De an.* ii,5, Aristotle speaks also of how, within that extensionless point, we can identify a bi-polar structure, although not one that involves (as in a movement) a passing from one point to another. These various ideas are useful in once again connecting Aristotle's analysis of human action to his analysis of movement in the *Physics*, but they are yet more useful for understanding Aristotle's analysis of character types.

Later in the chapter, I argue that, although in his analysis of human action Aristotle refers repeatedly to crafts (which give intelligibility to makings), it would be a mistake to conceive of φρόνησις, the intellectual virtue that presides over the practical realm, as a craft. But, again, recalling *Metaph.* ix,6, this ought not to be understood as a complete sequestering of φρόνησις from makings. Φρόνησις is about human acts, which includes the things done by craftsmen. This approach gives us insight into how a general conception of what constitutes good conduct might give unity to a multitude of human acts—and a multitude of types of human acts.

Chapter 6 finishes with some remarks on pleasure, as it relates to the φρόνιμος but also to ethical types whose lives are less orderly, such as the ἀκρατής and the ἀκόλαστος: the weak-willed and the wholly depraved man. Although, as Aristotle says in *De an.* ii,5, knowledge (including the general practical knowledge of φρόνησις) depends on the agent who thinks "when he wills to," falling away from virtue is not simply a matter of choosing to follow an alternative idea. It is rather a corruption: a relatively permanent state, like sickness or even death. It occurs when pleasure becomes detached from the human practice to which it is proper and is pursued for its own sake. When this occurs, a person's behavior becomes irrational, lacking in intelligibility; he is without the φρόνιμος's calm overview of what is per se best for man. This is not to say, however, that Aristotle regards pleasure as a bad thing. He follows rather the approach set out by Plato in the *Philebus*, according to which the calm pleasures—which inform the practices that are naturally and therefore rationally pursued by men—are good and positive. Pleasures turn bad and ultimately unpleasant when they pull away from such practices.

Chapter 7 ("Φρόνησις and the φρόνιμος") continues the previous chapter's discourse on φρόνησις and the φρόνιμος. To hark back to the analysis of chapter 5, the argument here is that Aristotle's φρόνιμος, an ideal character type, pursues the good per se: he is given over (so to speak) heart and soul to the pursuit of the practical good. In expounding this idea, the chapter makes use primarily of Plato's *Hippias minor* [*Hp. Mi.*], of remarks about *Hp. Mi.* in *Metaph.* v,29, and of *EE* viii,1.

Hippias Minor is an unusual Platonic dialogue in so far as its major character, Socrates, defends a thesis that most people would regard as non- or even anti-Platonic: that there is no difference between the upright man (represented by Achilles) and the deceitful man (represented by Odysseus). This does not, however, constitute an insuperable interpretative difficulty, since Socrates's argument is easily understood as ironical. It would seem, then, that Plato's own position is that a character type inclined (voluntarily) toward any sort of evil has nothing at all in common with the character type inclined toward the corresponding good—at least if one's attention is focused upon the intelligibility of such character types (as it should be in philosophical analysis). This is also Aristotle's position in *Metaph.* v,29: the φρόνιμος is infallibly φρόνιμος; the false man is similarly—but in the opposite direction—committed to that which is false.

In *EE* viii,1, Aristotle contrasts (as it seems at first, rather strangely) such practices as using one's eye in an abnormal way, by pressing down on it in order to see double, with using—or claiming to use—φρόνησις abnormally in order to be φρόνιμος. Aristotle holds that φρόνησις cannot be so used, although other capacities can be. A grammarian who deliberately employs the wrong case in order to see whether his students catch the mistake is in effect demonstrating his knowledge of grammar; a φρόνιμος, however, does not demonstrate his φρόνησις by committing unjust acts. The reason for this, argues Aristotle, is that practices such as deliberately seeing double or deliberately committing solecisms involve "contortion": working *against* a positive capacity in order to display—and remain within—the same capacity. Such a thing cannot be done with φρόνησις, since what would have to be contorted is the soul (and character) of the agent himself—and the φρόνιμος is defined (in a non-nominal way) as one whose whole soul heads toward the good and the just in an unequivocal way. This is the lesson to be learned from *Hippias minor*; it is also a criticism of the historical Socrates, who held that φρόνησις is a type of science.

A second passage in the *Eudemian Ethics* where Aristotle speaks of contortion is also useful in this regard. In *EE* ii,10, Aristotle does not suppose that someone might use the concept of contortion in order to excuse or account for unjust acts; his point is rather that deliberately pursuing the merely apparent good is a contortion of human nature itself—and, therefore, not good. Just as a doctor cannot demonstrate that he is a good doctor by damaging the very health of his patient, for that would be to go against the defining good of medicine itself, so an agent cannot deliberately pursue an apparent good without going against human nature, defined as it is by reference to the genuine good for man.

By acting in accordance with φρόνησις, the φρόνιμος pursues the true good for man. As Aristotle suggests in *Metaph.* v,29, this means that the φρόνιμος tells the truth (the practical truth). And, as is made clear in *EN* vi, this truthfulness has as its object not private concerns—or, at least, not those alone—but primarily the concerns of the city and of ethical behavior in general. This emphasis on truth does not mean that, if the φρόνιμος deliberates on behalf of the larger group and that which he counsels turns out badly (to be, that is, not *truly* to the benefit of the group), he is not φρόνιμος. The φρόνιμος's truthfulness will prevent him from promoting or effecting actions that go contrary to the basic principles of ethics themselves—for this would be to imply that those principles are not true—but he can also be said to be an honest and truthful man when his (by definition) wise counsels go awry, for his truthfulness has to do with his character rather than with what occurs in spite of his reasoned and reasonable decisions.

The main character type discussed so far in the second half of the book (especially in chapters 6 and 7) is the φρόνιμος, although other character types that fall short of embodying φρόνησις have also made the occasional appearance. In chapter 8 ("Some other character-types"), the last of the book, I consider these latter characters more deliberately. The two major types are the ἀκρατής and the ἀκόλαστος (as identified above, the weak-willed and the wholly depraved man). The vehicle used to expound especially the former is a passage in *EE* vii,6 where Aristotle exploits a device employed by certain sophists of his day; according to this device, aspects of a person are referred to as if they were persons themselves. Coriscus in the agora, for instance, would be different from musical Coriscus; there would, therefore, be no musical man named Coriscus in the agora. Such puzzles or riddles certainly appeared to Aristotle as ridiculous as they appear to us today; but he finds useful the idea of dividing a moral character, especially a less than upright moral character, into aspects—or the soul of a man with such a character into "parts."

This interpretation makes use of the concept of "quantities," as understood and explained by Aristotle in the *Categories* and in the fifth book of the *Metaphysics*. His remarks in *EE* vii,6 about the non-φρόνιμοι—and especially about the minor character types—are very brief, so we do not learn a great deal about them; but we do learn at least that they must be regarded as harboring within their souls—or perhaps we might say 'in their personal histories'—characteristics arising from actions that the principle of non-contradiction (as it operates in the practical realm) does not allow to exist comfortably together. They are, in short, conflicted personalities.

One issue that arises in the course of expounding *EE* vii,6 is how Aristotle would explain the fact that some such conflicted types occasionally commit suicide. This is a problem for him since, although recognizing that they are conflicted, he also recognizes that there is a core "unit" in each which considers itself good and is therefore an object of desire to itself (and not, therefore, as something to be destroyed). I offer a solution to this problem which involves a comparison between *EE* vii,6 and the closely parallel fourth chapter of *EN* ix. This analysis also provides further insight into how the principle of non-contradiction bears upon character types.

Toward the end of this chapter, I consider the ἀκόλαστος, making use of some ideas put forward by Elizabeth Anscombe. The main issue here is the nature of his προαίρεσις (often translated 'choice') and whether the ἀκόλαστος, having committed himself to the pursuit of "the present pleasure," actually believes that the life he pursues is a morally upright life. Anscombe describes him as saying in effect, "a fig for moral virtue," and this interpretation seems to me to be the correct one. I also discuss some other character types who might seem to be related to the ἀκόλαστος; they are really, however, quite different from him because they do not make the same evil προαίρεσις.

II. Texts, Conventions, and Acknowledgments

For the Greek text of the works of Aristotle I generally use the Oxford Classical Texts, when available,[1] although for the *Eudemian Ethics* I prefer the Susemihl edition,[2] and for the *Nicomachean Ethics* I often prefer the Susemihl-Apelt edition.[3] For *De motu animalium*, I use Nussbaum; for the *Magna moralia*, I use Susemihl.[4]

For translations from Aristotle, I sometimes make use of the *Revised Oxford Translation*, occasionally altering it without (at that point) notifying the reader.[5] Usually, however, I give my own translations. For translations of Plato, I have made use of Cooper,[6] but, again, usually the transla-

---

[1] For the *Metaphysics*, I generally use the text in W. D. Ross, *Aristotle's* Metaphysics: *A revised text with introduction and commentary*, 2d ed. (Oxford: Clarendon, 1953). When following Jaeger [Werner Jaeger, ed., *Aristotelis Metaphysica*, Oxford Classical Texts (Oxford: Clarendon, 1957)], I have indicated this.

[2] Franciscus Susemihl, ed., *Aristotelis Ethica Eudemia (Eudemi Rhodii Ethica)* (Teubner: Leipzig, 1884); the OCT (which is occasionally better than Susemihl) is R. R. Walzer and J. M. Mingay, *Aristotelis: Ethica Eudemia*, Oxford Classical Texts (Oxford: Clarendon, 1991).

[3] Franciscus Susemihl and Otto Apelt, eds., *Aristotelis Ethica Nicomachea* (Teubner: Leipzig, 1912). The standard alternative is Ingram Bywater, ed., *Aristotelis Ethica Nicomachea*, Oxford Classical Texts (Oxford: Clarendon, 1894).

[4] Martha Nussbaum, *Aristotle's* De motu animalium (Princeton: Princeton UP, 1978); Franciscus Susemihl, ed., *Aristotelis quae feruntur Magna moralia* (Teubner: Leipzig, 1883).

[5] Jonathan Barnes, ed., *The Complete Works of Aristotle: The Revised Oxford Translation* (Princeton: Princeton UP, 1984); for translations of *APo.*, however, I have made use of Barnes's revised translation [Jonathan Barnes, translator & commentator, *Aristotle:* Posterior Analytics, Oxford Aristotle Series (Oxford: Clarendon, 1994)].

[6] John M. Cooper, ed. *Plato: Complete Works* (Indianapolis/Cambridge: Hackett, 1997).

tions are my own. My own translations are frequently very literal; often I use terms that are traditional and technical. In chapter 6, for example, I translate πάσχειν as 'suffering,' that is 'being passive with respect to something active.' My reason: I am writing for scholars and the traditional language often allows one to reproduce more easily the word-order and precise sense of the Greek.

In citing Plato and Aristotle and other ancient authors, I use the table of abbreviations found in the front matter of any edition of the Liddell-Scott-Jones *Greek-English Lexicon*. The works of "other ancient authors" cited are primarily commentaries on the works of Aristotle. The standard abbreviation for these is *in* plus the Liddell-Scott-Jones abbreviation for the Aristotelian work. Thus, a commentary on the *Prior Analytics* is abbreviated *in APr*. In referring to chapters in the *Nicomachean Ethics*, I employ the primary scheme of chapter division in Bywater's edition: that is, the chapters as identified with Arabic numerals at the top of a page and with Roman numerals in the center column between two bodies of text. In the Susemihl-Apelt edition, these chapter divisions are marked just with Roman numerals. The scheme I follow is the scheme followed by the Revised Oxford Translation but not, for instance, by Gauthier and Jolif.[7] In some editions and translations, the last three chapters of the *Eudemian Ethics* are referred to as vii,13–15; in others, as viii,1–3—in the Susemihl edition, for example. I follow the latter in recognizing an eighth book.

I adopt the convention, now common in philosophical circles, of reserving double inverted commas ("...") for genuine quotations and things to which I wish to call attention as surprising or non-standard—that is, as scare quotes. I use single inverted commas ('...') for all other appropriate uses, such as for the mention of a term or a concept or for quotations within quotations.

When I speak of chapters and sections (e.g., "chapter 4, sections II to V") without further specification, the reference is always to chapters and sections of the present book.

In order to keep italic text to a minimum, quotations in foreign languages but written in the Latin alphabet appear in double inverted com-

---

[7] René-Antoine Gauthier and Jean Yves Jolif, *L'Éthique à Nicomaque: Introduction, traduction et commentaire* (Louvain-la-neuve: Éditions Peeters, 2002²).

mas. When I (as opposed to another) employ a foreign word or phrase written in the Latin alphabet or when I am discussing such particular foreign words or phrases or when I interject the latter into a larger quotation translated into English, I do use italics. Some Latin expressions commonly used in English and frequently used in this book (such as 'per se' and 'per accidens'), I do not put in italics.

Since this book contains much Greek script and since it would be distracting to be switching back and forth between Greek characters and transliterated Greek, I do not employ the latter. Also, in order to avoid terminological difficulties attaching to the standard English translations, I frequently use Greek terms. Examples of this would be the words φρόνησις, φρόνιμος, ἀκρατής, and ἀκόλαστος. When doing this, I employ the nominative form as if it were an English (non-inflected) substantive.

For the most part, the material in this book has not been published before. Significant portions of chapter 2 appeared in the English edition of *Nova et Vetera*,[8] but the argument that appeared there has been altered in important ways—thanks largely to a remark made by my friend and constant philosophical interlocutor, Stephen Brock. Chapter 3 contains sections of a paper that appeared in the *Proceedings of the Boston Area Colloquium in Ancient Philosophy* and owes much to Michael Pakaluk, who as director of BACAP was my host when I spoke at Clark University; his remarks on that occasion helped me to understand more clearly some of the issues raised in my paper.[9] Chapter 7 contains bits and pieces of an essay to be published in a volume containing a number of papers on practical reason that were given by various scholars in the Fall of 2003 at the Catholic University of America;[10] chapter 8 contains bits and pieces of an essay on Elizabeth Anscombe published in *Christian Bioethics*.[11]

I have many people and institutions to thank. I thank the Notre Dame

---

[8] Kevin L. Flannery, "Aristotle and Human Movements," *Nova et Vetera* 6 (2008): 113–38.

[9] Kevin L. Flannery, "Force and Compulsion in Aristotle's Ethics," in *Proceedings of the Boston Area Colloquium in Ancient Philosophy*, ed. John Cleary and Gary Gurtler, vol. 22 (2006) (Leiden: E. J. Brill, 2007), 41–60. A predecessor of *this* paper is Kevin L. Flannery, "Ethical Force in Aristotle," *Vera Lex* 6 (2005): 147–62.

[10] Kevin L. Flannery, "Aristotle's Infallible Φρόνιμος," in *Studies in Practical Reason*, ed. Bradley Lewis (Washington, D.C.: The Catholic University of America Press, forthcoming).

[11] Kevin L. Flannery, "Anscombe and Aristotle on Corrupt Minds," *Christian Bioethics* 14 (2008): 151–64.

Center for Ethics and Culture, where I was the Mary Ann Remick Senior Visiting Fellow for the academic year 2006–2007 and where I did the bulk of the research that has gone into this book. I also thank the Institute for the Psychological Sciences, which appointed me Senior Fellow at the IPS Centre for Philosophical Psychology (Oxford) for Trinity Term, 2007. I thank the Pontifical Gregorian University and the Faculty of Philosophy here for granting me a leave in order to take up the fellowships at Notre Dame and Oxford. I thank the Detroit Province of the Society of Jesus for its generous support. I thank John O'Callaghan, Michael Pakaluk, Pavlos Kontos, David Solomon, Ralph McInerny (*requiescat in pace*), Alasdair MacIntyre, Stephen Brock, Jonathan Barnes (who taught me about ancient texts), David Charles, Daniel McInerny, Paul Mankowski, William and Elizabeth Kirk, Joy Lynn, Matthew Levering, Raymond Hain, Sean Walsh, Karen Chan, Kurt Pritzl (*requiescat in pace*), Susan Needham, David McGonagle, James Kruggel, Elizabeth Benevides, Trevor Lipscombe, Theresa Walker, Brian Roach, Terence Irwin, Christopher Shields, Ursula Coope, Leslie Brown, Richard Sorabji, Alfonso Gómez-Lobo (*requiescat in pace*), Richard Finn, Robert George, Thomas Berg, and the White Russians (where not already named). Finally, I thank the Fathers and Brothers of the Congregation of Holy Cross at Corby Hall and especially Brother Frank Gorch for their friendship and hospitality during my time at Notre Dame.

Action & Character
according to Aristotle

One

Logic, Perception, and the Practical Syllogism

ARISTOTLE TELLS US any number of times that ethics does not admit of the methods of analysis proper to the sciences.[1] This is largely due to the fact that the character of one's moral acts depends directly upon how one understands what one is doing. Since one's understanding of what one is doing depends in turn upon the particular circumstances in which one acts—which accept of infinite variety and can, indeed, alter in a trice—there is an inherent unpredictability or fluidity in the very subject matter of ethics which excludes it from science. And yet there are passages in Aristotle where he appears to speak of human (moral) acts in the language proper to his syllogistic, which would make them at least candidates for inclusion in a science. The passages where he speaks of human action in such terms are often associated with the so-called "practical syllogism."[2] I argue in this first chapter that these passages are not about syllogisms of the type set out in the syllogistic. They are about the relationship be-

---

[1] See, for instance, *EN* i,3, 1094b11–27; i,4, 1095a30–b3; i,7, 1098a26–b8; ii,2, 1103b34–1104a10, and ii,9, 1109b20–26.

[2] Kevin L. Flannery, *Acts Amid Precepts: The Aristotelian Logical Structure of Thomas Aquinas's Moral Theory* (Washington, DC / Edinburgh: The Catholic University of America Press / T & T Clark, 2001), 8–12.

tween universals, which are the staple of the scientific, and an underlying domain of perceptual singulars, which are excluded from the scientific.³

The first three sections of the chapter depict, primarily from the perspective of thinking that is non-practical, the domain of perceptual singulars and the domain of the syllogistic, and also the relationship between them. In section I, I consider the discussion early in the *Metaphysics* of the difference between perception [αἴσθησις] (and the experience based primarily upon it) and the properly scientific. In section II, I consider Aristotle's identification in the *Prior analytics* of a domain below the syllogistic. As mentioned in the introduction to the present work, Aristotle considers in *APr.* a possible objection to the method of logical proof called ἔκθεσις. This method would appear to stray beyond the limits of the syllogistic's subject matter; but Aristotle responds that, correctly understood, it does not do so: it simply takes something from the singular domain and treats it in a perfectly syllogistic way, that is to say, it treats it *as* a universal (or as a possibly plural part of a universal). This is not the way that Alexander of Aphrodisias understands ἔκθεσις; but, as I argue, his account is confused. I also argue that understanding ἔκθεσις as the use of a perceptual singular as a universal allows us to connect the *APr.* proof method with remarks in the *Sophistici elenchi* on the "third man argument." In section III, I offer a description of the domain of the perceptual, first as it exists in the speculative realm but then also as it exists in the practical.

In the next three sections (sections IV through VI), I move decidedly into the practical realm properly speaking, examining three passages in the *Nicomachean Ethics* often associated with the practical syllogism: the first is found in *EN* vi,7 and the other two are in *EN* vii,3.⁴ My analyses

---

3 In what follows, I speak of speculative and practical reason as sharing a "domain," that is, the domain of perceptual singulars; but I also distinguish between the speculative "realm" and the practical "realm." The speculative realm includes, besides perceptual singulars, the properly scientific, from which such singulars are excluded; the practical realm exists primarily at the level of singulars, that is, singular actions, although it is not unconnected with universals of which an agent may have a grasp. I permit myself a bit of ambiguity in the use of the expressions 'singular' and 'perceptual singular.' A genuine singular such as Socrates is also a perceptual singular, for he can be perceived, but not all perceptual singulars are genuine singulars: a prospective action, for instance, which belongs to the practical realm and to the realm of perceptual singulars, is not a genuine singular. Still, I speak occasionally of a prospective action as simply a singular.

4 There is also a pertinent passage in *De motu animalium* (*MA*) vii which I discuss in connection with the second of the *EN* vii,3 passages.

of these texts all make the same point: that they are best understood as talking about the relationship between the two domains: the perceptual, understood as the proper locus of action, and the syllogistic, the proper locus of universals. The second and third of these passages are especially useful for understanding what goes wrong in the thought and behavior of the ἀκρατής (the weak-willed man). His problem is basically that he does not press the universal knowledge that he has of what he ought to do down into the domain of perceptual singulars (practically conceived) where action takes place.

In the final section (VII), I return to *APr.*, in order to argue that, although the perceptual and the syllogistic domains are distinct, they are united by a single very important principle: the principle of non-contradiction. I look at a passage in *APr.* ii,15, and another in *APr.* i,21. Although they both involve propositions in speculative reason, they also both make reference to the good. The ideas discussed here will be of use in later chapters (especially 7 and 8), when we discuss the ἀκρατής, the φρόνιμος, and the ἀκόλαστος (the depraved man), for the verification of these character types depends upon the presence or absence of practical contradiction within the soul.

I. Levels of Thought

In the first chapter of the first book of the *Metaphysics*, Aristotle effects a division of the animal kingdom, a division that has as its goal the identification of the characteristics proper to human beings qua human beings. The chapter begins (famously) with the remark that "All men desire by nature to know," although Aristotle immediately adds a remark about perception: "An indication of this is the delight we take in our senses" [σημεῖον δ' ἡ τῶν αἰσθήσεων ἀγάπησις]. A few lines later he notes that all animals have perception: φύσει μὲν οὖν αἴσθησιν ἔχοντα γίγνεται τὰ ζῷα. This, in effect, locates man within the animal kingdom; but Aristotle is also careful to connect the perception that interests him with knowledge; we prize sight, he says, since "among the senses this makes us to know and brings to light many differences" [ποιεῖ γνωρίζειν ἡμᾶς αὕτη τῶν αἰσθήσεων καὶ πολλὰς δηλοῖ διαφοράς].

Animals are then divided into those which, in addition to perception, have memory, and those which do not; Aristotle says that those with memory (and which are therefore "more intelligent and more capable of learning" [φρονιμώτερα καὶ μαθητικώτερα]) are also those which can hear sounds. What distinguishes the race of men from that of animals is that, while animals live by "appearances and memories" [ταῖς φαντασίαις ζῇ καὶ ταῖς μνήμαις] (and "have but little of extended experience" [ἐμπειρίας ... μικρόν]), men do so also by "art and reasonings" [τέχνῃ καὶ λογισμοῖς].

'Extended experience' is a somewhat elusive concept.[5] The corresponding capacity is higher than the capacity for taking in perceptions of singulars (and higher even than the capacity to remember such perceptions), since it is "similar to science [i.e., reasonings] and art" [ἐπιστήμῃ καὶ τέχνῃ ὅμοιον]. It also involves a sort of abstraction of universals from singulars: "many memories of the same thing terminate in the capacity for one extended experience" [αἱ γὰρ πολλαὶ μνῆμαι τοῦ αὐτοῦ πράγματος μιᾶς ἐμπειρίας δύναμιν ἀποτελοῦσιν]. And yet it falls short of science and art, which are the proper marks of the human. One who has the capacity pertaining to a science or an art has the capacity to make a general *judgment* [ὑπόληψις] regarding the universals picked up by extended experience. In other words, one can make an intelligent decision about where in a science or art they fit (or ought to fit).[6]

As to perception [αἴσθησις], although Aristotle most often speaks of it with regard to singulars, he also holds that they are perceived *in* perceiving universals. This is apparent in a passage in the *Posterior analytics*, a passage parallel to the one we have been considering (*Metaph.* i,1). In the last

---

5 The Revised Oxford Translation renders ἐμπειρία as 'connected experience,' which is a good translation since it connotes a phenomenon occurring a level above that of taking in perceptions and even remembering them. I employ here the translation 'extended experience' in order to establish a connection with the 'extended quantities' of *EE* vii,6 and *Categories* vi, to be discussed in chapter 8. The word ἐμπειρία comes from πεῖρα, meaning attempt or experiment, and so it implies a certain heading toward an end over time (and in this sense ἐμπειρία would be "extended").

6 For an Aristotelian-inspired discussion of the characteristics that human animals share with other animals (especially dolphins) and the way in which, along the same scale, they exceed such animals, see Alasdair MacIntyre, *Dependent Rational Animals: Why Human Beings Need the Virtues* (Chicago: Open Court, 1999), 5–6, 21–28, 55–61, 81–83. On p. 82, MacIntyre writes: "The care for others that dolphins exhibit plays a crucial part in sustaining their shared lives. Yet this part is one that they themselves cannot survey, lacking as they do, any capacity to look back to infancy or forward to aging and death as humans do." See also Richard Sorabji, *Animal Minds and Human Morals: The Origins of the Western Debate* (London: Duckworth, 1993), 12–20. I discuss the difference between humans and mere animals in chapter 6, section II.

chapter of *APo.*, Aristotle compares perception to a group of soldiers who manage to make a stand in battle: "if one man makes a stand another does and then another, until a position of strength is reached" [100a12–13].[7] He even insists upon this point since, immediately after making the comparison to a stand in battle, he takes another run through the thesis, lest there be any misunderstanding:

What we have just said but not said clearly, let us say again. When one of the singulars [ἀδιαφόρων ἑνός] makes a stand, there is first a universal in the soul (for one *perceives* the particular but perception is of the universal: of man but not of Callias the man); again a stand is made in these, until things indivisible and universal make a stand; for instance, a particular animal stands, until animal does, and in this a stand is made in the same way. It is clear, therefore, that we must come to know the first things by induction; for perception too introduces the universal in this way. [*APo.* ii,19, 100a14–b5]

Aristotle has to recognize universals together with the singulars, since otherwise, when we recognize something as a type of thing, its being of that type would not belong to *it*. In section VII of the present chapter, we shall see that this connection between perception and universals is important for understanding what would be the state of soul of the perfectly virtuous man.

Also relevant to our present concerns is a passage at the end of *EN* vi,8, a passage that reveals a connection between the perception discussed at *APo.* ii,19 and the perception proper to the practical realm. The passage runs as follows:

That practical wisdom is not knowledge is clear, for it is of the last thing, as we have said; for the practical is such.[8] It corresponds, therefore, to comprehen-

---

7 This is from the Revised Oxford Translation, which reads in line 100a13 ἀλκὴν instead of ἀρχήν.

8 The back-reference is to *EN* vi,8, 1141b27–28. The word I have translated here as "practical" is πρακτὸν [1142a25]. In private correspondence, Pavlos Kontos has suggested to me that this translation is not entirely satisfactory. In a recent book, he argues that πρακτὸν (which he leaves untranslated) has a "twofold meaning," "designating either 'what is achievable within and through action' or 'what has already been brought into being through action'" [Pavlos Kontos, *Aristotle's Moral Realism Reconsidered: Phenomenological Ethics* (New York: Routledge, 2011), 10]. He laments the fact that the former meaning has often been preferred to the second, although the second is the primary meaning and more in line with Aristotle's moral realism. For want of an alternative, I leave 'practical' as the trans-

sion. Comprehension is about terms, of which there is not an account; practical wisdom is about the last thing, of which there is not knowledge but rather perception [αἴσθησις]—but not perception of the individual senses but perception of the sort by means of which we perceive in mathematics that the last thing is a triangle; for there will be a stand here too.[9]

This is a dense and elliptical passage, but the gist of it is not inaccessible. Practical wisdom [φρόνησις] is not knowledge [ἐπιστήμη], for that would impose upon it the limits of the syllogistic, and practical wisdom is about singulars (the "last thing" [ἔσχατον]). Practical wisdom is not unlike comprehension [νοῦς], wherein a person comes to grasp syllogistic terms (although terms not yet included in propositions).[10] Comprehension does involve perception but, as is clear in *APo.* ii,19, its accumulated perceptions finish in universals (in terms) which might go into science; practical wisdom, on the other hand, heads toward the last things, the objects of perception. This is not, however, the perception of the individual senses (the sense of sight, the sense of hearing, etc.) but a sort of intellectual perception, not unlike that whereby in a geometrical proof one considers a *particular* triangle, even though it is not a particular object of the senses. The quoted passage finishes with a remark that appears to be a reference to the passage in *APo.* ii,19 we examined just above. Having made the point that practical wisdom involves perception like that in geometry, Aristotle adds: "for there will be a stand here too."[11] Whether the point is that in geometry

lation of πρακτόν; I stipulate, however, that this translation should not be understood in a way that diminishes Aristotle's moral realism as generally understood by Pavlos.

9 τί δ' ἡ φρόνησις οὐκ ἐπιστήμη, φανερόν· τοῦ γὰρ ἐσχάτου ἐστίν, ὥσπερ εἴρηται· τὸ γὰρ πρακτὸν τοιοῦτον. ἀντίκειται μὲν δὴ τῷ νῷ· ὁ μὲν γὰρ νοῦς τῶν ὅρων, ὧν οὐκ ἔστι λόγος, ἡ δὲ τοῦ ἐσχάτου, οὗ οὐκ ἔστιν ἐπιστήμη ἀλλ' αἴσθησις, οὐχ ἡ τῶν ἰδίων, ἀλλ' οἵᾳ αἰσθανόμεθα ὅτι τὸ ἐν τοῖς μαθηματικοῖς ἔσχατον τρίγωνον· στήσεται γὰρ κἀκεῖ. [*EN* vi,8, 1142a23–29]. The chapter actually finishes with the following enigmatic words: ἀλλ' αὕτη μᾶλλον αἴσθησις ἢ φρόνησις, ἐκείνης δ' ἄλλο εἶδος ("But this is rather perception than practical wisdom, but of *that* it is another type" [1142a30]). I take this to be a marginal note, perhaps an afterthought by Aristotle himself, objecting to the previous passage's saying that it is φρόνησις that picks up the last thing (i.e., the singular). That is the role of perception, the note would sustain, although (and the previous passage is right on this count) it is a special *type* of perception, not the perception of the individual senses.

10 … ὧν οὐκ ἔστι λόγος [1142a26]; cp. *APo.* ii,19, 100b10. At *EN* vi,8, 1142a25, Aristotle says that practical wisdom "stands opposite" to comprehension [ἀντίκειται μὲν δὴ τῷ νῷ]. This can be understood as 'corresponding to,' as in my translation, rather than as 'being contrary to,' although it is also true that there are differences between the perception proper to the practical realm and comprehension.

11 στήσεται γὰρ κἀκεῖ [1142a29]; cp. *APo.* ii,19, 100a15 and 100b2.

there is also a stand (at the particular triangle thought of in the proof) or that in practical wisdom there is also a stand (although not at a universal induced from a number of singular perceptions) is unclear.

As obscure as it is, this passage establishes at least two things. First, that the perception proper to the practical realm is a sort of intellectual perception. This will be important in later chapters of the present work when we discuss the object of the human act—which may, indeed, be a physical object but only in so far as it is part of a moral act, that is, only as *understood* as the object of a moral act. Secondly (and this is more pertinent to the present discussion), that the perception proper to the practical realm is not distinct from that proper to the speculative realm—in particular, from that proper to geometry. This gives us a warrant for moving from Aristotle's remarks on perception in, for instance, the first chapter of *Metaph.* (examined above) and in other passages in *APr.* to similar remarks made in more practical contexts (such as the remarks in *EN* associated with the practical syllogism). Indeed, it is to passages in *APr.* that we now turn, looking forward, however, to applying the ideas found there to the practical syllogism passages.

II. The Distinction between Perception and Higher Levels of Thought

In two passages in the *Prior analytics*, i,6, 28a22–23 and i,8, 30a6–14, Aristotle employs a method of logical proof called ἔκθεσις.[12] The second of these passages (the more interesting of the two) concerns the validation of the syllogistic moods Baroco and Bocardo, which have apodeictic premisses and apodeictic conclusion. It says:

But in the middle figure when the universal is affirmative and the particular negative [i.e., when the mood is Baroco] and again in the third when the universal is affirmative and the particular negative [Bocardo], the demonstration will

---

[12] Alexander of Aphrodisias sees an ecthetic proof also at *APr.* i,2, 25a14–17, i.e., in Aristotle's proof that universal negative propositions convert (see Kevin L. Flannery, *Ways into the Logic of Alexander of Aphrodisias*, Philosophia Antiqua, vol. 62 [Leiden: Brill, 1995], 16–19, 25–30). Alexander's remarks on the Aristotelian passages pertaining to ἔκθεσις have become a lightning rod for scholarly treatments of the concept; see chapter 1 of Flannery, *Ways into the Logic of Alexander of Aphrodisias*.

not take the same form; but it is necessary for us, having set out [ἐκθεμένους—30a9] something of which each does not hold, with respect to this to make the syllogism; for the syllogism will be necessary using these. If the syllogism is necessary with respect to that which was set out, it will also be necessary with respect to the former 'some.' For that which was set out is something of the former sort. Each of the syllogisms is in its proper figure.[13]

What Aristotle has in mind is basically this. We know that, with the exception of two, all moods of the second and third figures that have apodeictic premises and conclusion can be reduced to moods of the first figure (also with apodeictic premises and conclusion) and thereby validated. The two exceptions are Baroco and Bocardo. With the other moods, reduction to the first figure is effected by means of the standard conversion rules ('if X holds of no Y, then Y holds of no X,' etc.),[14] nothing further being required; but in the case of Baroco and Bocardo, one must first perform an ἔκθεσις: literally, a "setting out" of terms. This process transforms Baroco and Bocardo into other moods in their own figure; these latter can then be reduced to first figure syllogisms by means of the standard conversion rules.

Consider Baroco: that is, the mood that runs: 'Y holds of all X; Y does not hold of some Z; therefore, X does not hold of some Z.' There are conversion rules for propositions of the form 'Y holds of no X,' 'Y holds of all X,' and 'Y holds of some X,' but no such rule exists for a proposition of the form 'Y does not hold of some X.' Suppose, then, the following syllogism in Baroco: 'B holds of all A; B does not hold of some C; therefore, A does not hold of some C.' In order to show that the conclusion is validly derived, the minor premise ('B does not hold of some C') must be made into a proposition of a form that can be converted. Aristotle, in fact, makes it into a proposition of the form 'Y holds of no X.' He does this by setting out something of which the term B does not hold. That is to say, given that the second premise is 'B does not hold of some C,' we take some C, calling it **c**. This can be considered a delimited class on its own; so, instead of 'B does not hold of some C,' we now have 'B holds of no **c**.' But now we have, in effect, premises of the form found in the second figure mood

---

13 *APr.* i,8, 30a6–14.
14 'X' and 'Y' here are place holders for actual terms 'A,' 'B,' 'C,' etc.

Camestres ('Y holds of all X; Y holds of no Z; therefore, X holds of no Z'): that is, we have the premisses 'B holds of all A' and 'B holds of no c.' From these premisses, we can conclude, 'A holds of no c.' Since this syllogism with the set out term is valid, so also is the original syllogism in Baroco, since that which was set out was some C.[15]

That is basically the type of proof that Aristotle has in mind in *APr.* i,8, 30a6–14.[16] For our purposes, however, more important than the proof itself is what Aristotle says near the end of the passage, in justification of the procedure of ἔκθεσις: "If the syllogism is necessary with respect to that which was set out, it will also be necessary with respect to the former 'some.' For that which was set out is something of the former sort."[17] When Aristotle uses here the word "former" (κατ' ἐκείνου τινός [30a12] and ὅπερ ἐκεῖνό τί [30a13]), he is referring to the "some C" of which A does not hold. So he is justifying the move from 'some C' to 'c' and back again (i.e., the move from the premise 'B does not hold of some C' to 'B holds of no c' and then from the conclusion 'A holds of no c' to 'A does not hold of some C') by saying that anything said of the thing set out is said also of 'some C,' because it is some such thing; that is say, it is a C.

A modern-day logician would worry about justifying the move from a particular to a universal, but Aristotle hardly adverts to that; for him, the possibly controversial move is from C to c. Any proposition of the form 'Y holds of some X' is in standard syllogistic form. To set out a term such as

---

15 The argument can perhaps be made more perspicuous by substituting actual terms for the letters. For Baroco, instead of 'B holds of all A; B does not hold of some C; therefore, A does not hold of some C,' we might say: 'Breathing holds of all Animals; Breathing does not hold of some Cars; therefore, Animal does not hold of some Cars.' (Since all Animals are separated from some Cars by virtue of their breathing, obviously 'Animal does not hold of some Cars.') One can prove this by setting out some Cars (for instance, CONVERTIBLES) and saying that 'Breathing holds of no CONVERTIBLES.' This gives: 'Breathing holds of all Animals; Breathing holds of no CONVERTIBLES; therefore, Animal holds of no CONVERTIBLES.' But this is a syllogism in Camestres, reducible to the first figure by means of e-conversion—and, therefore, valid.

16 Alexander gives a different, more complicated proof at *in APr.* 121.26–122.27; see Flannery, *Ways into the Logic of Alexander of Aphrodisias*, 24.

17 εἰ δὲ κατὰ τοῦ ἐκτεθέντος ἐστὶν ἀναγκαῖος, καὶ κατ' ἐκείνου τινός· τὸ γὰρ ἐκτεθὲν ὅπερ ἐκεῖνό τί ἐστιν [*APr.* i,8, 30a11–13]. It might be thought that, in speaking of syllogisms that are "necessary," Aristotle is referring to the modal character of the conclusions of Baroco and Bocardo and of Camestres and Felapton (into which they are transformed). But *APr.* i,41, which we shall be examining shortly, confirms the idea that he is talking rather about the necessity of the syllogism itself (*necessitas consequentiae*): in that chapter, in which he addresses possible objections to ἔκθεσις, he refers a number of times (49b17, 50a1, 50a3–4) to syllogisms, specifying no mode.

c is to step outside standard form since, properly speaking, singular things are excluded from the syllogistic. According to Alexander of Aphrodisias, to set out a term is to go from the level of logic (i.e., of the syllogistic) to the level of perception (αἴσθησις). Since sciences are made up of syllogisms—which, in turn, are made up of propositions in proper syllogistic form—to set out terms is to leave the realm of the properly scientific. Bearing in mind what Aristotle says in *Metaph.* i,1, this is (in some sense) to revert to a capacity that man shares with mere animals.

That Aristotle considered this move to be particularly controversial is evident some chapters later, where he says:

> We must not suppose that something absurd comes about because of the setting out [παρὰ τὸ ἐκτίθεσθαί]. For in no way do we make use of some particular thing's being [τῷ τόδε τι εἶναι]; rather, we do what the geometrician does who says that this particular line [τήνδε (γραμμὴν)] is a foot long and straight and without breadth, although it is not, but does not use them as if deducing anything from them. For in general, unless there is something related as whole to part and something else related to this as part to whole, the demonstrator does not demonstrate from them, and so no syllogism comes about <from them>. We use setting out [τῷ ἐκτίθεσθαι] as we do illustration [literally, 'making perceptible': τῷ αἰσθάνεσθαι], easing the way for the student. For it is not as if without them it were impossible to demonstrate, as it *is* impossible to demonstrate without the premisses of a syllogism.[18]

Aristotle's point here is that the use of set out terms is not illegitimate, even though it involves stepping out of the sphere of formal logic and into the sphere of singular perceptibles. What is being illustrated ("made perceptible") are not the set out terms themselves but the logical relationships they illustrate. His remarks apply not only to the passages, such as the one we just examined in which set out terms are integral to a method of proof, but also to the more numerous passages in which he sets out terms to show, for instance, that certain combinations of propositions are

---

18 *APr.* i,41, 49b33–50a4. Aristotle makes similar remarks at *APo.* i,10, 76b39–77a3: οὐδ' ὁ γεωμέτρης ψευδῆ ὑποτίθεται, ὥσπερ τινὲς ἔφασαν, λέγοντες ὡς οὐ δεῖ τῷ ψεύδει χρῆσθαι, τὸν δὲ γεωμέτρην ψεύδεσθαι λέγοντα ποδιαίαν τὴν οὐ ποδιαίαν ἢ εὐθεῖαν τὴν γεγραμμένην οὐκ εὐθεῖαν οὖσαν. ὁ δὲ γεωμέτρης οὐδὲν συμπεραίνεται τῷ τήνδε εἶναι γραμμὴν ἣν αὐτὸς ἔφθεγκται, ἀλλὰ τὰ διὰ τούτων δηλούμενα. See also *Metaph.* xiii,3, 1078a14–21.

not syllogistic.[19] But they apply especially to the former, since often the other instances do not involve valid syllogisms—and, here in *APr.* i,41, Aristotle clearly does have in mind valid syllogisms: "the demonstrator does not demonstrate from them, and so no syllogism comes about"; "it is not as if without them it were impossible to demonstrate, as it *is* impossible to demonstrate without the premises of a syllogism."

A number of commentators—both modern and ancient—read this passage not as a justification of ἔκθεσις (in the sense described here) but of the use of letters (A, B, Γ, etc) instead of terms ('animal,' 'man,' 'rational,' etc.). (The passage just prior to 49b33–50a4, i.e., 49b14–32, is a farrago of letters and obscure argumentation.) The principal among these commentators is (again) Alexander of Aphrodisias, who argues that Aristotle uses letters rather than terms since terms lead more easily to error.[20] When presented with the propositions 'all men are animals' and 'all those capable of laughter are animals,' an inexperienced student is tempted to conclude that 'all men are capable of laughter'—which is true, of course, although it does not follow from the "premises," which are not syllogistic. What throws the student off is what he already knows about the relationships among the terms, in particular, about the relationship between 'capable of laughter' and 'men.' So, in order to avoid such errors, Aristotle (according to this interpretation) employs letters, which give no indication of the relationships among the terms.[21]

---

19 The instances are too numerous to list; good examples are found in *APr.* i,10 and 11, the chapters just following the proof of Baroco. (At *APr.* i,10, 30b31–35, he actually uses the phrase, κἂν ὅρους ἐκ θέμενον εἴη ... ; he writes there "Further, one might show by an exposition of terms that the conclusion is not necessary without qualification, though it is necessary given the premises. For example let A be animal, B man, C white, and let the propositions be assumed in the same way as before: it is possible that animal should belong to nothing white.") In the chapters just preceding *APr.* i,41, he sets out terms that are less closely associated with proofs. At *APr.* i,39, 49b6 he uses the phrase ἡ τῶν ὅρων ἔκθεσις; at *APr.* i,40, 49b11, the phrase θετέον τοὺς ὅρους.

20 In Alexander, see *in APr.* 379.14–380.27. A similar interpretation appears in Philoponus, *in APr.* 352.3–25 (although he has a more plausible interpretation of *APr.* i,41, 49b37–50a1). Alexander is followed (and cited) by Maier Heinrich Maier, *Die Syllogistik des Aristoteles* (Leipzig: K. F. Koehler, 1896–1900), 2.1 320 n.1] and also by Mignucci [Mario Mignucci, *Aristotele*, Gli analitici primi: *Traduzione, introduzione, commento* (Naples: Loffredo, 1969), 495]. Smith, I believe, has the right interpretation ("the problem is that this particular figure seems to enter into the proof, which purports to be universal" [Robin Smith, trans., *Aristotle: Prior Analytics* (Indianapolis: Hackett, 1989), 173]).

21 See Alexander of Aphrodisias, *in APr.* 380.5–11. See also Jonathan Barnes, *Truth, etc.: Six Lectures on Ancient Philosophy* (Oxford: Clarendon, 2007), 341–43.

If this interpretation were correct, it would be more difficult to make a connection between ἔκθεσις and perception (and, ultimately, between ἔκθεσις and the practical syllogism passages)—but it is not correct. There is a very subtle and elusive tangle in Alexander's account. Aristotle in fact is saying that ἔκθεσις uses terms that cause problems in that they bear with them quasi-material characteristics but that we can prescind from such characteristics and avoid the problems; Alexander interprets him as saying that ἔκθεσις employs letters which *avoid* problems because they do *not* have the quasi-material burdens of more concrete terms. But this latter hardly corresponds to the simile Aristotle uses of a geometer using concrete lines—that is, lines in matter—in order to indicate things mathematical. When Aristotle says at 49b37–50a1 that "unless there is something related as whole to part and something else related to this as part to whole, the demonstrator does not demonstrate from them, and so no syllogism comes about," he is *embracing* the part-whole relationship, without any suggestion that it makes for confusion. Alexander has things exactly reversed.[22]

Ross points to a passage in the *Sophistici Elenchi* [*SE*], which he says sheds a good deal of light on the *APr.* i,41 passage and the "problem" of ἔκθεσις in general.[23] The passage concerns the famous "third man argument," according to which, in order to know that two men are the same qua men, one must make use of the Form of man, which, since it must be like the first two, is itself a man.[24] The (technical and very dense) passage runs as follows:

Again, there is the argument that there is a third man above and beyond the man and individual men. But 'man' or any commonality [ἅπαν τὸ κοινόν] signifies not a determinate individual [τόδε τι], but some quality [τοιόνδε], or quantity [ποσὸν] or relation [πρός τι], or something of that sort. So also in the case of 'Coriscus' and 'musical Coriscus' and the question whether they are

---

22 At the end of the section, however, Alexander does say that the syllogisms with the letters are not the actual syllogisms, since a syllogism *does* have matter: *in APr.* 380.25–30.

23 W. D. Ross, *Aristotle's Prior and Posterior Analytics* (Oxford: Clarendon, 1949), 413.

24 The third man argument is an anti-Platonic argument, although it actually appears in Plato (as a piece of self-criticism). In the following passage, an adversary is conceived of (or presupposed) as maintaining that a third man exists, even though the third man argument is a *reductio ad absurdum*, the *absurdum* being the existence of a third man. On the third man argument, see Gail Fine, *On Ideas: Aristotle's Criticism of Plato's Theory of Forms* (Oxford: Clarendon), 203–41.

Logic, Perception, Practical Syllogism   13

the same or different. For the one signifies an individual [τόδε τι], the other a quality [τοιόνδε], so that it is not it [αὐτὸ] which was set out [ἐκθέσθαι].²⁵ It is not the setting out [τὸ ἐκτίθεσθαι] that creates [ποιεῖ] the third man, but the idea that the sort [τὸ ὅπερ] is a determinate individual [τόδε τι]. For the sort which 'man' is [ὅπερ ἄνθρωπός ἐστιν] cannot also be a determinate individual [τόδε τι], like Callias. Nor does it make a difference if one says that the thing set out [τὸ ἐκτιθέμενον] is not a determinate individual-sort [ὅπερ τόδε τι] but rather a quality-sort [ὅπερ ποιόν], for there will be the one something above and beyond the many—that is, the man.²⁶ It is clear, therefore, that one must not grant that what is predicated in common is a determinate individual [τόδε τι] but that it signifies either a quality [ποιὸν], or a relation [πρός τι], or a quantity [ποσὸν], or something of that sort.²⁷

The basic idea here is that the error of positing "a third man" (or something similar) arises only if one insists that that which we predicate of some individual (some τόδε τι)—whether we predicate the sort of thing it is or its quality or its quantity—be set out (or posited) *as* a determinate individual. Aristotle acknowledges that there is such a thing as setting out [τὸ ἐκτίθεσθαι], for instance, the sort 'man' [ὅπερ ἄνθρωπός], but he insists that this does not constitute creating a third man. We find similar language— and, in particular, the pivotal word ὅπερ—at the end of the ecthetic proof

---

25 In other words, once we hypostatize 'musical Coriscus' as a concrete individual, Coriscus the determinate individual (the τόδε τι) is necessarily not the same as that "which was set out": i.e., 'musical Coriscus.'

26 Lines 179a6–8 in Ross's OCT text are as follows:

    6: μενον μὴ ὅπερ τόδε τι εἶναι λέγοι ἀλλ' ὅπερ ποιόν, οὐδὲν δι-
    7: οίσει· ἔσται γὰρ τὸ παρὰ τοὺς πολλοὺς ἕν τι, οἷον τὸ ἄνθρω-
    8: πος. φανερὸν οὖν ὅτι οὐ δοτέον τόδε τι εἶναι τὸ κοινῇ κατ-

For line 7, Bekker has the following (... διοί-):

    σει· ἔσται γὰρ τὸ παρὰ τοὺς πολλοὺς ἕν τι, οἷον ὁ ἄνθρω-

He reports that, instead of ὁ, AD have τὸ. Ross's apparatus says that, with regard to the *first* τὸ in his line 7, **DAB²** have that reading, B¹cu have ὁ. (His **D** includes Bekker's D.) He must mean the second τὸ. Ross, who acknowledges [p. vii] that he has not looked at B but relies on Bekker and Waitz, is also inaccurate in reporting that the first hand in B has ὁ, a second has τὸ. As Waitz says in his apparatus, the ὁ in B is the result of the first hand correcting itself: "τὸ] ὁ *cu et pr B*, τὸ pr manu corr."

I prefer ὁ to τὸ since it makes better sense of the argument (expounded, as I understand it, below). With ὁ ἄνθρωπος, Aristotle is referring to the generation of a "third man"; he says just ὁ ἄνθρωπος because the "man" generated is not actually a *third* man: his talk of a third man is just a way of establishing a reference to the original Platonic problem.

27 *SE* xxii, 178b36–179a10.

of Baroco, where, as we have seen, Aristotle says, "For that which was set out is something of the former sort" [τὸ γὰρ ἐκτεθὲν ὅπερ ἐκεῖνό τί ἐστιν—*APr.* i,8, 30a12–13]. As there, the key here is "bracketing": one must look away from the way we speak of the sort 'man'—referring to it only, as we do, *as if* it were a stabile entity, enjoying a determinate existence of its own—just as, in the logical proof method, we must look away from particular characteristics of the thing set out.

Setting out something—in this case, an aspect of a thing, such as a man's being a man or six feet tall or musical—is tied up with perception: that is, with what we hold before the mind's eye. Because both a man qua individual and the same man qua a sort of thing (i.e., man-sort) can appear before our minds as separate thoughts—the individual man *here*, the man considered as a sort of man over *there*—we are led astray philosophically. We come to regard them as discrete individuals. Aristotle identifies perception as the culprit in *Topics* ii,7, where he also mentions Plato's theory of Forms (against which the third man argument is directed).[28] In so far as these Forms (or Ideas) exist in us, "they are perceptible [αἰσθητὰς] and thinkable [νοητὰς]" [113a27]. This is clear, he says, "for it is through perception by means of sight that we recognize the form present in each individual" [113a31–32]. But nothing perceived enters, qua perceived, into the realm of scientific knowledge.

As Aristotle suggests in his justification of ἔκθεσις in *APr.* i,41, thoughts qua thoughts should, therefore, be regarded as aids of the sort mathematicians provide when they use lines drawn with inexact physical utensils as illustrations of mathematical lines: our ideas qua perceived (that is to say, before the mind's eye) do not themselves constitute knowledge.[29] This gives us insight into what Aristotle means when, in various contexts, he speaks of perception. He does not necessarily have in mind data coming through the senses to the mind but can mean simply the way thoughts appear in the mind, that is, as if seen, as if sensed.

To sum up, what *SE* xxii, 178b36–179a10 shows is that *APr.* i,41 is after all about the setting out of terms (ἔκθεσις) (and not the use of letters) and

---

28 See also *Top.* vi,10, 148a14–18.

29 As with the third man, Aristotle does not think that these mathematical lines really exist as distinct individuals; see *Metaph.* xiii,2.

it gives us also an understanding of what is actually done in ἔκθεσις and why it needs to be justified. The procedure always involves somehow the use of an example or idea that has to be "looked past" in some way if its scientific import is to be understood in a correct manner. What needs to be justified is the use in scientific discourse of material that is not strictly speaking scientific: predicates that seem to pick out distinct individuals but do not really do so; individuals that seem to figure in logical proofs as individuals but are really just devices for grasping logical truths. In *APr.*, Aristotle is interested in showing that the perceptual does not enter into the discipline of formal logic (the syllogistic); in the passages associated with the practical syllogism, as we shall see, his aim is quite the opposite: to show that and how the perceptual is included. But this is what takes ethics outside of the properly scientific—so that the "practical syllogism" must be quite different from a syllogism of the syllogistic.

III. The Terrain of the Mind

What then is the domain of perceptual singulars, the level below the syllogistic, like? It is a domain in which sometimes there can be identified—by someone practiced in the syllogistic, for instance—a continuous line of reasoning but where often the reasoning, such as it is, is simply a matter of drawing together two or more thoughts, with no attempt to forge them into a syllogism or to connect them up with a full-fledged theory at all. Such thinking occurs within the domain of perception [αἴσθησις], in the sense isolated above. The simple—not necessarily sad—fact is that thinking is not always syllogistic or scientific. Like the thinking of mere animals, our thinking often involves no more than associating one distinct and disparate thought with another.

Let us say that a man is thinking about his livestock. He has before his mind's eye the fact that it comprises his cows and his horses. We might represent his thought in the way shown in Figure 1-1 (where L = livestock, C = cows, and H = horses). And we might say that the man has two propositions in his head: 'L holds of C' and 'L holds of H'. The propositions are arranged in his head in such a way that he knows too that 'C holds of no H' and 'H holds of no C'. We might even say that, given the facts, he can "derive" such conclusions.[30] But the complex of propositions 'L holds of C'; 'L holds of H'; therefore, 'C holds of no H' (and/or 'H holds of no C') is non-syllogistic: the man reasons perfectly well, but not syllogistically. There is no syllogism here, but simply an assembly of thoughts. If we make the standard scholastic distinction between logical form (the figure and mood in which three terms might be arranged) and logical matter (the terms themselves), all this thinking occurs at the level of matter, since there is no form (in the strict, syllogistic sense).[31]

Alternatively, a person might reason materially in a way that corresponds to a syllogistic figure but without really reasoning syllogistically. Aristotle gives an example in *APr.* i,33:

> Let A be 'everlasting,' B 'Aristomenes thought of,' C 'Aristomenes.' It is true then that A holds of B, for Aristomenes thought of is everlasting. But also B holds of C, for Aristomenes is Aristomenes thought of. But A does not hold of C, since Aristomenes is perishable. [47b21–26]

The term 'everlasting' must be understood here in a loose sense that makes it true to say that Aristomenes as *merely* thought of is eternal because it (i.e., the thought) is still around even when Aristomenes is dead and gone. The problem with this "syllogism," says Aristotle, is that the proposition 'A holds of B' ('Everlasting holds of Aristomenes thought of') ought to have been assumed as a universal [47b27]; that is to say, it ought to have been put in proper syllogistic form. Then it would have been seen that 'Everlasting holds of Aristomenes thought of'—or, more precisely, 'Everlasting holds of every Aristomenes thought of'—is false, since some instances of Aristomenes thought of are not everlasting: Aristomenes (the presently existing person), for example. But even though there is syllogistic error here, there is *thinking*: there is a bringing of ideas together into a succession. In giving an account of practical reasoning, that is all we are looking for—although when thought turns practical, another factor is introduced: ὄρεξις (or inclination) in its various manifestations.[32]

---

30 Alexander speaks in this fashion. See Flannery, *Ways into the Logic of Alexander of Aphrodisias*, 136–42.

31 Jonathan Barnes, "Logical Form and Logical Matter," in *Logica, mente e persona*, ed. A. Alberti (Florence: Leo S. Olschki, 1990), passim.

32 ... ἐν τε τῷ λογιστικῷ γὰρ ἡ βούλησις γίνεται, καὶ ἐν τῷ ἀλόγῳ ἡ ἐπιθυμία καὶ ὁ θυμός· εἰ δὲ τρία ἡ ψυχή, ἐν ἑκάστῳ ἔσται ὄρεξις [*de An.* iii,9, 432b5–7]. See also *de An.* iii,11, 434a5–15.

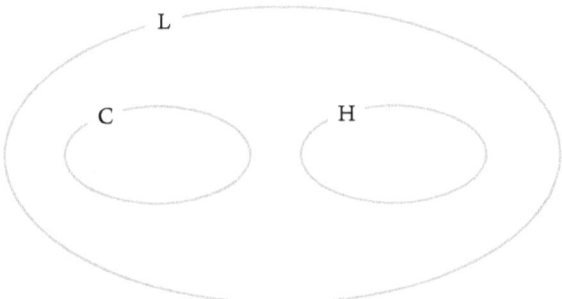

FIGURE 1-1. The Domain of Perceptual Singulars

It might be thought that widening the field of enquiry in this way makes philosophical psychology—in particular, as it regards the practical realm—hopelessly complicated and ultimately incomprehensible. This objection is, in a sense, sound: the human mind as it operates in the practical realm is, in an important sense, unfathomable; as noted above, Aristotle says any number of times that we simply cannot organize it as we organize, for instance, the science of geometry. But he does not throw up his hands and say that the practical realm is *wholly* incomprehensible.

This is apparent from the context of many of the *loci classici* for the practical syllogism. They often come within Aristotle's account of how people can go wrong in their practical reason—and, in particular, how the ἀκρατής goes wrong. Aristotle's fundamental principle is that a single soul cannot accommodate a genuine practical contradiction: that if there is inconsistency in an agent's behavior—if, for instance, he knows what he ought to do and does not do it—this can and must be explained by positing a lack of unity within his soul. The obverse side of this coin is that, if there were a person who had a good grasp of the basic principles of morality and who was in no way practically inconsistent, his soul would be unified.

Aristotle's investigation of the psychology of such figures as the ἀκρατής—his account of how it is possible for such a person to contradict himself—can provide at least a rough map of the terrain of the soul. Even if we cannot organize a man's thoughts as we might construct an axiomatic logical system, we are capable of understanding how the whole thing works: what happens to the soul if consistency is lacking; what has to happen if consistency is to be restored.[33]

IV. The Practical Syllogism: *EN* vi,7

Aristotle speaks about practical reasoning in terms of premisses and terms, primarily in two places in the *Nicomachean Ethics*; they have become, therefore, the *loci classici* for the practical syllogism: *EN* vi,7 and *EN* vii,3.[34] We will examine them in that order.

In *EN* vi,7, beginning at 1141b8, Aristotle speaks about φρόνησις, associating it especially with the ability to deliberate well.[35] He says that no one deliberates about things that are determined in advance, or about things that are not in some way associated with an end—that is, a practical good. The good deliberator, he says, simply speaking deliberates well with respect to the greatest practical good for man, although φρόνησις is not just about such universals but concerns itself also with perceptual singulars, since it is practical and the practical is about singulars. For this reason, he says, some persons who do not know are more practical than others who do; these non-scientific persons are the ἔμπειροι—or those who possess the "extended experience," discussed (as we have seen) in *Metaph.* i,1.

Aristotle explains:

For if someone knows that light meats are digestible and wholesome, but does not know which are light, he will not bring about health; but someone who knows that the meat of fowl is light and wholesome will rather do this.[36]

René-Antoine Gauthier's interpretation of this latter passage depends upon a syllogism he claims is alluded to in the passage.[37] The syllogism—

---

33 I deal with these issues in chapter 8.

34 Other remarks in Aristotle are also associated with the practical syllogism. In *EN* vii,3 (particularly in 1147a24–b9), he makes more remarks than we can examine closely here; there are also important remarks in *de An.* iii,11 and in *MA* vii (to be considered to some extent below).

35 In chapter 7 of the present work, φρόνησις treated in some detail.

36 εἰ γὰρ εἰδείη ὅτι τὰ κοῦφα εὔπεπτα κρέα καὶ ὑγιεινά, ποῖα δὲ κοῦφα ἀγνοοῖ, οὐ ποιήσει ὑγίειαν, ἀλλ' ὁ εἰδὼς ὅτι τὰ ὀρνίθεια κοῦφα καὶ ὑγιεινὰ ποιήσει μᾶλλον [*EN* vi,7, 1141b18–21].

37 René-Antoine Gauthier and Jean Yves Jolif, *L'Éthique à Nicomaque: Introduction, traduction et commentaire*, 2d ed. (Louvain-la-neuve: Éditions Peeters, 2002), 2.2 496–97.

Logic, Perception, Practical Syllogism 19

which he formulates by means of traditional syllogistic language—would have as its "major term" 'digestible (i.e., wholesome).'[38] Its "middle term" would be 'light' and as its "minor term" 'meat of fowl' (or simply 'fowl'). The syllogism itself (call it [A]) would, therefore, be:

[i] Digestible (wholesome) holds of light;
[ii] light holds of fowl;
[iii] ∴ digestible (wholesome) holds of fowl.

Gauthier says that Aristotle is simply wrong to say that the non-scientific man knows [ii]. If he knew that, he would be a scientific man—that is, the type of scientific man who knows not just the universal (premise [i]) but also the means (the middle) that brings one to the goal—in this case wholesomeness. What the non-scientific man does know is, therefore, the conclusion [iii]: 'Flesh of fowl is digestible,' the only proposition known through (extended) experience.

Gauthier's approach has the advantage—not shared by many modern editors—that it does not require cutting out the words 'light and' [κοῦφα καὶ] at line 1141b20; that is, his translation of the second clause of the above passage is effectively that given above ("but rather someone who knows that the meat of fowl is light and wholesome will do this") and not 'but rather someone who knows that the meat of fowl is wholesome will do this" [i.e., bring about health].[39] This is an advantage because the first clause of the passage says that what the merely scientific man lacks is knowledge of what meat is light: "For if someone knows that light meats are digestible and wholesome, but does not know which are light, he would not bring about health." The non-scientific man knows what the scientific man does not. But that still leaves the issue (raised by Gauthier)

---

38 Aristotle is somewhat vague about what this term is, wavering between 'digestible' and 'wholesome.'

39 His translation of the passage is actually as follows: "Si l'on sait en effet que les viandes légères sont faciles à digérer, c'est-à-dire bonnes pour la santé, mais qu'on ignore quelles viandes sont légères, on ne produira pas la santé. Mais celui qui sait que les volailles sont légères, c'est-à-dire bonnes pour la santé, celui-là, plutôt que l'autre, produira la santé" [Gauthier and Jolif, *L'Éthique à Nicomaque*, 1.2 171]. Bywater, following Trendelenburg, brackets the words κοῦφα καὶ in line 1141b20. A raft of others accept the Trendelenburg emendation, including Rassow, Bekker, Ramsauer, Susemihl (even with Apelt in their 1903 edition but not in 1912 edition), Stewart, and Greenwood. Citing Ross, who points to *EN* vi,11, 1143b3 and vii,3, 1147b9–10, Gauthier would leave the words κοῦφα καὶ in the text, attributing them to Aristotle's presumably misleading tendency to associate the minor term with the minor premiss.

that, if the non-scientific man knows that 'digestible (wholesome) holds of light' (as he apparently does) and that 'light holds of fowl,' he has all the knowledge necessary to be a wholly scientific man: that is, knowing not only the theory but also how to apply it.

The problem with Gauthier's interpretation is that it assumes that Aristotle has in mind primarily a syllogism of the general sort found in *APr.* and that the things known or not known by the various characters mentioned (the scientist and the non-scientist) are premises in that syllogism. In fact, the scope of Aristotles's attention—the factors that might play a part in his account—is larger than that. His point is that a learned and scientific man might know the proposition 'wholesome holds of all light meat' (because digestible), but knowledge that this particular meat is light is not the sort of knowledge to enter into a syllogism. Light meat *itself* is like the thing set out in the procedure ἔκθεσις: it is not properly syllogistic (or scientific) material—although it is proper "matter for thought." Aristotle might have gone on to make a similar point also about the meat of fowl. If a scientific man knows that 'wholesome holds of all light meat' and that 'light holds of all meat of fowl' but does not know which animals are fowl—or, for that matter, if he knows that chickens are fowl but not which animals are chickens—he will not be very good in the *practice* of medicine.

If we think of the theory held by the merely scientific man as occupying a level of understanding hovering above the domain of perception, where the non-scientific man's thoughts remain, the issue between the two men is not who has command of what syllogistic premises. The non-scientific man is more skilled at effecting cures than the scientific man because he operates at the lower level, where cures are effected. What the non-scientific man with extended experience has is not unlike what is available even to animals: that is, mere perception.[40] He, so to speak, keeps his nose to the ground. As rational, he can make use of the knowledge the scientific man has worked out in a universal way—so, he may indeed have a certain knowledge of the two premises of syllogism [A]—but he never presumes to "put it all together," that is, his concrete practical knowledge and the syllogistic premises in some sense at his disposal.[41]

---

40 *De An.* iii,11, 434a5–7.

41 In the last chapter of *Pol.* i, Aristotle speaks of the slave not having a deliberative faculty [τὸ

V. The Practical Syllogism: *EN* vii,3, 1146b35–1147a10

This approach is confirmed in the second place in which practical reasoning is couched in syllogistic language: *EN* vii,3; we shall look first at lines 1146b35–1147a10.[42] In what comes before this passage in book vii, Aristotle has been discussing various ethical character types, especially the ἀκρατής (the man who is weak of will).[43] The passage is part of a larger explanation of how such a man can know what he should do but not do it—and, in fact, do something quite different or even contrary to what he knows he should do. The argument is elliptical and crabbed:

Moreover, since there are two ways of propositions, nothing prevents someone who has both from acting against his knowledge, making use, however, of the universal but not the particular; for it is particular things that are done. And a universal also differs,[44] for one part pertains to someone himself, the other to

---

βουλευτικόν—1260a12] of his own. He shares rather in the pertinent faculty of his master: 1260a15–16, 39–40. I understand the relationship between the scientific and the non-scientific man along these general lines. See also *Pol.* iii,11, 1282a3–5, where Aristotle identifies three types of doctor, the last being merely taught *about* the craft.

42 Gauthier finds in *EN* vii,3 four major arguments: (a) 1146b24–35, (b) 1146b35–1147a10, (c) 1147a10–24, and (d) 1147a24–b10. He regards (b) (i.e., the passage we are examining here) as "purely dialectical" and maintains that Aristotle's definitive response to the problem of explaining the ἀκρατής only comes in (d) [Gauthier and Jolif, *L'Éthique à Nicomaque*, 2.2 605, 609–10]. This latter position depends on the idea that the word φυσικῶς at *EN* vii,3, 1147a24 is an allusion to the distinction between λογικῶς and φυσικῶς, according to which, to deal λογικῶς would be to mount a merely dialectical or verbal argument, whereas to deal φυσικῶς would get down to the "precise nature of the facts in question" [W. D. Ross, *Aristotle's* Metaphysics: *A revised text with introduction and commentary*, 2d ed. (Oxford: Clarendon, 1953), 2 168] (see *Metaph.* vii,4, 1029b13 and *Phys.* iii,5, 204b4 and 10). But it is unlikely that Aristotle has this sense of φυσικῶς in mind, since at the end of argument (d) he refers the reader to "students of natural science" [ὃν δεῖ παρὰ τῶν φυσιολόγων ἀκούειν—*EN* vii,3, 1147b8–9]. Moreover, argument (b) depends upon the idea that we can leave the realm of the merely logical, and the chapter's concluding remarks (1147b10–19) make a back-reference to a remark about Empedocles in argument (c) (see 1147a20 and 1147b12), but with no suggestion that that remark does not belong to his definitive account.

43 These character types are treated in some detail in chapter 6 of the present work.

44 Since Aristotle goes on to divide the proposition 'dry things are good for every man' internally into a part having to do with man, another having to do with dry things (i.e., food), the phrase διαφέρει δὲ καὶ τὸ καθόλου must refer to the two terms contained in a universal proposition. (See also *de An.* iii,11, 434a17–19.) In *de Interpretatione* (*Int.*) vii, Aristotle says that "there cannot be an affirmation in which a universal is predicated universally of a subject, for instance: every man is every animal"

the thing to be done.⁴⁵ Let us say, for instance, that dry things [i.e., food] are good for every man and that one is a man or that stuff of this sort here is dry; but whether this here is such, of this the person in question either has not the knowledge or is not exercising it. There will, then, be such a huge difference between these ways that to know in the one way [and not to act] would seem nothing strange; but to know in the other [and not to act] would be astonishing.⁴⁶

The passage begins rather awkwardly with the idea that propositions come in two "ways" [τρόποι—1147a1]. (One might have two types of proposition but not "two ways of propositions.") But eventually it becomes clear that the distinction here is not between types of propositions but between ways in which they might be known. By the end of the passage Aristotle is still speaking about ways [τρόπους—1147a8]—one associated with universality, the other with particularity—but the idea that we are dealing with distinct propositions has been set to one side (although it resurfaces later).⁴⁷ The analysis he performs is of a single universal proposition, said to contain a part referring to the person who entertains it, another referring to the act he might or might not do. That is, the universal proposition 'dry-food-being-good-for holds of every man' has, existing in—we might even say "below"—itself, the fact that the person entertaining it is a man and the fact that "stuff of this sort here is dry." The person in question either does not have knowledge of these latter facts or—and this corresponds more closely to the situation of the ἀκρατής—it is not

---

[17b14–16]; see also *APr.* i,27, 43b17–21. But this does not entail that a predicate cannot *be* universal. And, indeed, it is an often criticized characteristic of Aristotle's syllogistic that predicate terms serve also as subject terms, in which case other terms are said to be in them "as in a whole" [*APr.* i,1, 24b26–28]. In other words, we say that 'every man is an animal,' but then that 'every *animal* is mortal.' (For the criticism, see Peter Geach, "History of the Corruptions of Logic," in *Logic Matters* [Oxford: Basil Blackwell, 1972], 44–61.) One notes that Aristotle speaks at 1147a4 of τὸ καθόλου (διαφέρει δὲ καὶ τὸ καθόλου), although in 1147a2–3 he uses a feminine article: τῇ καθόλου, which refers to a universal proposition. It also appears that Aristotle speaks of 'dry things' [τὰ ξηρά: 1147a6] in order make it apparent that he conceives of the predicate term as a universal.

45 To an extent, I follow Gauthier here, who translates διαφέρει δὲ καὶ τὸ καθόλου· τὸ μὲν γὰρ ἐφ' ἑαυτοῦ, τὸ δ' ἐπὶ τοῦ πράγματός ἐστιν [1147a4–5] as, "l'universel est rapporté au sujet qui agit, et, d'autre part, à l'objet de l'action," in effect connecting πράγματός in 1147a5 with πρακτὰ in 1147a3—i.e., with the particular things that "are done."

46 *EN* vii,3, 1146b35–1147a10.

47 Notably at *EN* vii,3, 1147b9–10: ἐπεὶ δ' ἡ τελευταία πρότασις δόξα τε αἰσθητοῦ καὶ κυρία τῶν πράξεων.... There is nothing inaccurate about this; my point is simply that *EN* vii,3, 1146b35–1147a10 is not interested in identifying two distinct propositions.

present to him when he is falling prey to his dislike of dry food. That the knowledge is not present to him explains how he can both know what is good for him—and which, therefore, in that sense, he wants—and yet does not pursue it.[48]

It is apparent that Aristotle's concerns here are quite different from the concerns he has when constructing the system of the *Prior analytics* (with the exception of the remarks, already mentioned, in which he goes below the level of the syllogistic strictly speaking); and yet Gauthier, while appearing to recognize to some extent that Aristotle is taking into consideration here the terrain upon which the syllogistic is built, remains inclined toward the syllogistic model. "The problem to resolve," he says, "is the following: the incontinent man [the ἀκρατής] knows the premises but he does not know the conclusion. How is this possible?"[49] Gauthier's answer to his own question is that, although the ἀκρατής knows both the major premiss 'dry food is good for every man' and also the minor premiss 'food of such and such a quality is dry,' he does not know the latter—which he describes as universal—"in its full actuality." This is to not know "that the particular included in the minor enters into the universal," that is, that this food here *is* "food of such and such a quality." It is because of this failure in knowledge that the ἀκρατής does not put himself into action and eat the dry food.[50]

So, according to Gauthier, the syllogism that Aristotle has in mind would be something like the following:

'Good for every man' holds of 'dry' (food)
'Dry' holds of 'food of such and such a quality'
∴ 'Good for every man' holds of 'food of such and such a quality'

Since the point of practical reasoning is to bring good things (things good for every man) together with particular actions, presumably, if an agent connects 'food of such and such a quality' with this food here, he will eat it.

But this is to ignore all that Aristotle says about a part of the universal

---

48 I discuss the particular characteristics of the ἀκρατής in chapter 8.
49 Gauthier and Jolif, *L'Éthique à Nicomaque*, 2.2 605.
50 Gauthier and Jolif, *L'Éthique à Nicomaque*, 2.2 606. Aristotle says at *EN* vii,3, 1147a28 that action is the conclusion of a practical syllogism. But see also *MA* vii, 701a15–16, where he says that the agent acts immediately, *if* nothing impedes him or compels him to act otherwise.

that "pertains to someone himself" and the awareness "that one is oneself a man." Gauthier defends his approach by noting that elsewhere (i.e., at MA vii,701a26–28) Aristotle says that no one ever fails to recognize himself as the agent in his own practical reasoning; but one cannot simply ignore the fact that Aristotle analyzes "the universal" here into one part that pertains to the agent himself and another to the thing to be done. Moreover, in order to make the minor premise in the above syllogism a universal (as he must do, since it is within a universal term that the particular food before the agent is presumably located, although in this case inactively), Gauthier has to ignore the fact that τοιόνδε at 1147a6–7 is a demonstrative pronoun.[51] Gauthier's approach also forfeits the parallel between the phrase "that one is oneself a man" [ὅτι αὐτὸς ἄνθρωπος] and "that stuff of this sort here is dry" [ὅτι ξηρὸν τὸ τοιόνδε]—a parallel which is clearly intended by Aristotle. The agent obviously recognizes himself as a particular man; the material "here" which is dry should similarly be particular.

What sort of thought process does Aristotle then have in mind? He apparently starts with a proposition like 'dry-food-being-good-for holds of every man.' Since in the practical realm seemingly good things are brought together with individuals in action (or at least considered action), the conclusion would be that the agent (a man) goes for—perhaps only in his mind—the dry food. We might represent this in symbols as 'D ⇐ M,' where M represents every man, '⇐' represents 'theoretical going toward' (a relation moving from right to left), and 'D' represents a 'dry-food-as-good-for,' since Aristotle says that this part of the universal represents the thing to be done (i.e., the πρᾶγμα: 1147a5), but considered generally.[52] Below this—that is, below the level of universal propositions, which for Aristo-

---

51 Gauthier's translation of ξηρὸν τὸ τοιόνδε [1147a6–7] is "L'aliment qui présente telle et telle qualité est un aliment sec" [Gauthier and Jolif, L'Éthique à Nicomaque, 1.2 199, 2.2 606]. Aristotle's mention of a particular would come in, therefore, only in the subsequent clause: ἀλλ' εἰ τόδε τοιόνδε, which Gauthier translates, "mais, au contraire, que 'cet aliment-ci présente telle et telle qualité' ... ". The "au contraire" injects a second note of opposition with respect to the former clause that does not exist in the original. Aristotle's point is simply that the ἀκρατής in a certain sense knows that "stuff of this sort here is dry" [ὅτι ξηρὸν τὸ τοιόνδε] "but" that knowledge is not active. We find similar sortal mixed with singular language at de An. iii,11, 434a18–19: ἡ μὲν γὰρ λέγει ὅτι δεῖ τὸν τοιοῦτον τὸ τοιόνδε πράττειν, ἡ δὲ ὅτι τόδε τοιόνδε, κἀγὼ δὲ τοιόσδε.

52 The unusual direction of the arrow represents the fact that practical thinking proceeds toward the relevant end, which occupies the place occupied by the major term in a standard syllogism. See Flannery, Acts Amid Precepts, 8–12.

tle is static—we find a proposition that corresponds to 'D ⇐ M' but is the type of reasoned experience a man might have who is simply concerned to bring himself together with the dry food before him.[53] This is the domain of the perceptual, although the perceptual as characterized by the fluidity and directedness of the practical, fueled as it is by ὄρεξις.[54] We might represent the possible event in this fashion: 'd ← m,' where 'm' represents the individual man, '←' the right left relation of actually going toward (at least intentionally), and 'd' the actual object of the action (or intention): this dry food.

That gives us an argument—if it can be called an argument at all—that looks like this:

$$D \Leftarrow M$$
$$d \leftarrow m$$

This is not a syllogism, of course, but then human action does not occur at the level of syllogisms (although syllogistic premisses and conclusions may play a role in practical reasoning). This distinction of levels provides Aristotle with an explanation of what happens when the ἀκρατής fails to do that which be believes he should do. As Gauthier acknowledges, the ἀκρατής fails to push his universal belief down into the particular realm of action. It is impossible for a man to grasp the whole of what is represented by (what we might call) the DMdm diagram and to grasp it in such a way that he knows that 'd ← m' is part of 'D ⇐ M'—and not to act (or, at least, not to intend to act). But if we presume that he attends only to 'D ⇐ M'—which, as a universal of the sort that appears in the syllogistic, remains above the fray of the practical life—we presume nothing impossible.

VI. The Practical Syllogism: *EN* vii,3, 1147a24–b19

EN vii,3 adds two further explanations of what happens when the ἀκρατής fails to do that which he believes he should do. The first of these (1147a10–24) uses sleep, inebriation, and madness to account for the failure of the ἀκρατής to act according to his knowledge. Individuals in such

---

53 For the static character of the universal, see *de An.* iii,9, 432b26–29, iii,11, 434a16.
54 See above, note 32.

states may in a sense know what they should do, but their condition prevents them from calling it to mind. The fact that such individuals "use the language that flows from knowledge proves nothing," he says, "for even men under the influence of these passions utter scientific proofs and verses of Empedocles, and those who have just begun to learn can string together words, but do not yet know" [1147a17–22].

This argument does not contain much syllogistic-type language; but the argument that follows it does. There, in an argument that Aristotle calls "physical" [1147a24], he attributes ἀκρασία (weakness of will) to the presence of two "opinions" in the soul of the ἀκρατής:

(1) The one opinion [δόξα] is universal, the other is about particulars, of which [particulars] [αἴσθησις] already has the command. And when a single opinion is generated from these,[55] the soul necessarily at that point utters that which has been concluded [τὸ συμπερανθὲν]; and, in the case of productive opinions,[56] it must immediately act. (2) For instance, if one ought to taste of every sweet thing, and this is a sweet thing, that is, it is one of the particulars, one who can act and is not prevented from doing so must necessarily at the same time also act. (3) So, when the universal opinion is present hindering tasting and the other (that every sweet thing is pleasant and this here [τουτὶ] is a sweet thing) this one is active (desire happening to be present), the one opinion, therefore, says to flee this but desire leads forward, for it can move each of the parts.[57]

---

55 I.e., from the universal and the particular opinions.

56 Gauthier, citing *MA* vii, 701a23, says that Aristotle uses the word ποιητικαῖς [1147a28] in the sense of πρακτικαῖς.

57 μὲν γὰρ καθόλου δόξα, ἡ δ' ἑτέρα περὶ τῶν καθ' ἕκαστά ἐστιν, ὧν αἴσθησις ἤδη κυρία· ὅταν δὲ μία γένηται ἐξ αὐτῶν, ἀνάγκη τὸ συμπερανθὲν ἔνθα μὲν φάναι τὴν ψυχήν, ἐν δὲ ταῖς ποιητικαῖς πράττειν εὐθύς· οἷον, εἰ παντὸς γλυκέος γεύεσθαι δεῖ, τουτὶ δὲ γλυκὺ ὡς ἕν τι τῶν καθ' ἕκαστον, ἀνάγκη τὸν δυνάμενον καὶ μὴ κωλυόμενον ἅμα τοῦτο καὶ πράττειν. ὅταν οὖν ἡ μὲν καθόλου ἐνῇ κωλύουσα γεύεσθαι, ἡ δέ (ὅτι πᾶν γλυκὺ ἡδύ, τουτὶ δὲ γλυκύ) αὕτη δὲ ἐνεργεῖ (τύχῃ δ' ἐπιθυμία ἐνοῦσα), ἡ μὲν οὖν λέγει φεύγειν τοῦτο, ἡ δ' ἐπιθυμία ἄγει· κινεῖν γὰρ ἕκαστον δύναται τῶν μορίων ... [*EN* vii,3, 1147a25–35]. The text here is that given in Bywater, although I have altered the bracketing: now, instead of bracketing αὕτη δὲ ἐνεργεῖ in 1147a33, I bracket ὅτι πᾶν γλυκὺ ἡδύ, τουτὶ δὲ γλυκύ (1147a32–33) and also τύχῃ δ' ἐπιθυμία ἐνοῦσα (1147a33–34). This gives Aristotle a jerky second clause in the μὲν/δὲ construction—(1) ἡ μὲν καθόλου ἐνῇ κωλύουσα γεύεσθαι, (2) ἡ δέ (ὅτι πᾶν γλυκὺ ἡδύ, τουτὶ δὲ γλυκύ) αὕτη δὲ ἐνεργεῖ (τύχῃ δ' ἐπιθυμία ἐνοῦσα)—but Aristotle in effect acknowledges this when in the next phrase he indicates to the reader by means of a second οὖν that his thought is still moving forward: "the one opinion, *therefore*, says to flee this but desire leads forward ..." [ἡ μὲν οὖν λέγει φεύγειν τοῦτο, ἡ δ' ἐπιθυμία ἄγει ...]. As David Charles has pointed out to me, we find a similar idea at *de An*. iii,9, 433a31–3: ἔτι καὶ ἐπιτάττοντος τοῦ νοῦ καὶ λεγούσης τῆς διανοίας φεύγειν τι ἢ διώκειν οὐ κινεῖται, ἀλλὰ κατὰ τὴν ἐπιθυμίαν

This is a difficult passage, requiring careful consideration; for that reason I have divided it into sections. In (1) Aristotle sets out two elements in which he is interested: one universal, the other particular (and perceptual). One notices that they are not called premises or propositions but simply opinions. Moreover, as he says, sometimes these two become one, thereby producing an action. But it is not as if, when this does not occur, we are left with two distinct opinions. As in the argument we examined previously (*EN* vii,3, 1146b35–1147a10), the particular things are in the universal terms, but sometimes the thought of the universals is not pressed down into the perceptual domain. So, in the rest of the passage, Aristotle has in mind primarily individual universal opinions that sometimes do, sometimes do not, come down into the more material realm of action.

In (2), Aristotle gives an example of a universal that does press down into the practical: "if one ought to taste of every sweet thing, and this is a sweet thing, that is, it is one of the particulars, one who can act and is not prevented from doing so must necessarily at the same time also act." At first reading, this sounds as if Aristotle has in mind something like a syllogism in Darii (except, of course, that genuine syllogisms do not concern singulars, and this one does). Presumably it would go: 'OTT holds of every S; S holds of s; therefore, OTT holds of s'—where 'OTT' = 'ought to taste,' 'S' = 'sweet thing,' and 's' = a particular sweet thing. But there is no reason to see a syllogism in what Aristotle says and plenty of reason not to. As we saw in the earlier argument (*EN* vii,3, 1146b35–1147a10), the particulars associated with action reside within and below the universal terms of the propositions in question, as in the DMdm diagram. Moreover, in (3), which we shall analyze shortly, the event discussed here in (2) is referred to in the singular. So, it is more reasonable to think of "this sweet thing" [τουτὶ γλυκὺ: 1147a29], as residing within and below the universal term S (in effect, 'sweet things'). As we shall see shortly, near the end of *EN* vii,3, Aristotle refers to a particular opinion of the type mentioned in (1) indif-

---

πράττει, οἷον ὁ ἀκρατής. The parts mentioned at the very end of the quotation (1147a35) are probably parts of the soul, here the intellect and (as it appears) the passionate part (the ἐπιθυμία). See Gottfried Ramsauer, ed., *Aristotelis Ethica Nicomachea: Edidit et commentario continuo instruxit* (Leipzig: Teubner, 1878), ad 1147a35, who speaks of "et ὁ λόγος ὁ ἕνεκά τινος, et ipsa ἡ ἐπιθυμία." (I am grateful to Charles for this reference.)

ferently as a proposition [πρότασις: 1147b9] and as a term [ὅρον: 1147b14].

In the earlier argument, Aristotle was more explicit about how he conceives the structure of actually going for something. The universal opinion there was 'all men ought to go for dry food' (or D ⇔ M), which becomes active when the embedded 'd' and 'm' (*this* dry food and *this* man) are genuinely known; but we also noted that in *MA* vii Aristotle says we can usually dispense with mention of the M-m relation, since few people fail to realize that they themselves fall under the universal term that they employ in their own practical reasoning. The result of setting this latter consideration aside is a proposition of the sort mentioned in (2): "one ought to taste of every sweet thing" (or 'OTT holds of every S'), where the particular sweet thing the ἀκρατής actually goes for resides within and below the 'S.' When, as in the case of the ἀκρατής, going for the sweet thing actually ensues, we can speak of the two opinions mentioned in (1)—that is, the universal and the other, which is "about particulars"—as one.

In (3), therefore, Aristotle discusses two universals: the first, uttered by reason, discourages tasting sweet things; the second is the universal opinion expounded in (2). Most (but not all) commentators and translators have understood Aristotle to be setting out here the two premisses of another syllogism corresponding to what occurs within the ἀκρατής; the Revised Oxford Translation, for instance, has: " … and there is also the opinion that everything sweet is pleasant, and that this is sweet (now this is the opinion that is active), and when appetite happens to be present in us," etc.[58] But the tortured syntax of the Greek suggests that the words—"that every sweet thing is pleasant and this here [τουτί] is a sweet thing" [ὅτι πᾶν γλυκὺ ἡδύ, τουτὶ δὲ γλυκύ]—are a quick back-reference to the joining of 'one ought to taste of every sweet thing' and 'this is a sweet thing' mentioned in (2).[59] Thus, once again, the best explanation of what Aristotle is saying looks not to a (second) practical syllogism but to the relationship between the universal and the singular. What happens in the ἀκρατής is that he has in his head two universal opinions: one saying that

---

58 *EN* vii,3, 1147a32–34. The words 'everything sweet is pleasant' would be the major premise, 'this is sweet' the minor premise.

59 In the reformulation, "one ought to taste of every sweet thing" has become "every sweet thing is pleasant."

he ought not to taste sweet things, another saying the opposite; the latter gets activated because it makes contact with the perceptual level, because of the presence of desire.

Once a universal opinion—whichever it is—gets pressed down into the lower domain, the domain of the truly practical, the action necessarily follows—or, at least, a decision to act follows and the action itself will follow eventually unless something impedes it. Says Aristotle in the seventh chapter of *De motu animalium*:

> For when a man is *actually* using [ἐνεργήσῃ] perception or imagination or comprehension with respect to some end, he does at once that toward which he is inclined. For actualization of the inclination steps in for inquiry or thought. I want to drink, says appetite; this here is drink, says perception or imagination or comprehension; at once I drink. It is in this way that animals begin to move and to act: inclination being the last cause [ἐσχάτης αἰτίας] of movement, but inclination coming about either *through* perception or through imagination and thought. When animals are inclined to act, some act and some do not act, some through desire or spiritedness, some through will.[60]

Once matters are pushed into the domain of perceptual singulars, that is, once there is "actualization" of the capacity in question in the realm of inclination, animals—including rational animals—are all alike: they go toward their objects. That is simply what that realm *does*: it goes toward things. Aristotle makes this point a bit earlier in the same chapter. There he considers two contrary—or nearly contrary—universal propositions: 'all men ought to walk' and 'no man ought to walk now.' If the man in question presses one or the other universal to the material-level realization that 'I am a man,' there is action. "And he does both, if he is not prevented or coerced."[61] Aristotle's point is obviously not that the man does both things at once but that he does one or the other, depending on which universal is pressed down into the singular domain; but once at that level, the action is inevitable, provided it is not impeded. In rational animals, reason (in the above quotation, "comprehension" or νοῦς) may remain in charge, and then (to use the *EN* vii,3 example) the man abstains from tasting the sweet

---

60 *MA* vii, 701a29–b1. Aristotle makes similar remarks at *de An.* iii,11, 434a5–15.
61 αἱ ταῦτα ἄμφω πράττει, ἂν μή τι κωλύῃ ἢ ἀναγκάζῃ [*MA* vii, 701a15–16].

thing—although this too is an action of sorts, just as the man's not walking is the actualization of a thought. If the man goes for the sweet thing, this means that the opinion "one ought to taste of every sweet thing" has won through. In either case, however, it is inclination that brings about the action: it is the "last" (or proximate) cause.

In the concluding remarks of *EN* vii,3, Aristotle speaks once again of the second opinion of (1), although he now calls it "the last proposition" [ἡ τελευταία πρότασις: 1147b9]—or, alternatively, "last term" [τὸν ἔσχατον ὅρον: 1147b14]. Echoing what he says in (1), Aristotle says that this proposition both "is an opinion about that which is perceptible and commands actions."[62] But now he has in mind a perceptual singular residing within and below the universal uttered by *reason* in (3), that is, the universal "hindering tasting," for he says that the ἀκρατής, because of passion, either does not have this opinion or has it in a merely formal way: "as a drunken man may utter the verses of Empedocles." Because this "last term" is not (as such) a universal, he says, the basic principle of Socrates can be maintained: that knowledge is never dragged about by passion. What is dragged about is the perceptual faculty [τῆς αἰσθητικῆς: 1147b17], which is at a level of thought quite distinct from the level at which the syllogistic—which is involved in all genuine knowledge—is elaborated.[63]

VII. The Connection between the Perceptual and the Syllogistic

The realm of action (the realm of perceptual singulars) is, therefore, quite distinct from the realm of universal terms (the realm of the syllogistic). It is important to bear in mind, however, that it is not an utterly lawless realm. Far from it: for Aristotle, as I argue below, what might be called the supreme logical law of all, the principle of non-contradiction,

---

62 *EN* vii,3, 1147b9-10: δόξα τε αἰσθητοῦ καὶ κυρία τῶν πράξεων. The language recalls the language of (1): ἡ δ' ἑτέρα περὶ τῶν καθ' ἕκαστά ἐστιν, ὧν αἴσθησις ἤδη κυρία [1147a25–26].

63 αἱ διὰ τὸ μὴ καθόλου μηδ' ἐπιστημονικὸν ὁμοίως εἶναι δοκεῖν τῷ καθόλου τὸν ἔσχατον ὅρον καὶ ἔοικεν ὃ ἐζήτει Σωκράτης συμβαίνειν· οὐ γὰρ τῆς κυρίως ἐπιστήμης εἶναι δοκούσης περιγίνεται τὸ πάθος, οὐδ' αὕτη περιέλκεται διὰ τὸ πάθος, ἀλλὰ τῆς αἰσθητικῆς [*EN* vii,3, 1147b13–17]—following Stewart [J. A. Stewart, *Notes on the Nicomachean Ethics of Aristotle* (Oxford: Clarendon Press, 1892), II 163-64], who reads περιγίνεται instead of the MSS's παρούσης γίνεται in line 16.

Logic, Perception, Practical Syllogism   31

has its basis not in the syllogistic but in (or at) the perceptual level. Upon this pinciple depends the nature of virtue itself. Aristotle says in *EN* vi,7 that φρόνησις is not "concerned with universals only—it must also recognize the particulars [τὰ καθ' ἕκαστα]; for it is practical, and practice is concerned with particulars" [1141b14–16].) The attitude and the behavior of the φρόνιμος (the man possessed of φρόνησις) with respect to these particulars (or singulars) must be consistent, for φρόνησις is ultimately an intellectual virtue and intellectual virtue requires truth and consistency.[64]

There are a couple of passages in the *Prior analytics* where Aristotle discusses the relationship between the syllogistic and the perceptual realms; they help us to see the way in which the principle of non-contradiction belongs properly to the domain of perceptual singulars. We return now to matters having to do with speculative as opposed to practical reason, although even here Aristotle sometimes speaks of that which is good. The first passage is contained in *APr.* ii,15. In it, Aristotle argues that in two of the syllogistic figures (the second and the third) it is possible to derive a conclusion from propositions that are "opposed." Pairs of opposed propositions would include the pairs 'YeX'-'YaX' and 'YeX'-'YiX.'[65] Let us say that, in a syllogism in the second figure mood Festino ('YeX & YiZ ∴ XoZ'), the middle term (Y) is 'P' (meaning 'profitable') and both the major and the minor (X and Z) terms are 'G' (meaning 'good'). (Formally speaking, nothing prevents 'X' and 'Z' turning out to be the same thing.)[66] Since the premisses of Festino are of different quality (negative and affirmative) and since their terms (P and G) are identical, they are opposed. Given these opposed premisses we can validly derive the conclusion that some good thing is not good: GoG' ('PeG & PiG ∴ GoG'). But such a syllogism, as legitimately formulable as it is, can never produce a true conclusion. Says Aristotle: "And it is clear that from falsehoods it is possible to deduce a truth (as was said before),[67] but from opposed premisses it is not possible. For the syllogism is always contrary to the fact, e.g., if a thing is good, that it is

---

64 On φρόνησις and the φρόνιμος, see chapter 7.
65 I use the standard abbreviations: 'a' = 'holds of every,' 'e' = 'holds of no,' 'i' = 'holds of some,' and 'o' = does not hold of some'; the first term in a proposition is the predicate, the second the subject. As above, 'X' and 'Y' are place holders for actual terms 'A,' 'B,' 'C,' etc.
66 For the second figure moods with opposed premisses, see *APr.* ii,15, 63b40–64a19.
67 That is, in *APr.* ii,2–4.

not good ..." [*APr.* ii,15, 64b7–10]. Note that Aristotle even mentions here the conclusion we have just derived from the premisses 'profitable holds of no good' and 'profitable holds of some good.'

Thus, although it is possible to derive 'GoG' from 'PeG & PiG,' such a conclusion will always be false. At first, this might appear almost trivial, but it is a significant result. It shows that, for Aristotle, although at the perceptual level one can say and think what one wants, even at that level one is subject to the principle of non-contradiction: the conclusion 'some good thing is not good' is necessarily false. Moreover, although pertaining properly to the lower level, this principle has a bearing upon the higher, syllogistic level. Although one can put the terms P and G together into premisses of opposite quality, they can never yield a true conclusion. The reason for this is that the two premisses characterize their subject (which happens to be represented by the same term, G) in incompatible ways, saying both that P holds of it and that it does not. These latter cannot be brought together into a single coherent thought, since they go in quite opposite directions: they take away from a particular "logical spot" and add to it the same thing; that is, they take P *from* G and add P *to* the same. The two propositions ('PeG' and 'PiG') can be accepted into the same system (the syllogism 'PeG & PiG ∴ GoG') only in as much as one does not attend to the fact that the subject term is a single term. But once one does attend to this, one sees that they refer—or seek to refer—to a thing that could not be. This thing *would* exist in the domain of perceptual singulars, but that domain can accept no such thing. It cannot contain a good thing that is both profitable and not profitable (at the same time and in the same respect), any more than it can contain some good thing that is not good, which the possibility of a thing that is both profitable and not profitable would entail. In other words, opposed propositions entail a subject that cannot be itself; obviously, such a thing cannot exist at all.

That this is the way Aristotle understands the relationship between the formally logical and the perceptual becomes apparent in *Metaph.* iv,4, where he discusses the soundness of the principle of non-contradiction. He acknowledges there that, in a sense, since this principle is the most basic of all principles, it cannot be demonstrated: other things are demonstrated by virtue of it, not vice-versa. But then he acknowledges that one can get some argumentative leverage on an interlocutor's intransigent denial of the principle by getting him to "at least signify something" [σημαίνειν γέ τι: *Metaph.* iv,4, 1006a21]. One cannot ask him to utter a proposition, he says, since a proposition's being true excludes its being false, and its being false excludes its being true—and this is exactly what the interlocutor (remaining necessarily at a formal level) disputes. But if he is willing to signify "something"—or, perhaps better, "some thing" [τι]—you've got him, since no such thing can ever possess contradictory qualities. Although Aristotle does not use the word αἴσθησις in this section of the *Metaphysics*, he is in effect leaving the realm of dialectical disputation—which at least wields the instruments proper to scientific knowledge—and descending to the level of the perceptual.[68] It is apparent that Aristotle believes that this level is more *evidently* bound by the principle of non-contradiction than the syllogistic level.

In *APr.* ii,21, Aristotle discusses matters similar to those discussed in *APr.* ii,15, although in ii,21 he is more concerned with simple error (as opposed to inconsistency). He says a number of things very reminiscent of what we have heard him saying about how it is possible for the ἀκρατής to act against his own knowledge. Consider a syllogism in the form of Barbara ('ZaY & YaX, ∴ ZaX'), in which the major term is 'has angles equal to two right angles' (R), the middle is 'triangle' (T), and the minor is 'perceptible triangle [αἰσθητὸν τρίγωνον: 67a14]' (p). Now suppose that a man denies that p (the "auld triangle" in the song about Mountjoy Prison) exists; but he knows that R holds of everything of which T holds. In this case, he both knows and does not know that R holds of p: he knows that it holds of every T, but he does not know that p is among the Ts, since he does believe that it exists. "For knowing that every triangle has angles equal to two right angles is not simple [ἁπλοῦν]: on the one hand, it is to

---

68 On the interpretation of this argument, see R. M. Dancy, *Sense and Contradiction: A Study in Aristotle* (Dordrecht: D. Reidel, 1975), 14–21, 79–91; Annamaria Schiaparelli, "Aspetti della critica di Jan Lukasiewicz al principio aristotelico di non-contraddizione," *Elenchos* 15 (1994): 43–77; also, Kevin L. Flannery, "Due sensi della logica in Aristotele," in *L'Attualità di Aristotele*, ed. Stephen L. Brock (Rome: Armando Editore, 2000), 73–84, and Kevin L. Flannery, "Logic and Ontology in Alexander of Aphrodisias's Commentary on *Metaphysics*, Book IV / Logica e significato nel commento di Alessandro di Afrodisia alla *Metafisica*, libro IV," in *Alessandro di Afrodisia e la «Metafisica» di Aristotele*, ed. Giancarlo Movia (Milan: Vita e Pensiero, 2003), 117–52.

have the universal knowledge; on the other, the particular."⁶⁹ Since these bits of knowledge occupy different levels, the person who knows the relevant geometry but does not (in this sense) know that the auld triangle has angles equal to two right angles, does not believe contradictory things. In other words, we cannot say that he *conceives* of a world in which all triangles contain two right angles but this one triangle does not—anymore than the ἀκρατής acts as he does because he believes the moral universe is simply contradictory.⁷⁰

In the last section of *APr.* ii,21, Aristotle applies such ideas (or procedures) to the good and the bad, and so apparently within the field of ethics.⁷¹ Just before the passage in question he has offered yet another explanation of how a person might manage to know and yet be mistaken about a matter pertaining to that very knowledge. The explanation might be, he says, that the knowledge is not actualized; it does not therefore come into direct conflict with the false belief. The erroneous belief in this case is "not contrary to knowledge," he says, "for error contrary to universal knowledge would have to be a syllogism."⁷² In other words, there is a break between a body of knowledge cast in syllogistic form and the occasional erroneous belief that even a scientist might hold on occasion; this break explains the latter's *lapsus* in such a way that we need not posit a contradiction within the system of knowledge itself.

But then Aristotle considers a difficulty. An objector maintains that in fact it is possible to construct a syllogism—indeed, a logically very tight and scientific syllogism—that contains such an error, since the various terms can be predicated of one another reciprocally. Such a syllogism is

---

69 *APr.* ii,21, 67a16–19. Recall the way we distinguished 'D' and 'd', and 'M' and 'm,' in section V, above.

70 Aristotle goes on immediately to apply these ideas to the example of the slave-boy in Plato's *Meno*: see *APr.* ii,21, 67a21–26.

71 Smith writes: "It seems probable ... that Aristotle has in mind some type of situation in which it is argued that a person has inconsistent beliefs as a result of thinking that the same thing is simultaneously good and bad (which could perhaps form the basis for an argument in Platonic fashion that this person confuses the nature of goodness with the nature of badness). This, in turn, may lend further support to the suggestion of a relationship between this passage and Greek discussions of the problem of weakness of will" [Smith, *Aristotle: Prior Analytics*, 216].

72 ... οὐδ' αὖ διὰ τὴν ὑπόληψιν ἐναντίαν ἀπάτην τῇ ἐπιστήμῃ· συλλογισμὸς γὰρ ἡ ἐναντία ἀπάτη τῇ καθόλου [*APr.* ii,21, 67b10–11].

clearly possible with respect to facts; it is possible, therefore, also when representing beliefs.

The passage reads as follows:

[1] But someone who believes that to be good is to be bad will believe that it is the same thing to be good and to be bad.[73] [2] For let A stand for 'to be good' and B for 'to be bad,' and again C for 'to be good.' Since then he believes that B and C are the same, he will believe that B is C; and again that A is in like manner B; and A is, therefore, also C. [3] For just as, if it is true that B holds of that of which C holds and that A holds of that of which B holds, it is also true that A holds of C, so it is with believing. And the same applies to being since, if C and B are the same, as are again B and A, C is the same as A—just as it was with opining.

[4] Is this then necessary if someone grants the first point? But perhaps *that* is false, that is, that some could believe that to be good is to be bad except accidentally,[74] for there are available various ways in which one can believe this. This must be investigated more thoroughly.[75]

The objector's basic thesis is contained in the first sentence ([1]): If "someone who believes that to be good is to be bad," he will necessarily "believe that it is the *same thing* to be good and to be bad." If this is true and the person in question can believe that to be good is the very same

---

73 Most commentators (following Philoponus: *in APr.* 467.2–4) say that the phrases τὸ ἀγαθῷ εἶναι and τὸ κακῷ εἶναι in this passage are meant to refer to definitions or essences; thus, the Revised Oxford Translation gives: "But he who believes the essence of good is the essence of bad," etc. [67b12–13]. But this is hard to reconcile with the structure of the general argument, which (as I argue below) starts from propositions containing subjects and predicates related to each other in the standard way and then argues *to* identity among the terms. To say that the essence of good is the essence of bad is already to assert an identity.

74 Waitz says of this phrase: "Quamquam non fit, ut quis ponat res contrarias unam esse et eandem, tamen accidit, ut quis ponat contingere aliquando, ut quid recte praedicetur de aliqua re quod eius naturae contrarium sit" [Theodor Waitz, ed., *Aristotelis Organon Graece: Novis codicum auxiliis adiutus recognovit, scholiis ineditis et commentario instruxit Theodorus Waitz* (Leipzig: Hahn, 1844–46), I 527].

75 *APr.* ii,21, 67b12–26. The most detailed exegesis of this passage that I have found is at Maier, *Die Syllogistik des Aristoteles*, II.2 367 n. 1; see also Smith, *Aristotle: Prior Analytics*, 215–16, which is good on the general structure of the argument. Philoponus [*in APr.* 467.1–8] thinks that Aristotle has selected the terms of the objection's syllogism poorly, with the result that the objector maintains nothing objectionable. It is for this reason, according to him, that Aristotle says at the end of the chapter that the matter should be investigated "more accurately" [ἀκριβέστερον].

thing as to be bad, then there is no "wiggle room" left by means of which to explain away the simultaneous presence of contraries. One would have to acknowledge that a world in which good was not-good and not-good good was a genuine possibility; such a world would be believable. Aristotle cannot accept this, since it is tantamount to saying that one might conceive of a world in which Socrates might be standing and not standing at the same moment and in the same sense.

Most of the passage is a justification of the move from the protasis of the objector's basic thesis to the apodosis: that is, from someone's believing that to be good is to be bad, to his believing that it is the same thing to be good and to be bad. As suggested above, the transition from protasis to apodosis is effected by means of a syllogism, whose terms are shown to be reciprocally predicable.[76]

The objector sets out (in [2]) the terms of a fairly standard syllogism:[77]

'To be good' [A] holds of 'to be bad' [B];
'to be bad' [B] holds of 'to be good' [C];
∴ 'to be good' [A] holds of 'to be good' [C].

He then argues that the terms of the minor premise ('to be bad' holds of 'to be good') can be reversed; or, as he puts it, "Since then he believes that B and C are the same, he will believe that B is C" (i.e., that C holds of B) and not just that C is B (i.e., that B holds of C).[78] So also can the terms of the major premise and the conclusion be reversed—although in the latter case, it hardly makes much difference. In the next few lines (67b17–22) (i.e., [3]), the objector argues that the basic syllogism he has employed is valid whether one considers beliefs or facts. So, using it, plus the argument that the terms are predicable reciprocally, it can be deduced that "it is the same thing to be good and to be bad" (or that someone might be-

---

[76] That Aristotle is interested in this passage in reciprocal terms is confirmed in the subsequent chapter, *APr.* ii,22, which is about such terms.

[77] It is only "fairly standard" since it contains no quantifiers; perhaps the propositions are "indefinite": *APr.* i,1, 24a19–22.

[78] The protasis of this sentence, i.e., "he believes that B and C are the same [ταὐτὸν: 67b15]," does not make reference to the identity found in the apodosis of the objector's basic thesis (that is to say, "it is *the same thing* [τὸ αὐτὸ: 67b12–13] to be good and to be bad") but to the protasis of that basic thesis: "someone... believes that to be good is to be bad."

lieve that "it is the same thing to be good and to be bad"), which was the proposition to be proved.

Then (in [4]) comes Aristotle's objection to the objection—and it is this that interests us most. He says: "Is this then necessary if someone grants the first point?" The "first point" is the protasis of the objector's basic thesis.[79] Without this protasis, the argument that follows it is never generated. In other words, Aristotle calls into doubt whether someone could actually believe that to be good is to be bad. In a way somewhat similar to what we saw in *APr.* ii,15, one can put either proposition—either "'to be good' holds of 'to be bad'" or "'to be bad' holds of 'to be good'"— into a syllogism, but only because they both meet the most formal of requirements for syllogistic premises: each has two terms held together by a canonical connector, 'holds of.' But one cannot really believe that either states the truth. In a sense, we can think what we want—and make plans and act as we want—but there are some thoughts (etc.) to which the world cannot logically correspond.

If this is the case, it is important for our understanding of moral psychology. Assuming (as is reasonable to assume) that consistency of belief is something to be desired, if one cannot believe that to be good is to be bad or that to be bad is to be good, there is good reason to avoid moral inconsistency in general, for moral inconsistency always comes down to a claim that that which is bad is good (or vice-versa). Not only can such a claim not be true but (and this is what is important for moral psychology) one's soul cannot accommodate the idea. This would all apply not only to the ἀκρατής but also to another figure we shall meet anon, the depraved man or ἀκόλαστος. The idea that the ἀκρατής—the man who is weak of will, doing what he knows he ought not to do—is torn or divided internally is not terribly controversial; but this passage at the end of *APr.* ii,21 suggests that also this other ethical type, the ἀκόλαστος—the man who is utterly steeped in evil practices—cannot have it all together either, for even he cannot genuinely believe that to be good is to be bad. We shall return to this issue, especially in chapter 8.

The φρόνιμος—that is, the ethical type that possesses perfect φρόνησις

---

79 See Ross, *Aristotle's* Prior and Posterior Analytics, 476.

—possesses also consistency of soul. Whether or not it is actually possible for one individual to achieve this state, it is very useful to know what the logical properties of such a soul might be; this would be like having at least a model of a consistency proof for the soul.[80] Of course, given the soul's complexity and changeableness, it would be impossible in any case ever to prove that a person's soul (or mind) is consistent. But having at least an idea of what perfect psychological consistency would be gives us an idea of what might go wrong within the soul and what might sometimes be put right.

VIII. Conclusion

To conclude, then, the major point of this first chapter is that the subject matter of the philosophical psychology of action is singular: it is not the practical syllogism, at least in the way typically conceived. Syllogisms are made up of universals, not of perceptual singulars. Universals are relevant to the philosophical psychology of action, but what needs to be studied first are human acts, which have their existence at a level lower than the syllogistic, a level that excludes them from the realm of science, properly considered. Accordingly, in the next three chapters, we shall be concerned with how singular human acts are shaped, characterized, qualified, etc. In subsequent chapters we shall come back to more general issues, such as how the failure to actualize one's universal moral beliefs in action adversely affects one's psychology (one's soul); but there is, in the meantime, a good deal of work to be done just in order to understand what an action is for which one might be held responsible. Even in the present chapter, we have been preparing the ground for the subsequent consideration of more general themes, for, as we have just seen, if it is true that the domain of perceptual singulars and the domain of the syllogistic are distinct, nonetheless they are held together by means of the principle of non-contradiction, which governs both domains, although it resides more basically—that is, as a principle—in the domain of perceptual singulars.

---

80 Regarding a methodology in Aristotle for proving the consistency of logical systems, see Jonathan Lear, *Aristotle and Logical Theory* (Cambridge: Cambridge University Press, 1980), 90–97.

Two

The "Physical" Structure of the Human Act

WE ESTABLISHED in chapter 1 that the proper subject matter of ethics is the singular human act and that, as such, it ought not to be conceived of as part of a syllogism such as those studied in *Prior analytics* (the syllogistic). We begin now the task proper of analyzing singular human acts, showing first of all, in section I, how Aristotle treats them in his *Physics*, where he often uses human acts as examples of movements (κινήσεις).[1] Although human acts depend upon human beings, this does not mean that the entirety of what it is to be a human act—all that one needs to take into account in order to understand a human act—is necessarily located in the human being who performs it. Like simple physical movements, the typical human act's point of arrival is different from its point of origin. The point of origin makes the act human; the hoped-for point of arrival is, in a certain sense, the agent's, that is, *he* has it in his mind; but the fact that he may not get to it shows that what it is to be such an act does not come just from him. Aristotle investigates these matters in *Phys.* iii,3, by means of a multiplex

---

1 Regarding the themes treated in section I (and especially the interpretation of *Phys.* iii,3), I have found very enlightening section B (6–30) of chapter 1 of David Charles, *Aristotle's Philosophy of Action* (London: Duckworth, 1984). See also Mary Louise Gill, "Aristotle's Theory of Causal Action in *Physics* iii,3," *Phronesis* 25 (1980): 129–47.

aporia. He shows that an act of teaching always corresponds to an instance of learning. Thus, there are two lines of intelligibility involved: the way the teacher understands what he is doing and the way the student understands what he himself is experiencing; but both are part of a single intelligible event: a "teaching-learning," we might say. The upshot of Aristotle's very dense argument is that the various pieces of intelligibility at work in such acts as teaching and learning interact in a way that ensures objectivity. Such a human act is connected to the objective world: a teacher teaches only if a student learns; or, as Aristotle says at the beginning of the chapter in question, "movement is in the movable" [*Phys.* iii,3, 202a14–15].

In section II, we bring the same set of ideas to bear upon a passage in the final book of the *Physics* in which, as part of his proof that there exists a first unmoved mover, Aristotle argues against the thesis that everything that is moved is moved by something that is moved. His response to this thesis is that, since the very intelligibility of movement involves an agent and a patient (an active element and a passive), this bi-polar structure, necessary to make sense of causality in the universe, would be nullified if either (1) movements were self-contained (if heating, for instance, did not involve, besides heating, something's being heated) or (2), in the chain of caused events, two actions of the same type could occur without the occurrence of that type of action's passive coordinate.

In section III, I show how Aristotle, in *Metaph.* iv,4, understands the bearing of the principle of non-contradiction upon human action; I argue that the bi-polar structure of human action is demanded by the principle of non-contradiction and is much tied up with it. This helps us to understand how Aristotle can speak of a bi-polar structure even in "perfect" actions such as seeing and thinking that involve no temporal or spatial extension (in so far as the moment that seeing or thinking is present, so also is the appropriate object).

How Aristotle understands seeing and thinking, as opposed to such "imperfect" acts as building a house, has, however, been much discussed in contemporary Aristotelian studies, so in the final section (section IV) I look at the passage that has been at the center of this discussion, the back section of *Metaph.* ix,6, where Aristotle makes the distinction between perfect and imperfect actions (or πράξεις). I argue that, in interpreting the passage, our emphasis ought not to be upon linguistic issues (the verbs mentioned in the passage: 'thins' and 'has thinned,' 'thinks' and 'has thought,' etc., in their various forms) but rather upon metaphysical issues and in particular upon the question, where in the sequence of an act its intelligibility is located. In perfect actions, we see in the act itself its intelligibility, for such actions are complete in themselves and for the entire duration of their existence. By contrast, in imperfect actions, such as building a house, the intelligibility arrives only once that imperfect action is past, that is, once the house is completed and the builder has ceased to perform the action we call 'building a house.' This distinction will prove important later in the present book, that is to say, beginning with chapter 6, where I argue that perfect acts are the ideas and attitudes that potentially make sense of imperfect acts and in terms of which we judge a person's character as morally good or less than that.

I. Human Movements

Aristotle does not hesitate in the *Physics* to speak of human acts as movements. An objection to this approach would be that it amounts to introducing the non-intelligible into the intelligible sphere: the merely physical into the sphere of human reason. But Aristotle finds intelligibility also in the physical world and so finds no radical incompatibility between the two spheres. There is an intelligible structure to a cylinder's rolling down a slope, for instance, even if no one notices its rolling: it is a rolling, with points on top moving below, then to the top, then below, until it gets to the bottom. This is a different species of physical movement from sliding (for example), where points down below stay there.[2] A key feature of the intelligibility of a rolling or a sliding is the fact that each has a beginning and an end, both in time and in space. The rolling cylinder may not reach that end, but, as we shall see more clearly below, the end that it would have reached, had it not been impeded, fixes its particular species.[3]

---

2 Plato distinguishes these two types of motion in this way: Τὰ δέ γε κινούμενα ἐν πολλοῖς φαίνῃ μοι λέγειν ὅσα φορᾷ κινεῖται μεταβαίνοντα εἰς ἕτερον ἀεὶ τόπον, καὶ τοτὲ μὲν ἔστιν ὅτε βάσιν ἑνὸς κεκτημένα τινὸς κέντρου, τοτὲ δὲ πλείονα τῷ περικυλινδεῖσθαι [*Laws* x, 893d6–893e1].

3 See, for instance, *Phys.* v,1, 224b7–8. On the "individuation of capacities for change," see

Such basic, bi-polar intelligibility is present also in human acts. Aristotle frequently uses the example of teaching: an act of teaching finishes in a student taught.[4]

The account of teaching is different from the account of learning; that is, "the account which states the essence [τὸν λόγον ... <τὸ> τί ἦν εἶναι λέγοντα—202b12]," is in each case different; but presupposed by both accounts is a single event. This fact is itself indication that teaching and learning exist not simply in the minds of their agents. Aristotle compares the single shared event to the road between Thebes and Athens, which can be considered by someone standing in Thebes or by someone standing in Athens, although from either perspective it is the same road.[5] In other words, to be the way from Thebes to Athens is not the same as to be the way from Athens to Thebes, although the road is the same. Similarly, even though teaching and learning are in essence quite different, they share a common event.[6]

Aristotle investigates these matters in *Phys.* iii,3, depicting the way in which the intelligibility of teaching is related to the intelligibility of learning; the very interrelatedness of these two allows him to bring into relief their common dependence on a single identifiable event. The chapter begins (conveniently) with a statement of its own conclusions. Aristotle says that a potential mover (a κινητικὸν) has its actualization (ἐνέργεια) in the movable (ἐν τῷ κινητῷ). On the other hand, the mover is the "actualizer" [ἐνεργητικὸν] *of* the movable thing, so it is as if [ὁμοίως—202a18] there were just one actualization of both mover and movable.[7] Similarly,

---

Charles, 22–27. For a contrasting view (also to my own), see Sarah Waterlow, *Nature, Change and Agency in Aristotle's* Physics: *A Philosophical Study* (Oxford: Clarendon, 1982), 127–28.

4 Besides the passage to be examined below, teaching [τὸ διδάσκειν] (paired with learning [τὸ μανθάνειν]) is discussed in *Phys.* viii,5 (see e.g. 257a12–14). Learning is also mentioned at *Metaph.* ix,6, as an example of a imperfect practice.

5 The example occurs at 202b13–14 and (partially) at *Phys.* vi,1, 231b30–232a1; at *Phys.* iii,3, 202a19–20, Aristotle speaks of the ascent being identical to the descent, which is essentially the same example.

6 The parallel with the teaching-learning example is not exact; with reason, therefore, David Charles refers to the Thebes-Athens example as the "distance *analogy*" (my emphasis) [Charles, 12]. Cebes's going to Athens (from Thebes) is presumably quite independent of Socrates's going to Thebes (from Athens); Aristotle's teaching Alexander (a particular point on a particular occasion) is not so independent of Alexander's learning from Aristotle.

7 In *Phys.* iii,3, Aristotle sometimes speaks as if there were just one actualization involved in teaching-learning, sometimes as if there were two. And yet other times he suggests that the one actual-

the interval from one to two on the number line is the same interval traversed when going from two to one; and a slope's ascent is the same thing as its descent, "for these are one, although the account [λόγος] is not one" [202a20–21].

Aristotle then deals with a "dialectical difficulty" [ἀπορίαν λογικήν—202a21–22]; or, actually, what he presents is a series of difficulties.[8] He first (202a22–36) assumes that teaching and learning involve two distinct actualizations [ἐνέργειαι] and shows that this assumption has undesirable consequences; he then (202a36–b5) assumes that they involve just one actualization and shows that this assumption too presents problems. He then (202b5–22) resolves the difficulties following from the assumption that there is just one actualization, but in such a way that—although he does not spell this out—the problems arising from the assumption that there are two are also resolved. The solution (to repeat) is contained in the idea that the actualizations of teaching and learning are in a sense the same, in a sense different.

Going through these difficulties will help us to appreciate the strength of Aristotle's position and also its importance for his philosophical psychology of action. The passage begins with the words just alluded to, "This view has a dialectical difficulty," the view being that set out in the introductory remarks of *Phys.* iii,3, to the effect that movement is in the movable and that, therefore, that which can cause movement actualizes the moved thing, qua movable, even as it is actualized itself, qua moving thing, in so doing. Aristotle then explains what the dialectical difficulty is:

Perhaps it is necessary that the actualization [ἐνέργειαν] of the agent and that of the patient should not be the same.[9]

---

ization has two "ways of being" (see e.g. 202b8–9). This same ambiguity shows up in a similar context at *de An.* iii,2, 426a15–19.

8 Ross argues that the word λογικήν means here "that the question is a superficial or dialectical one, turning on the verbal difference between ποίησις and πάθησις and failing to see that these are but two ways of describing the same event from two different points of view" [W. D. Ross, *Aristotle's Physics: A Revised Text with Introduction and Commentary* (Oxford: Clarendon, 1936), 540]. Be that as it may, Aristotle's exploration of the difficulty reveals the unacceptable consequences of denying that reciprocal actions such as teaching and learning share an actualization that pertains in a special way to the patient (in this case, the learner).

9 Here at *Phys.* iii,3, 202a22–24, Ross's 1950 Oxford Classical Text gives ἔχει δ' ἀπορίαν λογικήν· ἀναγκαῖον γὰρ ἴσως εἶναί τινα ἐνέργειαν τοῦ ποιητικοῦ καὶ τοῦ παθητικοῦ. But in the 1930 Hardie and

(I) So, there is agency [ποίησις] and there is patiency [πάθησις]; the outcome and end of the one is an action, of the other a passion. Since then they are both movements [κινήσεις], if their actualizations are different,[10] *in what are they?* Either (A) both are in what is acted on and moved, or (B)[1] the agency is in the agent and (B)[2] the patiency in the patient. (If we must call also the latter an 'agency,' the word would be used in two senses.)

But, if the latter (B) is the case, the movement [κίνησις] will be in the mover, for the same account [λόγος] will hold of mover and moved, with the result that either every mover will be moved, or, having movement, will not be moved.

If, on the other hand (A), both are in what is moved and acted upon—that is, both the agency and the patiency (both teaching and learning, being two, are in the learner)—then, first, the actualization of each will not be in each; moreover, it will be strange that two movements are moved together. For what will these two alterations [ἀλλοιώσεις] of one thing into one form [εἶδος] *be*? But this is impossible.

(II) But will there be one actualization [ἐνέργεια]?[11] But (a) it would be contrary to reason if, for two movements different in kind [εἴδει], there should be one and the same actualization—and (b) this will be the case if teaching and learning (and agency and patiency) are the same, that is, if to teach is the same as to learn and to act as to be acted upon, with the result (c) that necessarily the teacher will learn in every respect and the agent be acted upon [*Phys.* iii,3, 202a22–b5].

Gaye translation [R. P. Hardie and R. K. Gaye, trans., "Physica," in *The Works of Aristotle*, ed. W. D. Ross, vol. 2 (Oxford: Clarendon, 1930)], he follows Bekker's text, which gives ἔχει δ' ἀπορίαν λογικήν· ἀναγκαῖον γὰρ ἴσως εἶναί τινα ἐνέργειαν ἄλλην τοῦ ποιητικοῦ καὶ τοῦ παθητικοῦ. (In his introduction to the Hardie-Gaye translation, Ross discusses his own work on the project: " ... I have on the basis of a study of the reported manuscript readings and of the Greek commentators adopted a good many changes of reading in the Greek text and altered the translation to suit them. All divergences from Bekker's text are mentioned in the notes" [Hardie and Gaye, iii]). I follow the 1930 Hardie-Gaye translation for these lines (202a22–24); the same sense can be got out of the Ross's 1950 text, although with some effort.

10 πεὶ οὖν ἄμφω κινήσεις, εἰ μὲν ἕτεραι, ἐν τίνι; [202a25]. The antecedent of ἕτεραι has to be ἐνέργειαι since Aristotle is developing the idea introduced at 202a22–23 ("Perhaps it is necessary that the actualization of the agent and that of the patient should not be the same"). In the second leg of the argument (where he assumes not two ἐνέργειαι but one), Aristotle speaks explicitly of an ἐνέργεια (at 202a36 he says, ἀλλὰ μία ἔσται ἡ ἐνέργεια), maintaining the supposition that the κινήσεις are two: ἀλλ' ἄλογον δύο ἑτέρων [κινήσεων] τῷ εἴδει τὴν αὐτὴν καὶ μίαν εἶναι ἐνέργειαν [202a36–b2].

11 I understand ἀλλὰ μία ἔσται ἡ ἐνέργεια [;] [202a36] as a question.

"Physical" Structure of the Human Act   45

Some of the obscurity of this passage is cleared up once one understands that Aristotle has tacitly eliminated two of the four logical possibilities presented to him by the dialectical difficulty at issue. The question would be whether one might not be able to say that in an action such as teaching-learning there are two actualizations, the two being distributed between the agent and the patient in various ways. The first possibility (A) would have agency [ποίησις] and patiency [πάθησις] both in the patient; the second (B) would have agency in the agent and patiency in the patient.[12] The two possibilities tacitly eliminated are (C) agency and patiency both in the agent, and (D) agency in the patient and patiency in the agent. Aristotle sees some plausibility in possibilities (A) and (B). He apparently regards possibility (C) as obviously implausible. This will seem strange to many modern philosophers, used to locating human acts within the agent himself; but Aristotle's instinctive approach to such matters is quite different. In fact, his final position, as he tells us right from the beginning, is that a mover has its actualization in the movable, the passive element. Possibility (D) so reverses one's intuitions that Aristotle quite reasonably decides not to mention it.[13]

So then, in *Phys.* iii,3, 202a21–b5, Aristotle takes up possibility (B) before taking up possibility (A). If we accept this thesis, he says, movement is always going to be in the agent, for both (B)¹ and (B)² are constructed according to the same model (or account [λόγος]), that of a mover whose object is itself. But assuming this model, it is impossible to say, in speaking of movers, whether they are waiting to move or are already moving, since there is no external point toward which any movement is headed; that is, there is no such thing as accomplishing the movement or bringing it into actualization. But if this is so, we are left with two equally unacceptable possibilities: either every mover is not moving now but will be moved

---

12 For a broader textual basis regarding "passive and active δυνάμεις," see Mary Louise Gill, "Aristotle on Self-Motion," in *Self-Motion: From Aristotle to Newton*, ed. Mary Louise Gill and James G. Lennox (Princeton: Princeton UP, 1994), 17–24.

13 Possibilities (A), (B) and (C) appear in the Arabo-Latin translation studied by Augustin Mansion [see Augustin Mansion, "Étude critique sur le texte de la *Physique* d'Aristote (L.I–IV)," *Revue de philologie, de littérature et d'histoire anciennes* 47 (1923): 24]; that translation was used by Averroes. Mention of (C) is reported by Simplicius as a variant reading [*in Phys.* 441.31–33] and was apparently read by Themistius [*in Phys.* 76.28–77.4]. The latter two commentators discuss possibility (D), arguing that because of its obvious absurdity Aristotle does not mention it.

in the future, in which case there will be no unmoved movers, or every mover is already moving and so will not be moved in the future, in which case every mover will be an unmoved mover. Either possibility gives us an unintelligible universe: the first because the regression from moved to mover goes on into infinity,[14] the second because the intelligibility of every movement is isolated from every other: there would be no such thing as explaining an effect in terms of a cause to which it is subordinate.

Someone might object, What gives Aristotle the right to say that the options fall out in this exclusively disjunctive way? Why must it be the case that either every mover must be moved or every mover, already having movement, must not be moved? Might there not be some moved movers and some unmoved? Aristotle's reply would doubtless be that here he is investigating the concept of agency and its actualization. If we are to posit two (or more) classes of "agents and/or patients" in this way, there must be a reason for positing them; but, under the present assumptions, there is no such reason. Indeed, the difficulty presents itself precisely because there is no way to decide between an account that renders a mover moved and an account that renders a mover unmoved.

Moving on (or back) to alternative (A), if we say that both agency and patiency are in the patient, "then, first, the actualization of each will not be in each; moreover, it will be strange that two movements are moved together [ἅμα]" [202a34–35]. This initial expression of the difficulties connected with alternative (A) is likely to strike one as question-begging and unconvincing. Of *course* the actualization will not be present in each: that is what makes (A) the alternative that it is; and what is wrong with saying that two movements occur together? But the two points are interrelated, and why together they constitute a problem is explained—very cryptically—in the subsequent sentence: "For [γὰρ] what will these two alterations of one thing into one form *be*?" (Aristotle is using the term 'form' [εἶδος] here in its non-Platonic sense, according to which any power or potency impresses a form upon that which it affects; see *Phys.* iii,2, 202a9–12.)

The problem inherent in proposal (A) is that, given that both actualizations are placed in the patient (not one actualization in each: agent and patient), the whole usually complementary relation 'teaching-learning'

---

14 See *Phys.* vii,1, 242b71–72.

occurs in the one thing (the patient), which has a single structure: that of receiving a form. But that structure must now accommodate two forms: that which teaching impresses (which pertains no longer to an agent but—absurdly—to a patient) and that which learning impresses. And both these forms finish simultaneously [ἅμα] at the same logical spot: that is, with the patient being impressed with those two forms, at the same time.[15] But two forms—that is, two distinct types of motion—cannot get into the same spot like this. It only adds to the absurdity that the two forms are complementary (and therefore contraries): teaching and learning.[16]

Why can two forms not get into the same logical spot? Let us say we have a lamp and a punch-press: the first impressing light upon a metal object, the second literally impressing an image upon the same object. The lamp does what it does (sheds light), thereby impressing its proper form (the object was dark, now it is bright); the punch-press does what it does (punches), thereby impressing its form (the object has now a different shape). But it is nonsense to suppose that the lamp and the punch-press could enact their respective alterations and finish up with the same form. What would this one form *be*? (Recall that Aristotle asks about teaching and learning: "what will these two alterations of one thing into one form *be*?" [202a35–36].) They will be, presumably, some hybrid of visual appearance and shape. But that is absurd: those two things cannot fit in there, that is, into the one form. Aristotle waves the notion away saying, "But this is impossible" [202a36].

That brings us to section (II) of the above quotation. Here Aristo-

---

15 I use the peculiar expression 'logical spot' here instead of 'logical space' since the word 'spot' seems to suggest (more than does the word 'space') the idea that the logical area referred to belongs just to the object: it fills it up and there is nothing there other than the object (so conceived). Charles formulates Aristotle's point in this way: "It is not possible that there should be two quality changes which end at the same point with the same object" [Charles, 12].

16 The Greek corresponding to "moreover, it will be strange that two movements are moved together" [202a34–35] is (according to Ross), εἶτα ἄτοπον δύο κινήσεις ἅμα κινεῖσθαι. Two MSS have εἶτα ἄτοπον τὸ δύο κινήσεις ἅμα κινεῖσθαι and one has εἶτα ἄτοπον τὰς δύο κινήσεις ἅμα κινεῖσθαι. It would appear, therefore, that at some point someone thought that the absurdity depended on *these two* movements being brought together in this way; i.e., that the absurdity resulted from their complementarity. But the subsequent sentence—τίνες γὰρ ἔσονται ἀλλοιώσεις δύο τοῦ ἑνὸς καὶ εἰς ἓν εἶδος;—makes it clear that the problem is getting two forms into one spot, i.e., the endpoint of a patiency. Attempting to get two forms into the same spot is equivalent to attempting to meld two forms into one; it is for this reason that Aristotle asks, "For what will these two alterations of one thing towards one form be?" [*Phys.* iii,3, 202a35–36].

tle changes the assumptions of the "dialectical difficulty," asking whether there might not be just a single actualization, as he had suggested in the introductory section of the chapter. There, as we have seen, he says that a mover is the actualizer [ἐνεργητικὸν] of the moveable thing, in such a way that it is "as if [ὁμοίως] there were one actualization for the two" [202a18]. But Aristotle expresses also an objection to this idea: under this assumption it would seem that teaching and learning are exactly the same thing, sharing the same characteristics (whatever these may be). This would mean, among other things, that "necessarily the teacher will learn in every respect and the agent be acted upon" [202b4–5]. As we shall see shortly, this is something that Aristotle very much wants to avoid: that (for example) the teacher qua teacher learns what he teaches.

At this point, Aristotle offers a solution to the problems associated with this altered assumption [*Phys.* iii,3, 202b5–14]:

(III) But, perhaps the contrary is the case, since:[17]

(a) It is not strange that the actualization of one thing should be in another, for teaching is the actualization of one who can teach, but *in* something; it is not cut off from its object but is the actualization of "this" in "that."

(b) There is nothing to prevent two things from having one and the same actualization (not in such a way that their being is the same but in the way that being in potency stands toward being in act).

(c) It is not necessary that the teacher should learn, even if to act and to be acted upon are the same, provided they are not thus in such a way that the account stating their essence is one (as are raiment and dress) but [they are one] rather in the way in which the road from Thebes to Athens and the road from Athens to Thebes [are one], as has been explained above.[18]

These three countervailing points clearly correspond to the three objections made in section (II) to the there newly introduced assumption that there is just one actualization; as I suggested earlier, however, they also address the difficulties expounded in section (I). In any case, in (II)

---

17 Behind this phrase, there is a single Greek word—in fact, a single Greek letter: ἢ (202b5), the conjunction 'or.' (For a similar usage, see *Phys.* v,4, 227b19.) This introduces a series of three periods, each beginning with οὔτε (or οὔτ'), the whole sentence concluding with the interrogative mark (... καὶ πρότερον;) [202b14].

18 *Phys.* iii,3, 202b18–20.

Aristotle says that it seems not right (a) to have one actualization corresponding to two specifically different movements, (b) to say that teaching and learning are the same thing, and (c) to say (therefore) that the teacher learns in every respect. He replies in (III) that: (a) one actualization pertains to two movements only in so far as the actualization of the agent is in the patient; (b) the oneness of the actualization is not one of being, such as would make teaching and learning to be the same thing, but the type of unity that exists between something's having a characteristic in potency and its having that same characteristic in act; and (c), similarly, the intelligibility of teaching need not be merged with that of learning (so that the one would be indistinguishable from the other), since one need not say that teaching and learning are one in essence (or account) but rather they are one only in so far as they share a common event.

(III)(a) is simply the idea that introduces this chapter; so clearly Aristotle is continuing to maintain that a mover, qua mover, is not complete in itself but finds that completion in its object; its very intelligibility is partially outside of itself, this being especially apparent when the movement fails to reach its completion. In (III)(b), the comparison of the unity of actualizations with the unity of potency and act appears maladroit, until one recalls that what makes that unity less than a full unity of being is precisely a difference of actualization: seated Socrates is not standing Socrates. Despite this difference, however, there is a certain unity: Socrates seated *is* Socrates standing (in potency).[19] (III)(c) allows Aristotle to acknowledge that a teacher might learn—might even learn precisely what he teaches—while denying that which it is necessary to deny, that in so far as he is teaching he is learning. The teacher does not learn "in every respect," since teaching and learning are different in being.

As to the difficulties adduced in (I), where the assumption was that there are two actualizations, possibility (A) (both agency and patiency in the patient) gave rise to the difficulty that two forms or alterations are forced (*per impossibile*) into the same logical spot. The approach offered in (III) gets us past this difficulty also, since it acknowledges the presence of two genuine actualizations, each with a proper object (or patient). Sec-

---

19 See *Phys.* iii,1, 201a29–201b2.

tion (III) does insist on the unity of (e.g.) teaching and learning but also says that this is merely the type of unity attributable to the movement from Thebes to Athens and the movement from Athens to Thebes in so far as they share the same a road. Saying these two are one is not to say that going from Thebes to Athens is the same thing as going from Athens to Thebes.[20] The only things to which such equivalency might be attributed—that is, equivalency in which all attributes are identical—is the road itself, which is the way from Thebes to Athens or (alternatively) the way from Athens to Thebes. Applying these ideas to the teaching-learning example, when Aristotle teaches Alexander a particular concept on a particular occasion, what Aristotle does and what Alexander experiences take place upon a single "road": the contact that they have with each other. This contact is seen in an emblematic way in the fact that a teacher's teaching is not complete in himself but in his student.[21] But none of this is to assert that teaching is not different from learning.

Aristotle indicates all this in the continuation of the section we quoted just above—the continuation, in fact, of (III)(c):

For it is not the case that things which are in *any* way the same have everything the same [ταὐτὰ], but only those whose being is the same. Clearly it is not the case that, if teaching is the same thing as learning, *to* learn is also the same as *to* teach, just as it is not the case that, if there is one distance between distant places, being here at a distance from there and being there at a distance from here are one and the same thing. Speaking generally, teaching is not in the strict sense the same thing as learning, nor agency as patiency, but that [is the same thing] of which the same things hold—that is, the movement [κίνησις][22]—for

20 This approach would, I believe, be consistent with Irwin's understanding of the teaching-learning example, according to which "this token teaching and this token learning are one ...but the being of teaching is not the being of learning" [Terence H. Irwin, "Aristotelian Actions," *Phronesis* 31 (1986): 72–73]. When Irwin says that "this token teaching and this token learning are one," he means that they are identical, that is, one token. John O'Callaghan has pointed out to me a disanalogy between the teaching-learning example and the Athens-Thebes example: no actual trip involves both movements, the one from Athens to Thebes and the one from Thebes to Athens.

21 See above, note 6.

22 δ' εἰπεῖν οὐδ' ἡ δίδαξις τῇ μαθήσει οὐδ' ἡ ποίησις τῇ παθήσει τὸ αὐτὸ κυρίως, ἀλλ' ᾧ ὑπάρχει ταὐτὰ, ἡ κίνησις [202b19–21]. I emend the ταῦτα in line 202b21 to ταὐτὰ, understanding this as an allusion to the earlier point that "it is not the case that things which are in *any* way the same have everything the same [ταὐτὰ] [202b14–15]." Keeping the ταῦτα (and translating as does, for example, the Revised Oxford Translation: "To generalize, teaching is not the same as learning, or agency as patiency,

the actualization of this thing in that and of that thing through this are different in account. [*Phys.* iii,3, 202b14–22]

The "account" [λόγος], in Aristotle's language here, is the account of the individual movements or actualizations, teaching and learning; the account of any such thing cannot finish in one and the same spot, otherwise there would be no difference between going to Thebes and going to Athens.

One will recall that in section (I) possibility (B) is split into (B)^1 (agency in the agent) and (B)^2 (patiency in the patient). Aristotle apparently posits this split because of its surface plausibility: since two actualizations and two individuals are in play, it seems reasonable to put one independently intelligible actualization in each. But this leads, as we have seen, to the anomaly that either all movers are moved or all movers are unmoved. How does Aristotle's solution in (III) address this difficulty? It does so in as much as it recognizes that in a sense activities such as teaching and learning share a single actualization: "teaching is the actualization of one who can teach, but *in* something; it is not cut off from its object but is the actualization of 'this' in 'that'" [202b6–8]. What ultimately assures this passage from agent to patient is the (often quite physical) "road" the agent has to travel in order to accomplish that which makes it to be the type of agent it is. Assuming this, we also allow into the universe unmoved movers, movers that are moved, and things that are just moved, since now there is a direction of intelligibility, from initial (or relatively initial) cause to ultimate (or relatively ultimate) effect.

Aristotle's position, then, in *Phys.* iii,3 is a carefully balanced one. If one maintains that the proper analysis of events such as teaching-learning involves two separate and distinct actualizations—whether one asserts that the actualization of both agency and patiency are in the patient, or that the actualization of agency is in the agent, the actualization of patiency in the patient, or any other combination of the same factors—one eliminates true patients and ultimately the intelligibility of the universe. And if one maintains that such reciprocal actions involve a single actualization

---

in the full sense, though they belong to the same subject, the motion …") suggests that teaching and learning are to be considered one movement. See also Charles, 28.

(and understands 'singularity' here in the strict sense), it becomes impossible to distinguish teaching from learning, agency from patiency. But if one recognizes that actions like teaching and its corresponding learning are in a sense two, but are also one in so far as they have to do with a single event, human action can be rendered in this regard intelligible.

All this entails, among other things, that the structure of such actions is objective, for their proper account does not depend (for instance) just on the teacher or just on the learner. Of course, teaching and learning are in another sense "subjective": one cannot do either without intending to do so; nonetheless, the action that, for instance, a teacher intends to perform when intending to teach has a structure that depends not just on that intention.

II. The Intelligible Units of the Universe

We find similar ideas in the very rich fifth chapter of *Phys.* viii. It is a useful passage to consider—and to understand—since it helps us to see how Aristotle's analysis of human action is of a piece with his understanding of the structure of the universe more generally. Although often (and correctly) considered part of Aristotle's proof of the existence of a first unmoved mover (God), the chapter is, in fact, replete with examples of human acts: agents wielding sticks, teachers teaching, etc. Playing a key part in this account is an idea we have just seen: the—in fact, absurd—idea of a movement in which agency and patiency are the same thing, that is, a movement without a whence and a whither.

The position that Aristotle sets out to refute maintains that everything that is moved is moved by something that is moved. For Aristotle, on the contrary, although he acknowledges that some things are both moved and mover (but not in the same sense), eventually we must arrive at something that is *just* mover, without being moved. Such a thing stops the regress: if an unmoved mover is in the system under consideration, an infinite regress cannot be generated. So, if someone wants to argue for an infinite regress, he has two options. He can say that all movement is accidental and lacking in intelligibility, that is, things do move "but not because of the being moved itself" (that is, not because they are on the passive end of movements intelligible as movements of that particular type).²³ This would be the first horn of the dilemma. Alternatively (the second horn), he can say that there are things that are both moving and moved because of the being moved itself: that is, because moving *is* being moved.²⁴ In either situation there would be no ultimate thing that was just mover; an infinite regress would be possible.

Aristotle's refutation of the first horn of the dilemma does not interest us at the moment. It will surprise no one to learn that he denies that the movements we encounter in the world are ultimately haphazard and without intelligibility. But his refutation of the second horn contains a proof that any full explanation of a movement must come down eventually to a movement-type structure. He argues as follows:

Now, if the mover is not accidentally but necessarily moved and, if it were not moved [κινοῖτο], it would not move [κινοίη], then the mover in so far as it is moved [τὸ κινοῦν ᾗ κινεῖται] must necessarily be moved either (a) with the same kind of motion, or (b) with a different kind. I mean [regarding (a)], the

---

23 τοι τοῦτο ὑπάρχει τοῖς πράγμασιν κατὰ συμβεβηκός, ὥστε κινεῖν μὲν κινούμενον, οὐ μέντοι διὰ τὸ κινεῖσθαι αὐτό ... [*Phys.* viii,5, 256b5-7].

24 ... ἢ οὔ, ἀλλὰ καθ' αὑτό [*Phys.* viii,5, 256b7]. This tag is best understood in its immediate context. The οὔ in 256b7 cancels the οὐ in κινεῖν μὲν κινούμενον, οὐ μέντοι διὰ τὸ κινεῖσθαι αὐτό [256b-6-7] (which serves to characterize κατὰ συμβεβηκός causality). The result of the cancellation is that the second horn of the dilemma is about τὸ κινεῖν κινούμενον διὰ τὸ κινεῖσθαι καθ' αὑτό: the moved thing's moving by means of the being moved *in itself* or *alone*. Of the types of καθ' αὑτό relationship among terms mentioned in *APo.* i,4, this is closest to the fourth type, expounded at 73b10–16. In the latter passage Aristotle remarks: "But if through itself [δι' αὑτό], then in itself [καθ' αὑτό]—for instance, if something slaughtered dies, it also does so in [κατὰ] the slaughtering, since it does so through [διὰ] being slaughtered; and it does not just happen that the thing slaughtered dies" [73b13–16]. Aristotle is depicting a very compact line of intelligibility, much bound up (in the slaughtering case) with related linguistic expressions: slaughtered thing [σφαττόμενον], to be slaughtered [σφάττεσθαι], and slaughtering [σφαγή]. What is special, however, about the type καθ' αὑτό relationship discussed in the second horn (*Phys.* viii,5, 27ff.) is that it has no proper patient. In a slaughtering, an animal is slaughtered; in the second horn, the problem is that the relationship is compressed so far that agent becomes patient (and vice-versa). As we shall see, Aristotle also posits a second type of objectionable καθ' αὑτό relationship in *Phys.* viii,5, in which different types of change are involved (healing, being carried, growing [256b31–33]); this too must be understood as an extended sense of the fourth type of καθ' αὑτό. In other words, we must understand that there is an intelligible relationship among the terms, i.e., that the relationship is not κατὰ συμβεβηκός, but that the intelligible distance among the terms is greater than in the slaughtering example. Since Aristotle is not putting forward the second horn of the dilemma as his own position (and, in fact, he argues against it), neither need we include the "καθ' αὑτό relationship" discussed there among the genuine types of καθ' αὑτό relationship (as in *APo.* i,4).

heating thing would itself be heated and the thing making healthy made healthy and the transporting thing transported. [*Phys.* viii,5, 256b27–34]

In this first possibility, (a) within the second horn, Aristotle is supposing that, whatever (for example) heating is, its analysis never goes beyond concepts that somehow involve heat: that is to say, the concepts 'heating thing' and 'heated thing' (although in the end this first possibility also undermines any actual attempt to distinguish 'heating thing' and 'heated thing'). So, according to this conception, "the heating thing would itself be heated"; but, says Aristotle, "it is obvious that this is impossible" [*Phys.* viii,5, 256b34]:

For one must break things down to the smallest components [μέχρι τῶν ἀτόμων]: for instance, if someone teaches how to do something in geometry, this same thing in geometry must be taught; and, if something casts off, it is cast off in the same sense of casting.[25]

In other words, it is somewhat plausible to say, for example, that the fire iron is both heater and heated—even intending always the same sense of heating and not meaning, for instance, that the fire iron is heater in the sense of heating other things but heated as heated by something else—since we can in effect posit some "smallest component" within the fire iron by which it heats, another in which it is heated.[26] But then the question becomes whether, in the effort to make sense of such actions as heating, the smallest components—literally, "atoms"—can themselves be split. Aristotle's implicit answer is that no: they are atoms and therefore unsplittable.

So, the two consequences in the above passage are obviously absurd: that is, for that which teaches x, it itself to be learning precisely x and in the same sense; or for something that casts off to be cast off in that same sense of casting. Even if in some sense we can say (for example) that the teacher learns while he teaches, if we are looking to analyze the act of teaching and if we are applying the analysis to individual units of intelligibility, we are going to have to identify someone or something taught:

---

25 *Phys.* viii,5, 256b34–257a3: δεῖ γὰρ μέχρι τῶν ἀτόμων διαιροῦντα λέγειν, οἷον εἴ τι διδάσκει γεωμετρεῖν, τοῦτο διδάσκεσθαι γεωμετρεῖν τὸ αὐτό, ἢ εἰ ῥιπτεῖ, ῥιπτεῖσθαι τὸν αὐτὸν τρόπον τῆς ῥίψεως.

26 See *Metaph.* ix,2, 1046b4.

a patient. In this case, the patient would be another aspect of the teacher's own soul—the point being, however, that, if we are not to violate the principle of non-contradiction and forfeit all intelligibility, we cannot include this being taught (this patiency) in the teaching (the agency) itself.

The other possibility (b) within the second horn—that is, the other way of saying that we do not ever have to arrive at an unmoved mover standing opposite its object (even as we maintain that causality is not utterly haphazard)—is to say, not that the lines of intelligibility are compressed in the way we have just seen (that is, so compressed that there is no difference between agent and patient), but that they are more extended: they go on and on, one line of intelligibility actually being part of another, that one (of which the first is part) part of another, and so on. In introducing his refutation, Aristotle first restates the position he opposes:

Or [regarding (b)] if things are not thus [as in (a)], one kind [of change] comes from another distinct kind: e.g. the transporting thing is augmented, the thing augmenting this is altered by something else, the thing altering this is moved with respect to some other movement.[27]

According to this scenario, the process of augmenting something's size results not in a bigger thing (which would be for the augmentation to have a true—and its proper—patient) but in something that (actively) transports: τὸ φέρον; also, according to this scenario, that from which the augmenting thing issues has itself no conceptual connection with augmentation. It is important to note that, although in the translation the transporting thing is said to be "augmented," in the Greek there appears no passive participle; unfortunately, however, there is no other way to render the idea into understandable English. The phrase 'is augmented' corresponds to the Greek passive infinitive αὐξάνεσθαι. So, Aristotle never speaks even remotely of an augmented *thing*. His imaginary interlocutor (under this possibility) is allergic to passive objects of agency: for him, there are just agents and verbs.[28]

---

27 οὕτως μὲν μή, ἄλλο δ' ἐξ ἄλλου γένους, οἷον τὸ φέρον μὲν αὐξάνεσθαι, τὸ δὲ τοῦτο αὖξον ἀλλοιοῦσθαι ὑπ' ἄλλου, τὸ δὲ τοῦτο ἀλλοιοῦν ἑτέραν τινὰ κινεῖσθαι κίνησιν [*Phys.* viii,5, 257a3–6]. Just previously [256b33–34] he has represented the position more succinctly: "or (b) the healing thing is transported, the transporting thing augmented" [ἢ τὸ ὑγιάζον φέρεσθαι, τὸ δὲ φέρον αὐξάνεσθαι].

28 Towards the end of this more general passage (*Phys.* viii,5, 256b27–257a14), Aristotle does

Aristotle's stated objection to all this is not what someone might at first think: that is, his objection is not to the permutation and fusion of types of change (which is certainly objectionable in its own right and which Aristotle certainly does not accept),[29] but to the fact that even such an analysis eventually generates two agents—*sans* patients—of the same type. The reason why these must be generated, says Aristotle, is that the types of change are limited in number [257a7]. To use his own example, in working back from "transporting thing" [τὸ φέρον] to augmentation (which involves an "augmenting thing" [τὸ αὖξον]), to alteration (and an "altering thing" [τὸ ἀλλοιοῦν]), and so on, since there are a limited number of types of change, eventually the analysis must arrive at another "transporting thing" [τὸ φέρον]. And to have such a pair in the system, says Aristotle, is no better than to say that the teacher learns qua teaching [257a12–14].

The problem conclusion is generated, of course, by excluding from the outset true patients; and the reason for doing that was to avoid ever saying that there is something that is just mover and not moved. So, we see, Aristotle's doctrine of an unmoved mover is not unconnected with his doctrine that any movement has an object distinct from the movement itself. Not only must an unmoved mover have an object, but its unidirectional character (always and only toward something else) allows there to be an end to any possible regress.

Aristotle's argument in *Phys.* viii,5 also gives us a glimpse into the philosophical satisfactoriness to be expected from his analysis of movements (and therefore of human acts). Since each unit of intelligibility is self-contained and can be understood fully as what it is (this action going toward that object), once one understands that unit, one can rest assured that at least some genuine knowledge has been gained. One can then ratchet up to yet more extensive knowledge by adding intelligible units. One need not worry that, for instance, since the intelligibility of transportation itself is embedded in the intelligibility of augmentation, the latter in the intelligibility of alteration (and so on), that one can never really un-

---

speak of a κινούμενον [257a11], but there he is speaking in his own voice, saying that in a rightly conceived theory the moving thing comes before the thing moved.

29 This fusion (and confusion) of types of change would fall under the haphazard (κατὰ συμβεβηκὸς) change excluded at *Phys.* viii,5, 256b7–27.

derstand any change. Even if it is true that we can frequently add to what we know of a particular change, either by investigating a level of a particular change not yet considered or by fitting a change more adequately into the larger picture, we are adding to what we already really know. What knowledge we have, therefore, can be solid—and incrementally increased.

III. Action and the Principle of Non-contradiction

There remain, however, a number of issues to sort out if we are to achieve an adequate grasp of Aristotle's understanding of the relationship between human acts and movements. One of the central ones has to do with the fact that Aristotle utilizes his analysis of movement—the model of something going toward an object or end-state that completes it as movement—much more widely than would seem to be warranted. Even such acts as seeing and thinking, which do not work toward anything but, at every moment of their existence, have their objects within themselves—to see is at every stage in the seeing to see something and to think is at every stage in the thinking to think a thought—involve two components standing somehow at a distance from each other.[30]

As a preliminary step to understanding Aristotle's doctrine in this regard, it is necessary to say something about how the principle of non-contradiction has a bearing not only upon speculative truths, propositions, etc., but also upon actions. The fourth book of the *Metaphysics* is largely devoted to the investigation of this principle ("the PNC").[31] Its earliest formulation in that book is found toward the end of the third chapter: "the same attribute cannot at the same time hold and not hold of the same subject in the same respect" [*Metaph.* iv,3, 1005b19–20]. Ar-

30 See *de An.* iii, 2, 426a2–3, and 4, 429a17–18.
31 Aristotle has various ways of formulating the same principle; Jan Łukasiewicz identifies, in fact, three: the ontological, the logical, and the psychological—although one should bear in mind that Aristotle never speaks of more than one principle of non-contradiction and, so, these various formulations can be considered various aspects of—or ways of understanding—a single principle. See Jan Łukasiewicz, "Aristotle on the Law of Contradiction," trans. Jonathan Barnes, *Articles on Aristotle, vol. 3: Metaphysics*, ed. J. Barnes, M. Schofield, and R. Sorabji (London: Duckworth, 1975), 51; but see also Schiaparelli, passim; Fernando Inciarte, "Aristotle's Defense of the Principle of Non-contradiction," *Archiv für Geschichte der Philosophie* 76 (1994): 129–50, and Isaac Husik, "Aristotle on the Law of Contradiction and the Basis of the Syllogism," *Mind* 15 (1906): 215–22.

istotle immediately adds a word of explanation regarding the qualifying phrase "in the same respect": "and let us presuppose, in the face of dialectical objections, any further qualifications that might be added" [*Metaph.* iv,3, 1005b19–22]. If an Aristotelian says, for instance, that it is impossible for a person to be knowledgeable and not knowledgeable at the same time and another person objects that Theaetetus knows what a polyhedron is but does not know how to fight, the Aristotelian can reply that the PNC allows one to add whatever qualification (or specification) needed in order to deal with such an objection. Thus, the Aristotelian can always say something like, 'To be more precise, it is impossible for a person to be knowledgeable regarding polyhedrons and, at the same time, to be not knowledgeable regarding polyhedrons.' If the objector is persistent and says, 'Well, he can be knowledgeable regarding some polyhedrons and not knowledgeable regarding others,' the Aristotelian can reply: 'It all depends on what I meant: I meant that Theaetetus is knowledgeable regarding all polyhedrons; therefore, I cannot claim—without violating the principle of non-contradiction—that he is not knowledgeable regarding all.'

There are a number of possible objections that might be addressed in order to bring out how Aristotle understands the PNC, but we are interested here not in defending the principle but in understanding how it bears upon human acts. And, in this connection, of great importance is the fact that the PNC, as Aristotle understands it, is not primarily about, for the sake of truth, avoiding propositions that contradict one another. He does say in book iv that "the most indisputable of all beliefs is that contradictory statements are not at the same time true,"[32] and beliefs are certainly propositional, but that remark comes later (in chapter 6) and is best understood as an aspect of the PNC as enunciated earlier rather than as the principle itself in its most basic formulation. Aristotle's PNC is not the modern (p & p) but has to do rather with what attributes can simultaneously go *into* the same logical spot: "the same attribute cannot at the same time hold and not hold of the same subject in the same respect." The word(s) translated here as "hold of [something]" is ὑπάρχειν [τινί]. Linguistically—and in our minds—it connotes one thing going toward an-

---

32 βεβαιοτάτη δόξα πασῶν τὸ μὴ εἶναι ἀληθεῖς ἅμα τὰς ἀντικειμένας φάσεις [*Metaph.* iv,6, 1011b13–14].

other, even though the attribute in question and its subject may in fact not be separable in either space or time. That is the way our minds work: by bringing together and dividing.[33] If this leaves the analysis of "holdings" in which no distance of any sort is actually traversed still a delicate matter, it makes understanding how movements can be subject to the PNC quite a bit easier.

The PNC so formulated is also suited to the sort of analysis done in philosophical psychology, for it allows one to understand as falling under the principle the fact that a particular individual employing one and the same faculty cannot at the same time both want and not want x in the same respect. At one place in *Metaph.* iv, Aristotle actually applies the PNC within the field of human acts, using an example of a type frequently found in the *Physics*. As he does throughout *Metaph.* iv, he is arguing here against the notion that something and its contradictory might be simultaneously the case. "Why," he asks, "does a man, who thinks he ought to, walk to Megara and not remain inactive?" [*Metaph.* iv,4, 1008b14–15]. This man's intending to head toward Megara excludes his intending to remain where he is. This thesis of Aristotle's presupposes that the man has already come to the material (or perceptual) level of the "practical syllogism," as discussed in chapter 1 of the present work: a decision has already been made. If there is any intelligibility at all in someone's intending to go to Megara, it excludes his not intending to go there. The "attribute" at issue here is 'intending to go to Megara'; Aristotle is saying that that attribute cannot hold and not hold at the same time and in the same respect of the relevant faculty of the man in question. The contrary attributes here are conceived of as applying to the man (or to the relevant faculty), but they are also about his going *out* in one direction or not. Contradiction is not just about thoughts but about what can be the case in the world. If a man cannot both intend to go to Megara and not intend to go (at the same time and in the same respect), that is because so doing is impossible: his being at Megara and his remaining here cannot abide one another.

This brings us to our main question in this section: How can Aristotle attribute a bi-polar structure to non-movements? The answer is that the

---

33 *De Interpretatione* i, 16a12–16; *Metaph.* vi,4, 1027b18–34.

intelligible structure even of movements can be reduced to the PNC. A movement's having the intelligible structure it has is part and parcel of its being impossible for an agent's heading toward one object to be reconciled with his not doing that. What is important is not so much there being literal distance between the *terminus ab quo* and the *terminus ad quem* as the fact that going to Megara and not going there cannot get into the same logical spot together.

To show that the present claim is sound, it must be shown that even non-movements such as seeing involve two distinct intelligible entities, related to one another as opposing but complementary partners.[34] In other words, we must show that there is a one-directional line of intelligibility, a relationship between faculty and object. We find such relationships throughout Aristotle's philosophy, whenever he talks about things (physical objects, events, concepts, etc.) "qua" this or that, for he typically uses this locution to identify a distinct line of intelligibility. An animal, Aristotle acknowledges, is in a sense generated from an animal; but it comes, he says, from an animal "not qua animal, for that is already there" [*Phys.* i,8, 191b22]. What then does it come from? From its progenitor: not qua animal, however, but qua progenitor. And a progenitor is distinct—even conceptually—from its offspring. This distinction between progenitor and offspring establishes a line of intelligibility along which the action travels. Similarly, a patient is cured by a doctor not qua living body but qua sick body. Not only does a living body qua living body have no need of curing but, since there is nothing wrong with a living body qua living body, even to speak of curing it (qua living body) makes no sense. That is, such talk lacks intelligibility; there is no line of intelligibility here.

We find such a logical disposition of component factors also with non-movements. Even if the object of an act of seeing is always present while a man is seeing it, so that seeing something is never a matter of one thing's going toward another thing not yet there, still the object of seeing must be different from that which sees (the faculty of seeing). Of course, an object could come toward a person and only eventually be seen, but we are considering here rather the period during which the object is actually

---

34 Aristotle speaks of the faculty and its object as ἀντικείμενα [*de An.* i,1, 402b15 and ii,4, 415a20], "opposites."

seen, and during that period both seeing and the seen are necessarily present. As Aristotle puts it in *de An.* iii,2:

> Since the actualization of the sensible object and of the sensitive faculty is one, although the being [τὸ εἶναι] of each is different, necessarily the so-mentioned hearing and sounding perish and come to life at one and the same moment, also flavor and tasting, and so forth. [426a15–19]³⁵

It is difficult to separate the seeing from the object as seen, and yet we must posit a distinction—a certain distance, if only a conceptual one—if we are to make any sense of an action such as seeing. One notices, indeed, the resemblance of language between this passage and that of the passage in *Phys.* iii,3 we examined above, where Aristotle also speaks of one actualization but distinct "beings" of the same.³⁶ As with teaching and learning, the one "being" of the actualization of seeing, the faculty of seeing, depends upon the other: something visible.

If there were not these complementary poles to seeing, that activity would not have as its object any particular object and a particular seeing could be seeing anything or everything or nothing, since there would be nothing to delimit what that act of seeing was about. As with the man who, were it not for the PNC, could both intend to head toward Megara and not, a particular act of seeing could be seeing Socrates and not seeing him (at the same time and in the same respect) and/or seeing something quite different, whatever it might be. "It is not possible," says Aristotle, "for something to be at once white and black, and so it not possible for something to be affected at one and the same moment by the forms [τὰ εἴδει] of both, if sensation and thinking are as stated" [*de An.* iii,2, 427a8–9]. In the last phrase, Aristotle is referring to his previous analysis of those non-movements (sensation and thinking) in terms of potency and act: although they do not move toward a distinct product or end state, we must posit a certain coming into act, and that entails the separate beings of faculty and object.

The thing toward which any such activity moves must not only be

---

35 In speaking of the "so-mentioned hearing and sounding" [τὴν οὕτω λεγομένην ἀκοὴν καὶ ψόφον—426a17–18], Aristotle is referring to *de An.* iii,2, 426a12: οἷον ἡ ψόφησις καὶ ἡ ἄκουσις...

36 See *Phys.* iii,3, 202b9 and 16; see also *de An.* iii,2, 427a4–5. As we have seen, also in *Phys.* iii,3, Aristotle sometimes speaks as if teaching-learning involved one actualization. (See above, note 7.)

distinct from it but must also be something intelligible: a *logical* spot and not, for instance, some merely physical object. As we have seen, the coherence of even movement (the most intuitively accessible type of action) depends upon the idea that diverse forms cannot fit into the same logical spot. This is obviously true also with respect to non-movements, since the object is just the other end of an intelligible construct. The concept 'object of sight' has no sense independently of the concept 'seeing': there is a path of intelligibility from one to the other that holds the two together; without that path, neither component would be. At the other end of the stick, so to speak, there is a logical spot: and there is room at that spot for nothing that would violate the principle of non-contradiction.

As already suggested, the present argument has to do not simply with logic but with the logical structure of reality itself. If something (for instance, doing something) is something (that is, doing that), it is not *not* that something (that is, it is not not doing that). As Aristotle remarks in *Metaph.* iv, "not to have one meaning is to have no meaning at all …, for it is impossible to think of anything if we do not think of one thing."[37] If *per impossibile* we could get doing something and not into the same logical spot, whatever that would be would have no shape: no form. The latter truth holds not just of movements, such as going to Megara, but also of things like seeing and thinking. If someone sees Socrates coming toward him, he does not not see him—unless senses in which he both sees and does not see are presupposed or specified. ("I see the front of Socrates but not his back.")

It is important to note, however, that the direction of the activity within the bi-polar relationship—if indeed we can speak properly of direction within this context—might be described as not from the faculty to the object but rather from object to faculty.[38] Aristotle speaks of either faculty (seeing or thinking) as the passive partner in the relationship with its respective object, thereby indicating that the actualization occurs in the

---

37 τὸ γὰρ μὴ ἓν σημαίνειν οὐθὲν σημαίνειν ἐστίν … οὐθὲν γὰρ ἐνδέχεται νοεῖν μὴ νοοῦντα ἕν [*Metaph.* iv,4, 1006b7–10].

38 *de An.* iii,2, 426a2–6 and iii,4, 429a13–15 and 429b24–25. In iii,4, regarding thinking, Aristotle is somewhat tentative in saying that it is a passive faculty, although he clearly does think that its operation must be something like the reactive and passive operation of the senses (ἢ πάσχειν τι ἂν εἴη ὑπὸ τοῦ νοητοῦ ἤ τι τοιοῦτον ἕτερον—429a14–15).

faculty rather than in the object, just as, in *Phys.* iii,3, the actualization of teaching occurs in the student rather than in the teacher. As in that other case, where he does speak of the actualization of teaching itself, here too he recognizes that either faculty (again, seeing or thinking) is active;[39] in certain crucial contexts, however, especially where the unity or (we might even say) the identity of faculty and object is at issue, the passivity of the faculty becomes more prominent. The passivity of the faculty makes it apparent that seeing and thinking are never a matter of working toward an object, as when a builder builds a house. Since the action in non-movements is on the part of the object, the faculty is never in the position of having to get *to* it. As a consequence and as we have seen, the end or object of an activity such as seeing and thinking is present at every moment that the activity is present.

This idea, that is, that non-movements have a special logical character, due to their "accepting" objects from outside of themselves rather than producing them, will prove to be important beginning especially in chapter 6 of the present work. But because the relationship of movements to non-movements has been controversial in contemporary Aristotelian studies, and since the present chapter argues that movements and non-movements are similar in structure, I would like to conclude it with a word or two about the passage that has been the main source of the controversy.

IV. About *Metaphysics* ix,6

In the last third of *Metaph.* ix,6, Aristotle appears to make a sharp distinction between action [πρᾶξις] properly speaking—which he also calls 'actualization' [ἐνέργεια]—and movement [κίνησις]. The passage reads as follows:

Since (1) of the actions which have a limit none is the end itself but all are relative to the end, e.g., of 'to thin,' 'making thin,' and since (2) the things them-

---

[39] Regarding the senses, see *de An.* ii,5, 417a12–14; regarding thinking, see *de An.* iii,5. This chapter (*de An.* iii,5), is meant to explain how intellect is not only passive (as suggested in *de An.* iii,4) but also active. At one point in this difficult chapter [*de An.* iii,5, 430a23–25], Aristotle suggests that, whereas the passive side of the faculty is corruptible (this explaining memory loss), the active side is immortal; this, it seems to me, is to give the active side more prominence than the passive.

selves, when one is thinning in such a way that they are in movement, are not that at which the movement aims, *these* are not the action [πρᾶξις] or at least not the complete one (for there is no end), but in *that* exists the end (that is, [in] the action). For example, one sees (but also: one thinks), and one understands and *has* understood; but it is not true that at the same time one learns and has learnt, or one is being cured and has been cured. One lives well and has lived well, but also one thrives and has thrived. If not, the process would have had at some time to break off, as when someone thins; but, as it is, there is no such thing: one lives and has lived.

Of these, then, some are to be called movements [κινήσεις], others actualitizations [ἐνεργείας]. For every movement is incomplete: making thin, learning, walking, building. These are movements, and they are indeed incomplete. For one journeys and has journeyed not at the same time; nor does one build and has built, nor does something come to be and has come to be, nor is moved and has moved—but each is different (that is, 'moves' and 'has moved'). But it is the same thing that at the same time has seen and sees, or thinks and has thought. The latter such action, then, I call an actualization [ἐνέργειαν], the former a movement [κίνησιν].[40]

Part of what Aristotle is saying here is certainly linguistic. Consider the process of thinning something, that is, making something thin, such as a human body.[41] The thinning of that particular body is only accomplished once it is thinned to the desired dimensions. So, while engaged in the process one can say that one is thinning (the body) but not that the thinning has been accomplished. Moreover, once the body is thinned, it is no longer true that one is thinning it. On the other hand, with respect to activities such as seeing or thinking, one can look back on earlier stages in the process in which one is currently engaged and say truthfully that also during those stages one was doing what one is doing now; for instance, one is thinking now and has been thinking for ten minutes. But also before

---

40 This passage, *Metaph.* ix,6, 1048b18–35, is extremely difficult from a textual point of view; the textual difficulties are treated in Appendix 1 to the present book.

41 In a parallel passage in *Phys.* ii,3, in which Aristotle is discussing causality and, in particular, final causality, he speaks of curing or making healthy (ἵνα ὑγιαίνῃ—194b34) and of thinning (ἡ ἰσχνασία—194b36). (See also *Metaph.* v,2, 1013b1.) Both concepts appear in *Metaph.* ix,6, 1048b18–35 (although the latter employs the verb ὑγιάζειν instead of ὑγιαίνειν). It would seem, therefore, that in *Metaph.* ix,6 Aristotle has in mind regimes of weight loss, engaged in ultimately for the sake of health.

now (e.g., in the ten minutes between starting to think and now), thinking was entirely (completely) there. The reason for this, as Aristotle explains, is that activities such as seeing and thinking are wholly present whenever and as long as one engages in them, since the end of either activity need not be waited for but is present in every moment of the activity. One is reminded of the distinction made in the *Nicomachean Ethics* between things good in themselves and things good for the sake of other things: seeing and understanding are good in themselves;[42] thinning is for the sake of something else: health, for instance.

But, as John Ackrill famously pointed out some forty years ago, Aristotle's argument in *Metaph.* ix,6 is not without its problems.[43] Most people would say that listening to a piece of music is an action strictly speaking and not a movement, since presumably one enjoys the piece throughout its playing. One's satisfaction—and therefore one's end—is present in every moment and does not arrive only when the piece is finished. And yet the piece of music does have an end: a moment when it concludes, a point at which it hopes to arrive. Strictly speaking, one cannot claim truthfully to have heard Bach's first Brandenburg Concerto until the concerto is finished; thus, listening to a concerto is not unlike thinning something and yet it is an action (a πρᾶξις).[44]

But, although there is no denying that Aristotle employs the distinction between the present and the imperfect tense repeatedly in *Metaph.* ix,6, 1048b18–35 in order to establish his general point, there is more go-

---

42 *EN* i,6, 1096b13–14; see also *Metaph.* i,1, 980a21–26, i,2, 982b20–21, where seeing and thinking are said to be pursued for their own sake.

43 J. L. Ackrill, "Aristotle's Distinction between *energeia* and *kinēsis*," in *New Essays on Plato and Aristotle*, ed. R. Bambrough (New York: Humanities Press, 1965), 121–41.

44 The literature on the issues raised by Ackrill is huge. See, for instance, Terry Penner, "Verbs and the Identity of Actions: A Philosophical Exercise in the Interpretation of Aristotle," in *Ryle: A Collection of Critical Essays*, ed. O. Wood and G. Pitcher (New York: Anchor Books [Doubleday], 1970), 393–460; Daniel W. Graham, "States and Performances: Aristotle's Test," *Philosophical Quarterly* 30 (1980): 117–30; Kathleen Gill, "On the Metaphysical Distinction between Processes and Events," *Canadian Journal of Philosophy* 23 (1993): 365–84; Robert Heinaman, "Aristotle on Housebuilding," *History of Philosophy Quarterly* 2 (1985): 145–62; Alexander P. D. Mourelatos, "Aristotle's *kinēsis/energeia* Distinction: A Marginal Note on Kathleen Gill's Paper," *Canadian Journal of Philosophy* 23 (1993): 385–88; Cynthia A. Freeland, "Aristotelian Actions," *Nous* 19 (1985): 397–414, and Charles, 35–44. In my own interpretation of *Metaph.* ix,6, 1048b18–35, I am much indebted to the section of David Charles's book just mentioned and to chapters 2 through 7 of Carlo Natali, *L'action efficace: Études sur la philosophie de l'action d'Aristote*, Aristote: Traductions et Études (Leuven: Peeters, 2004).

ing on in the passage than that—and ultimately his point is not linguistic but metaphysical, having to do, that is, with the metaphysics of human action.[45] This is especially apparent in the first (very difficult) sentence of the passage: "Since of the actions which have a limit ... that is, [in] the action." One difficulty in interpreting this sentence lies in the expression "the things themselves" [αὐτά] at 1048b20, referred back to in the subsequent line as "these" [ταῦτα] (which is emphasized in the translation: "*these*"). Bonitz suggests that "the things themselves" [αὐτά] are τὰ πράγματα—which can also mean "the things" but in a concrete or definitive sense: Aristotle would be speaking thus about the completed things (or actions).[46] But the αὐτά seem rather to be stages in the (so to speak) "life" of a movement or of a moved thing qua moved.[47] These stages, Aristotle says, occur before the end (e.g., the thinned body) is actually present; they are present, that is, while the thing is still "in movement" [ἐν κινήσει—1048b20]. They are to be distinguished from the action properly speaking, referred to in our first sentence as "to thin [τοῦ ἰσχναίνειν]," which is itself distinct from the "making thin [ἡ ἰσχνασία]." The action properly speaking is picked out as distinct from the stages of the movement also in the subsequent sentence (according to my translation): "but in *that* exists the end (that is, [in] the action)."

The idea is that with some actions we can consider their various stages—that is, "the things [αὐτά]" in the various states in which they find themselves along the way—and see that they are distinct from the "essence" of the action itself, which does not contain in itself stages along the way but is simply doing that thing. These stages (considered as parts of an action) are not yet the action properly speaking, which gets its intelligibility from the completed action. In other words, our idea of 'to thin something' comes from our knowledge of things that have been thinned and this idea is transferred also to the process of making thin, ἡ ἰσχνασία— *even though*, if we look at any stage in the process of making thin, we will not see the thinned thing. No stage in the process of getting to the end

---

45 See Charles, 38–39, 43–44.
46 Hermann Bonitz, *Aristotelis* Metaphysica (Bonn: 1848–1849), vol. 2, 397.
47 In this passage, Aristotle allows himself to move seamlessly from talk of movements to talk of things qua moved.

"Physical" Structure of the Human Act   67

can, therefore, be called the action—nor can the whole process itself, qua process, be so called—since, while the action is being executed, the end is not yet present. The action itself, that is, "to thin" [τοῦ ἰσχναίνειν], is the action, properly speaking, because it does have the end right in its own intelligibility; but that action is not there in its full intelligibility until its stages are completed ... and in the past.[48]

That *Metaph.* ix,6, 1048b18–35 is making such points is confirmed by looking a couple of chapters ahead, at *Metaph.* ix,8, the main theme of which is that actualization [ἐνέργεια] (mentioned also at *Metaph.* ix,6, 1048b34) is prior to potentiality [δύναμις], which Aristotle closely associates with movement (see 1050a14; also *Metaph.* v,12, 1019a15–20). Actualization is prior, he says, "in substance" [οὐσίᾳ—1050a4], "because everything that comes to be moves toward a principle, that is an end" [*Metaph.* ix,8, 1050a7–8]. He goes on to use some of the very examples he uses in *Metaph.* ix,6, 1048b18–35:

While in some cases the exercise is the ultimate thing (for instance, of sight seeing,[49] and nothing comes into being other than the activity [ἔργον] of sight) and in other cases something comes into being (for instance, from the art of building [οἰκοδομικῆς], besides the act of building [παρὰ τὴν οἰκοδόμησιν] there comes into being a house), nonetheless [the actualization: ἐνέργεια] is in the former case the end and in the latter more the end than the potentiality is. For the act of building [οἰκοδόμησις] is in the thing built [ἐν τῷ οἰκοδομουμένῳ], and it comes to be—and is—at the same time as the house [1050a23–1050a29].

Ironically, the building—that is, that which is expressed by the gerund 'building' (as in the phrase 'building such a structure is exhausting') and

---

48 See Mary Louise Gill, "Aristotle's Distinction between Change and Activity," *Axiomates* 14 (2004): 10: "So construed, the definition of change captures the object at all moments up to but excluding the moment at which it is actually φ."

49 ὄψεως ἡ ὅρασις [*Metaph.* ix,8, 1050a24]. It is instructive to compare this expression to that at ix,6, 1048b19: οἷον τοῦ ἰσχναίνειν ἡ ἰσχνασία. While to 'seeing' [ὅρασις] there corresponds the abstract term 'sight' [ὄψις], making it even more apparent that seeing (or sight) can be (and is) present at every step along the way of seeing, there is no such abstract term corresponding to ἰσχνασία; nor, as with the act of building [οἰκοδόμησις] and the craft of building [ἡ οἰκοδομική], is there a corresponding craft of thinning. There is a *word* that captures the intelligibility of (a) thinning [ἡ ἰσχνασία], but it is the verb itself: τὸ ἰσχναίνειν. So, in *Metaph.* ix,8, 1050a24, Aristotle had not many linguistic options for expressing the intelligibility of ἰσχνασία.

68   "Physical" Structure of the Human Act

which is in some sense the action (or πρᾶξις)—arrives only when the process of building is past.⁵⁰

This approach takes us beyond the linguistic distinctions Aristotle makes in *Metaph.* ix,6 and to the metaphysical ideas more prominently in his mind in this book of the *Metaphysics* devoted to showing that actuality is prior to potency because of its fuller intelligibility.⁵¹ Those ideas include the following: (1) that, if the end is not present in an action's stages, neither is that action's full intelligibility—that is, its essence (or "substance"); (2) that, if, on the other hand, in some cases there are no stages leading up to whatever (that is, in cases in which the end is never absent), all that there is to the action is present when it is engaged in: to use Aristotle's examples, whenever one sees or thinks, all there is to seeing and thinking is present at that moment. Or, as Aristotle puts it, using yet another example, at the moment when a man "has lived well," it was (is) true to say that he lives well. Were this not the case, "the process would have had at some time to break off, as when someone thins"—that is to say, there would have had to be a terminus such as constitutes a distinction between thinning and its full intelligibility, which latter arrives only with the end (which is a "breaking off" of the action). But, "as it is," says Aristotle, "there is no such thing: one lives and has lived."⁵²

When, therefore, Ackrill notes that we can posit an end in the various moments of listening (for instance) to a concerto, he misses the point. What he says is true, but still 'listening to concertos' derives its intelligibility as a concept from concertos; and concertos are not finished until they are finished. Ackrill is confusing the end made present by the pleasure we take in listening with the completion (the end) of the concerto. It is note-

---

50 At *EN* x,4, 1174a20–21 Aristotle calls attention to this. Speaking again of housebuilding, he says that it is complete when it has done what it set out to do. It is complete, therefore, "either in the whole time or at that moment" (i.e., when the house is built).

51 See *Metaph.* ix,8, 1049b5: ... πρότερον ἐνέργεια δυνάμεώς ἐστιν ....

52 It is possible that this phrase (i.e., εἰ δὲ μή, ἔδει ἄν ποτε παύεσθαι ὥσπερ ὅταν ἰσχναίνῃ—*Metaph.* ix,6, 1048b26–27) means, 'If not, the process would have had at some time to stop, as when someone thins ...,' the idea being that a movement can be stopped at any point short of (and without) achieving its end; but, besides containing the difficult notion that a movement must stop or pause, this understanding does not fit well with what comes just after: "but, as it is, there is no such thing: one lives and has lived" [νῦν δ' οὔ, ἀλλὰ ζῇ καὶ ἔζηκεν]. The contrast here is between there being a distinction between the movement and the end and there not being such a distinction (or break); such a break is necessary, given the nature of κινήσεις.

worthy that Aristotle addressed this precise issue in the last book of the *Nicomachean Ethics*:

> We have discussed movement with precision in another work [i.e., the *Physics*], but it seems that it is not complete [τελεία] at any and every time, but that the many movements are incomplete [ἀτελεῖς] and different in form [εἴδει], since the whence and whither give them their form [τὸ πόθεν ποῖ εἰδοποιόν].[53] But of pleasure the form is complete [τέλειον] at any and every time. Plainly, then, pleasure and movement must be different from each other, and pleasure must be one of the things that are whole and complete [τῶν ὅλων τι καὶ τελείων]. This would seem to be the case, too, from the fact that it is not possible to move otherwise than in time, but it is possible to be pleased; for that which takes place in a moment is a whole. [*EN* x,4, 1174b2–9]

The point of the remark about the "whence and the whither" is that, in the case of movements, the completed form arrives only at the point whither [ποῖ] the movement is headed. But all this is quite independent of one's enjoying the movement while it is yet incomplete.

V. Conclusion

We are now in position to give at least a preliminary account of the structure of the human act—to be filled out in subsequent chapters. The modern temptation is to view the human act as without structure—or, at least, not to attend too closely to what structure might have to be acknowledged. Is a general to be blamed for ordering the bombing of a heavily populated city? Are the consequent deaths to be attributed to his will? We cannot give a precise answer to such questions (it is argued or tacitly assumed) since choices, wants, and so on, are amorphous, unstable things. All that could matter morally is the state of the general's mind: his desires, what he wanted to accomplish. An analysis of the external act contributes nothing to our understanding of the moral character of his behavior.

Such approaches or attitudes are hard to argue against. If an interlocutor is disinclined to regard even acknowledged structure in what someone

---

53 In speaking of form here, Aristotle is referring to a movement's intelligibility (to employ the language employed above).

does as relevant ethically, the best we can do is simply to depict the structure in as perspicuous a manner as possible and hope that this will lead him to acknowledge that that does correspond to what the agent does. Aristotle was faced with similar interlocutors in his own day: those who expended every effort to discover infinity—the unknowable—in movement (see, for instance, *Phys.* vi,7). His response was always patiently to break into intelligible bits and to order that which they claimed was not orderable.

In this chapter I have argued for—depicted—a movement-like structure for any human act, whether the completion of the act comes only once the act can no longer be referred to by means of a progressive form of its proper verb (such as the imperfect) or whether the act is complete even while such a verb applies (that is, while the person is performing the act). I have also argued that the movement-like structure of any action depends upon distinct lines of intelligibility: each with a whence and a whither, each going from one to another logically related spot, in accordance with the principle of non-contradiction. That we are able to individuate such lines is a good thing. It constitutes the ability to identify the basic unit of moral character: intelligibility, that upon which character depends. So, we know what to look for. But before getting to such issues of larger scope, issues having to do with moral character, in the next two chapters, we shall continue to consider individual acts and the multifarious ways in which they are open to qualification morally.

Three

Internal Articulation and Force

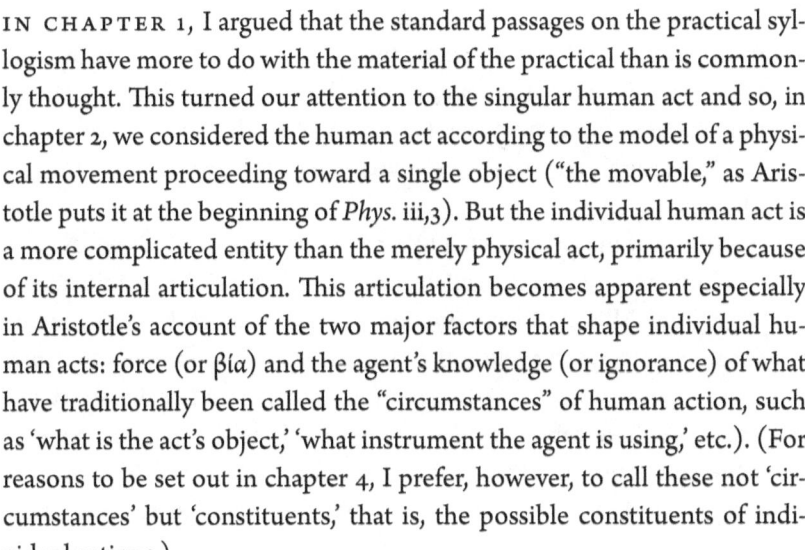

IN CHAPTER 1, I argued that the standard passages on the practical syllogism have more to do with the material of the practical than is commonly thought. This turned our attention to the singular human act and so, in chapter 2, we considered the human act according to the model of a physical movement proceeding toward a single object ("the movable," as Aristotle puts it at the beginning of *Phys.* iii,3). But the individual human act is a more complicated entity than the merely physical act, primarily because of its internal articulation. This articulation becomes apparent especially in Aristotle's account of the two major factors that shape individual human acts: force (or βία) and the agent's knowledge (or ignorance) of what have traditionally been called the "circumstances" of human action, such as 'what is the act's object,' 'what instrument the agent is using,' etc.). (For reasons to be set out in chapter 4, I prefer, however, to call these not 'circumstances' but 'constituents,' that is, the possible constituents of individual actions.)

The *locus classicus* for these two factors is *EN* iii,1, where Aristotle discusses first force and then knowledge (or ignorance). But this discussion presupposes something not mentioned there in *EN* iii,1: that human acts are internally articulated in such a way that aspects of them might be forced, while other aspects are not, or some constituents might be known (and, therefore, fall within the moral responsibility of the agent), while others might be unknown (and, therefore, fall outside the same). The only discussion of this essential presupposition is found in the less well known *Eudemian Ethics*, book two, chapters six through nine. There is a problem, however, with these chapters—a problem not unconnected with the fact that they are not well known. The argument put forward in *EE* ii,6–9—in particular, over the course of *EE* ii,7 and 8—is extremely dense and obscure. Among commentators it has given rise to great controversy and disagreement, making it difficult to exploit as a source of substantive Aristotelian theory.[1] So, pulling out of these chapters Aristotle's account of the internal articulation of the human act is going to require some work. We will be obliged to expend a good deal of effort just in order to bring to light the argumentative structure of *EE* ii,6–9. A coherent account is recoverable here, however, and it provides much insight into Aristotle's philosophical psychology of action.

Aristotle's argument in favor of the internal articulation of acts incorporates a number of theses regarding force; as a consequence, the present chapter, especially toward the end, has much to say about the role of force in human action. In the next chapter, we consider the other major factor, knowledge (or ignorance), especially knowledge (or ignorance) of the circumstances.

Section I of the present chapter sets out the structure of what I call "the preliminary argument," which takes up all of *EE* ii,7 and finishes a short way into *EE* ii,8. (I have provided a translation of *EE* ii,6–9 in appendix 2, inserting markers into the text corresponding to the indications given in the present chapter.) The preliminary argument begins by saying that there are three candidates for the status of the defining characteristic of the voluntary (and therefore also of the involuntary). By means of an assortment of arguments, Aristotle eliminates two of these candidates.

---

1 *EE* ii,7 has itself been described by commentators as aporetic, dialectical, and even sophistical. See Anthony Kenny, *Aristotle's Theory of the Will* (London: Duckworth, 1979), 21–22; Susan Sauvé Meyer, *Aristotle on Moral Responsibility: Character and Cause* (Oxford: Blackwell, 1993), 59–91; and Franz Dirlmeier, *Aristoteles*, Magna Moralia (Berlin: Akademie, 1958), 234. Speaking of both *EE* ii,7–8 and *MM* 1,12–16, Dirlmeier says, "Die Argumente über ἑκούσιον-ἀκούσιον haben geradezu sophistischen Charakter, man kann auch sagen: sokratischen, insoferne kein eindeutiges Ergebnis herauskommt." Dirlmeier thinks that Aristotle is out, not to deceive us, but rather to offer traditional statements ("traditionelle Aussagen") regarding the voluntary, in the style of the Δισσοὶ λόγοι.

The issues mentioned in these arguments are all resolved in *EE* ii,8, but, strangely, this has no effect upon the general argument, for in *EE* ii,9 Aristotle speaks of the two as still eliminated. All of this is puzzling, until one realizes that in *EE* ii,7 Aristotle is assembling ideas he will use later.

In section II, I examine the first two (of three) parts of what I call the "force and compulsion argument" (entirely contained in *EE* ii,8). In the first part of that argument, Aristotle asks how it has come about that people understand the voluntary and the involuntary in the simplistic manner that lends plausibility to the dialectical arguments he has discussed in the preliminary argument. One such argument maintains, for instance, that the desired corresponds to the voluntary and so the painful corresponds to the involuntary. His reply is that the very simplicity of physical force seduces us into assimilating all force to such a model, even though it is clear that humans are more complicated than even other animals, as is indicated by the fact that their reason can come into conflict with their appetite. In the second part of the force and compulsion argument, Aristotle applies the gains of the previous part to issues having to do with the continent and the incontinent man. The main lesson to be learned from the puzzles in the preliminary argument, he says, is that one must distinguish the analysis of individual acts from the analysis of whole souls: a man might suffer force within and yet still perform individual voluntary acts.

In section III, I confront the question mentioned above, that is, how Aristotle's resolution in *EE* ii,8 of various contradictions—contradictions that in *EE* ii,7 appeared to eliminate various candidates for the status of 'defining characteristic of the voluntary'—affects his general argument. The technical answer to this question is that the contradictions identified and then resolved have little to do with whether something (such as 'that which is according to desire') can serve as a differentia specifying the voluntary within the genus of movement. What eliminates the candidates is that they can be associated with *either* the voluntary or the non-voluntary; it is for that reason cannot serve as the differentia of the voluntary. In section III, I offer an additional explanation of why Aristotle has included *EE* ii,8 where he does. This explanation looks back to the agenda set in *EE* ii,6, where Aristotle speaks of principles ("sovereign principles") that have a direct and necessary effect upon their consequences. In *EE* ii,8,

Aristotle shows that man, as sovereign principle of his own acts, controls them completely, so that he is responsible for all—and only—that which is voluntary in them. This accounts for the fact that the term 'voluntary' applies in the first instance to whole acts but that such acts are also internally articulated. Human acts are, by definition, voluntary, so the voluntary takes them in—qua acts—necessarily; but the voluntary is also discriminating, being strictly delimited by the knowledge proper to itself and by its own genuine involvement in what it does (for that which is voluntary is "up to" the person who acts). Within a voluntary act there can be no aspects of which the agent is not the "sovereign principle."

In section IV, I go through the third part of the force and compulsion argument, where Aristotle begins to apply the ideas put forward in the first two parts of the same argument (which parts in turn depend upon the preliminary argument). Here Aristotle moves (to a certain extent) away from consideration of the continent man and the incontinent man and toward a consideration of the agent in whom there is no conflict between reason and appetite; he also draws a distinction between that which is due to force (βία) and that which someone does having been compelled (ἀναγκαζόμενος), the former involving that which is not up to such an agent, the latter involving such cases as performing a disgraceful act in order to rescue hostages. Bearing this distinction in mind, it is possible to resolve a number of textual issues, for it helps to make sense of the text as it stands and so to avoid emendation. Also useful in resolving a textual issue is the idea, discussed in both the preliminary argument and in the first part of the force and compulsion argument, that the continent man "forces" himself to follow not his desires but reason. Aristotle also discusses in this last part of the force and compulsion argument cases in which a person is overcome by natural—and even supernatural—movements of the soul.

Section V looks at a number of passages outside of *EE* ii,6–9 in which Aristotle uses the ideas presented there. These passages all have to do with the internal articulation brought to individual acts because of force.

I. The Preliminary Argument
(*EE* ii,7 and the beginning of *EE* ii,8)

Aristotle's stated goal in *EE* ii,6–9 is to ascertain "what is the voluntary and what the involuntary" [*EE* ii,7, 1223a21], prior to ascertaining what is choice, which he does in *EE* ii,10 and 11 (the last chapters of the book). Basically, he is seeking a definition of the voluntary and, accordingly, he is considering various candidates as its differentia.[2] He suggests at *EE* ii,6, 1222b29 that the voluntary's genus is 'movement' [κίνησις]. The progress of this argument turns to a certain extent on a limitation of options set out at the beginning of *EE* ii,7. Aristotle says that the voluntary is just one of the following things: (1) that which is according to appetite (κατ' ὄρεξιν), (2) that which is according to choice (κατὰ προαίρεσιν), and (3) that which is according to thought (κατὰ διάνοιαν).[3] That which is according to appetite is declared a non-candidate at the end of *EE* ii,7, apparently on the grounds that it leads to a number of contradictions that present themselves especially when considering two of the subdivisions of appetite, ἐπιθυμία (desire) and θυμός (aggression). That which is according to choice is also dismissed with a very brief argument at the beginning of *EE* ii,8, at which point Aristotle launches a discussion of force (τὸ βίαιον) and compulsion (τὸ ἀναγκαῖον), over the course of which the contradictions that supposedly doomed desire and aggression are resolved. But this apparently has

---

2 On definitions, see especially Marguerite Deslauriers, *Aristotle on Definition*, Philosophia antiqua (Leiden: Brill, 2007), cited below. Besides Deslauriers, see also Jean Marie Le Blond, "Aristotle on Definition," in *Articles on Aristotle: 3. Metaphysics*, ed. Jonathan Barnes, Malcolm Schofield, and Richard Sorabji (London: Duckworth, 1979), 63–79; D. M. Balme, "Aristotle's Use of Division and Differentiae," in *Philosophical Issues in Aristotle's Biology*, ed. Allan Gotthelf and James G. Lennox (Cambridge: Cambridge University Press, 1987), 69–89; D. M. Balme, "The Snub," in *Philosophical Issues in Aristotle's Biology*, ed. Gotthelf and Lennox, 306–12, and Robert Heinaman, "Frede and Patzig on Definition in *Metaphysics* Z.10 and 11," *Phronesis* 42 (1997): 283–98.

3 It is important to follow Aristotle's phraseology fairly closely here. He is not suggesting that the voluntary *is* appetite, choice, or thought, but that it is "according to"—κατὰ—them. What sort of relationship this might be is made sufficiently clear in a passage that comes later, after he has set aside the first two candidates, 'that which is according to appetite' and 'that which is according to choice.' He says: "But if necessarily the voluntary was one of these three—either that which is according to appetite or according to choice or according to thought—and it is not two of these, all that is left is that the voluntary consists in somehow doing that which is thought" [*EE* ii,8, 1224a4–7].

no effect on their candidacy for the status of defining factor of the voluntary since, at the beginning of *EE* ii,9, Aristotle again says that the voluntary is not to be defined by either appetite or by choice but by that which remains: thought.[4]

What I shall call "the preliminary argument" of the pages that interest us comprises the whole of *EE* ii,7, plus the very first piece of *EE* ii,8. *EE* ii,7 divides fairly easily into four parts. First (a) comes an introductory section in which (as I have said) Aristotle identifies three candidates for the status of differentia of the voluntary. Then the first, appetite, is divided into three types: will [βούλησις],[5] aggression [θυμός], and desire [ἐπιθυμία].[6] In what then follows, these are treated in reverse order. So, in the next section (b), Aristotle considers desire (1223a29–b17); in section (c), aggression (1223b18–28); and, in section (d), will (1223b29–36). The first piece of *EE* ii,8 contains the fifth section (e) of the preliminary argument.

Section (b) divides into four arguments, the first two of which (1223a29–36, 1223a36–b3) are in favor of the idea that the voluntary is that which is according to desire, the remaining two (1223b5–10, 1223b10–17) against. The two positive arguments—let us call them P1 and P2—are fairly straightforward (even simplistic). According to P1 (1223a29–36), the painful and forced are involuntary, and that which is painful (or forced) goes against desire [παρὰ τὴν ἐπιθυμίαν]. Since the painful and the desired

---

4 *EE* ii,6–9 contains a large number of controversial claims having to do with the necessary and sufficient conditions of voluntary action. I will discuss some of these, especially when they have a bearing upon the general structure of Aristotle's argument; others I leave either unaddressed or addressed only by means of a note and/or reference. More detailed analysis of the problems can be found in Robert Heinaman, "The *Eudemian Ethics* on Knowledge and Voluntary Action," *Phronesis* 30 (1986): 128–47; Robert Heinaman, "Compulsion and Voluntary Action in the *Eudemian Ethics*," *Nous* 22 (1988): 253–81; Terence H. Irwin, "Reason and Responsibility in Aristotle," in *Essays on Aristotle's Ethics*, ed. Amélie O. Rorty (Berkeley: University of California Press, 1980), 117–55; and Michael Woods, *Aristotle: 'Eudemian Ethics,' Books I, II and VIII*, 2d ed. (Oxford: Clarendon, 1992). Heinaman, "The *Eudemian Ethics* on Knowledge and Voluntary Action" is mostly about *EE* ii,9; Heinaman, "Compulsion and Voluntary Action in the *Eudemian Ethics*," is mostly about *EE* ii,8.

5 In today's English translations, the word βούλησις is often rendered as 'wish'; I employ here rather the more traditional 'will,' since Aristotle suggests at one crucial point (ii,7, 1223b29) that the βουλόμενον might be identical to the voluntary. This thesis sounds more plausible if we translate βούλησις 'will' (and its derivatives accordingly). See also notes 11 and 44 (below).

6 Woods points out that Aristotle's dividing desire into three and then considering each of the three separately vitiates his argument, since the more likely definition of the voluntary is that which is in accordance with *some* desire (whichever of the three it might be) [Woods, *Aristotle: 'Eudemian Ethics,'* 121].

are opposed and since the painful is involuntary, that which is according to desire must be voluntary, for the voluntary is opposed to that which is involuntary.[7] It is apparent here that Aristotle is not putting forward ideas with which he necessarily agrees, for he certainly holds that that which is painful to do can be voluntary.[8] The ideas smack rather of ancient sophistry. But that does not mean that they are not genuine working parts of Aristotle's argument. If 'according to desire' were the differentia of the voluntary, we should have to conclude that that which is painful stands outside of the voluntary, for no one voluntarily seeks pain (in itself).[9]

According to P2 (1223a36–b3), ἀκρασία (i.e., incontinence, or acting in accordance with desire but against reason) is a type of vice, and vice makes one more unjust. Anything that makes one unjust is voluntary, so action involving ἀκρασία is voluntary. Thus, once again, the voluntary is associated with desire, since the ἀκρατής follows desire rather than reason.

What is notable about the next two, that is, the negative, arguments—let us call them N1 and N2—is that they both finish with the idea that, if the voluntary is that which is according to desire, the same agent will act at the same time [ἅμα: 1223b9, 1223b17] both voluntarily and involuntarily. This language reminds one of Aristotle's first (and primary) formulation of the principle of non-contradiction: "the same attribute cannot at the same time [ἅμα] hold and not hold of the same subject in the same respect."[10]

In N1 Aristotle posits an effective equivalence between the voluntary and the willed: "all that a man does voluntarily [ἅπαν γὰρ ὃ ἑκών τις πράττει] he does willingly [βουλόμενος πράττει], and what he wills he does voluntarily."[11] No one wills that which he thinks bad; the person,

---

[7] Aristotle describes the basic form of such an argument at APo. ii,6, 92a21–23: "for things which have a contrary, being their contrary is being contrary to what they are" [τῷ δ' ἐναντίῳ τὸ τῷ ἐναντίῳ εἶναι, ὅσοις ἔστι τι ἐναντίον]. (This is to adopt Barnes's rejection of Ross's emendation and to return to the MSS readings.) See also Top. vi,9, 147a29–b25; vii,3, 153a26–b24.

[8] See, for instance, EE ii,8, 1224b15–17 and EN iii,1, 1110a8–12.

[9] We see a similar exploitation of sophistic argumentation at EE vii,6, 1240b21–28, discussed in chapter 8. See Kevin L. Flannery, "The Aristotelian First Principle of Practical Reason," Thomist 59 (1995): 459–63 (although the general argument of this essay now seems to me wrongheaded).

[10] τὸ γὰρ αὐτὸ ἅμα ὑπάρχειν τε καὶ μὴ ὑπάρχειν ἀδύνατον τῷ αὐτῷ καὶ κατὰ τὸ αὐτό [Metaph. iv,3, 1005b19–20].

[11] This observation can serve as confirmation of Terence Irwin's thesis that Thomas Aquinas is correct to say that Aristotle's βούλησις is involved even in merely voluntary acts (i.e., τὸ ἑκούσιον). See Terence H. Irwin, "Who Discovered the Will?" Philosophical Perspectives 6 (1992): 461–67. On p.

however, who has become incontinent does that which he does not will, since, influenced by desire, he does that which he thinks not the best thing to do (i.e., the bad). But, according to P2, the ἀκρατής acts voluntarily; so the same person would be acting involuntarily (because not according to his will) but also voluntarily. But, if this is the case, "it will follow [συμβήσεται] that the same man acts at the same time [ἅμα] both voluntarily and involuntarily," and that is impossible.

Just as N1 borrows a premise from P2, so also N2 borrows one from P1; that is to say, it makes use of the proposition that that which goes against desire [παρὰ τὴν ἐπιθυμίαν] is involuntary [1223a33–35]. (It also makes use of the proposition 'that which makes one just is voluntary,' which is part of the general principle alluded to in P2, where it is said that anything that makes one unjust is voluntary.) Aristotle argues that ἐγκράτεια (continence) is virtuous and virtue makes one just; it also voluntary, since that which makes one just is voluntary. But ἐγκράτεια also goes against desire, since the ἐγκρατής (the continent man) follows reason in preference to desire. Since, as per P1, that which goes against desire is involuntary, we have a contradiction: the same person (ὁ αὐτός) is said to do at one and the same time (ἅμα) the same thing (τὸ αὐτό) both voluntarily and involuntarily [1223b17]. Again, one recognizes the language of the principle of non-contradiction.

So, the attempt to define the voluntary in terms of that which is according to desire finishes in apparent perplexity. But, says Aristotle [1223b18–24], entering phase (c) of the argument, a similar set of considerations is generated if we say that the voluntary is that which is according to aggression [θυμός], since the basic concepts that generated the aporia regarding desire—in particular, ἀκρασία and ἐγκράτεια [1223b18–19]—are present also with respect to aggression. He indicates in very brief fashion how such a demonstration of this might go ("what goes against aggression is painful ...," etc. [1223b19–21]), cites Heraclitus in support, and then finishes with the following remark:

467, he says: "While Aquinas at first seemed to be mistaken in intruding his own concept of the will into Aristotle's discussion of voluntary action, further examination shows that he actually explains Aristotle's intention more clearly than Aristotle explains it himself. For some of Aristotle's claims about voluntary actions are difficult to defend unless Aristotle relies on something like Aquinas's concept of the will."

But if it is impossible for the same man voluntarily and involuntarily at the same time [ἅμα] to do the same thing and with respect to the same aspect of the act, then that which is according to the will is more voluntary than that which is according to appetite or aggression; and a proof of this is that we do many things voluntarily without anger or desire.[12]

This is apparently meant to serve as both a conclusion to section (c) and as reason to go on to section (d), the treatment of will [βούλησις]. Aristotle would be saying, therefore, that the proposal to use aggression as the defining characteristic leads to contradiction—indeed the language here is especially close to the formulation of the principle of non-contradiction at *Metaph*. iv,3, 1005b19–20—and that, therefore, we ought to move on to the last candidate (among types of appetite), will.

The passage [1223b24–28] raises a couple of issues. First, it would seem that the idea called for here is not that "that which is according to the will is more [μᾶλλον] voluntary than that which is according to appetite or aggression," but that 'that which is according to the will is voluntary rather [μᾶλλον] than that which is according to appetite or aggression.' Of the three types of appetite, only will at this point is left; accordingly, Aristotle begins the next section (d) with the words, "It remains, therefore, [λείπεται ἄρα] to be investigated whether the willed [τὸ βουλόμενον] and the voluntary are the same thing" [1223b29]. In fact, Michael Woods translates 1223b26–27 as "what is in accordance with wish [τὸ κατὰ βούλησιν] is voluntary rather than what is in accordance with spirit or desire."[13] But that cannot be right, since it implies that 'according to will [κατὰ βούλησιν]' is (alas) the differentia Aristotle has been seeking—but it is not: 'according to thought [κατὰ διάνοιαν]' is.[14] One is tempted to interpret 1223b26–27 as Aristotle's concluding that there is more *reason* to believe that that which is according to will is the voluntary (since 'according to desire' and 'according to aggression' lead to such contradictory conclusions); but it is quite reasonable to understand Aristotle as meaning just

---

12 *EE* ii,7, 1223b24–28. See Appendix 2 below, including the note at 1223b28 (note 2).
13 Woods, *Aristotle: 'Eudemian Ethics,'* 24.
14 Perhaps Woods might be defended by arguing that he is not suggesting that that which is according to βούλησις is *the* voluntary but just that it is voluntary. But, if this is the point, Aristotle would be saying that that which is according to desire and/or aggression is clearly not voluntary; and that is not his position.

what he says: that that which is according to will is more voluntary than the others, for the preceding argument has shown that that which is according to desire (or aggression) sometimes is voluntary, sometimes not, and, on the other hand, he is prepared to assert quite straightforwardly that "all that a man does voluntarily he does willingly, and what he wills he does voluntarily" [1223b5–6].[15] We shall also see that in *EE* ii,8 Aristotle is very much interested in degrees of voluntariness.

Secondly, the final bit in the passage before us [1223b24–28]—"and a proof of this [i.e., that that which is according to will is more voluntary than the others] is that we do many things voluntarily without anger or desire"—seems to render unnecessary the very complicated arguments that have preceded it. Anthony Kenny says of that bit the following:

> This passage makes clear that Aristotle thinks that quite independently of the arguments he has just patiently rehearsed he has a proof that voluntariness is not in accord with temper [θυμός = aggression] or appetite [ἐπιθυμία = desire]: the simple and obvious fact that we often act voluntarily without being in a state of passion.... It is this brief but adequate argument, and not the dubious dialectical ones, which entitles him to conclude that voluntariness cannot be defined in terms of temper or appetite.[16]

Kenny is right to say that in some sense the arguments that precedes this more straightforward proof are dialectical; but they do serve a function: they allow Aristotle to sort through the various factors associated with the voluntary and the involuntary. We have before us at this point a good number of ideas touching upon the voluntary and the involuntary; what Aristotle is doing is assembling a tool box of ideas about the internal workings of the voluntary, ideas that will be useful later on. So, Kenny may be right to say to say that 1223b24–28 provides the same conclusion as the preceding argument, but he misses the point of the larger argument (*EE* ii,6–9), which is to give an account of the voluntary *by way* of a search for its differentia.

That brings us to section (d) of *EE* ii,7, where Aristotle argues that

---

[15] The association of frequency of occurrence and "degree of presence" of an attribute is apparent also in *Metaph.* ii,1, 993b28–31.

[16] Kenny, *Aristotle's Theory of the Will*, 22–23.

will [βούλησις] too can be discounted as the differentia of the voluntary. With respect to appetite [ὄρεξις], the one possibility that remains, suggests Aristotle, is that the willed [τὸ βουλόμενον] is the same thing [ταὐτό] as the voluntary [1223b29]. This is clearly a different thesis from the one mentioned earlier that simply asserted that "all that a man does voluntarily he does willingly, and what he wills he does voluntarily."[17] For one thing, the present thesis is an object of query, whereas the previous one was asserted as if requiring no argument. But that there is a significant difference between the two theses is clear also on the face of things. For the voluntary and the willed to be the same thing would exclude one's ever doing anything voluntarily that involved an aspect not actually wanted (willed) by the agent. It would be as if βούλησις involved only directly willing or nilling particular objects and that these two corresponded exactly to the voluntary and the involuntary. But, in fact, one often voluntarily performs actions that involve things that one considers bad and, therefore, does not will.

In any case, the argument in section (d) of *EE* ii,7 is again about ἀκρασία. It is assumed, Aristotle says, that wickedness makes a person more unjust; and, since ἀκρασία is a type of wickedness, it would seem to have to have the same effect. Now, no one wills [βούλεται] what he believes to be evil, but he does do such a thing when he becomes ἀκρατής (incontinent). So, if to act unjustly is voluntary and the voluntary is that which is according to the will [βούλησις], when a person becomes ἀκρατής, he does not act unjustly but becomes, in fact, more just than before he became ἀκρατής.[18] This is obviously impossible, so that which is according to will cannot serve as the differentia of the voluntary. Since will is the last remaining sector of appetite (aggression and desire having been eliminated previously), 'that which is according to appetite' cannot be the differentia of the voluntary.

17 πᾶν γὰρ ὃ ἑκών τις πράττει, βουλόμενος πράττει, καὶ ὃ βούλεται, ἑκών [*EE* ii,7, 1223b5–6].

18 ... ἀλλ' ἔσται δικαιότερος ἢ πρὶν γενέσθαι ἀκρατής [1223b35–36]. Woods says of this remark: "the conclusion actually stated is that the incontinent man will cease acting unjustly when he becomes incontinent (and so be juster than before)" [Woods, *Aristotle: 'Eudemian Ethics,'* 127]. But it is not clear why we have to assume that the man in question *ceases* to act unjustly. It is easier to believe that Aristotle is simply exaggerating here in order to make the contrast with the comparative of 1223b31 (ἀδικωτέρους) more apparent.

The beginning of *EE* ii,8 (1223b38–1224a7), section (e) of the preliminary argument, deals very peremptorily with the second major candidate for the status of defining characteristic of the voluntary: choice [κατὰ προαίρεσιν]. The passage reads as follows:

> That [the voluntary] is not that which is according to choice is clear again from the following considerations: for it has been demonstrated [ἀπεδείχθη] that that which is according to will is not involuntary but rather that all that is willed is also voluntary (but it has been shown only that one can do voluntarily even what one does not will). But we willingly do many things suddenly; no one, however, chooses anything suddenly.[19]

The argument here is obscure, probably because of the way that the text has been passed down. The claim is made that it has been demonstrated that all that is willed is also voluntary; this is immediately followed by an objection to the same: "but it has been shown only that one can do voluntarily even what one does not will" [1224a2–3]. I take it that this latter is a marginal note that has found its way into the text, since it is a comment *upon* the remark that immediately precedes it and, in fact, fails to appreciate the basis upon which Aristotle states here (at the beginning of *EE* ii,8) that all that is willed is also voluntary. The glossator has in mind *EE* ii,7, 1223b29–36, where Aristotle argues that the willed and the voluntary (τὸ βουλόμενον καὶ ἑκούσιον—1223b28–29) are not the same thing and that, therefore, something not willed can be done voluntarily; his objection is that this is not to demonstrate that the willed is voluntary. But the real basis of the remarks at *EE* ii,8, 1223b39–1224a2 ("it has been demonstrated that that which is according to will is not involuntary but rather that all that is willed is also voluntary") is Aristotle's assumption, expressed at 1223b5–6, that what a man wills he does voluntarily (and that the voluntary always involves the will). Of course, an assumption is not a demonstration; but Aristotle often uses the verb ἀποδεικνύναι (as at 1224a1) loosely.

At 1224a3–4 it is apparent that Aristotle's assumption is not just that that which is willed is voluntary but the more expanded assumption expressed at 1223b5–6 ("all that a man does voluntarily he does willingly,

---

19 *EE* ii,8, 1223b38–1224a4. See Appendix 2, including the note at 1224a4 (note 3).

and what he wills he does voluntarily"), for he says that "we willingly [βουλόμενοι] do many things suddenly; no one, however, chooses anything suddenly." This assumption is enough to establish that the voluntary cannot be that which is according to choice, for, presuming this wide influence of the will—so wide, that is, that it includes also things done suddenly—it is clear that 'according to choice,' which presumes time to deliberate, does not include all the voluntary. Since the question is whether 'according to choice' could serve as the differentia fixing the definition of the voluntary, obviously the voluntary is not equivalent to that which is according to choice.

II. The Force and Compulsion Argument

We come now to the main argument of *EE* ii,8, over the course of which Aristotle in effect resolves the contradictions identified in the preliminary argument. But, before addressing the issue of whether (as suggested above) by means of this resolution Aristotle undermines his own effort to determine the definition of the voluntary, we must have a good understanding of the argument that constitutes the resolution. The argument in question—let us call it the "force and compulsion argument"—is long, stretching from 1224a8 to 1225a33. Aristotle introduces it by saying that he will now "put a cap on the definition with respect to the voluntary and the involuntary."[20] This way of speaking—"put a cap on" [ἐπιθῶμεν τέλος τῷ . . .]—is an indication that Aristotle regards what follows as connected with but, strictly speaking, not integral to the argument that precedes it (i.e., the preliminary argument). Indeed, besides shedding light upon the preliminary argument, it puts forward some substantive theory in its own right.

The force and compulsion argument can be divided into three sections: (a) 1224a8–1224b15, (b) 1224b15–1225a1, and (c) 1225a2–1225a33. Near the beginning of section (a), Aristotle says that he is concerned with cases in which an agent's appetite and his reason are not in harmony [οὐ

---

20 . . . ἐπιθῶμεν τέλος τῷ περὶ τοῦ ἑκουσίου καὶ ἀκουσίου διορισμῷ. δοκεῖ γὰρ τὸ βίᾳ καὶ μὴ βίᾳ τι ποιεῖν οἰκεῖα τοῖς εἰρημένοις εἶναι [*EE* ii,8, 1224a8–10]. See Appendix 2, including the note at 1224a10 (note 4).

... συμφωνεῖ—1224a24–25], that is, cases of ἐγκράτεια and ἀκρασία.[21] At the beginning of (c), he announces a switch to cases in which the agent's appetite and his reason are in harmony [οὐ διαφωνοῦντος—1225a3]. This change at the beginning of (c) is a signal that Aristotle has moved even farther from a strict consideration of the issues of the preliminary argument, which had to do with ἐγκράτεια and ἀκρασία. For this reason, and since it also raises some textual issues, I consider section (c) later, that is, in part IV of the present chapter. So, here we are interested primarily in sections (a) and (b) of the force and compulsion argument.

In section (a), Aristotle is concerned to explain how the concepts of force [βία] and non-force [μὴ βία] come to be associated so simplistically with the voluntary and the involuntary in arguments about ἐγκράτεια and ἀκρασία.[22] (We saw such a simplistic approach above, in arguments P1 and P2 of the preliminary argument). He says that we—or, at least, some people—are led to make this association by the simplicity and consequent greater clarity of the force found, for instance, among inanimate things. This simplicity lies not just in the fact that such things go in a single direction—fire goes up, stones go down—but also in the fact that we do not even have a word for what they do when they go in their natural direction. If a stone is thrown up, we say that it is forced to go up, but when it goes down we do not say that it does so voluntarily: the antithesis of being forced has no name: it is ἀνώνυμος [1224a19]. By contrast, the force and compulsion with which Aristotle is concerned in *EE* ii,6–8 are opposed to namable (and named) phenomena: to the voluntary [τῷ ἑκουσίῳ] and to convinced preference [τῇ πειθοῖ] [1224a14–15].[23] Animate things not

---

21 Although in the preliminary argument Aristotle is scrupulous about distinguishing appetite [ὄρεξις] from desire [ἐπιθυμία], in the force and compulsion argument the two words are sometimes used interchangeably. See, for instance, *EE* ii,8, 1224b29–31, where the distinction is between λόγος and ἐπιθυμία, but a few lines later (1225a3) between λόγος and ὄρεξις.

22 δοκεῖ γὰρ τὸ βίᾳ καὶ μὴ βίᾳ τι ποιεῖν οἰκεῖα τοῖς εἰρημένοις εἶναι· τό τε γὰρ βίαιον ἀκούσιον, καὶ τὸ ἀκούσιον πᾶν βίαιον εἶναι φαμέν [*EE* ii,8, 1224a9–11]. The words τοῖς εἰρημένοις refer to the voluntary and involuntary mentioned also in 1224a8–9: ἐπιθῶμεν τέλος τῷ περὶ τοῦ ἑκουσίου καὶ ἀκουσίου διορισμῷ.... "The main theme of this section [1224a13–30]," says Woods, "is the close connection between the notions of compulsion and necessity" [Woods, *Aristotle: 'Eudemian Ethics,'* 129]. I do not think that this is right.

23 The word πειθώ is usually translated 'persuasion,' but persuasion would seem rather to be something that comes from outside (as a sort of intellectual force). Here (and in what follows) Aristotle has in mind something internal.

endowed with reason in addition to appetite—or not yet endowed with it (as is the case with children)—are also relatively simple, says Aristotle. Although we can identify opposite poles in them—that is, the forced and the voluntary (see *EN* iii,1, 1111a25–26)—they are simple when compared to adult humans, since adult humans have appetite but also reason, which is sometimes opposed to appetite.[24]

The consequence of the relative simplicity of force as found among inanimate and simple animate things is that, whenever the slightest suggestion of the involuntary appears in the action of even adult humans, the tendency (at least among those of a sophistic bent) is to say that the whole of the action is forced.[25] That this is the gist of section (a) of the force and compulsion argument is evident from what Aristotle says at 1224b2–5: "That, therefore, these [that is, the ἐγκρατής and the ἀκρατής] seem to act only due to force and involuntarily and why this is so (because they act according to a likeness of acting due to force, according to which likeness we say the same also of inanimate things) has been stated."[26] In concluding (a), Aristotle offers a way of avoiding any such confusion and/or sophistry: one employs the word 'forced' of acts only when speaking of something that comes wholly from without [ἔξωθεν—1224b7], as when someone takes up the hand of another—whose is unwilling and resistant—and strikes a third person [1224b13–14]. Since the ἐγκρατής and the ἀκρατής, despite any internal force they might experience or impose upon themselves, ultimately act on their own, it is incorrect to put their characteristic acts into the category of the forced (or compelled). "When ... the principle [ἡ ἀρχή] is internal, the action is not due to force" [1224b14–15]. We shall see shortly, however, that, although Aristotle sticks to this terminological injunction, it is still possible for him to speak of force within the soul.

In section (b) (1224b15–1225a1), having sorted out the proper mean-

24 See Appendix 2, the note at 1224a30 (note 5).
25 *EE* ii,8, 1224a30–36. Aristotle adds here (1224a36–b2) a quick argument to the effect that, even on the surface of things, the difference with respect to voluntariness between the ἐγκρατής and the ἀκρατής is apparent: the ἀκρατής acts *more* voluntarily than the ἐγκρατής, since he acts with less pain. Aristotle acknowledges, though, that the ἐγκρατής does act voluntarily, since he follows convinced preference, which is opposed to force and compulsion.
26 τι μὲν οὖν δοκοῦσιν οὗτοι μόνον βίᾳ καὶ ἄκοντες ποιεῖν, καὶ διὰ τίν' αἰτίαν, ὅτι καθ' ὁμοιότητά τινα τοῦ βίᾳ, καθ' ἣν καὶ ἐπὶ τῶν ἀψύχων λέγομεν, εἴρηται [*EE* ii,8, 1224b2–5].

ing of the term 'force' (or 'forced'), Aristotle now feels free, in his analysis of human acts, to make use of factors exploited by sophists in order to sow confusion. For there does exist, he argues, real force or compulsion within the souls of men—within, for instance, the souls of the ἐγκρατής and the ἀκρατής—and there is genuine knowledge to be gained from considering such force, as long as it is not confused with the force that makes an entire action involuntary. It is not unreasonable [ἔχει λόγον—1224b22] to say that either of these two character types acts under force and involuntarily, the one on account of desire, the other on account of reasoning, "for these [appetite and reason], being separated, are dominated one by the other" [1224b23–24]. The ἐγκρατής forces his desires into their proper place,[27] the ἀκρατής resists reason.

We can admit all this—and, indeed, it constitutes theoretical progress to do so—as long as we maintain that the action of the whole soul is to be analyzed in a distinct manner. "The whole soul of both the incontinent man and the continent acts voluntarily; neither acts due to force, but something in each does, for even by nature we have both."[28] This latter clause is a reference once again to appetite and reason. Aristotle understands that both of these are present in the soul independently of that soul's will (we do not *will* to have intellect). "For reason exists by nature for, once genesis is allowed and not impeded, it is present; and so is desire, for it follows immediately upon birth and is then present" [1224b29–31].

As we shall see shortly, this approach—this exploitation of sophistical observations—allows Aristotle to put forward in *EE* ii,8 a more articulated analysis of moral force and compulsion than we find anywhere else in the corpus. It allows Aristotle to work into his theory the role of natural "forced" tendencies of both a rational and an irrational (a-rational) sort. But his wielding of terms is often very subtle and open to misunderstanding. His use of the term 'natural,' which plays such a large role in the passage we are currently considering, is a case in point. Like 'voluntary' or 'involuntary,' 'natural' can be used in a local sense, as when the particular

---

27 Note that at 1224b8, that which forces from without either moves (something) or makes it to remain inactive: κινῇ ἢ ἠρεμίζῃ. See also 1224b12: τὴν παρὰ τὴν ὁρμὴν ἢ ἐμποδίζουσαν ἢ κινοῦσαν.

28 δ' ὅλη ἑκοῦσα ψυχὴ καὶ τοῦ ἀκρατοῦς καὶ τοῦ ἐγκρατοῦς πράττει, βίᾳ δ' οὐδέτερος, ἀλλὰ τῶν ἐν ἐκείνοις τι, ἐπεὶ καὶ φύσει ἀμφότερα ἔχομεν [*EE* ii,8, 1224b26–29].

effect of desire within an act is said to be natural, or in a more global sense, as when an entire act is characterized by and attributed to a natural desire. He acknowledges such linguistic dangers in this very passage. Speaking of the ἐγκρατής and the ἀκρατής and summing up his reflections about the naturalness of reason and desire, he says: "So that each acts *not according to* nature and, simply speaking, *according* to nature, although not the same nature" [1224b35–36], by which he means that the ἐγκρατής acts according to reason but not desire, the ἀκρατής vice-versa. He might also have added (what he will add later) that, when there is no such thrusting out of one impulse by the other, the whole of an action might be according to nature, involving reason or desire or both together.

Aristotle concludes section (b) with the following remarks:

> The puzzles then about the incontinent and continent man—about whether both or one of them act due to force, so that, acting either not voluntarily or at the same time due to force *and* voluntarily, supposing that force is involuntary, they act at the same time [ἅμα] voluntarily and involuntarily—how these are to be addressed is reasonably clear from what has been said.[29]

These remarks are redolent of the contradiction concerns we have already seen in *EE* ii,7. Their more immediate reference is certainly to the problems discussed in section (a) of the force and compulsion argument (*EE* ii,8, 1224a30–b15); but, since the latter contains no explicit mention of contradiction, it is reasonable to maintain that Aristotle still has in mind the arguments in *EE* ii,7, especially sections (b) and (c). The remarks, therefore, bring to a head the problem of the interpretation of the preliminary argument. How, if Aristotle *solves* here the puzzles (the ἀπορίαι) of the preliminary argument, can that argument be sound, given that certain candidates for the role as differentia of the voluntary are eliminated there on the grounds that positing them as differentiae leads to contradiction?

Consider, for example, the argument identified above as N1 (1223b5–10). There, having previously argued (in P2) (1223a36–b3) that the ἀκρατής acts voluntarily (since he can be criticized for what he does and no one is criticized for what he does involuntarily), Aristotle argues, to the contrary,

---

29 *EE* ii,8, 1224b36–1225a1. See Appendix 2, including the note at 1225a1 (note 7).

that, when the ἀκρατής following desire does what he does not want to do [οὐχ ἃ βούλεται], he acts involutarily, since no one does voluntarily what he thinks is evil [*EE* ii,7, 1223b5–9]. Thus, "it will follow that the same man acts at the same time both voluntarily and involuntarily; but that is impossible" [1223b9–10]. This apparent contradiction has now been resolved by the force and compulsion argument: part of the ἀκρατής is "forced" by desire to do that which, in another part of his soul, he does not want to do, but the whole of his soul does act voluntarily.

Or consider another of the *EE* ii,7 arguments that finish with the language of contradiction, N2 (1223b10–17). Aristotle argues there that the ἐγκρατής acts virtuously and that this entails that he acts voluntary; but he also acts against his desires, and this is involuntary; so "the same man at the same time does the same thing voluntarily and involuntarily" [1223b17]. This is now resolved, since it is now apparent that it is possible to perform an act in its entirety even while, within one's soul, there are parts that are not so inclined (i.e., are not willing). In the soul of the perfectly virtuous man, there is no such reluctance (involuntariness); but both types—the ἐγκρατής and the virtuous man—might perform this sort of act.

III. Understanding the Preliminary Argument: The Agenda Set in *EE* ii,6

We have already sufficient evidence that the peculiar strategy of the preliminary argument is useful for the assembling of ideas; the question before us, however, is whether the argument is valid. Not all of its subarguments finish with remarks about contradiction; that type of move is limited to the earlier arguments eliminating 'that which is according to desire' and also, by implication, 'that which is according to aggression' (in sections II (b) and (c)). But if those arguments are not sound, they bring into question the validity of the preliminary argument, since its general strategy is one of exclusion (see *EE* ii,7, 1223a23–28). If even one element in it is resolved, one is not forced to conclude that the differentia of the voluntary is that which is according to thought.

But perhaps we have this all wrong? The implicit task of the preliminary argument is not to say how things stand (and so to avoid contradiction) but whether the voluntary can be defined by means of the differentia 'according to desire' (or 'according to aggression').[30] And whenever an effort of the latter sort arrives at the idea that something falling within the scope of the voluntary can be described as both voluntary and involuntary, it is apparent that that candidate will not do as a differentia for the voluntary. Aristotle never denies—indeed, as we have just seen, he straightforwardly asserts—that force can also bring involuntariness to an internal aspect (or part) of the soul. A differentia obviously ought not to take in things that are not included in the species one is seeking to define. So, the eliminative preliminary argument is perfectly sound as it stands, since 'according to desire' (and later 'according to aggression') are rejected not on the grounds that they lead to contradiction but because they cannot serve as differentiae—as they obviously cannot do, since that would be to allow within the species of the voluntary the involuntary. The resolution of contradictions in section (b) of the force and compulsion argument has, therefore, no real bearing upon the validity of preliminary argument; the force and compulsion argument itself is more of an independent excursus, although one that exploits and develops the bundle of ideas assembled by Aristotle over the course of the preliminary argument.

But why does Aristotle take this approach? That is best explained by backing up and considering especially *EE* ii,6 and its bearing upon what

---

30 A legitimate question at this point would be, What type of definition does Aristotle have in mind in the preliminary argument? Does he have in mind simply a genus-differentia combination, as in the *Topics*? (See *Top.* i,4 and vi,4–6.) Or does he have in mind a definition like those discussed in *Metaph.* viii,6, where the genus becomes matter and the differentia form? And, since the definition of the voluntary (or voluntary acts) falls within the genus 'movements,' it is not to be immediately discounted that he has in mind the definitions of events ("noise in the clouds") in terms of cause and effect, as in *APo.* ii,8. There is, however, no indication in *EE* ii,7–8 that Aristotle has in mind the latter. As to the former two options, the *Metaph.* approach does not eschew genus-differentia language (see, for example, *Metaph.* vii,12 passim and *Metaph.* viii,1, 1042a13–21 and viii,2, 1043a19–21), although, as Marguerite Deslauriers has shown, there is a difference between the *Top.* and *Metaph.* approaches. The former understands a differentia as an attribute of the corresponding genus; the latter is especially concerned with the unity of definitions (see *Metaph.* viii,6)—a concern that is obscured by speaking of attributes [Deslauriers, *Aristotle on Definition*, 210]. Since in section (d) of the preliminary argument, Aristotle slips so easily into language suggesting that the voluntary and that which is according to will are "the same thing," it seems to me that in the argument in general (*EE* ii,7–8) he must have in mind the *Metaph.* approach.

follows.³¹ In *EE* ii,6, Aristotle discusses the relationship between principles [ἀρχαί] and their consequences. At the beginning of the chapter, he speaks about plants, mere animals, and man, noting that only man is the principle of actions [πράξεών ... ἀρχὴ—1222b19] (by which he means human actions, in the technical sense). He then singles out a subset of the principles, which he calls ἀρχαί κύριαι: "sovereign principles," which are fully responsible for—and in command of—their effects;³² the primary example of such a principle is God [1222b23].

In order to illustrate the character of such principles, he uses as an example the principles in mathematical proofs, which, although not strictly speaking sovereign principles, can be said to be such because of a certain resemblance [1222b24–25].³³ Given that a triangle has interior angles equal to two right angles, a quadrilateral will have angles equal to four right angles. The triangle's having angles equal to two right angles is, therefore, the cause of the quadrilateral having angles equal to four right angles, so that, if the triangle had angles equal to three right angles, the quadrilateral would have angles equal to six right angles. But if there is no such alteration and the principle (the essence of triangle) remains as it is, the other (the quadrilateral) necessarily remains as it is.³⁴

Aristotle is obviously interested here in combining both necessity and change. And it becomes apparent eventually that his reason for doing so is that he sees both in human action: the relationship between a man as sovereign principle [ἀρχὴ καὶ κύριος—1223a5] and the characteristics of his own actions is necessary, although anything that a man does (by way of a human action) he might also not do. If at the point of origin, there is voluntariness, there *must* be a corresponding voluntariness in the act; but what is related thereby in a necessary manner are contingencies: if the sovereign principle changes its (his) mind, the act also changes.

---

31 On this chapter, see especially Heinaman, "The *Eudemian Ethics* on Knowledge and Voluntary Action."

32 See Woods, *Aristotle: 'Eudemian Ethics,'* 191.

33 Aristotle says of this relationship between mathematical principles and their consequences: "In any case, however, this is meant as an analogy, for also here, if the principle is altered, all the things demonstrated from it would certainly change, but the things demonstrated do not change one another, one destroyed by the other—except in the case of the destruction of an assumption, by means of which something is demonstrated" [1222b24–28]. See Appendix 2, the note at 1222b28 (note 1).

34 *EE* ii,6, 1222b34–37.

Why Aristotle should be interested here in contingency is not hard to understand: he is about to launch a discussion of the voluntary; but no less important is his insistence on necessity. Man, being a sovereign principle, is responsible for everything that falls within the scope of his own voluntariness—and only those things.[35] Thus, if there are aspects of his own action that are forced upon him, they cannot be connected (attributed) to him morally. The same can be said of aspects of an action of which he is non-culpably ignorant, as Aristotle goes on to explain in *EE* ii,9. One might know, for instance, who the person is to whom one gives a drink but not that the drink is poisoned [1225b1–8]; or one might have knowledge of an obligation not to behave in a certain way but, through no fault of one's own, not be able to activate it—"bring it up"—at the crucial moment [1225b11–16].[36] All this is the converse of the necessity that binds the agent to the voluntary aspects—or entire acts—of which he is sovereign. When he shakes, they shake; but he has no moral connection with what does not enter into this nexus. If it is true, as we saw in chapter 1, that human acts occur in the perceptual realm, that is, in the realm below the syllogistic, there is still a sort of syllogistic necessity tying a man's will to the things he does: to his acts with all their particular characteristics. This is the reason why Aristotle draws the mathematical (or geometrical) analogy he does in *EE* ii,6. The will's reach is as extensive—and as precise—as the reach of mathematical principles: where it enters, there is moral responsibility; where it does not enter, there is none: there is no human action.[37]

It is clear from all this that Aristotle has to look at everything to which the voluntary might attach but also to delineate the limits of this field of moral action: he is dealing (but in a discriminating way) with a phenomenon—the voluntary—that has an inherent propensity to expand. His standard methodology for conducting any such an investigation is first

---

35 At *de An.* ii,8, 419b18–22, having acknowledged that sound can be heard in water but not so well as in air, Aristotle notes, however, that neither air nor water is κύριος of sound. What *is* κύριος of sound is the "impact of two solids against one another," but even that principle is not κύριος over the material in which the sound is received.

36 See below, chapter 4, section I.

37 By the will here, I mean βούλησις, the combination of intellect and appetite, as in *de An.* iii,9, 432b3–7 and iii,10, 433a23–25.

to include as much information as is feasible within a given field of enquiry—the so called ἔνδοξα—and then to sift through it all, organizing it according to the principles of scientific enquiry.[38] The word ἔνδοξα is often translated 'reputable opinions,' but, in this case, as we have already seen, he uses puzzles originating in an apparently eristic context in order to see how far the phenomenon extends that he must subsequently organize.[39] That the ἔνδοξα are conflictual is to be expected; even so, they tell us a good deal about how far the voluntary extends. Aristotle is able to take them all into account in a way that, by distinguishing the force that affects an act itself from the force that might affect a part of one, does not violate logic.

IV. The Force and Compulsion Argument, section (c)

We come now to the final section of the force and compulsion argument, which like the others is dense and controversial. With the ideas presently at hand, however, I believe that we can pull some solid and useful theory from this last section of *EE* ii,8. But before we enter the thicket, it would be good to review some of those ideas. The fundamental idea—and the chief gain of Aristotle's argumentation up to this point—is the idea that in the analysis of acts we must distinguish the act itself from its internal aspects (see *EE* ii,8, 1224b26–29). The predicates 'voluntary' and 'involuntary' can be attributed to internal aspects of an act—aspects important for a complete understanding of the act—without being attributed to the act itself. Secondly, we can, therefore, say that even the typical actions of, for instance, the ἐγκρατής involve force, since he has to force himself to resist his own desires ("for he is pained as he fights against countervailing appetite") (see 1224a33–36). Thirdly, the force within such character types as the ἐγκρατής and the ἀκρατής depends on the (in their case) countervailing tendencies of desire and reason.[40] Fourthly, taking

---

38 On ἔνδοξα, see especially Jonathan Barnes, "Aristotle and the Method of Ethics," *Revue Internationale de Philosophie* 34 (1980): 490–511.
39 See above, note 9.
40 See 1223a37–38, 1223b12–14, 1224a24–25, and 1224a36.

into consideration the internal complexity of an act and the various voluntary and involuntary aspects, we can speak of degrees of voluntariness, so that the ἀκρατής can be said to act more voluntarily and less by force than the ἐγκρατής (see 1224a36–38). Fifthly, both reason and desire are inborn and are, therefore, in so far as they are inborn, independent of the will of the individual agent (see 1224b29–31). Finally, in this latter connection, we might mention the presupposition of sections of the preliminary argument that there is a difference between what the will (βούλησις) might want in a specific way and its general influence upon human action (although at issue is always one and the same faculty of the soul).[41]

It will be good to have before us a translation of section (c) [*EE* ii,8, 1225a2–33], broken down into four subsections:

[i] In another way, too, men are said to act due to force and to be compelled to act, without any disagreement between reason and appetite in them, that is, when they do what they consider both painful and bad, but should they not do it, there would be lashings or chains or deaths. For they say that they acted having been compelled. Or is that not right but all do the thing itself voluntarily? For they had it in them not to act and to endure the alternative affliction.

[ii] Moreover, perhaps someone might say that, of these acts, some are voluntary, some not. For of the things that depend on a man whether they come about or not, those which he does without willing them he always does voluntarily and not due to force; but those that do not depend on him, he in a sense does due to force but not simply speaking, for he does not choose that itself which he does but he does choose the end for which it is done (since also among these there is a certain difference).

[iii] For, if in order not to be seized someone groping about were to slay another, it would be ridiculous if he were to say that he acted due to force, that is, that he was compelled, but there must always be some greater and more painful evil which will befall the one not acting (for in this way one *is* compelled and acts not due to force, or not by nature, when he does something evil for the sake of good, or for the sake of release from some greater evil); in any case, he acts involuntarily, for these things do not depend upon him.[42] So, many regard love and some outbursts of aggression—that is, natural things—as involuntary be-

---

41 See 1223b5–6, 1223b26–27, 1223b29, and 1223b32–36.
42 See Appendix 2, the note at 1225a19 (note 8).

cause stronger even than nature; these admit of forgiveness, as they are things by nature capable of forcing nature.

[iv] A man would seem *more* to act from force and involuntarily if he acts in order not to experience strong than in order not to experience light pain, and if in order not to experience pain generally than in order not to take pleasure.[43] For that which depends on him—and everything comes down ultimately to this—is the following: what his nature is able to bear. What it cannot bear, nor pertains by nature to his appetite or reason, does not depend on him. Therefore those who are inspired and prophesy, although they perform a work of reason, even still we do not say that it depends on them not to say what they said, not to do what they did. Nor do they act due to desire. So, some thoughts and affections—or the acts performed according to such thoughts and reasonings—also do not depend on us, but, as Philolaus said, some arguments are stronger than we are.

Let us go through the subsections in order. In subsection [i], Aristotle moves explicitly away from the issues raised in the preliminary argument, which were all generated by the sophistic—but not to be dismissed out of hand—analysis of the ἐγκρατής and the ἀκρατής. Here in [i], there is no "disagreement between reason and appetite"—although, as we shall see, the natural operation of reason and appetite (λόγος and ὄρεξις) themselves are still very much at issue. Also at this point, Aristotle begins to distinguish force [βία] and compulsion [ἀνάγκη], which up until this point have been rather run together (see *EE* ii,8, 1224a13ff.). Here Aristotle says that when people do things because they are threatened with whipping, imprisonment, etc., they say they acted on compulsion [φασιν ἀναγκασθέντες πρᾶξαι—1225a6]. So, a main theme of section (c) will be the distinction between such acts—spoken of as "mixed acts" in *EN* iii,1—and other acts that involve (as we shall see) force. At the end of subsection [i], Aristotle establishes a bit of distance between himself and what these people say: "Or is that not right ... ?" he asks, suggesting that talk of compulsion is out of place, since these individuals do, after all, act voluntarily.

At the beginning of subsection [ii], Aristotle suggests that the category of acts that do not involve conflict between reason and appetite

---

43 See Appendix 2, the note at 1225a25 (note 9).

is more complicated than he has been suggesting: "Moreover, perhaps someone might say that, of these acts, some are voluntary, some not" [ἔτι ἴσως τούτων τὰ μὲν φαίη τις ἂν τὰ δ' οὔ—1225a8–9]. The expression "these acts" [τούτων—1225a8] refers to the category of acts that do not involve conflict between reason and appetite—not, that is, to the compelled acts he has just discussed; the ἔτι ("Moreover") which introduces this division of "these acts" indicates a point distinct from the one that precedes it. The same is also apparent in what immediately follows, for Aristotle does not divide the *compelled* acts into those that are voluntary and those that are involuntary, but he explains (among other things) why the compelled acts are all voluntary. In compelled acts one does what one does not will [ἃ μὴ βούλεται], but one *does* these things, that is, "voluntarily and not due to force" [ἑκὼν πράττει, καὶ οὐ βίᾳ—1225a11].[44] Here he is clearly speaking of things done by people threatened with whipping, imprisonment, etc. He distinguishes such acts from those due to *force*: unlike the person who, for instance, betrays his comrades in order to save his family, the forced (or quasi-forced: βίᾳ πώς—1225a12) person does not choose to do "that itself which he does" [αὐτὸ τοῦτο ... ὃ πράττει—1225a12–13] but only the end for which it is done.[45]

What are these things? As we shall see, they are things that one does when so under the influence of a natural force that one cannot but so act. At this point (i.e., at the very end of [ii]), Aristotle adds: "since also among these there is a certain difference" [1225a13–14]). The difference referred to is the difference between the act itself and its end. Aristotle acknowledges that in forced acts the act and the end run together, but the distinction can be made. By contrast, the unwilling betrayer is acutely aware that his act and his end are distinct; he does *do* something, which he would not do otherwise, in order to get to the desired end.

Subsection [iii] begins with the words, "For, if in order not to be

---

44 We see perhaps here (in particular at 1225a10–11: ἃ μὴ βούλεται) the distinction between particular things willed and the general operation of will (or βούλησις). If all that one does voluntarily one does with the involvement of the will [1223b5–6], a compelled act depends on the will, even though what one is compelled to do one may not will to do.

45 On "quasi-forced acts," see Kevin L. Flannery, "Force and Compulsion in Aristotle's Ethics," in *Proceedings of the Boston Area Colloquium in Ancient Philosophy*, vol. 22 (2006), ed. John Cleary and Gary Gurtler (Leiden: E. J. Brill, 2007), 53. (For this section of the present chapter, I have lifted a few paragraphs from this article.)

seized someone groping about were to slay another, it would be ridiculous if he were to say that he acted due to force, that is, that he was compelled, but there must always be some greater and more painful evil which will befall the one not acting" [1225a14–17]. Here Aristotle is clearly still talking about the distinction we have just seen. If we are to talk about compulsion, there must be some genuine act which one would not do unless so compelled. The word translated "groping about" [ψηλαφῶν—1125a14] is translated in the Revised Oxford Translation as "[playing] blind man's bluff."[46] This is a misleading, since it suggests that what is ridiculous is applying the word 'force' to what occurs in a mere child's game. What Aristotle seems to have in mind rather is a person who, groping about in the dark, is seized by another; such a person quite naturally lashes out. The ridiculousness has nothing to do with the game but with the linguistic usage: saying that instinctive lashing out involves force or compulsion.[47]

But why would Aristotle say that it is ridiculous to speak of force, since he has already suggested that such a way of speaking is acceptable (βίᾳ πώς—1225a12)? Well, he does not really say that speaking of force is ridiculous. Crucial in this respect is the "that is" in the phrase, "if he were to say that he acted under force, *that is*, that he was compelled." Other translations employ instead the conjunction 'and'; the Revised Oxford Translation, for example, has, "...if he were to say that he acted by force, and on compulsion." But it is perfectly legitimate to translate the word καὶ not as 'and' but epexegetically, as I have done. The idea is that it would be ridiculous if the man were to say that he acted under force *in the sense that* he was compelled.[48] So, we could indeed say that the man who lashes

---

46 The Revised Oxford Translation is Jonathan Barnes, ed., *The Complete Works of Aristotle: The Revised Oxford Translation* (Princeton: Princeton University Press, 1984). See also Woods, *Aristotle: 'Eudemian Ethics,'* 134: "The reference seems to be to a game like blind man's bluff." Dirlmeier agrees, citing Rackham and Jackson [Franz Dirlmeier, *Aristoteles* Eudemische Ethik (Berlin: Akademie, 1962), 284]. A game something like blind man's bluff called χαλκῆ μυῖα ("bronze fly") is described at August Friedrich Pauly, Georg Wissowa, and others, eds., *Paulys Real-Encyclopädie der classischen Altertumswissenschaft: Neue Bearbeitung* (Stuttgart: Metzler, 1893), 3.2068.

47 Although "groping about" seems to imply a certain degree of ignorance of what is going on, Aristotle is not interested here in that aspect of the action. In another philosophical context, he could (or might) very well say that such a slaying of another is involuntary because the agent does not know that his lashing out could slay someone or that his thrust of the dagger would kill a comrade (as opposed to an enemy); but Aristotle is interested here not in ignorance but in force and compulsion.

48 Gauthier finds a similar usage at *EN* vi,9, 1142b18 [René-Antoine Gauthier and Jean Yves Jolif, *L'Éthique à Nicomaque*, 2.2 516].

out was forced to do what he did; but it would be ridiculous to say he was compelled to do so, which would require the presence of "some greater and more painful evil which will befall the one not acting." Aristotle immediately adds as a parenthesis: "for in this way [i.e., when one acts to avoid "some greater and more painful evil"] one *is* compelled and acts not due to force, or not by nature, when he does something evil for the sake of good, or for the sake of release from some greater evil" [1225a17–19]. He then comes back the "naturally forced" agent, saying that in any case *he* acts involuntarily, for the things he does "do not depend upon him" [1225a19].[49] "So," Aristotle says, "many regard love and some outbursts of aggression—that is, natural things [τὰ φυσικά]—as involuntary because stronger even than nature [ὑπὲρ τὴν φύσιν]; these admit of forgiveness, as they are things by nature capable of forcing nature [βιάζεσθαι τὴν φύσιν]" [1225a19–22]. In this remark, Aristotle acknowledges the ambiguous character of words like 'nature' [φύσις] and 'natural' [φυσικός]: natural things [τὰ φυσικά] (i.e., natural propensities) can be above nature [ὑπὲρ τὴν φύσιν] and can even force nature.

Aristotle makes the distinction between force and compulsion also in his lectures on ethics—or, at least, so reports a student's notes, now known as the *Magna moralia*.[50] That is, in book one, chapters 14–15, he makes a distinction between the forced [τὸ βίαιον] and the compelled [τὸ ἀναγκαῖον], the former (as in *EE* ii,8, 1224a15–18) finding its primary analogue in the stone that is forced to go up or the fire that is forced to go down, the latter comprising cases in which, for instance, "a man receives some damage by way of alternative to some other greater, when compelled by circumstances" [*MM* i,15, 1188b19–21]. This would correspond to the "some greater and more painful evil which will befall the one not acting" here in [iii] (*EE* ii,8, 1225a16–17). It appears that in the Greek of his time the words βία and ἀνάγκη (and cognates) were very close in meaning, so that Aristotle needed occasionally to tell his audience which technical sense he had in mind.

---

49 See above, note 42, for my repunctuation of Susemihl's text.
50 See John M. Cooper, "The *Magna Moralia* and Aristotle's Moral Philosophy," *American Journal of Philology* 94 (1973): 327–49. Cooper maintains that *MM* was not penned by Aristotle but is a collection of student notes on lectures given by Aristotle. But see also C. J. Rowe, "A Reply to John Cooper on the *Magna Moralia*," *American Journal of Philology* 96 (1975): 160–72.

Subsection [iv] is impossible to understand without bearing in mind what we have seen in the force and compulsion argument, especially section (a), where it becomes apparent that Aristotle accepts the idea, taken over from the sophists, that there is force within the souls of both the ἐγκρατής and the ἀκρατής, although it is not force that so overwhelms nature as to constitute force "from without" [ἔξωθεν] (see *EE* ii,8, 1224b7–8). As we have seen, at one point Aristotle even says that the characteristic acts of the ἐγκρατής involve force, since he has to force himself, by means of his own reason, away from the pleasures that tempt him (1224a33–36).

Bearing this last point especially in mind, we see that a textual emendation accepted by all modern commentators is unnecessary and, in fact, obscures Aristotle's theoretical point. In the first sentence of [iv], Aristotle is sketching out a scale of measurement for the involuntary and the voluntary. At either end of the scale is a limit case: on the left (let us say) there is full involuntariness or force, on the right full voluntariness. In the first sentence of [iv] Aristotle says that a man would be assigned a place closer to the fully involuntary "if he acts in order not to experience strong than in order not to experience light pain." This makes good sense, but it is the next phrase that causes the difficulty. A man is also assigned a place closer to the fully involuntary if he acts in order not to experience pain (however strong) "than in order not to take pleasure" [ἢ ἵνα μὴ χαίρῃ—1225a24–25]. The scale would be as is shown in Figure 3-1. The two pairs (avoid great pain–avoid light pain and avoid pain–avoid pleasure) are not positioned relative to each other; Aristotle's point is just that the left members of either pair are closer to the involuntary and the right ones to the voluntary.

Modern texts and translations, however, have all cut out the 'not' (μὴ) at 1225a25, so that, in the Revised Oxford Translation, for instance, we read: "A man would more seem to act from force and involuntarily if he acted to escape violent than if to escape gentle pain, and generally if to escape pain than if to get pleasure" [1225a22–25].[51] But this all comes of a failure to see that Aristotle is fitting the compelled man into the larger scheme of the force and compulsion argument. All three types involve

---

51 See above, note 43. Bekker deletes the μὴ, as do Rackham, Woods, and Dirlmeier; Susemihl and Walzer-Mingay both put it in brackets; Kenny describes its deletion as "imperative" [Kenny, *Aristotle's Theory of the Will*, 46, n. 1].

fully involuntary	to avoid great pain	to avoid light pain	fully voluntary
	to avoid pain	to avoid pleasure	

FIGURE 3-1.

some degree of force (although not the degree that would allow for a judgment of 'involuntary'): the compelled man, obviously, but also the ἀκρατής, who is diverted from his better intentions even by the prospect of light pain—*and* also the ἐγκρατής, who, as we have seen, must force himself to go against his own desires. Earlier (at 1224a39–b1) Aristotle acknowledges that the ἐγκρατής does act voluntarily, but the fact that he is not simply a voluntary agent owes to the fact that his actions involve some degree of involuntariness.

The next piece of [iv]—"For that which depends on him—and everything comes down ultimately to this—is the following: what his nature is able to bear. What it cannot bear, nor pertains by nature to his appetite or reason [μηδ' ἐστὶ τῆς ἐκείνου φύσει ὀρέξεως ἢ λογισμοῦ—1225a26–27], does not depend on him"—is also difficult; but, bearing in mind again the scale of measurement just depicted, it yields tolerable sense. The far left side of the scale represents what a man's nature is unable to bear, that is, that which is (in some sense) beyond the natural; what appears to the right of that extreme is by nature bearable, in grades tending toward the completely voluntary (the other end of the scale). As we have seen a number of times in the force and compulsion argument, the natural capacities at issue—in particular, within the ἐγκρατής and the ἀκρατής—are reason and desire (or appetite). Both can be associated with either the voluntary or the involuntary; but they are also both natural,[52] so they do not allow one to judge an action performed under their influence totally involuntary.

The force and compulsion argument finishes with a specification of

---

52 αἱ γὰρ ὁ λόγος φύσει ὑπάρχει, ὅτι ἐωμένης τῆς γενέσεως καὶ μὴ πηρωθείσης ἐνέσται, καὶ ἡ ἐπιθυμία, ὅτι εὐθὺς ἐκ γενετῆς ἀκολουθεῖ καὶ ἔνεστιν [*EE* ii,8, 1224b29–31].

the preceding point, a specification that makes it apparent that Aristotle holds that it is possible for a person to do something that is natural even when he has no choice in the matter and his act is, therefore, involuntary. Aristotle says that "those who are inspired and prophesy" should be put on the far left extreme of the scale, "although they perform a work of reason [διανοίας ἔργον—1225a28]." It is possible for us to be so overwhelmed intellectually as to be literally incapable of thinking otherwise; or, as the Philolaus says, "some arguments are stronger than we are."[53] But thinking and thoughts and arguments are all natural to man.

V. Other Passages

We have before us now the substance of Aristotle's theory regarding the way in which force shapes the interior contours of the voluntary act. The other shaping factor is the factor toward which the preliminary argument is directed and at which the general argument eventually arrives: reason or "that which is according to thought," discussed in *EE* ii,9. In that chapter Aristotle discusses the knowledge of an act's constituents that an agent might or might not enjoy. I will consider this issue in chapter 4. To conclude the present chapter, I would like to examine a number of passages outside of *EE* ii,6–9 that yield, I believe, more sense when one bears in mind the theory presented in those chapters.

The first passage is found in *EN* iii,1; in it, Aristotle introduces the elements that might impede voluntariness, including (especially) force:

Those things are thought involuntary which take place due to force or owing to ignorance; and that is forced of which the moving principle is from without, being a principle in which nothing is contributed by the one who acts or is acted upon—if, for instance, the wind were to convey one or men have one in their power.

---

53 Aristotle's citing Philolaus is not irrelevant to the voluntary-involuntary scale he has just set out, for one of the Pythagorean philosopher's main theses is that nothing would be knowable if all things were without limit (see H. Diels and W. Kranz, eds. and trans., *Die Fragmente der Vorsokratiker*, 6th ed. [Dublin/Zurich: Weidmann, 1951], 44.B.3). In another fragment [Diels and Kranz, *Die Fragmente der Vorsokratiker*, 44.b.17], Philolaus speaks of the universe as fixed by extremes, between which everything else falls. Applied in the present context, the idea would be that, in order to make sense of the cases in which the voluntary and the involuntary are mixed, we must posit the extremes 'full involuntariness' and 'full voluntariness.'

As, however, to things that are done for fear of greater evils or for something noble (if, for instance, a tyrant should order one to do something base, having one's parents and children in his power, and if one does the action they will be saved, but if not they will die), there is some question whether such actions are involuntary or voluntary. Something of the sort happens also with regard to things jettisoned during storms, for simply speaking no one throws goods away voluntarily but, in order to preserve oneself or the others, anyone who has sense does so. Such actions are, therefore, mixed, although they are more like voluntary actions. For they are worthy of choice at the time they are performed, and the end of an action is relative to the occasion. [1109b35-1110a14]

Where in the theory set out in *EE* ii,6–9 would the matters discussed here—things forced upon individuals and "mixed acts"—fit? Not among the actions by individuals whose reason and appetite are not in agreement—the acts discussed, that is, in sections (a) and (b) of the force and compulsion argument—for at issue here is neither ἐγκράτεια nor ἀκρασία. So, they would be treated, if anywhere, in (c), the section devoted to cases in which there is no conflict between reason and appetite. There is no difficulty whatsoever fitting the mixed acts into that discussion, for they are explicitly mentioned in the first sentence of (c): "In another way, too, men are said to act due to force and to be compelled to act, without any disagreement between reason and appetite in them, that is, when they do what they consider both painful and bad, but should they not do it, there would be lashings or chains or deaths" [1225a2–6]. Things are not so clear, however, with respect to forced acts, since all the things discussed in (c) are positive acts, while the force discussed in *EN* iii,1 appears to be force that deprives an agent of action. In other words, the first paragraph above appears to be talking about what we might call "brute force": cases in which the subject of force does absolutely nothing and all the movement comes from another source.

But there is an easily missed indication here that Aristotle has in mind a broader category. He says that when force is present, "nothing is contributed by the one who *acts* or is acted upon" [ὁ πράττων ἢ ὁ πάσχων—1110a2–3]. So, one can *do* something that is forced. What sort of action might Aristotle have in mind? It is now fairly widely accepted that Aristotle's remark about the wind conveying someone somewhere refers to an event at sea (as does, of course, the jettisoning of goods). According to Alexander of Aphrodisias, Aristotle himself elucidates his definition of force by saying that "this happens in the case of voyagers when they are forced off course by some wind."[54] And Gauthier points to a passage at *Metaphysics* v,30, 1025a25–27, which gives this same general idea: "Going to Aegina was an accident, if the man went not in order to get there, but because he was carried out of his way by a storm or captured by pirates."[55] It could be that a pilot very deliberately maneuvers his ship into the harbor at Aegina; even still, it can be said that he was forced to do that.

There is not an exact correspondence between section (c) of the force and compulsion argument and the above paragraphs from *EN* iii,1. Although (c) discusses mixed acts, the only example it gives of an act that falls into the category of the fully involuntary is the example of the person groping about in the dark who, frightened, lashes out. But this is not a great problem, since Aristotle does mention a case of brute force earlier in *EE* ii,8, when he uses as an example of forced action someone who, "grabbing the hand of one who resists and neither wills nor desires this, should strike someone [else]" [1224b13–14]. So, Aristotle would certainly not resist putting *EN* iii,1's forced acts—whether brute or somewhat less than brute—together with the lashing out example of (c). And, indeed, it is instructive to compare the lashing out example to acts such as bringing the ship into Aegina. In placing such examples together in the same category, we see that there is no theoretical difficulty in saying that the natural propensities figuring in an act classed as involuntary might involve also calm, deliberate action on the part of the agent. One thinks, in general, of acts of personal self-defense. The need to defend himself is forced upon an agent ("comes from without"), since he has no say in his nature's containing a propensity toward self-preservation and since the immediate cause of his

---

54 ἔδειξεν γινόμενον ἐπὶ τῶν πλεόντων, ὅταν ὑπὸ πνεύματός τινος ἐξωσθῶσιν (*Quaestiones* 133.2–3). Alexander understands Aristotle's words εἰ πνεῦμα κομίσαι ποι as saying *that* this happens in the case of voyagers. One notices Alexander's word ἐξωσθῶσιν: he is clearly trying to associated being forced off course with being subject to something "from without" [ἔξωθεν].

55 Gauthier and Jolif, *L'Éthique à Nicomaque*, 2.1 172. Gauthier is also good here on the misunderstandings of the wind example in medieval times (in particular by Robert Grosseteste and Albert the Great).

having to defend himself is another person's attack. The agent's act of killing (or harming) the other might be described as involuntary (or *praeter intentionem*) as long as a genuine threat remains and as long as the self-defender employs proportionate means.[56]

There is also an instructive comparison to be made between how in *EN* iii,1 Aristotle analyzes the structure of mixed acts and how in *EE* ii,8 he does the same for the lashing out example. He says that mixed acts are "more like voluntary actions" since "they are worthy of choice at the time they are performed, and the end of an action is relative to the occasion" [*EN* iii,1, 1110a12–14]; and he says that in forced acts—Aristotle eventually gives the lashing out example—a person "in a sense" acts due to force "but not simply speaking, for he does not choose that itself which he does but he does choose the end for which it is done" [*EE* ii,8, 1225a12–13]. It is apparent that the difference between a mixed act (such as jettisoning goods) and a forced act (such as lashing out) has to do with the relationship between the act performed and its end. In the mixed act, the end is proper to the moment and therefore distinguishable. As Aristotle says a couple of lines previously, "simply speaking, no one throws goods away voluntarily" [1110a9–10]; indeed, the end is *determined* by the moment (it is κατὰ τὸν καιρόν [1110a13–14]; "relative to the occasion"). With a forced act, the emphasis is exactly the reverse. As we have seen, Aristotle acknowledges that, when a person does something which does not depend upon him [1225a11], it is a task even to make out a distinction between the end and what he does. ("What did you do?" "I saved my own life!") The end of self-preservation was implicitly in the agent's nature before the incident, it was present during it, and continues thereafter.

The second pertinent passage outside of *EE* ii,6–9 is *EN* v,8. Most commentators accept the thesis that *EN* v, being one of the "common books," belongs properly to *EE*; there is confirming evidence for this thesis in *EN* v,8.[57] At *EN* v,8, 1135a23, Aristotle makes a back reference to

---

56 See Kevin L. Flannery, "Capital Punishment and the Law," *Ave Maria Law Review* 5 (2008): 404. See also John Finnis, "Allocating Risks and Suffering: Some Hidden Traps," *Cleveland State Law Review* 38 (1990): 196–99. In the former (and at the reference), I discuss proportionate means as they come into personal self-defense; the Finnis article discusses mantraps and spring-guns, which are not proportionate means, precisely because their use is not forced upon the agent.

57 Anthony Kenny maintains that the common books belong properly to *EE* and that *EE* is a

"what was said earlier" about the voluntary. In so far as it refers to a discussion of the voluntary, this could be a reference to *EN* iii,1, but there are indications in what immediately follows that point rather to *EE* ii,6–9. First of all, at *EN* v,8, 1135a27–28, Aristotle gives the following example of a forced act: " ... if someone taking the hand of someone should strike someone else, the second man would act not voluntarily, since it did not depend upon him." This is virtually identical to the example given at *EE* ii,8, 1224b13–14 and significantly different from the parallel examples given in *EN* iii,1. (One notes that it is also about brute force.) Also, a couple of lines later in *EN* v,8, Aristotle mentions that one attributing voluntariness or involuntariness to an act must take into consideration the "whole act" [περὶ τὴν πρᾶξιν ὅλην—1135a31]. There is no such concern in *EN* iii,1; but there is, as we have seen, in *EE* ii,8 (1225a7, 12–13).

But Aristotle's concerns in *EN* v,8 are somewhat different from those of *EE* ii,6–9. Book v of *EN* is about justice and injustice, and in that chapter he is especially interested in the distinction between "unjust things" [ἄδικα—1135b8] that a person might do, without necessarily being an unjust person. In order to be an unjust person, he says, one must actually choose to do the unjust thing [1135b8–11]. For instance, someone coerced [ἀναγκαζόμενον—1135b7–8] into not returning "a deposit" [παρακαταθήκην—1135b8] (i.e., something left in one's trust with the expectation that it would be returned by a particular time) does something that is objectively unjust but he is not, by reason of doing that, unjust. This is not to deny, however, what we have seen in *EE* ii,8: that such compelled acts are voluntary.

---

more mature work than *EN*: see Anthony Kenny, *The Aristotelian Ethics: A Study of the Relationship between the* Eudemian *and the* Nicomachean Ethics *of Aristotle* (Oxford: Clarendon, 1978). But see John M. Cooper, review of *The Aristotelian Ethics* by Anthony Kenny, *Noûs* 15 (1981): 383–88 ("On balance, then, the best working hypothesis seems to be that the common books are indeed originally Eudemian books, but that as we now have them Aristotle has reworked them for inclusion in the Nicomachean Ethics" [388]). See also C. J. Rowe, review of *Aristotle's Theory of the Will* by A. Kenny, *Journal of Hellenic Studies* 102 [1982]: 250–53; see also Terence H. Irwin, review of *The Aristotelian Ethics* and *Aristotle's Theory of the Will* both by Anthony Kenny, *The Journal of Philosophy* 77, no. 6 [June 1980]: 342–44; Woods, *Aristotle: 'Eudemian Ethics,'* xii). Rowe and Irwin say things similar to what Cooper says (above). Pakaluk has doubts about the Aristotelian authorship of *EE* [Michael Pakaluk, "The Egalitarianism of the *Eudemian Ethics*," *Classical Quarterly* 48 (1998): 411–32]. See also C. J. Rowe, *The* Eudemian *and* Nicomachean Ethics: *A Study in the Development of Aristotle's Thought*, in *Proceedings of the Cambridge Philological Society, supplement no. 3* (Cambridge: Cambridge Philological Society, 1971).

Aristotle then [*EN* v,8, 1135b11ff.] discusses three types of injury that enter into an account of justice and injustice but do not entail that the person involved is unjust.[58] An injury that occurs due to factors that are abnormal [παραλόγως] is called a 'misadventure'—or, literally, an event "without luck" [ἀτύχημα—1135b17]; one that occurs due to factors that are not abnormal but simply unknown to the agent is called a 'mistake' [ἁμάρτημα—1135b18]. Aristotle says that a mistake involves no vice on the part of the agent [ἄνευ δὲ κακίας—1135b17–18]. A mistake is, therefore, the result of some factor that could (theoretically) be known but is not, as when a soldier in the course of his duties, and with no negligence on his part, kills a fellow soldier, thinking that he is an enemy.

This second type of injury, says Aristotle, has its origin in the agent, the first outside: "for one makes a mistake when the origin [ἡ ἀρχὴ] of the cause [τῆς αἰτίας] is in him; one is subject to misadventure when it is outside."[59] The Revised Oxford Translation reads ἀγνοίας for αἰτίας in 1135b19 ("for a man makes a mistake when the ignorance [ἀγνοίας] originates in him, but is the victim of accident when its origin lies outside him"), apparently worried about the awkwardness of speaking about the origin or principle of a cause.[60] But it is difficult to grasp how an unlucky event might be the origin of a man's *ignorance*. This reading also suggests that the agent who makes a mistake is the cause of his own ignorance and therefore culpable, which is contrary to what Aristotle says at 1135b17–18.[61] In saying that when a man makes a mistake the origin of the cause is in him, Aristotle means that ignorance—which is always in a subject—causes the

---

58 At *EN* v,8, 1135b11, Aristotle speaks of three types of injury. He eventually gives us a three part division—ὅταν μὲν [1135b16], ὅταν δὲ [1135b17], ὅταν δὲ [1135b19]—and uses the terms ἀτύχημα, ἁμάρτημα, and ἀδίκημα. But before entering into the division (i.e., at 1135b12–16) he discusses the second category. (Note the word ἁμαρτήματα at 1135b12.) The first two categories involve ignorance; the third does not. At *Rhetoric* i,13, 1374b4–10, Aristotle makes a similar three-part division but, as he presents it, he is not interested in the distinction between unjust things done and unjust agents, so the ἀδικήματα are culpable (... ἀπὸ πονηρίας τέ ἐστιν· τὰ γὰρ δι' ἐπιθυμίαν ἀπὸ πονηρίας ... [1374b9–10]).

59 μαρτάνει μὲν γὰρ ὅταν ἡ ἀρχὴ ἐν αὐτῷ ᾖ τῆς αἰτίας, ἀτυχεῖ δ' ὅταν ἔξωθεν [1135b18–19].

60 Jonathan Barnes, ed., *The Complete Works of Aristotle: The Revised Oxford Translation*, 2.1792. Cp. Terence H. Irwin, *Aristotle: Nicomachean Ethics* (Indianapolis: Hackett, 1985), 138.

61 The ἀγνοίας for αἰτίας reading originates with Henry Jackson, who calls ἡ ἀρχὴ τῆς αἰτίας "a strange phrase" [Henry Jackson, ed., *The Fifth Book of the* Nicomachean Ethics *of Aristotle* (Cambridge: Cambridge University Press, 1879), 44.20–21, 110–11]. Jackson interprets the man who makes a mistake as culpable.

injury, although in this case the agent is not the cause of the ignorance.⁶²

The third type of injury is the act of someone who is not ignorant of the probabilities of harm, etc., but does not deliberate about what he does. Such an act, says Aristotle, is an "unjust thing" [ἀδίκημα—1135b20] but it does not make the person performing it an unjust man. Since non-culpability (of whatever degree) has only two sources—ignorance and force—and ignorance has been excluded, this third category of injuries are non-culpable by virtue of force. Aristotle gives as examples "anger and other passions," which he describes as natural things [τὰ φυσικά]—or natural propensities—which come upon men. The same term (τὰ φυσικά) occurs at *EE* ii,8, 1225a21. He then makes the following remark: "So, things issuing from anger are rightly judged not to issue from foreknowledge, for it is not the man who acts in anger but the one who enraged him who started things."⁶³ Aristotle apparently has in mind a pair of litigants who have come to blows over an insult or some other provocation. The one who deliberately initiates the quarrel is to blame. The act of the other man is another example of an act that is involuntary due to force; it is analogous to the act of the man startled in the dark.

Shortly after this—in the last few lines of the chapter and before taking up a new theme—comes a much disputed passage. It exploits a distinction between that which is done in ignorance, or we might even say "ignorantly" [ἀγνοῶν], and that which is done due to ignorance [δι' ἄγνοιαν]. This distinction appears also in *EN* iii,2 and in *EE* ii,9, as shall see in section I of chapter 4. Things done due to ignorance (ignorance, for instance, of the fact that the cup contains poison instead of wine) are involuntary; things done "ignorantly" are culpable. In *EN* iii,1 gives as examples of the latter persons who are drunk or angry.⁶⁴ At the end of *EN* v,8, in the passage we are about to examine, Aristotle uses the expression 'due to ignorance' [δι'

---

62 As the Susemihl-Apelt edition points out [Franciscus Susemihl and Otto Apelt, eds., *Aristotelis Ethica Nicomachea* (Teubner: Leipzig, 1912), 115], in the prooemium to *Mechanica* (which is spurious but included in the Aristotelian *corpus*) there is also talk of an origin of a cause: πάντων δὲ τῶν τοιούτων ἔχει τῆς αἰτίας τὴν ἀρχὴν ὁ κύκλος [847b15–16]. Also, several times in *EE* ii,6 Aristotle associates ἀρχή with αἰτία: 1222b30, 1222b40, 1223b15–18.

63 διὸ καλῶς τὰ ἐκ θυμοῦ οὐκ ἐκ προνοίας κρίνεται· οὐ γὰρ ἄρχει ὁ θυμῷ ποιῶν, ἀλλ' ὁ ὀργίσας [*EN* v,8, 1135b25–27]. On anger as less culpable than concupiscence, see also *EN* vii,6, 1149a24–1150a8.

64 *EN* iii,1, 1110b26; see also *EE* ii,9, 1225b15–16.

ἄγνοιαν] to refer apparently to the first two types of injury discussed earlier in the chapter, misadventure [ἀτύχημα] and mistake [ἁμάρτημα]. He then refers to some things that are done not due to ignorance but ignorantly. In the Revised Oxford Translation, the passage is rendered as follows:

> Of involuntary acts some are forgivable, others not. For the mistakes which men make not only in ignorance [ἀγνοοῦντες] but also from ignorance [δι' ἄγνοιαν] are forgivable, while those which men do, not from ignorance but (though they do them *in* ignorance) owing to a passion which is neither natural nor such as man is liable to, are not forgivable. [*EN* v,8, 1136a5–9]

The observation at the very end about things performed "owing to passion which is neither natural nor such as man is liable to" [1136a8–9], which are apparently not forgivable, has caused particular difficulties for commentators.

Anthony Kenny maintains that it clashes not only with *EN* iii,1, 1109b31–32 ("on voluntary passions and actions praise and blame are bestowed, on those that are involuntary forgiveness") but also with *EE* ii,8, 1225a19–22 ("So, many regard love and some outbursts of aggression—that is, natural things [τὰ φυσικά]—as involuntary because stronger even than nature; these admit of forgiveness as they are things by nature capable of forcing nature"). He might also have mentioned another passage in *EN* iii,1 where Aristotle says that forgiveness is bestowed "when one does what he ought not under pressure which overstrains human nature and which no one could withstand" [1110a24–26]. In any case, in order to avoid the inconsistency, Kenny argues that at the end of *EN* v,8 Aristotle must be speaking about a different type of unnatural passion, that is, "a perverted passion of the kind described in *EN* vii,5, unnatural cruelty or lust amounting to brutishness (1148b15ff.)."[65] Similarly, John Burnet says that Aristotle is speaking about the utter forfeiture of humanity: "a state in which moral insensibility and temporary mental obscuration have been caused by an access [*sic*] of brutality."[66]

---

65 Kenny, *Aristotle's Theory of the Will*, 62. In *EN* vii 5, Aristotle refers, for example, to "the female who, they say, rips open pregnant women and devours the infants" [1148b20–21], to "the man who sacrificed and ate his mother," and to "the slave who ate the liver of his fellow" [1148b25–27].

66 John Burnet, *The Ethics of Aristotle: Illustrated with essays and notes* (London: Longmans, Green, and Co., 1895), II 132.

But Aristotle has discussed no such extreme states in *EN* v,8, so such an observation would be inappropriate in this concluding passage. Moreover, there is a way of reading the Greek that connects it not only with the earlier remarks about actions performed from and actions performed in ignorance but also with the remark about the pair of litigants who come to blows. It would seem that Aristotle mentions actions performed under the influence of natural passions only in order to distinguish them from actions performed *in* ignorance (or ignorantly) and not subject to forgiveness. The concluding passage could, therefore, be translated with slightly different emphases and so also with different punctuation (in the translation), along these lines:

> Of involuntary acts some are forgivable, others not. For the mistakes that men make not only in ignorance but also due to ignorance are forgivable, while those which they do, not due to ignorance but in ignorance owing to a passion (one, however, which is neither natural nor simply human), are not forgivable.[67]

The passions that are "natural" and "simply human" would include righteous and spontaneous anger. Both the person who picks a fight and the person who reacts are influenced by passions; but the first is moved by hatred or envy (or whatever) to perform a voluntary action, the second is moved by the natural human passions that arise when one is dealt with unjustly. The act of the first is not forgivable, that of the second is. This is so because the latter is not due to the agent himself but to his nature.

VI. Conclusion

The argument in *EE* ii,6–9—and, in particular, in *EE* ii,7–8—is difficult, but we can draw from it important ideas regarding the role of force in the analysis of human acts. Of particular usefulness is the idea that, although each human act is *itself* voluntary, within it there might be identi-

---

67 τῶν δ' ἀκουσίων τὰ μέν ἐστι συγγνωμονικὰ τὰ δ' οὐ συγγνωμονικά. ὅσα μὲν γὰρ μὴ μόνον ἀγνοοῦντες ἀλλὰ καὶ δι' ἄγνοιαν ἁμαρτάνουσι, συγγνωμονικά, ὅσα δὲ μὴ δι' ἄγνοιαν, ἀλλ' ἀγνοοῦντες μὲν διὰ πάθος δὲ μήτε φυσικὸν μήτ' ἀνθρώπινον, οὐ συγγνωμονικά [*EN* v,8, 1136a5–9]. The last couple of lines might be translated very literally as, "... while those which men do, not from ignorance but in ignorance—owing on the one hand to a passion, on the other not to a natural or to a [simply] human one—are not forgivable."

fied aspects that are more or less under the influence of force (aspects that are wholly due to force being, however, not part of the human act strictly speaking). Also useful is the argument put forward in *EE* ii,6 to the effect that a man's sovereignty over his own acts is not dissimilar to the relationship between mathematical principles and the things following from them. This argument helps us to understand why he says the things he says in *EE* ii,7–8 and, in particular, why the human act must be regarded as internally articulated. The internal articulation of human acts concerns, however, not just force but also the knowledge (or ignorance) an agent brings to an act. This is the subject of the next chapter.

Four

The Constituents of Human Action and Ignorance Thereof

WE CONTINUE IN this chapter to explore the perceptual realm of practical reason, in contrast with what I referred to in chapter 1 as the realm of the syllogistic, whose coin is the universal term. So, as in chapter 2, we are concerned here with the type of human act which is analyzable straightforwardly as an Aristotelian movement (or κίνησις). In chapter 3, we considered the first of two factors that shape and internally articulate individual human acts: force (or βία); in this chapter we consider the second, knowledge (or ignorance) of what have traditionally been called the "circumstances," which include things like 'what instrument the agent is using,' 'what the likely effect of his action is,' etc. It should by now be clear that, whatever its connection with his *Physics*, Aristotle's philosophical psychology of action is anything but physicalist; but this becomes pellucidly apparent in attending to what he says about the circumstances, for his overall thesis is that one cannot be held responsible for an aspect of an act of which one has no knowledge or has no possibility of having knowledge.

Again, our strategy is simply to provide an Aristotelian alternative to the often only partially articulated view that, because of its inherent fluidity, any attempt to understand the structure of the human act can never arrive at results utilizable in the moral evaluation of individual acts. Our chosen way of dealing with such a view (or attitude) is not to argue directly against it but simply to depict the structure that is there, with the hope—even the expectation—that, once a person sees the structure, he will acknowledge that it is tied up with what an act is and, therefore, with what a person is doing, what he is responsible for, when he performs an act.

Section I of the present chapter is concerned with the types of ignorance that exonerate one of responsibility for an act or for an aspect of an act fixed by one of its circumstances. The general lines of this doctrine are set out in *EN* iii,1, although not especially clearly; more clarity is gained by combining ideas set out more explicitly in *EE* ii,9. The basic issue here is the involvement of will in an agent's ignorance of what he is doing. The more complete theory recognizes that, if the agent's will is involved—in particular, if his own negligence has caused the ignorance—the ignorance is not exonerating.

Having discussed what Aristotle says about ignorance, in section II we begin the consideration of the circumstances themselves, dealing first of all with the question of what to call them. Since among the so-called circumstances are what the agent is doing when he acts and since the word 'circumstance' would seem to signify that which "stands around" what the agent is doing, the term 'circumstance' is inappropriate. I propose 'constituent' (of an act) as a substitute. Another question is just what the (as I now call them) constituents are. I argue that, although Aristotle presents them in *EN* iii,1 as things of which an agent might be ignorant, he understands them also—even primarily—as things of which an agent might be aware and, therefore, as things susceptible to philosophical analysis by someone wishing to understand the structure and components of a particular act.

The list of constituents in *EN* iii,1 contains seven items, so I will speak of seven constituents, even though (as I argue below) two of them are really one. In section III of the present chapter, I consider constituent (1), "who," and constituent (2), "what." The first constituent is a good example of a constituent of which an agent is not unaware, for, as Aristotle himself notes, no agent is unaware of who is performing his own acts; and, indeed, in the analysis of acts, it is often important to understand who is doing the acting and what role he fills in society. The second constituent represents what objectively an agent is doing—but not in any sense that would make it irrelevant to moral analysis ("the merely physical act"); the 'what' is simply an objective "take" on what one is doing, prescinding from such other factors as why one is doing it. Section IV goes into this point in some detail, attending especially to the examples that Aristotle gives in *EN* iii,1 of constituent (2), examples having to do with revealing secrets and launching catapults. Some of these examples refer to things of which the agent is aware, some do not.

In section V, I look at constituents (3) and (4): "about what [περὶ τί]—or in regard to what [ἐν τίνι]—someone acts" [*EN* iii,1, 1111a4]. I note that these singular expressions—that is, the prepositions περί and τίνι plus their respective singular objects, τί and τίνι—are parallel to the plural expressions by means of which Aristotle refers to all the constituent as he begins his exposition of them, that is to say, to the expressions "about which" [περὶ ἅ] and "in which" [ἐν οἷς]. This suggests that René-Antoine Gauthier's effort to distance the interpretation of this general passage from the medieval idea of circumstances that "stand around" an action does not go far enough. Instead of understanding "about what" and "in regard to what" as he does, that is, as conditions within which an act is performed, we should (as I have already said) regard them as constituents of the act.

At *EN* iii,1, 1111a18–19, Aristotle speaks of constituents that are the "most important" constituents. The Greek text in which he does this has been subject to emendation by modern editors, since, as it stands, it appears to say that, among the constituents, the two most important are the action's end and the constituents themselves. Of course, saying that an action's end is an important constituent makes good sense: the end for which a person performs an action can change it from good to bad, as when a person tells the truth in order to wound; but to say that the constituents are *a* constituent is nonsense. I propose in section VI, therefore, an emendation to the text different from the one that several modern editors accept; I propose, that is, a less intrusive emendation that has Aristotle saying that the two most important constituents are the sixth, the action's end, and the fourth, 'that in regard to which' the act is (or its subject matter). These are both clearly important constituents, since they must be taken into consideration in the moral analysis of any action.

In section VII, I trace a connection between this fourth constituent and the object toward which a physical movement proceeds (discussed also in chapter 2). In studying the lists of constituents that Aristotle gives in *EN* and *EE*, one notices that, where *EE* ii,9 and *EN* v,8 identify one of the constituents as 'whom' (the object, for example, of an act of striking), the *EN* iii,1 list speaks of that about which or in regard to which an action is (that is to say, the subject matter). It appears, then, that Aristotle abandons the language of objects—or, more precisely, that he realizes that the object, considered as end point of a movement, does not give information about an action sufficient to fix its species; required is rather an understanding of the subject matter, which includes more of the intelligibility of the action (but includes also the object). Aristotle discusses this issue in *Phys.* v,4, so, here in section VII, I look at that passage.

In section VIII, I consider constituents (5), (6), and (7): the instrument, the end, and how (the act is performed). With regard to (6), I argue against Gauthier's position that in *EN* iii,1 Aristotle does not have in mind the end with which an agent performs an act but rather the result at which the act will arrive, considered independently of what the agent had in mind. As in other sections in the present chapter, the argument here is that the end can be either mistaken by the agent or known by him. In the interest of providing a full analysis of human action, Aristotle takes into consideration not only cases in which there is a disconnect between what the agent has a mind to do and what he in fact does but also cases in which there is no such disconnect. I make similar points regarding the instrument used in an act and the manner in which an act is performed.

I. Excluded Types of Ignorance

In *EN*, Aristotle introduces the circumstances at iii,1, 1111a3–21. As mentioned, however, these are much bound up with the ignorance that an agent brings to a particular action since, at least in some cases, ignorance of a circumstance exonerates an agent of any evil effect connected with that circumstance. So, immediately before introducing the circumstances,

Aristotle clears away some types of ignorance that do not put an act or an aspect of an act into the category of the involuntary. This section of *EN* iii,1 on exonerating and non-exonerating ignorance is not a complete account of the matter—or, at least, Aristotle does not state the whole account explicitly. The parallel passage *EE* ii,9 helps us to fill it out.

The *EN* iii,1 passage runs as follows:

All that is done 'due to ignorance' is not voluntary, but the involuntary is that which is painful and produces remorse. For one who does something due to ignorance but is not disturbed on account of the act, it is true, he does not do voluntarily that of which he has no knowledge, but, not being disturbed by it, neither does he do it *in*voluntarily. Regarding, therefore, that which is done 'due to ignorance,' it would appear that the man who experiences remorse acts involuntarily; he who is without remorse, since he is different, let us say that he acts 'non-voluntarily,' for, since there is a difference, it is better that he have his own name.

It would seem that acting 'due to ignorance' is different from someone's acting ignorantly. For the man who is drunk or furious does not appear to act *due* to ignorance but due to one of the things mentioned, not knowingly but also not involuntarily. Every rascal is ignorant of what he ought to do and what he ought to refrain from doing, and it is due to such error that he acts unjustly and becomes wholly evil. 'Involuntary' is normally used not of someone who is ignorant of what is good for himself, for ignorance by choice is not the cause of the involuntary but rather of rascality—and neither is ignorance of the universal (for people are blamed because of that)—but rather ignorance regarding the particulars in which and about which an action is, since with respect to these there is mercy and forgiveness, for the man who is ignorant of one of these acts involuntarily. [*EN* iii,1, 1110b18–1111a2][1]

The first type of ignorance excluded from the involuntary in this passage—the type discussed in the first paragraph—we might be inclined to associate *with* it, since it has to do with acts that stand outside the volun-

---

[1] τῶν δ' ἀκουσίων τὰ μέν ἐστι συγγνωμονικὰ τὰ δ' οὐ συγγνωμονικά. ὅσα μὲν γὰρ μὴ μόνον ἀγνοοῦντες ἀλλὰ καὶ δι' ἄγνοιαν ἁμαρτάνουσι, συγγνωμονικά, ὅσα δὲ μὴ δι' ἄγνοιαν, ἀλλ' ἀγνοοῦντες μὲν διὰ πάθος δὲ μήτε φυσικὸν μήτ' ἀνθρώπινον, οὐ συγγνωμονικά [*EN* v,8, 1136a5–9]. The last couple of lines might be translated very literally as, "... while those which men do, not from ignorance but in ignorance—owing on the one hand to a passion, on the other not to a natural or to a [simply] human one—are not forgivable."

tary; in fact, however, Aristotle does not do this. This category includes acts performed "due to ignorance" [δι' ἄγνοιαν—1110b18] but for which, when discovering what one has done, one experiences no remorse. For Aristotle the ignorance that causes involuntariness must result in an act or an effect that goes against one's wishes, and so he calls non-repented acts not 'involuntary' but 'non-voluntary.'[2]

Significant in this first paragraph is the expression 'due to ignorance.' In what follows here in *EN* iii,1 (and also in the *EE* ii,9), being per se due to ignorance is the mark of the involuntary; all other manifestations of ignorance are excluded from the involuntary in so far as ignorance is not involved per se.[3] But here, in the first paragraph of the above quotation (1110b19–20), the non-voluntary—which is not involuntary—is said to be "due to ignorance." In order to resolve this problem and also to make general sense of Aristotle's position in these matters, it seems to me that we have to understand the expression 'due to ignorance,' as employed in *EN* iii,1, as only *eventually* incorporating the idea that the ignorance goes contrary to the wishes (or will) of the person acting. In other words, at the beginning of the *EN* iii,1 passage, since Aristotle has not yet established the point about the 'non-voluntary' (as being distinct from the involuntary), the expression δι' ἄγνοιαν does not yet bear with it the connotation 'and quite against the wishes of the agent.'

In the second paragraph of the above quotation, the role and meaning of the expression 'due to' (in Greek, διὰ or δι') becomes more apparent. Says Aristotle: "For the man who is drunk or furious does not appear to act *due* to ignorance but due to one of the things mentioned, not knowingly but also not involuntarily." The things mentioned are inebriation and

---

2 At 1110b23, the person so acting is described as οὐκ ἑκών. I have tried to convey the idea of an action or aspect of an action going contrary to the wishes of the agent by occasionally emphasizing the word 'due' in expressions like 'due to ignorance.' The idea would be that the relevant moral character of the act comes *just* from the ignorance and quite against the will of the agent. Anthony Kenny describes the "connection between involuntariness and repentance or remorse" as "slightly puzzling" "It seems clear," he writes, "that a person's subsequent state of mind can have very little to do with whether a particular action is voluntary, involuntary, or neither" [Anthony Kenny, *Aristotle's Theory of the Will*, 53].

3 I discuss the per se (and the per accidens) extensively in chapter 5. For now, it should suffice to say that an instance of involuntariness is per se due to ignorance when the ignorance itself is the sole cause of the involuntariness.

anger: it is these things that characterize the respective acts per se, not ignorance itself. The same sort of analysis applies also to the "rascal" (the μοχθηρὸς), although here the role of will is more apparent: the rascal is ignorant but his ignorance is due per se not to the ignorance itself but to his error in not knowing what he ought to be doing. The error in this instance is a willful error.[4] The ignorance that is present is not connected to the act per se; that through which the act comes about is the willfulness.

Continuing to speak of the rascal, Aristotle also notes that the term 'involuntary' is normally used with respect to someone who is ignorant of "what is good for himself" (ignorant, that is, of τὰ συμφέροντα). The use of this expression, τὰ συμφέροντα, indicates that Aristotle still has in mind the willful error (ἁμαρτία) made by the rascal: that which is good for one is that toward which one would direct one's efforts, were it not for willful error. Aristotle identifies two ways in which such error might come about: either by choice (that is, the man makes a definite choice to live an immoral life) or for want of the relevant universal (as when a man does not know what the moral law requires).[5] In this last point, we see the incompleteness—or, at least, the inexplicitness—of Aristotle's account here in *EN* iii,1. What about ignorance of the universal that was or is beyond one's power to remedy? Aristotle is concerned here with ignorance that *is* willful, so perhaps we can take it as implicit that ignorance of the universal that is not willful results in acts (or aspects of acts) that are involuntary, even though the ignorance here concerns not particular circumstances but general principles. In any case, in *EE* ii,9, Aristotle acknowledges explicitly that ignorance of what the moral law teaches does not entail culpability when it involves no negligence.[6]

So, let us turn to *EE* ii,9. Aristotle begins that chapter by remarking that the voluntary is the opposite of the involuntary and that someone's acting with knowledge of the circumstances is the opposite of someone's

---

4 An error [ἁμαρτία] of this type is quite different from a mistake [ἁμάρτημα] as discussed in *EN* v,8 and in chapter 3, section V. Here in *EN* iii,1 Aristotle says that the rascal διὰ τὴν τοιαύτην ἁμαρτίαν ἄδικοι καὶ ὅλως κακοὶ γίνονται [1110b29–30]. As we have seen, the person who makes a mistake [ἁμάρτημα] does so ἄνευ κακίας [*EN* v,8, 1135b18–19].

5 Aristotle's mention of ignorance of the universal recalls his presentation of the practical syllogism: see chapter 1, sections IV through VI.

6 He makes the point also at *EN* iii,5, 1113b33–1114a3.

acting in ignorance [τῷ ἀγνοοῦντα—1225b5] of the same. He specifies (as in *EN* iii,1) that an action, in order to be considered involuntary, must be performed "due to ignorance." Here he is more explicit than in *EN* iii,1 about the meaning of the phrase, for he specifies that such acts are "due to ignorance, not per accidens" [δι' ἄγνοιαν, μὴ κατὰ συμβεβηκός—1225b6].[7] In other words, it must be the ignorance itself that makes the act involuntary and not any willfulness on the part of the agent, which would make the presence of ignorance accidental to the moral assessment of the act.

EE ii,9 then continues:

So, whatever a man, in whose power it is not to act, does not unknowingly and *due* to himself, this must needs be voluntary—and this is what the voluntary is; but whatever he does unknowingly and *due* to the ignorance is involuntary. Since, however, 'to understand' or 'to know' has two meanings: one being 'to have' knowledge, the other 'to use' it, the man who has but does not use would in a sense justly, in a sense not justly, be called 'unknowing,' for instance, if it is *due* to negligence that he does not use it. Similarly, the man who does not even have knowledge would be blamed if, *due* to negligence or pleasure or pain, he has not knowledge that was easy or necessary to have.[8]

Unlike the *EN* iii,1 passage, here in *EE* ii,9 Aristotle acknowledges explicitly that negligence is a factor in the moral assessment of ignorance with respect to acts. In the first sentence, 'due to ignorance' is in opposition to 'due to himself.' Anything a man does due to negligence is clearly 'due to himself,' so Aristotle goes on to discuss negligence. He distinguishes four types of case in which negligence might or might not be involved: (1) cases of having knowledge but, due to negligence, not using it; (2) cases of having knowledge but not using it, although not due to negligence; (3) cases of, due to negligence, not having knowledge; (4) cases of not having knowledge but not due to negligence. The cases in (1) and (3) are blamable, because the ignorance is due to negligence and not due to ignorance itself. The cases in (2) and (4) are not blamable; they are involuntary, since the bearing of the ignorance upon the act is not per accidens [κατὰ συμβεβηκός] but per se.[9]

---

7 Cp. *EN* v,8, 1135a26.   8 *EE* ii,9, 1225b8–16.
9 It is not immediately apparent what sort of cases might be represented by type (2). Remarks

There is one final point regarding ignorance and the involuntary that needs to be stated clearly before we go on to our discussion of the circumstances of particular acts. Aristotle speaks about ignorance that might or might not remove an act from the realm of the culpable because he is interested in the moral evaluation of these particular acts. So, when he speaks, for instance, about ignorance of what the moral law says as not exonerating the agent if such ignorance involves negligence, his primary point is not that the negligence is culpable (although he would certainly say that it is) but that the acts done while in the grips of such ignorance are culpable. Thus, if someone, who might have known and accepted the moral law in the relevant respect, performs an immoral act but claims that the act is not immoral because he acts in good conscience, he is wrong; and the immorality affects not just his ignorance but the act itself.

To summarize this section, Aristotle's teaching on the bearing of knowledge and ignorance upon the voluntary and the involuntary is (at best) stated very elliptically in the passage of *EN* iii,1 that comes just before his discussion of the circumstances. The central idea of that teaching is that that which is per se *due* to ignorance and against the wishes of the agent is non-culpable, independently of whether such ignorance concerns particular circumstances or aspects of the moral law itself. The full implications of this idea are set out more explicitly in *EE* ii,9.

II. Circumstances or Constituents

So, having described at least in outline the types of ignorance that cause involuntariness with respect to "the particulars in which and about which an action is," Aristotle says that "perhaps it would not be a bad idea to set these [particulars] out: what and how many they are" [*EN*

---

in the *Magna moralia*, in a section introduced by the remark, ἔστι γὰρ τὸ ἐπίστασθαι διττόν, ὧν τὸ μέν ἐστι τὴν ἐπιστήμην ἔχειν (ἐπίστασθαι γάρ φαμεν τότε, ὅταν τις ἐπιστήμην ἔχῃ), τὸ δ' ἕτερον τὸ ἐνεργεῖν ἤδη τῇ ἐπιστήμῃ [*MM* ii,6, 1201b11–13], suggest some examples: (a) that of a man who sleepwalks and commits an otherwise blamable act [*MM* ii,6, 1201b17–19]; (b) that of a man who knows that he ought not to strike his father but, because he does not know that this man is his father—that is, because he is not using the knowledge he has with respect to the particular man before him—he strikes his father [*MM* ii,6, 1201b24–1202a1]; (c) that of a man who is made drunk and has the knowledge that would prevent his committing a bad act but commits it because of the drunkenness [*MM* ii,6, 1202a1–7].

iii,1, 1111a3]. In the passage that follows, there would appear to be seven of them:

So: (1) who, (2) what, (3) about what—or (4) in regard to what—someone acts, sometimes also (5) with what (e.g. what instrument), (6) to what end (e.g. for safety), (7) and how (e.g. whether gently or violently).[10]

The Greek terms corresponding to the seven are as follows: (1) τίς, (2) τί, (3) περὶ τί, (4) ἐν τίνι, (5) τίνι, (6) ἕνεκα τίνος, and (7) πῶς. In other places in Aristotle the list is shorter. In *EE* ii,9, for instance, they are given as ὅν (whom), ᾧ (by what means), and οὗ ἕνεκα (to what end) [1225b2], and then (twice) as ὅν (whom), ᾧ (by what means), and ὅ (what) [1225b6, 1225b7]. The first of these *EE* lists appears also at *EN* v,8, 1135a25; it is followed in the same chapter by a four-member list made up of all the list members of *EE* ii,9: ὅν (whom), ὅ (what), ᾧ (by what means), and οὗ ἕνεκα (to what end) [*EN* v,8, 1135b13] and then by another list from which ὅ (what) is again absent [1135b15–16].

The lists, therefore, break down as follows:

EN iii,1: τίς, τί, περὶ τί, ἐν τίνι, τίνι, ἕνεκα τίνος, πῶς [1111a3–6]
    (6 or 7 members)
EE ii,9: ὅν, ᾧ, οὗ ἕνεκα [1225b2] (3 members)
EE ii,9: ὅν, ᾧ, ὅ [1225b6] (3 members)
EE ii,9: ὅν, ᾧ, ὅ [1225b7] (3 members)
EN v,8: ὅν, ᾧ, οὗ ἕνεκα [1135a25] (3 members)
EN v,8: ὅν, ὅ, ᾧ, οὗ ἕνεκα [1135b13] (4 members)
EN v,8: ὅν, ᾧ, οὗ ἕνεκα [1135b15–16] (3 members).

The similarity of the lists in *EN* v,8 and *EE* ii,9 is evidence that the so-called "common books," *EN* v–vii, belong properly to the *Eudemian Ethics*, as books iv–vi.[11] The element ὅν—which appears in the *EE* and *EN* v,8

---

10 ... τίς τε δὴ καὶ τί καὶ περὶ τί ἢ ἐν τίνι πράττει, ἐνίοτε δὲ καὶ τίνι, οἷον ὀργάνῳ, καὶ ἕνεκα τίνος, οἷον σωτηρίας, καὶ πῶς, οἷον ἠρέμα ἢ σφόδρα [*EN* iii,1, 1111a3–6]. I have interjected the numbers for easier reference. The Revised Oxford Translation translates the passage as follows: "A man may be ignorant, then, of (1) who he is, (2) what he is doing, (3) what or (4) whom he is acting on, and sometimes also (5) what (e.g., what instrument) he is doing it with, and (6) to what end (e.g. for safety), and (7) how he is doing it (e.g., whether gently or violently)." I argue below that περὶ τί ἢ ἐν τίνι ought not to be translated "what or whom he is acting on."
11 See note 57 in chapter 3.

lists but not in the *EN* iii,1 list—refers to the person acted upon, not the agent; it is to be associated, as I argue below, with an action's subject matter, represented in circumstances (3) and (4).

It is important to understand what these lists represent in general, and the best way of doing that is to look (in a preliminary way) at one of the particular members: in the *EN* iii,1 list, number (2), τί (what), which appears in some of the other lists as ὅ. Aristotle describes it in this fashion:

> But of what he is doing a man might be ignorant, as for instance people say 'it slipped out of their mouths as they were speaking,'[12] or 'they did not know it was a secret,' as Aeschylus said of the mysteries, or a man might say he 'let it go off when he merely wanted to show its working,' as the man did with the catapult.[13]

I deal more extensively with the meaning of the τί below; for now it is sufficient to say that it is the external act performed by the agent or "what he does," although in this case he is not fully aware of what it is.

Now the seven members of the *EN* iii,1 list are traditionally called "circumstances," probably because Aristotle refers to them a number of times in that chapter [1110b33–1111a1; 1111a16, 18, 24] as that "in which" [ἐν οἷς] an act is. The expression is suggestive of things "standing around" (*circumstantes*) an act.[14] But this is hardly compatible with the inclusion of τί

---

12 The Revised Oxford Translation (making no change to Ross) follows Ramsauer [G. Ramsauer, *Aristotelis* Ethica Nicomachea: *edidit et commentario continuo instruxit* (Leipzig: Teubner, 1878), 142] in reading λέγοντάς φασιν ἐκπεσεῖν αὑτούς at 1111a9.

13 *EN* iii,1, 1111a8–11 [Revised Oxford Translation]. Note that τί becomes ὅ δὲ πράττει at *EN* iii,1, 1111a8; this is the basis of the Revised Oxford Translation's reading (with Gauthier and with Richards) of κυριώτατα δ' εἶναι δοκεῖ ἐν οἷς ἡ πρᾶξις ὅ καὶ οὗ ἕνεκα (instead of Bywater's κυριώτατα δ' εἶναι δοκεῖ ἐν οἷς ἡ πρᾶξις καὶ οὗ ἕνεκα) at 1111a18–19. This passage is to be discussed below (see Gauthier and Jolif, *L'Éthique à Nicomaque*, 2.1 187–88).

14 Gauthier associates the expression with Greek and Latin rhetoric: περίστασις and *circumstantia* respectively, mentioning Hermagoras of Temnos, Nemesius, and Boethius [Gauthier and Jolif, *L'Éthique à Nicomaque*, 2.1 185]. In general, Gauthier attempts to drive a wedge between what Aristotle means with his constituents in *EN* iii,1 (and elsewhere) and the use to which they are put by Greek and Latin rhetoricians and by theologians (he mentions explicitly the Fourth Lateran Council, Albert the Great, and Thomas Aquinas). I believe that he is correct to reject Albert's and Thomas's claim to have discovered in Aristotle's list at *EN* iii,1, 1111a3–6 'where' and 'when'; and he is correct to insist that the members of Aristotle's list are not to be considered accidents with respect to the act itself; but he is wrong when he says that "the point of view of the rhetorician and that of the theologian are in effect entirely different from that of Aristotle" [Gauthier and Jolif, *L'Éthique à Nicomaque*, 2.1 186]. The rhetorician and the theologian—not to mention the moral philosopher interested in the analysis of human action—have interests different from those of Aristotle in *EN* iii,1, but they make use of his presuppositions, which occasionally come to the surface in his remarks about ignorance of constituents.

in the list. How can *what* the agent does be a circumstance, that is, stand around itself? The sense rather in which an act is "in" the members of the list is that it *consists* in those things. This is confirmed by the already-quoted remark that immediately precedes Aristotle's presentation of the *EN* iii,1 list, where he says that the only ignorance that bears upon the involuntary is "ignorance regarding the particulars in which and about which an action is": ἡ καθ' ἕκαστα [ἄγνοια] ἐν οἷς καὶ περὶ ἃ ἡ πρᾶξις [1110b33–1111a1]. Here the things "in which" (ἐν οἷς) an action *is* have to be those in which it consists. In what follows, therefore, I refer to what are traditionally referred to as circumstances as constituents. An act consists of its constituents.[15]

But there is a further twist to the remark we have been considering. As we have just seen, the constituents are described not only as the things "in which" but also "about which" the act is [1110b33–1111a1]. Aspasius says a number of times in his commentary on this section that Aristotle understands the expression "in which" in this section as equivalent to "about which."[16] In 1110b33–1111a1, both phrases refer to all the constituents so that all seven—or, however many there are—are not only things in which actions consists but also "about which" their identification or definition turns.[17] This is connected with the fact that the voluntary is defined in terms of reason or thought. The constituents give species to actions, since they are what actions are "about"; and to be "about" something is to be

---

15 Or, to be more precise, it consists of its per se constituents; I discuss this issue in chapter 5. One could argue that what appear in the various lists ought to be called '*possible* constituents' since, if one is unaware of a "constituent," it is not part of the human act performed. But speaking always of the "possible constituents" would be extremely awkward; it is sufficient to join Aristotle in pointing out that the components of a particular *action* are its per se constituents.

16 Aspasius, *in EN* 64.34 (τὸ δὲ περὶ τί καὶ ἐν τίνι ἐφ' ἓν ἔοικε φέρειν); also 65.29–30 (τὸ δ' ἐν οἷς ἡ πρᾶξις ταὐτὸν λαμβάνει τῷ περὶ ὃν ἡ πρᾶξις· καὶ διὰ τοῦτο ἐφαμεν τὸ περὶ τί ἢ ἐν τίνι ἐκ παραλλήλου εἰρῆσθαι). See also *in EN* 64.23 and 26, where Aspasius first speaks of the ignorance of the particulars περὶ ἃ an act is—i.e., not using the phrase ἐν οἷς—but then he paraphrases this remark itself with the words Διορίζει δὲ καὶ τίνα ἐστίν, ἐν οἷς ἡ ἄγνοια. See also Kenny, *Aristotle's Theory of the Will*, 51 and 55.

17 It is not clear how this could be, under Gauthier's interpretation. He understands the particulars ἐν οἷς an action is as the conditions within which an action unfolds and the particulars περὶ ἃ an action is as the objects ["c'est-à-dire des conditons dans lesquelles se déroule l'action et des choses qui en sont les objets" [Gauthier and Jolif, *L'Éthique à Nicomaque*, 2.1 184]; the same phraseology appears in his translation of the passage. By 'objects' he apparently means simply the plural of what is referred to in the singular in constituent (4): ἐν τίνι. But the phrase ἐν οἷς, like περὶ ἃ, is meant to refer to all the members of the list that immediately follows. Gauthier does not explain how, for instance, the first constituent (τίς) and the seventh (πῶς) are to be understood as objects.

part of an account or an explanation of what that thing is. Stories, for example, are about families and language and plotlines, etc.; cars are about speed, drivers, and engines. Actions are about the τίς, the τί, and so on; these are the things in which they consist. Aristotle says something similar in the *Physics* v,4, where he refers to the things "with respect to which" [περὶ ἅ] we speak of motion. The Revised Oxford Translation renders this passage rather poetically as, "There are three *textures* in connection with which we speak of motion—what, where, when."[18]

III. Constituents (1) and (2)

Let us now go through the *EN* iii,1 list in order. Immediately after giving the list, Aristotle says of its first member (τίς), "Of all of these no one who is not mad could be ignorant, and clearly no one could be ignorant of the agent—for how could someone not know himself?" [*EN* iii,1, 1111a6–7]. It is very apparent that in the first constituent Aristotle is referring not to the person upon whom or with respect to whom an act is performed ("the patient") but rather to the agent; but his very inclusion of τίς is not without exegetical and philosophical interest. If no one could be ignorant of τίς, what is τίς doing in the list? For this is a list of things ignorance of which causes involuntariness. It would seem that Aristotle understands the constituents as pertaining not just to the account of exonerating ignorance but also to something more positive and objective; that is to say, to a straightforward account of how acts that do not involve exonerating ignorance are structured.

We get a strong suggestion of just this in the corresponding passage in *EE* ii,9:

The voluntary, therefore, seems to be the contrary of the involuntary and one's having known either 'whom,' 'by what means,' or 'to what end' . . . to one's being ignorant due to ignorance and not per accidens of 'whom,' 'by what means,' and 'what.'[19]

---

18 τρία γάρ ἐστι τὸν ἀριθμὸν περὶ ἃ λέγομεν τὴν κίνησιν, ὃ καὶ ἐν ᾧ καὶ ὅτε [*Phys.* v,4, 227b23–24]; I discuss this section of the *Physics*—and, in particular, the meaning of ἐν ᾧ—below (in section VII).

19 δοκεῖ δὴ ἐναντίον εἶναι τὸ ἑκούσιον τῷ ἀκουσίῳ, καὶ τὸ εἰδότα ἢ ὃν ἢ ᾧ ἢ οὗ ἕνεκα (ἐνίοτε γὰρ οἶδε μὲν ὅτι πατήρ, ἀλλ' οὐχ ἵνα ἀποκτείνῃ, ἀλλ' ἵνα σώσῃ, ὥσπερ αἱ Πελιάδες, ἤτοι ὡς τοδὶ μὲν πόμα, ἀλλ'

So, there are two types of account—one of a knowing, the other of an unknowing agent—to either of which the list of constituents might be applied. In the positive account, it is not a matter of wondering whether one is the agent and knows with what means one is operating, and so on, but of realizing that an act consists of things known and that one of those things is who one is, another is what means one is using, and so on. If the constituent τίς is to have any significance even in the positive account, it must refer to the agent in a way that could make a difference to the moral analysis of an act, as when a king's saying "Off with his head" differs from a pauper's saying the same thing. For Aristotle, therefore, who performs an act would be an important factor in its analysis: a pauper cannot be tried for unjust sentencing, since paupers cannot effect sentences.[20]

The basic meaning of the next member of the list, τί ("what"), is also fairly apparent, but it too points to a broader issue. We recall from above that Aristotle explains the meaning of τί in terms of a person who might say, 'It slipped out of my mouth as I was speaking,' or 'I did not know it was a secret,' or 'in firing the catapult, I was just showing how it worked.' The τί here would then be the act that one performs, considered independently of (among other things) the end for which it is performed: the τί is what the person did, although he did not mean to. The people who revealed the secrets really did reveal them, although they did not know that they were secrets; similarly, the man who fired the catapult did *something* (τὶ), for example, he showed the mechanism to someone, although he did not mean for it to actually fire. The mistaken firing of a catapult could also fall under ignorance of the instrument used ("I did not know it was loaded"), but here Aristotle is clearly interested in "the what": what the agent did.

ὡς φίλτρον καὶ οἶνον, τὸ δ' ἦν κώνειον) τῷ ἀγνοοῦντα καὶ ὃν καὶ ᾧ καὶ ὃ δι' ἄγνοιαν, μὴ κατὰ συμβεβηκός [*EE* ii,9, 1225b1–6]. I have left the words in the parenthesis out of the translation; they will be discussed below. In *Magna moralia* i,33, 1195a16–18, knowledge of the constituents is put even more positively (that is, in terms of what is known rather than unknown).

20 Cp. Gauthier and Jolif, *L'Éthique à Nicomaque*, 2.1 186. At *EN* iv,2, 1122b23–26, Aristotle says: "But in all cases, as has been said, we have regard to the agent as well and ask *who* he is and what means he has; for the expenditure should be worthy of his means, and suit not only the result but also the producer" [ἐν ἅπασι δ' ὥσπερ εἴρηται, καὶ πρὸς τὸν πράττοντα ἀναφέρεται τὸ τίς ὢν καὶ τίνων ὑπαρχόντων· ἄξια γὰρ δεῖ τούτων εἶναι, καὶ μὴ μόνον τῷ ἔργῳ ἀλλὰ καὶ τῷ ποιοῦντι πρέπειν (emphasis added to the Revised Oxford Translation)]. The back reference is apparently to *EN* iv,2, 1122a25–26: τὸ πρέπον δὴ πρὸς αὑτόν, καὶ ἐν ᾧ καὶ περὶ ὅ. In these passages we see Aristotle making use in a positive way of various constituents.

The broader issue raised by this second constituent has already been touched upon—in talking, that is, about the positive account presupposed by what Aristotle says in *EN* iii,1. The constituents are listed there in order to explain how mistakes are made, that is, how what an agent thinks he is doing might not correspond to what he does. Aristotle's approach is parallel to his understanding of truth and falsity as correspondence or not to the facts spoken of:

> To say of what is that it is not, or of what is not that it is, is false, while to say of what is that it is, and of what is not that it is not, is true; so that he who says of anything that it is, or that it is not, will say either what is true or what is false ... [*Metaph.* iv,7, 1011b26–27][21]

In a parallel way, Aristotle is saying in *EN* iii,1 that the ignorance that causes involuntariness is due to a disconnect between (in the present case) the τί that an agent thinks he is doing and the τί he does. Aspasius is again good on this. The man who injures his friend with the catapult, he says, "in doing one thing has done another; he did not know, therefore, what he did."[22] But, obviously, the analysis of the τί need not always involve error. In the more straightforward case, the τί becomes simply what one does. That is an element in the analysis of acts, one of the things human action is "about," one of the things in which the agent's act consists; in short, it is one of the constituents.

IV. Slips and Shots

Let us consider more attentively the examples that Aristotle uses in the passage quoted above [*EN* iii,1, 1111a8–11]: that is, people who "say 'it slipped out of their mouths as they were speaking,' or 'they did not know it was a secret,' as Aeschylus said of the mysteries, or a man might say he 'let it go off when he merely wanted to show its working,' as the man did with the catapult." These examples are carefully selected. Regarding the first, there are a couple of things to bear in mind. First of all, as is true of

---

21 On Aristotle's understanding of truth in this passage, see Paolo Crivelli, *Aristotle on Truth* (Cambridge: Cambridge University Press, 2004), 134–35.

22 οὖν πράττων ἄλλο ἔπραξεν· ἠγνόει οὖν ὃ ἔπραξε [*in EN* 64.33].

any constituent, this one *can* be known by the agent. We ought not to assume that Aristotle takes the people who say 'It just slipped out' at their word: such sayings are a way people have of distancing themselves from their own utterances and thereby claiming (half-serious themselves) that they ought not to be held responsible for what they have said. Aristotle's point, therefore, would seem to be simply that what a person does can be viewed in isolation from what he intends. This does not mean that it would ever be possible for 'the what' of a moral act to exist without an intention but only that it is possible to consider just what the person did independently of why he did it. (This latter is, of course, a constituent in its own right, the sixth; we shall examine it shortly.)

Secondly, although the expression 'it slipped out of my mouth' is typically disingenuous, Aristotle does think that one could be ignorant of 'the what' (or, at least, know it only per accidens), for he says this explicitly: "of what he is doing a man might be ignorant" [1111a8]. The first example, however, seems ill-suited to bringing out this aspect of 'the what,' for one typically says 'it slipped out of my mouth' when one knew what one was saying when one said it but was not exercising sufficient restraint or perspicacity at that moment (and so "it slipped out"). It is probably for this reason that Aristotle immediately adds the other two examples, which refer to things that one could genuinely be ignorant of, although the second example may still bear with it the connotation of something that 'just slipped out.'

The second example ("or 'they did not know it was a secret,' as Aeschylus said of the mysteries") is explained by Gauthier in this fashion:

Aeschylus was accused before the Areopagus of having revealed the secrets of the Mysteries; he defended himself saying that he had not yet been initiated and that, as a consequence, he had said what came to his tongue without knowing that it was secret. He was acquitted.[23]

---

23 Gauthier and Jolif, *L'Éthique à Nicomaque*, 2.1 186. Gauthier cites for this information Clement of Alexandria's *Stromata* (II, xiv, 60) and also the anonymous paraphrast [Gustavus Heylbut, ed., *Eustratii et Michaelis et anonyma in Ethica Nicomachea commentaria*, Commentaria in Aristotelem graeca, vol. 20 (Berlin: G. Reimer, 1892), 145.23–146.3]. But Heliodorus is also pertinent: ἐνδέχεται δέ τινα τούτων ἀγνοεῖν καὶ σωφρονοῦντα· ὥσπερ ἀγνοεῖ τις πολλάκις αὐτὸ τὸ πρᾶγμα ὃ πράττει, καθάπερ οἱ ἐξειπόντες τὰ μυστήρια. λέγοντας γὰρ περὶ ἄλλων συγχυθῆναί φασι καί τι καὶ περὶ τῶν μυστηρίων παραφθέγξασθαι, μὴ συνορῶντας ὃ λέγουσιν ἢ καὶ ἀγνοοῦντας ὅτι ἀπόρρητα ἦν. οὗτοι γὰρ αὐτὸ τὸ

Aeschylus was likely born at Eleusis; it is likely too that "the Mysteries" he was accused of revealing were the Eleusian mysteries, elements of which he would have picked up from his native environment. If Gauthier is right, we have here again a case of something which, in a sense, "slipped out of someone's mouth,"[24] but this time there is less suggestion that the speaker knew that it could do harm. We find here, therefore, the same way of objectifying that which is (or was) done—as when one who, going through a recording, says at one point, '*There* is the speech act'—but less suggestion that the person knew *what* he was in effect doing (e.g. revealing a secret) in doing what he did.

The third example ("or a man might say he 'let it go off when he merely wanted to show its working,' as the man did with the catapult") bears with it many of the characteristics of the second, especially the suggestion that the agent does not know what he is doing, although 'the what' (of which the agent here is ignorant) is more closely connected with a physical movement. A literal translation of the very concise Greek would be: "or, wanting to show, to discharge, as someone [might] a catapult."[25] Gauthier notes that Aristotle informs us at one point that in Athens there were special masters in charge of teaching young men the handling of catapults.[26] Here one supposes that the instructor does not realize that the catapult's pouch contains a rock, but the point is not so much that the instructor does not realize this, for that would collapse this constituent into the fifth: knowledge (or ignorance) of the instrument used (the "with what"); the point again is rather that the instructor does not realize (or understand) *what* he is doing. What he is ignorant of is a piece of behavior. He does not realize, for instance, that releasing the trigger amounts to,

---

πρᾶγμα γινόμενον ἀγνοοῦσιν· οὐ γὰρ γινώσκουσιν, ὅτι τὰ μυστήρια ἐξάγουσι [Gustavus Heylbut, ed., *Heliodori in Ethica Nicomachea paraphrasis*, Commentaria in Aristotelem graeca, vol. 19.2 (Berlin: G. Reimer, 1889), 44.9–14]. The word παραφθέγξασθαι seems to suggest something that "just slipped out." Testimonies relative to Aeschylus's revelation of the mysteries are gathered at Stefan Radt, *Tragicorum graecorum fragmenta*, vol. 3, *Aeschylus* (Göttingen: Vandenhoeck & Ruprecht, 1985), T 93a–d, 94.

24 Gauthier [Gauthier and Jolif, *L'Éthique à Nicomaque*, 2.1 186] cites *Republic* viii, 563C1–2, where Socrates is being particularly candid in his criticism of democracy: "Are we to say with Aeschylus 'that which just now came into the mouth'?".

25 δεῖξαι βουλόμενος ἀφεῖναι, ὡς ὁ τὸν καταπέλτην [*EN* iii,1, 1111a10–11].

26 ειροτ[ο]νεῖ δὲ καὶ παιδοτρίβας αὐτοῖς δύο καὶ διδασκάλους, οἵτινες ὁπλομαχεῖν καὶ τοξεύειν καὶ ἀκοντίζειν καὶ καταπάλτην ἀφιέναι διδάσκουσιν [*Constitution of Athens* 42.3.3–5]; Gauthier and Jolif, *L'Éthique à Nicomaque*, 2.1 186.

in fact, firing the catapult. So, again the idea is that we can look at a piece of behavior and describe it as such. An instructor whose catapult is not loaded can also look at his releasing the trigger as simply that.

So, the second constituent, 'the what,' is really just a way of looking at an action. One is tempted to say that one "abstracts" from the act its objective or external characteristics; but that would be to suggest that one is referring not to an aspect of a concrete action but rather to an idea, or that 'the what' is somehow non-intentional, a merely physical description of the action. But that is not what Aristotle has in mind. Saying something that will hurt another or revealing a secret or demonstrating the working of a catapult are all intentional events, human actions; but in speaking about 'the what' we prescind from that aspect and attend just to "what is done." 'The what' has its own intelligibility.

V. Constituents (3) and (4)

The next two constituents—(3) περὶ τί and (4) ἐν τίνι—should be considered as in some way one. Ignoring the interrogative aspect, the phrase περὶ τί can be translated 'that about which';[27] by analogy with ἐν οἷς in 1110b33–1111a1, ἐν τίνι could be translated 'that in which' (an action consists). 'That in which an action consists' might be conceived of as a sort

---

27 Aristotle is apparently speaking about this (the περὶ τί) at EN iii,1, 1111a11–12 when he speaks of someone's mistaking his son for an enemy combatant. (Elsewhere, e.g. at EN. v,8, 1135a25, he speaks of such cases as mistaking the ὄν.) In that case, it might seem more appropriate to speak of περὶ τίνα, but περὶ τί can be understood as including such non-neuter subject matters.

One might wonder why, given that e.g., a son might be that περὶ ὅ an action is, he does not simply speak here of the object, using, for example, the expressions εἰς ὅ (as at Phys. v,1, 224b7; see also 5, 229a22–27) or ἀντικείμενον (as at de An. i,1, 402b15 and 5, 411a4, and especially ii,4, 415a20–22). One is tempted to say that his reason is that, since (as he argues in Phys. v,4) the ἐν ᾧ gives the species of a movement [227b29–30] and ἐν ᾧ is roughly equivalent to περὶ ὅ, he wants to avoid speaking of the object of an act, for that would take us out of the realm of species and into concrete particulars. But this cannot be the answer, since he very clearly signals at EN iii,1, 1110b33–1111a1 that he has moved away from general considerations to particulars. The answer is rather to be found in Phys. v,4, 227b14–20, as I argue below. Aristotle's point there is that the bare object is not sufficient to give the species of a movement, although it does give a movement its name [Phys. v,1, 224b7–8, 5, 229a25].

Aristotle uses περὶ + the accusative to refer to the object of a power a number of times in the de An.: ii,6, 418a12 (περὶ ὅ μὴ ἐνδέχεται ἀπατηθῆναι), iii,3, 428a13 (ὅταν ἐνεργῶμεν ἀκριβῶς περὶ τὸ αἰσθητόν), iii,3, 428b25 (περὶ ἃ μάλιστα ἤδη ἔστιν ἀπατηθῆναι κατὰ τὴν αἴσθησιν), and iii,6, 430a26 (περὶ ἃ οὐκ ἔστι τὸ ψεῦδος). In most (but not all) of these passages the objects referred to are the proper objects of the power in question; that is, they are that "about which" the power functions.

of matter, although it is not like the matter of a house, wood and stone, that might just as well become something else: statues, for instance. This matter arrives on the scene only once there is present some sort of moral entity: perhaps just the thought of doing something. It is the *intelligible* matter of the act. Traditionally, constituents (3) and (4) have been understood as distinct, but that is hardly compatible with the syntax of the list in which they appear, where all the other members are joined by the conjunction 'and' (καί) but these two by 'or' (ἤ).[28] This understanding is confirmed by the virtual equivalence of the plural counterparts of (3) and (4) at 1110b33–1111a1, where (as we have seen) Aristotle speaks of the particulars "in which" [ἐν οἷς] an action consists and "about which" [περὶ ἅ] it is.

But although the expressions ἐν οἷς and περὶ ἅ in that introductory remark help with the interpretation of ἐν τίνι and περὶ τί here, the parallel has also engendered confusion. The easiest way to summarize the ancient and modern interpretative situation is to quote Gauthier's observations on *EN* iii,1, 1111a4 (περὶ τί ἤ ἐν τίνι πράττει), which he translates, "what is the object or the domain of [the agent's] action"). He remarks:

Aspasius, the Anonymous, Grant, Stewart, Burnet, Ross and Dirlmeier understand: "what thing or what person is the object of his [the agent's] action." That which renders this interpretation plausible here is that, in this context, ἐν τίνι appears to have a sense more restricted than ἐν οἷς in 1110b33, 1111a16, 18, 24. Instead of designating, as does ἐν οἷς, *all* of the actual conditions of the action, it designates only one, approximately equivalent to περὶ τί. We believe, however, with Richards and Rackham, that τίνι is neuter and ought to be interpreted by analogy with ἐν οἷς: Aristotle does not distinguish between *thing* and *person* but between *object* and *domain* of the action, although this domain is restricted here in fact to the object. In any case, as emphasized by Aspasius, ἐν τίνι certainly does not signify "in what place," and even less "at what time"—contrary to the interpretation of St. Albert, adopted by St. Thomas.[29]

28 ... τίς τε δὴ καὶ τί καὶ περὶ τί ἤ ἐν τίνι πράττει, ἐνίοτε δὲ καὶ τίνι, οἷον ὀργάνῳ, καὶ ἕνεκα τίνος, οἷον σωτηρίας, καὶ πῶς, οἷον ἠρέμα ἤ σφόδρα [*EN* iii,1, 1111a3–6].

29 Gauthier's comment [Gauthier and Jolif, *L'Éthique à Nicomaque*, 2.1 185] is as follows: "1111a4 περὶ τί ἤ εν τίνι πράττει—quel est l'objet ou le domaine de son action." He goes on then to remark: "Aspasius, l'Anonyme, Grant, Stewart, Burnet, Ross et Dirlmeier comprennent: «quelle chose ou quelle personne est l'objet de son action». Ce qui rend ici cette interprétation vraisemblable, c'est que, dans ce contexte, ἐν τίνι semble avoir un sens plus restreint que ἐν οἷς de 1110b33, 1111a 6, 18, 24. Au lieu

There is much in Gauthier's approach that is right. He is right, for instance, to reject the notion that περὶ τί refers to a thing, ἐν τίνι to a person, and he is right to associate ἐν οἷς (from 1110b33–1111a1) and ἐν τίνι. He is right too to see an equivalence between περὶ τί and ἐν τίνι (as also between περὶ ἅ and ἐν οἷς). The last line in his comment is part of his more general argument that the constituents are not accidental to the act: they do not "stand around" the act, but, as he sometimes puts it, they are "the conditions in which an action unfolds"; or, as he puts it here, they constitute the "domain" of the act.[30] This, I think, is partly right and partly wrong—or, perhaps better, not taken far enough. Gauthier's term 'conditions' still connotes things that are external to something else, and a domain is still that *in* which something occurs. In other words, both terms continue to smack of 'circumstances' (understanding that word in its Latin literalness). But any sort of "standing around," as I have argued, is impossible to reconcile with Aristotle's inclusion in the list of τί: what the agent does.[31]

So, what does ἐν τίνι mean? Gauthier and the others he mentions are right to see τίνι as a more restricted correspondent of οἷς. And Gauthier is right to assign the same basic meaning to the two. But that meaning must be different from what he says it is: the dual reference is not to the conditions of an act and a single condition, nor (to use his alternative phraseology) to "the entire domain" [*le domaine tout entier*] and a single domain "restricted" to the singular object—indeed, it is not clear what this could possibly mean—but to those (plural) particulars in which an act consists and *this* particular, one of several in which the act consists. This latter, as Gauthier acknowledges, must be regarded here as equivalent in some way

---

de désigner comme ἐν οἷς *toutes* les conditions de fait de l'action, il en désigne une seule, à peu près équivalente au περὶ τί. Nous croyons cependant, avec Richards, *Aristotelica*, p. 5–6, et Rackham, que τίνι est un neutre et doit s'interpréter par analogie avec ἐν οἷς: Aristote ne distingue pas entre *chose* et *personne*, mais entre *objet* et *domaine* de l'action, même si ce «domaine» est ici restreint en fait à l'objet. En tout cas, comme le soulignait déjà Aspasius, p. 65, 1, ἐν τίνι ne signifie certainement pas «en quel lieu», et encore moins «en quel temps», contrairement à l'interprétation de saint Albert, adoptée par saint Thomas."

30 Gauthier's translation of 1110b33–1111a1 is "mais bien l'ignorance des faits singuliers, c'est-à-dire des conditions dans lesquelles se déroule l'action et des choses qui en sont les objets." But in his commentary he writes: "c'est le *domaine* tout entier de l'action, englobant toutes les conditions de fait qu'elle requiert" [Gauthier and Jolif, *L'Éthique à Nicomaque*, 2.1 185; emphasis his].

31 In the *EN* iii,1 list, the interogative form is used: τί ("what does he do?") [1111a4].

to the particular object (or, as I would put it, subject matter) of the act: the περὶ τί. In setting out the particular constituents, Aristotle equates that in which an act is (ἐν τίνι) with that about which it is (περὶ τί), just as earlier he equated the (plural) particulars "in which (ἐν οἷς) and about which (περὶ ἅ) an action is." So, in a manner similar to what we saw in 1110b33–1111a1, Aristotle is saying that the single subject matter of an act is—more than any of the other constituents—that in which the act consists.

VI. The "Most Important" Constituents

This has a bearing upon a problem in the conclusion to this section on the ignorance of constituents. Aristotle begins the section by saying that the ignorance with which he has been concerned "may relate, then, to any of these things in which [ἐν οἷς] an action is, and the man who was ignorant of any of these is thought to have acted involuntarily, especially if he was ignorant regarding the most important" [*EN* iii,1, 1111a15–17]. Then comes an apparently corrupt sentence: κυριώτατα δ' εἶναι δοκεῖ ἐν οἷς ἡ πρᾶξις καὶ οὗ ἕνεκα, translated by Ross (in the original Oxford translation) in this way: "and these are thought to be the most important constituents of the action and its end."

The problem here is that *among* the "most important" constituents are said to be the constituents! So, some more recent scholars follow Richards in inserting ὅ into the text after πρᾶξις, thus: κυριώτατα δ' εἶναι δοκεῖ ἐν οἷς ἡ πρᾶξις ὅ καὶ οὗ ἕνεκα ("and the important things in which an action consists seem to be 'what' and 'to what end'").[32] But, as with all such emendations that depart from the manuscript evidence, there are alternatives; one could, for instance, change the οἷς to ᾧ, giving κυριώτατα δ' εἶναι δοκεῖ ἐν ᾧ ἡ πρᾶξις καὶ οὗ ἕνεκα ("and the important things seem to be 'that in which' the action is and 'to what end'"). Linguistically, this emendation is at least as possible as that proposed by Richards and avoids

---

[32] Herbert Paul Richards, *Aristotelica* (London: G. Richards, 1915), 6; see also Gauthier and Jolif, *L'Éthique à Nicomaque*, 2.1 187–88. The Revised Oxford Translation follows Richards. Gauthier's translation is as follows: "... or, les principales des conditions de fait dans lesquelles se déroule l'action, ce sont, de l'aveu unanime, l'acte que l'on fait et le résultat auquel il aboutit" [Gauthier and Jolif, *L'Éthique à Nicomaque*, 1.2 60].

the rather leaden repetition of ἐν οἷς ἡ πρᾶξις in lines 16 and 18. With the phrase ἐν ᾧ Aristotle would be talking about the subject matter, but using the equivalent expression. The emendation is less intrusive in as much as it does not introduce an entirely new word into the text. It is also easy to imagine a scribe seeing ἐν ᾧ ἡ πρᾶξις, thinking it wrong and changing it to ἐν οἷς ἡ πρᾶξις in imitation of the ἐν οἷς ἡ πρᾶξις in line 1111a16.

There are as well other less textual reasons for preferring this emendation over that proposed by Richards. First of all, it would be strange for Aristotle virtually to equate περὶ τί and ἐν τίνι—the latter, like ἐν οἷς in 1110b33–1111a1, referring in some way to that in which the act consists—and not include one or the other among the most important constituents. Secondly, in the six other lists of constituents (in *EN* v,8 and *EE* ii,9), τί (or its equivalent) is three times left out, while the subject matter—which makes its appearance in those lists as ὅν—is never absent.[33]

VII. Object As Subject Matter

Let us consider more attentively the constituent spoken of in some of the lists of constituents (discussed above in section II) as ὅν (whom). As noted, ὅν does not appear in the list of constituents in *EN* iii,1, but it does appear in all of the other lists (which are all found in either *EE* or one of the common books):

[a] *EN* iii,1: τίς, τί, περὶ τί, ἐν τίνι, τίνι, ἕνεκα τίνος, πῶς [1111a3–6]
[b] *EE* ii,9: ὅν, ᾧ, οὗ ἕνεκα [1225b2]
[c] *EE* ii,9: ὅν, ᾧ, ὅ [1225b6]
[d] *EE* ii,9: ὅν, ᾧ, ὅ [1225b7]
[e] *EN* v,8: ὅν, ᾧ, οὗ ἕνεκα [1135a25]
[f] *EN* v,8: ὅν, ὅ, ᾧ, οὗ ἕνεκα [1135b13]
[g] *EN* v,8: ὅν, ᾧ, οὗ ἕνεκα [1135b15–16]

---

33 It must be acknowledged that the end (οὗ ἕνεκα), which at *EN* iii,1, 1111a18–19 is clearly said to be one of the "most important" constituents, does not appear in two of the lists in *EE* ii,9, that is, the list at 1225b6 and the one at 1225b7. Kenny suggests that in these two ὅ may actually refer back to οὗ ἕνεκα in 1225b2 [Kenny, *Aristotle's Theory of the Will*, 55], in which case οὗ ἕνεκα would appear in all the lists. Kenny acknowledges that at *EN* v,8, 1135b14–16 ὅ and οὗ ἕνεκα are distinguished [55 n. 1].

When ὄν appears in *EE* ii,9 ([b], [c], and [d]), it is the object, that is to say, the finishing point of the movement or action; the example given at *EE* ii,9, 1225b2 is that of the agent's father. In *EN* v,8 ([e], [f], and [g]), ὄν is identified as a person struck [1135a25] (so, again, the object), that is, "the striker's father," of whom the striker may be aware as a person in his presence but not as his father (1135a28–30). At 1135b14–16 the ὄν is again identified as a person struck, the striker thinking that object is another person. Presuming that Aristotle does not simply eliminated ὄν as a constituent when he sets out the *EN* iii,1 list ([a]) but includes it rather under another description, it clearly does not appear there as τίνι (the instrument) or ἕνεκα τίνος (the end), since these appear together with ὄν in [b], [e], [f], and [g]. (In these lists the instrument is represented as ᾧ.) A similar point can be made with respect to *EN* iii,1's τί, which appears in lists [c], [f], and [g] as ὅ. *EN* iii,1's πῶς is also obviously not the ὄν. That leaves τίς, περὶ τί, and ἐν τίνι, that is to say, *EN* iii,1's constituents (1), (3), and (4). But (1) or τίς is also eliminated since, as we have already seen, Aristotle identifies τίς in *EN* iii,1 as the agent of the action, not its object [1111a7–8].

So, by the time of the composition of *EN* iii,1, ὄν must have become in Aristotle's mind περὶ τί and/or ἐν τίνι.[34] Why is this? He gives an explanation in the *Physics*. In that work, since it is primarily about physical movement, the object is often spoken of not as ὄν but by means of the expression such as εἰς ὅ: 'that toward which the movement goes.'[35] Early in *Phys.* v, Aristotle is still speaking in this fashion, saying that a change is typically designated with reference to its object (that 'toward which' [εἰς ὅ] a change proceeds).[36] But in *Phys.* v,4 he explains why, strictly speaking, the mere object (understood simply as the point of arrival of an action) cannot serve as that which specifies the action.

34 This is presuming, of course, that *Nicomachean Ethics* (excluding the common books) is later. But this is accepted as a strong possibility by many scholars today: See note 57 in chapter 3.
35 See, for instance, *Phys.* iv,9, 217a5.
36 "For it is with respect to that toward which rather than that from which something is moved that a change is named [ὀνομάζεται—*Phys.* v,1, 224b7–8]; see also *Phys.* v,4, 229a22–27. In the continuation of the *Phys.* v,1 passage, Aristotle seems to hedge a bit. Having said that that toward which a change moves gives the change its name, he acknowledges, however, that perishing and coming to be are to be understood by looking not just to their end points but also to their points of origin: "So, perishing is 'change into not-being,' although that which perishes changes 'from being' and a coming to be is 'into being' but also 'from non-being'" [*Phys.* v,1, 224b8–10].

Constituents of Human Action 133

Phys. v,4 is about the oneness of acts; in order for something to be one, it has to be one something: that is, one thing of a certain type or species (εἶδος). But the object alone often does not allow us to identify a single species, even with respect to mere physical movements. Aristotle explains why:

> Someone might wonder whether a motion is one in species [εἴδει μία] when the same thing changes from the same point to the same point [ἐκ τοῦ αὐτοῦ τὸ αὐτὸ εἰς τὸ αὐτό], for instance, when one mathematical point goes from this place to this place over and over again. If that is the case, however, circular motion will be the same as rectilinear motion, and rolling the same as going. [*Phys.* v,4, 227b14–18]

The language Aristotle uses here [εἰς τὸ αὐτὸ—227b15–16] makes it apparent that he does indeed have in mind the object. Imagine a globe that turns perpetually with a circular motion. Its object—where it is headed—is all of the points on its surface. But the same points serve as the object of the motion of a globe that turns in one direction, up to a point, and then reverses direction (without lapse of time, since the turning is in an instant), proceeding in that direction until it reaches the same point again, when it reverses direction, proceeding in *that* direction until it reaches the same point again … and so on. In other words, the points on the surface, which are the object of either motion, say nothing at all about the type (the species) of motion involved. A similar thing can be said of the cylinder that rolls down an incline: its rolling down the incline has as its point of arrival point z at the bottom of the incline, but so also does a cylinder that does not roll down but simply *goes* down without rolling. (We can ignore friction: Aristotle is talking about mathematical models of motion.) In either case, rolling [κύλισις] or going [βάδισις], the object (z) is the same but the species—rolling and going—are different.

So, if we are to account for the oneness of a movement or an action, it is not sufficient to consider the object—as important as the latter might be for defining the movement (or action) (see chapter 2); we must look rather—or especially—to that 'about which' or 'in regard to which' the movement (or action) is: to its subject matter. Here in *Phys.* v,4, Aristotle uses the same language we find in *EN* iii,1,[37] that is to say, he uses the

---

[37] That is, ἐν τίνι at 1111a4 and (as I would claim) ἐν ᾧ at 1111a18.

expression ἐν ᾧ to refer to that which gives the species (τὸ εἶδος) to the act [*Phys.* v,4, 227b29–30]. This is not to deny, however, that the object is often so bound up in the subject matter that to refer to the object *is* to refer to the subject matter. This is the case with 'father,' as the object of parricide. If a son fails to strike his father—who stoops to tie his shoe just as the son launches a rock at his head—he cannot have committed parricide. This shows that the object (ὅν or 'whom') does give—or, in this case, would have given—species to that act. An unfortunate father with a stone creasing his forehead would have cast his influence (intelligibility) back upon the whole act, making it an act of parricide. The father gives the species, however, not qua end point of the physical movement but qua father. Had the stone hit a tree—or even the thrower's brother—the thrower would not have committed parricide.

So, the shift in language from the lists in *EE* ii,9 and *EN* v,8 (lists [b] through [g] in the above chart) to the list in *EN* iii,1 (list [a]), that is, the shift from talk of ὅν to talk of περὶ τί and ἐν τίνι, ought not to surprise us, for we find the same sort of shift in the *Physics*. We also find there (that is, in *Phys.* v,4) an explanation of the shift.

VIII. Constituents (5), (6), and (7)

To return to the list of constituents, number (5) τίνι clearly refers to the means or instrument employed. In his explanations after the list, Aristotle speaks of someone who thinks his sword is tipped, although it is bare, or that the stone he throws is of pumice, although it is actually of harder material [1111a12–13]. There is not much that needs to be said about this constituent, except to repeat what has already been said with respect to the first two. In *EN* iii,1, the agent's beliefs about his instrument are false: the construct in his mind does not correspond to the fact in the world. But an agent can obviously also have true beliefs about the instrument he uses, and then such disparity is not an issue: the τίνι becomes simply a constituent aspect of what the agent does. If a man knowingly uses an instrument disproportionate to the task at hand, that can change the moral character of his action so that it becomes a different type of action. If a man could effectively defend himself from an assailant by picking up his small-caliber pistol and wounding him but reaches instead for his assault weapon which blows him away, that changes what he does from an act of justifiable self-defense to murder.

Similar issues comes up with the next constituent, ἕνεκα τίνος ("to what end"), which Aristotle himself glosses as "e.g., for preservation [οἷον σωτηρίας]" [1111a5]. Despite this example, which certainly seems to represent why someone would do something or use some instrument, Gauthier maintains that Aristotle is not speaking here about the end that the agent proposes for himself: "in whatever case, he cannot be ignorant of that! It is a matter of the *result* at which this action will in fact arrive."[38] This brief argument is hardly compelling—as we have seen, Aristotle himself acknowledges that no one can be ignorant of the first constituent ("who") [iii,1, 1111a6–8]—but there is reason to go along with Gauthier, to an extent. In a parallel passage in the *Eudemian Ethics*, Aristotle uses the example of the daughters of Pelias who, relying on Medea, who wants Pelias dead, believe that in dismembering their father and boiling the body parts they will make him young [*EE* ii,9, 1225b2–3]. Here the end that is mistaken is not the daughters' end (or intention) in killing and boiling their father but the end—the "result"—of that action viewed objectively.[39] But in *EN* v,8, Aristotle explains this same constituent in a way that shows that he does not mean to exclude from consideration the end that an agent has in mind as he performs an act.

There are various ways in which a person can make a mistake [ἁμάρτημα], says Aristotle in *EN* v,8.[40] Sometimes the person does not think

to strike or to do it with that or at him or for that end, but what happens is either that the end [οὗ ἕνεκα] was not what he supposed [ᾠήθη] (e.g. not 'that [ἵνα] he might wound' but 'that [ἵνα] he might prick') or that the person struck or that the means with which he struck were not what he supposed. [1135b13–16]

---

38 Gauthier and Jolif, *L'Éthique à Nicomaque*, 2.1 185; emphasis Gauthier's. See also Kenny, *Aristotle's Theory of the Will*, 51: "a doctor prescribing a wrong drug may be mistaken about its *effects* (confusingly called here by Aristotle its οὗ ἕνεκα or purpose)" [emphasis his].

39 For a criticism of this type of position, see Cynthia A. Freeland, "Aristotelian Actions," 400–401 One notices, incidentally, that that Pelias would simply be killed (and not rejuvenated) was the end of Medea.

40 On mistakes, see chapter 3, section V.

Obviously, Aristotle is speaking here about a number of constituents; we are interested, however, in what he says about the end. Regarding the latter, Aristotle speaks, as we have come to expect, of two ends, each falling within the scope of the word ᾠήθη, that is, within the scope of the agent's supposition (the first negatively, the second positively), and each signalled by the word ἵνα. One end is "to prick"—and, had the action been such that it would just prick, this would have been unproblematically "the end": the agent's striking would have had the effect he intended it to have. The other is "to wound," and that was in no one's mind, says Aristotle; it is similar to the end toward which the dismembering and boiling of Pelias is ordered. It is noteworthy that in *EE* ii,9, where Aristotle speaks of the mistaken end of the daughters of Pelias, he says that they did not act in order to kill but in order to save.[41] The killing is something that *might* have been the daughter's end but was not.

To mistake the end, therefore, is for there to be a disconnect between these two types of end; but if there is no mistake, the end is simply the reason why the agent does what he does. Obviously, in a mistake, the end that comes about is independent of the end the agent had in mind; but, in order for there to have been a mistake, the agent has to have had something in mind. When there is not a mistake, that is because the end the agent has in mind and the result coincide. When intention and result do not coincide, the agent presumably experiences remorse (*EN* iii,1, 1110b22–23 and 1111a19–21); when they do, he is simply acting voluntarily (at least with respect to that which he knows). This more straightforward case is the more useful for identifying the structure of a simple act: it is what the agent has in mind in doing what, in fact, he does.

Much more needs to be said about 'the ἕνεκα τίνος'—it is, after all, one of the two "most important" constituents—but I shall put off further remarks until chapters 5 and 6. The meaning of the last of the constituents, 'how [πῶς]' (the act is performed) is not terribly controversial, but it too is not without wider exegetical importance. Aristotle again provides his own gloss: "e.g. softly or strongly" [1111a6], apparently with the thrust of

---

41 ... ἀλλ' οὐχ ἵνα ἀποκτείνῃ, ἀλλ' ἵνα σώσῃ, ὥσπερ αἱ Πελιάδες [*EE* ii,9, 1225b4–5]. At *EN* iii,1, 1111a5, that is, in his list of the constituents, Aristotle uses similar language: καὶ ἕνεκα τίνος, οἷον σωτηρίας.

a weapon especially in mind. A hoplite might think that his sword thrust will stop short of fatally wounding but, as it sinks into his opponent's flesh, he realizes he was wrong: the 'how' in his mind and the 'how' in reality do not correspond. But they *could* correspond; and in that case the 'how' would come to characterize the act morally, even essentially. If a private citizen wants to thrust his sword right through the heart of his neighbor and succeeds in doing so, that is different from warding the other off with a mere flesh wound.

Again, a person might mistake how he is doing something—"gently or violently" [1111a6]—but he might also know this full well. Teasing or ribbing someone may be a perfectly innocent thing to do; but sometimes—and with some people—it can be done in too strong or rough a manner. A person might mistake how close to the "rib" his comments cut, but he can also know this perfectly well and deliberately continue. On the other hand, sometimes a person cannot have known that he was going too far, in which case he is not culpable for what he does; but, when he does recognize what he is doing, that is, *that* it makes a moral difference, then 'the how' is a genuine (per se) constituent.

IX. Conclusion

We have now a good idea of what the constituents of acts are (who, what, about what, etc.) and of what type of things they are (not circumstances but rather constituents). Such an understanding is obviously an aid in nailing down pieces of theory regarding the structure and moral character of individual acts; but it is also important to recognize that much escapes nailing down and that human acts have an essentially temporary and improvisational nature. The constituents are beings of reason. If a person leaves a room abruptly (that being the 'how' [πῶς] of his act), the abruptness with which he leaves can make that act an act of an entirely different type from that of just leaving a room. Or, if an officer of the law begins his task of restraining an unruly citizen in a measured way, using only as much force as necessary, but then grows angry and uses unnecessary force, that can change his action from 'preserving the peace' to 'unjust assault.' Such sudden and radical changes, brought about by apparently secondary factors, are not found among natural objects. The essential nature of a tree remains the same throughout its life and is not altered, for instance, when its sap runs faster than usual. But in the realm of human action, reason—as manifest especially in the constituents—is everything; it can change the nature of an act.

But even the constituents of human action—as unstable and unpredictable as they are—admit of truth. This is apparent in Aristotle's presupposing in his exposition of them the possibility of mismatches: the possibility that in doing one thing one does another. In showing to another its firing mechanism, a man causes the catapult to go off. The possibility of such a lack of correspondence entails also the possibility of correspondence, which is to say, the truth of the claim that 'that is what I did.'

Five

Intelligibility and the Per Se

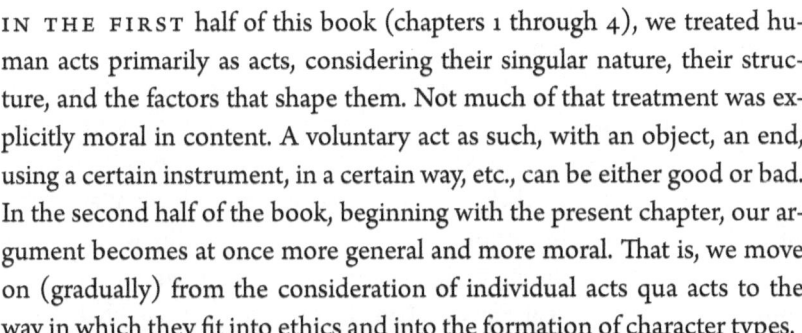

IN THE FIRST half of this book (chapters 1 through 4), we treated human acts primarily as acts, considering their singular nature, their structure, and the factors that shape them. Not much of that treatment was explicitly moral in content. A voluntary act as such, with an object, an end, using a certain instrument, in a certain way, etc., can be either good or bad. In the second half of the book, beginning with the present chapter, our argument becomes at once more general and more moral. That is, we move on (gradually) from the consideration of individual acts qua acts to the way in which they fit into ethics and into the formation of character types.

The present chapter presupposes the movement-like structure of actions such as was depicted in chapter 2. It also considers the way in which actions head toward ends. This, in effect, widens our scope of interest, since the end of a movement not only helps to define that movement but it also connects it with other structures of intelligibility. In chapter 6, we discuss how the ideas set out in *Metaph.* ix,6 (and discussed in chapter 2, section IV) help us to understand how individual acts understood as movements fit into larger systems such as crafts and sciences and even human lives themselves. The last two chapters are about such human lives—or, to be more precise, about human character types: first (in chapter 7) the φρόνιμος, then (in chapter 8) the less well-ordered character types, such as the ἀκρατής and the ἀκόλαστος. But in the present chapter we are concerned with the lines of intelligibility that contribute in various ways to these larger systems.

A key tool in the analysis of larger systems of intelligibility (whether they be sciences or crafts or other practical systems) is the distinction between the per se and the per accidens, and so we begin the present chapter with a review of Aristotle's remarks in book one of the *Posterior analytics* on the per se.[1] What is distinctive about these remarks is that, although they introduce Aristotle's philosophy—or, perhaps, logic—of the sciences, they include examples that are not only singulars (and, therefore, not properly scientific) but human actions. The main point in this section, however, is that the per se is about units of intelligibility, the clearest examples of which are linguistically related terms. This will come as no surprise since it is the job of language to pick out and to organize bits of intelligibility. The intelligibility on offer in ethics is less extensive than in the proper sciences—but it is there and identifying it is crucial for understanding the ethical realm's structure.

Section II begins with a brief discussion of Aristotle's remark in *EN* v,8 that the constituents, in order to be constituents in the strict sense, must be understood—which is to say that they cannot be constituents per accidens. In the present chapter we do not consider with equal attention all of the constituent but study primarily the two "most important" ones [*EN* iii,1, 1111a18], beginning in this section with 'that in which' an action consists. We look again at *Phys.* v,4 (considered also above, in chapter 4), where Aristotle expresses dissatisfaction with the idea that the mere *terminus ad quem* of an action might give it its species. In the passage that interests us, Aristotle establishes criteria for an action's being one; and, again, intelligibility is of central importance. If a movement is truly one movement, there will be a per se unit of intelligibility at its core. Such a movement will be per se then in a double sense: in so far as it is a per se unit of intelligibility and in so far as it is understood by the agent.

In section III, we take a more decisive step into the properly ethical by considering the per se as it concerns the end, the second of the most important constituents. We saw in chapter 4, section VII, that 'the end'

---

1 I employ in this chapter (and also elsewhere) the common Latin expressions per se and per accidens; in the present context, they correspond to the Greek καθ' αὑτό and κατὰ συμβεβηκός.

can be understood in two senses, either as the end which the agent possibly fails to understand (as when Pelias's daughters do not understand that dismembering and boiling him will kill him) or as the end which the agent does understand. Given what Aristotle says in *EN* v,8, when the former possibility is realized, that is, when the agent fails to understand where his act is headed, this end must be regarded as a per accidens constituent; in the latter case, the end is a per se constituent. This amounts to saying that the agent's own understanding of what he is doing establishes a line of intelligibility between himself and the end in this second sense. The existence of such a line of intelligibility does not preclude there being per accidens relationships among factors falling under such a per se intention. Some of these will be part of the moral act in question, some not. That within a piece of behavior with the status of overall per se intelligibility there might be found the per accidens is possible because human action occurs at the perceptual level (see chapter 1, *passim*); this could not happen in an Aristotelian science.

But, although in order to be a per se constituent 'the end' must be known, there are ends that are per se but not known, as when a person pursues a merely apparent good, that is, an apparent good that does not correspond to the genuine good. An example of this would be a man who thinks that happiness consists in the accumulation of money. In two distinct passages, one in *EN* vii,9, the other in *EN* iii,4, Aristotle maintains that in such cases the per se end is the end that is *not* known, the apparent good being sought only per accidens. This can be the case, since in these two passages Aristotle has in mind primarily not the end of a human act (the constituent 'the end') but rather the end of human nature. This may or may not correspond to the end pursued by a human agent; when it does, that is a good thing. Aristotle calls the good man, whose end does correspond to the true good, the "norm and measure" of all human action. (At this point we have clearly entered the realm of the ethical.)

Having established that ethics has to do not only with the ends of particular human acts but also with the end of human nature, in section IV we show how these ideas give us insight into the dynamic contours of the ethical. In *EN* ix,2, Aristotle speaks of various types of deliberation that cannot be made in a mechanical way. In discussing such deliberations and their subsequent actions, Aristotle employs the language of archery. Good deliberations and good actions in such matters involve the delicate task of taking aim well and hitting the center of the target that gives species to virtuous behavior. But although good ethical judgment is very often a matter of taking good aim and hitting the target in this way, there are parameters within which such aiming and shooting is performed; outside these parameters, any talk of aiming makes no sense. Aristotle mentions in *EN* ii,6, adultery, theft, and murder, but we might add also lying, which Aristotle says is per se evil. As Aristotle says in *EN* ii,6, determining that certain actions are not to be performed is not a matter of deliberative aiming, for it is not possible ever to go right with them, "one must always go wrong." Such acts lack practical intelligibility at their very core, so there is no way in which they could be part of a per se aiming at the genuine good for man.

In section V we discuss some difficult moral questions mentioned in *EN* ix,2 (such as whether someone who has been ransomed from pirates ought to ransom his ransomer or his own father), in order to show that even with respect to such questions genuine knowledge is available. It is important to make this point, lest the reader be left with the erroneous impression that, according to Aristotle, the only clarity and precision on offer in ethics is that having to do with the intrinsic immorality of acts such as adultery, theft, or murder.

I. The Per Se–Per Accidens Distinction

Aristotle tells us any number of times that ethics lacks the exactitude of (for instance) mathematics: he cannot offer us a science of ethics in the sense of a system that would state the principles or laws of human behavior in such a way that their consequences (human acts), with all their characteristics, would be derivable. As we saw in chapter 1, human acts occur at the level of perceptual singulars; as such, they resist scientific treatment in the strict sense. But, unlike his teacher Plato, Aristotle does not throw up his hands in despair of discovering intelligibility in the realm of human actions.[2] Rather, while acknowledging that each human action must be

---

2 In the first book of the *Republic* [331C1ff.], Plato discusses two of the classical "hard cases," whether one is always obliged to return something given to one in trust (a "deposit") and whether one

considered on its own,[3] he realizes too that human actions can be and are understood, especially by the person acting, and that they can be assessed with respect to how reasonable they may or may not be. In this enterprise, the per se–per accidens distinction is a very useful tool, put at our disposition by Aristotle, as a means of identifying pieces of intelligibility.

The distinction's role in Aristotle's moral theory ought not to be overestimated, as if the evaluation of a human act were solely a matter of identifying what in it is per se (or intended per se). There are few ethical questions which the distinction, by itself, resolves. Much more important is the way in which a human act, analyzed by means of the per se–per accidens distinction, fits into the larger scheme of human reason. That said, however, the distinction can be said to typify Aristotle's approach to human knowledge in general, including the analysis of human acts; it allows him to say how and where the things that are relevant to a particular discipline fit into its general scheme.

What is special about this approach is best brought out by contrasting it with some more modern approaches to causality. Without entering into specifics, we might say that a common presupposition of some (especially early modern) theories of causality is that, although in any one instance we might not be able to specify all the causal factors that lead to a particular event, such a complete account is theoretically possible, since the universe is structured in such a way that any event has a completely determinative causal explanation.[4] The aspect of Aristotle's approach we would emphasize here is not so much that he is not a determinist but that he would never, even implicitly, accept such a universal principle as a starting

---

is always obliged to tell the truth. (The two cases show up again at *R.* ii, 382C7ff.) Should a weapon be returned when it is clear its owner is out of his mind [331C5–7]? Are not falsehoods sometimes "useful" [382D4]? It is cases such as these that lead Plato to posit a world of forms independent of the world of human affairs. He believes, that is, that such examples show that in the actual political-ethical world, genuine knowledge and true exceptionless precepts are not to be found.

3 See *EN* i,4, 1095b4–8; i,7, 1098a33–b3. See also J. A. Stewart, *Notes on the Nicomachean Ethics of Aristotle*, I, 54–57.

4 This characterization of some modern conceptions of causality is put forward in G. E. M. Anscombe, "Causality and Determination," in *Metaphysics and the Philosophy of Mind*, vol. 3 of *Collected Philosophical Papers*, G. E. M. Anscombe (Minneapolis/Oxford: University of Minnesota Press/Basil Blackwell, 1981), 133–47; for a corrective to Anscombe's own ideas on causality (but not necessarily to her characterization of modern theories), see Stephen L. Brock, "Causality and Necessity in Thomas Aquinas," *Quaestio* 2 (2002): 217–40.

point. He begins not with the presupposition of an ultimate and universal order, knowledge of which we lack (but "could" have) but rather with pieces of causality whose intelligibility we can grasp now in a secure manner. He looks primarily to that which stands immediately before him (as investigator of whatever field of study) and especially to the most tightly compressed bits of intelligibility, into which doubt and ignorance have less room to interject themselves; he then adds one bit to another, explaining their mutual connections or lack thereof. Particularly in the field of ethics, Aristotle is less interested in building the pieces of intelligibility he discovers into a system than in bringing as many pieces of intelligibility as possible to bear upon that which he is studying at any one moment. For reasons set out in chapter 1 of the present work, our knowledge of the practical world is especially subject to limitations: since it subsists at the perceptual rather than the syllogistic level, large sectors of it will always resist the per se ordering characteristic of proper sciences.

Aristotle expounds the per se–per accidens distinction in a number of his works, but especially in the *Posterior analytics*.[5] In the latter, Aristotle deals primarily with propositions—combinations of terms—that represent genuine knowledge and that can, therefore, be included in larger structures of knowledge (the sciences); such propositions have various characteristics, including that of being per se. When dealing with propositions, it is natural to speak of the per se as a relationship (between two terms); but some of the examples Aristotle uses in *APo.* to explain the per se are not easily spoken of as relationships, so we will speak more generally here of "situations." So, in *APo.* i,4, Aristotle identifies four types of per se situation: {1} the situation that exists when a predicate represents something that belongs to the essence of a subject; {2} the situation that exists when a subject represents something that contributes to the definition of a predicate; {3} the situation that exists when the issue is not so much how a predicate holds of a subject as how something *is* that which it is qua itself (a walking thing, for instance, qua walking thing is walking but it is not, qua walking thing, white); {4} the situation that exists when something happens that pertains to a thing itself, "as when something sacrificed dies, that is, *because* of the sacrifice: the sacrificed thing dies be-

---

5 See *APo.* i,4, 73a34–b24; see also *Metaph.* v,6, 18, and 30.

cause of the being sacrificed and not just by chance."⁶ The examples offered by Aristotle to illustrate {3} and {4} are not well suited to sciences as conceived of by Aristotle, for they refer not to universals but to singular events; they are much better suited to ethics and the consideration of human behavior. Indeed, they correspond rather closely to what Aristotle identifies at *EN* iii,1, 1111a18–19 as the two "most important constituents" of human action.⁷

The first two situations represent formal and material causality and are proper to the sciences, strictly speaking; the other two are associated more readily (although not so straightforwardly) with efficient and final causality. Aristotle's way of describing type {4} is especially illuminating for a couple of reasons. First, he makes it apparent that the per se is bound up with intelligibility. Three of the words he uses—'sacrificed thing' [(τι) σφαττόμενον], 'the sacrifice' [τὴν σφαγήν], and 'the being sacrificed' [τὸ σφάττεσθαι]—are obviously closely related linguistically; there can be no mistaking the relationship of intelligibility between sacrificed things and sacrificing. Secondly, in expounding {4}, Aristotle clearly has in mind an intentional situation of some sort, that is, an action together with its constituent 'to what end.'⁸ He uses [73b11–13] also the example of lightening occurring while someone is walking: it is not because of the person's walking that it lightens, so the lightening occurs per accidens; but it is because of the person's walking that he gets to where he is going, so that occurs per se. Similarly, if during a sacrifice an animal should die of natural causes, then we cannot say that the relationship between its death and the sacrifice is per se; a sacrificed thing is always (per se) the object of someone's sacrificing.

We find similar ideas and preoccupations elsewhere in Aristotle's writings. One of his standard examples of a per se relationship is that existing between a sculptor and his statue, discussed, for instance, at *Metaph.* v,2, 1013b34–1014a1. It is no coincidence that Aristotle employs in this

---

6 εἴ τι σφαττόμενον ἀπέθανε, καὶ κατὰ τὴν σφαγήν, ὅτι διὰ τὸ σφάττεσθαι, ἀλλ' οὐ συνέβη σφαττόμενον ἀποθανεῖν [*APo.* i,4, 73b13–16]. Says Jonothan Barnes, "The fourth use involves a connection between *events*: 'E_1 occurs kata E_2.'" [Jonathan Barnes, trans. and comm., *Aristotle: Posterior Analytics*, Oxford Aristotle Series (Oxford: Clarendon, 1994), 117, his emphasis].

7 τατα δ' εἶναι δοκεῖ ἐν ᾧ ἡ πρᾶξις καὶ οὗ ἕνεκα ("and the important things seem to be 'that in which' the action is and 'to what end'"); see above, chapter 4, section VI.

8 See above, chapter 4, section VIII.

example two words, ἀνδριάς (statue) and ἀνδριαντοποιός (sculptor or "statue-maker"), connected to one another linguistically, for (as we have just seen) such a connection virtually ensures a meeting of intelligibilities. Although a per se relationship can exist in the absence of such linguistic closeness, when it is present, there is almost always a connection of intelligibility between the two things so brought together: in this case the intelligibility of 'statue' is contained in the very intelligibility—the meaning—of the word statue-maker (ἀνδριαντοποιός). Here is no promissory note of a connection to a hypothetical universal system of causal explanation but a small piece of intelligibility of which an investigator can be sure (and build upon).

In *Metaph.* v,30, Aristotle's philosophical "dictionary entry" on the per accidens, the first example he gives is of someone digging in a field and finding a treasure. If the farmhand "is digging a hole for a plant" [1025a16] and discovers treasure, that discovery is per accidens. On the other hand, his accomplishing the task of digging the hole would be per se related to his digging. As in the sacrifice example of *APo.* i,4, here the term 'per se' qualifies an action together with its end. In this same chapter [1025a25–30], Aristotle speaks of a ship that ends up in Aegina; if it does not end up there because it was going there, it does so by accident. Aristotle says of the accident of ending up in Aegina that it "comes about or is—not qua itself, however, but qua something other; for the storm is the cause of [the ship's] coming to where it was not sailing" [1025a28–30]. A ship *qua ship* or sailing vessel arrives where it is sailing. It does this qua what it is: a ship, or a sailing vessel, which is to be a vessel with a particular destination, for ships are human artifacts and are built for getting to particular destinations. As we shall see, this is connected with man's pursuit of the good. Although because of human action's perceptual nature, "in between" a particular action and the ultimate good sought, there may intervene stages related only per accidens to the action and/or that end, engaging in a human act is per se related to the good, since, like sailing vessels sailing, human pursuits (acts) pursue the pursued, that is to say, the good.[9] Similarly,

---

9 Virtues tend per se toward performing the acts by which they are produced: Κοινῇ μὲν οὖν περὶ τῶν ἀρετῶν εἴρηται ἡμῖν τό τε γένος τύπῳ, ὅτι μεσότητές εἰσιν καὶ ὅτι ἕξεις, ὑφ' ὧν τε γίνονται, ὅτι

however complex and flexible human action might be, the connection between the act of the will and that act's end is as necessarily unifying as anything in the harder sciences.

II. The Unity of an Act

It is very apparent, therefore, that, although Aristotle sets out his understanding of the per se within the context of his philosophy of science, the per se–per accidens distinction is also employable within the practical sphere and at the perceptual level.[10] We would expect, therefore, to find Aristotle employing the distinction with respect to the constituents of human acts, since the practical sphere is ultimately made up of these. And, indeed, we do find him doing just that. In *EN* v,8, he says the following:

By 'the voluntary' I mean, as was said previously,[11] whatever of those things that are 'up to him' a man does and which he does knowingly, that is, (1) not in ignorance of the person acted upon or of the means used or of the end, e.g. whom he is striking, with what means, and for what end, each of these being not per accidens, and (2) not due to force (for instance, if someone should take

---

τούτων πρακτικαὶ καθ' αὑτάς, καὶ ὅτι ἐφ' ἡμῖν καὶ ἑκούσιοι, καὶ οὕτως ὡς ἂν ὁ ὀρθὸς λόγος προστάξῃ [*EN* iii,5, 1114b26–30 (following Franciscus Susemihl and Otto Apelt, eds., *Aristotelis Ethica Nicomachea* [Teubner: Leipzig, 1912])]. Bywater, citing Aspasius (ἔτι εἴρηται, ὡς ὑφ' ὧν γίνονται ἕξεις, τούτων πρακτικαὶ καὶ καθ' αὑτάς [*in EN* 80.7–9:]) inserts καὶ (in pointed brackets) in line 28 (giving ὅτι τούτων πρακτικαὶ <καὶ> καθ' αὑτάς). But the καὶ in Aspasius's paraphrase is substituting for the τε in 1114b27, so Bywater's conjecture is not supported by Aspasius, and the passage makes good sense without it.

Aspasius goes on [*in EN* 80.8–18] to offer two possible accounts of Aristotle's use of the phrase καθ' αὑτάς. (1) Aristotle could have in mind the courageous man who performs temperate acts: he performs them not per se but per accidens, that is to say, not qua courageous but qua temperate. Courage effects courageous acts and temperance temperate acts, just as sacrifices are of sacrificed things and sculptors sculpt sculptures (see *APo.* i,4, 73b13–16 and *Metaph.* v,2, 1013b34–1014a1). (2) Aristotle could have in mind the fact that, e.g., a temperate man might perform an act characteristic of the intemperate. Aspasius uses the example of a temperate man who seduces the wife of a tyrant in order to save the city: "He will do this per accidens; temperate things he will do per se" (τοῦτο δὲ ποιήσει κατὰ συμβεβηκός, καθ' αὑτὰ δὲ τὰ σώφρονα [*in EN* 80.17–18]). For reasons to be set out in chapter 7 in connection with *EE* viii,1 (and in particular with 1246a29–31), it seems to me unlikely that Aristotle has in mind this second type of account.

10 See above, chapter 1, *passim*.

11 Since *EN* v is one of the common books and since in this brief list of constituents there appears ὄν (rather than περὶ τί or ἐν τίνι), this is probably an allusion to *EE* ii,9. See chapter 4, section VII. On the common books, see note 57 in chapter 3.

someone's hand and strike another, not voluntarily, for it is not 'up to him'). [*EN* v,8, 1135a23–28]¹²

The phrase "each of these being not per accidens" (κἀκείνων ἕκαστον μὴ κατὰ συμβεβηκὸς—1135a26) is epexegetical, as if Aristotle were saying, "*that is*, each of these features is to be understood per se, or as known."¹³ He is not saying that, among the constituents there are some that are per se, others per accidens, but rather that in order to be a constituent in the strict sense a feature must be known or understood. We are obviously now within the realm of human action, since it is no longer sufficient that there merely *be* a piece of intelligibility at the core of the action (as when a white thing becomes dark)¹⁴ but the intelligibility must be understood as such by its agent: a per se "constituent" of a physical act might not be a per se constituent of the corresponding human act. It is true, as we saw in chapter 4 (sections III and VIII), that Aristotle does speak of constituents of which an agent might be ignorant ("a man might say he 'let it go off when he merely wanted to show its working,' as the man did with the catapult" [*EN* iii,1, 1111a10–11]); but these cannot be constituents in the strict sense, that is, they cannot be per se constituents.

Aristotle is concerned here in *EN* v,8, with the performance of just and unjust acts. He uses the example of the returning of deposits.¹⁵ He as-

---

12 δ' ἑκούσιον μέν, ὥσπερ καὶ πρότερον εἴρηται, ὃ ἄν τις τῶν ἐφ' αὑτῷ ὄντων εἰδὼς καὶ μὴ ἀγνοῶν πράττῃ μήτε ὃν μήτε ᾧ μήτε οὗ <ἕνεκα>, οἷον τίνα τύπτει καὶ τίνι καὶ τίνος ἕνεκα, κἀκείνων ἕκαστον μὴ κατὰ συμβεβηκὸς (μηδὲ βίᾳ ὥσπερ εἴ τις λαβὼν τὴν χεῖρα αὐτοῦ τύπτοι ἕτερον, οὐχ ἑκών· οὐ γὰρ ἐπ' αὐτῷ) ... [*EN* v,8, 1135a23–28]. This piece of text is punctuated differently in both the Bywater and the Susemihl-Apelt editions; they begin the parenthesis in line 26 with the word ὥσπερ (instead of μηδὲ). I believe, however, that it is best to follow Kenny [Anthony Kenny, *Aristotle's Theory of the Will*, 57, n. 1] and punctuate as I have done. The phrase κἀκείνων ἕκαστον μὴ κατὰ συμβεβηκὸς seems not to refer to acts (that is, the τῶν ἐφ' αὑτῷ ὄντων of 1135a24), since no acts have been *listed* such as would give rise to the back reference "each of these." Beginning the parenthesis with μηδὲ makes the association of μὴ κατὰ συμβεβηκὸς with the constituents easier; a constituent might be per accidens but only acts are forced. The word μηδὲ in line 26 would, therefore, be coordinate not with the μὴ before κατὰ συμβεβηκὸς (in line 26) but with the μὴ in line 24: μὴ ἀγνοῶν. Indeed, if one wanted to make the syntax unmistakable, the whole passage might be punctuated in this fashion: ὃ ἄν τις τῶν ἐφ' αὑτῷ ὄντων εἰδὼς καὶ μὴ ἀγνοῶν πράττῃ (μήτε ὃν μήτε ᾧ μήτε οὗ <ἕνεκα>, οἷον τίνα τύπτει καὶ τίνι καὶ τίνος ἕνεκα, κἀκείνων ἕκαστον μὴ κατὰ συμβεβηκὸς) μηδὲ βίᾳ (ὥσπερ εἴ τις λαβὼν τὴν χεῖρα αὐτοῦ τύπτοι ἕτερον, οὐχ ἑκών· οὐ γὰρ ἐπ' αὐτῷ) ... [1135a24–28].

13 See *EE* ii,9, 1225b5–6, where the phraseology is strikingly similar: τῷ ἀγνοοῦντα καὶ ὃν καὶ ᾧ καὶ ὃ δι' ἄγνοιαν, μὴ κατὰ συμβεβηκός. See also above, chapter 4, section I.

14 For the example, see below, at note 22.

15 See above, note 2.

sumes that returning a deposit is per se a good thing to do; it is intelligible in itself. But if one returns the deposit reluctantly, says Aristotle, or for fear of otherwise being punished, one performs the just act only per accidens [1135b4–6]. Or, if one fails to return a deposit because of pressure and/or fear, one performs an unjust act but, again, only per accidens [1135b7–8]. This shows that the full intelligibility of either a just or an unjust act consists not solely in the physical act of (for instance) getting a deposit back to its owner (or failing to get it back), but in doing so in a certain manner: as the just man (or the unjust man) would do. This is not to say that the intelligibility of, for instance, the act of *returning a deposit* is not complete when the deposit is put into the hands of the owner by a reluctant former trustee but only to say that it is not complete qua just act, for the latter requires that one perform the act for the sake of justice itself.[16] Given that a man understands what he is doing, it is yet another issue whether the act is fully an act of justice. The wholly just man embraces the just acts he commits in all their intelligibility, that is, *as* just acts [*EN* ii,4, 1105b5–12]. A similar thing can be said of the unjust man in relation to his unjust acts; that is, that, in some sense, he must embrace them. The indecisive or conflicted parricide is different from the confirmed parricide. If on the grounds that he has always in principle opposed such acts as parricide he should protest, "I am *not* a parricide," he would not be talking nonsense—even though, having committed the act, in the legal but nonetheless real sense, he is a parricide.

Let us consider now the role of the per se in the first of the "most important" constituents mentioned at *EN* iii,1, 1111a18–19, the ἐν τίνι (the "in what?") or "'that in which' the action is."[17] As we saw in chapter 4, section VII, this constituent is connected in a special way with Aristotle's analysis of movements in *Phys.* v,4; as such, it has to do more directly with sin-

---

16 'Return deposits' is, of course, the standard example of a precept that admits of exceptions. (Again, see above, note 2.) The fact that the precept admits of exceptions does not mean that returning deposits is not per se a good and intelligible thing to do. Although admitting of exceptions (or non-application), an agreement with another to return a deposit has its natural end in the restitution of the deposit; the impeding of this natural progression is an interruption of intelligibility and is therefore, *prima facie*, not good.

17 This constituent is constituent (4) in the list given at *EN* iii,1, 1111a3–5; but, as we saw in chapter 4, sections V and VI, it is to be closely associated also with constituent (3), 'that about which' an act is—indeed, so closely associated as to be virtually identical to it.

gular human acts than with the way such acts fit into psychological types and into ethics. But, since movements have ends and ends are connected to other ends (see *EN* i,1, 1094a14–16, iii,3, 1112b17–19), consideration of the per se with respect to this constituent can bring us a step toward consideration of these more general issues.

We have seen that in *Phys.* v,4 Aristotle insists that the mere object (in the sense of a physical point of arrival) is not sufficient to give an action its species.[18] He sets out there the criteria for saying that a movement (or κίνησις), such as a human act, is itself numerically one. One might have thought that identifying an act's subject matter—the 'about what' [περὶ τί] and 'in regard to what' [ἐν τίνι] it subsists—would be sufficient to guarantee its numerical oneness; but in fact the subject matter gives us only the species of the act and a species can have numerous instances. The subject matter of an act of parricide is a father, which is only to say that parricide is about father-killing; Aristotle needs still to hone in on what it is to be an individual act of parricide.

In *Phys.* v,4, Aristotle gives three criteria for the "numerical and substantial" oneness of a κίνησις:[19] (a) what [ὅ] moves or is moved must be one; (b) 'that in regard to which' [ἐν ᾧ] the κίνησις is must be one; and (c) the time at which [ὅτε] the κίνησις occurs must be one.[20] Taken individually, each is a necessary condition of the oneness of a movement; taken together, they constitute a composite sufficient condition of the same. Regarding (a), one might wonder whether a flock of geese flying south would count as one thing in movement. Aristotle gives as examples of (a), "a man or gold" [227b25], examples he also uses at *Phys.* i,7, 190b24–25,

---

18 See chapter 4, section VII.

19 Aristotle speaks of movement that is simply speaking [ἁπλῶς] one as being one τῇ οὐσίᾳ μία καὶ τῷ ἀριθμῷ [*Phys.* v,4, 227b21–22].

20 *Phys.* v,4, 227b23–24: τρία γάρ ἐστι τὸν ἀριθμὸν περὶ ἃ λέγομεν τὴν κίνησιν, [a] ὅ καὶ [b] ἐν ᾧ καὶ [c] ὅτε. An equivalent formulation is found at *Phys.* v,4, 228b1–3 [διὸ ἀνάγκη τὴν αὐτὴν εἶναι [b] τῷ εἴδει καὶ [a] ἑνὸς καὶ [c] ἐν ἑνὶ χρόνῳ τὴν ἁπλῶς συνεχῆ κίνησιν καὶ μίαν ...]. (For this understanding of [b], see *Phys.* v,4, 227b27–30.) At *Phys.* v,4, 228b26, [b] seems to be identified with the object (the εἰς ὅ), which, as we saw above in chapter 4, section VII, is *associated* with the object but not identical to it. Ross writes: "One is tempted to read ἐν τῷ ἐν ᾧ for εἰς ὅ, but there is no evidence to support this, and the terminus may easily be named instead of the path as the third element in movement (cf. 224a35, 236b3). I therefore read ἐν τῷ εἰς ὅ" [W. D. Ross, *Aristotle's Physics*, 633]. This seems right: ἐν τῷ εἰς ὅ is just a loose way of saying ἐν τῷ ἐν ᾧ. See above, note 36 in chapter 4 (and the surrounding text).

where he refers to them as 'countable matter' [ἡ ὕλη ἀριθμητή].²¹ And later in *Phys.* v,4 Aristotle denies that two men restored to health in the same way would have the unity necessary for asserting the presence of a movement that is numerically one [228a1–3]. So, since a flock of geese, unlike a lump of gold or a single man, is made up of more than one substance, clearly the flock would not count as one thing in the sense required.

More important for our purposes, however, is the fact that Aristotle understands the numerical and substantial oneness mentioned in (a) as oneness of something over the course of a per se change (or movement). 'What [ὅ] moves or is moved,' says Aristotle, must be one in the way that the white thing having become dark is one and not in the way that Coriscus having become dark is per accidens one.²² (It just happens that the darkened white thing is Coriscus. There is no intelligible connection between Coriscus and darkness, as there is between whiteness and darkness. A white thing's becoming dark—brown, for instance—is connected with what white is: a color, as is also brown.) So, the human actions at the basis of ethics must involve some unit of intelligibility that characterizes the thing moved itself, qua moved in that way.²³ If a man steals an object, intending that the theft be blamed on another whom he dislikes intensely, although the act of theft and the act of injury to the good name of the other occur (or might occur) at one and the same time—in one and the same motion—there are two acts involved: theft and defamation. This is so because theft and defamation have distinct intelligibilities. Without

---

21 μὲν γὰρ ἄνθρωπος καὶ ὁ χρυσὸς καὶ ὅλως ἡ ὕλη ἀριθμητή· τόδε γάρ τι μᾶλλον, καὶ οὐ κατὰ συμβεβηκὸς ἐξ αὐτοῦ γίγνεται τὸ γιγνόμενον· ἡ δὲ στέρησις καὶ ἡ ἐναντίωσις συμβεβηκός [*Phys.* i,7, 190b24–27]. Aristotle's point here is that countable matter is per se related to that which comes of it; its relationship to the privation or contrary is per accidens.

22 .... καὶ τὸ κινούμενον ἓν εἶναι μὴ κατὰ συμβεβηκός, ὥσπερ τὸ λευκὸν μελαίνεσθαι καὶ Κορίσκον βαδίζειν (ἓν δὲ Κορίσκος καὶ λευκόν, ἀλλὰ κατὰ συμβεβηκός)... [*Phys.* v,4, 227b31–33].

23 Although it is tempting to draw the parallel, we should avoid associating *Phys.* v,4, 227b23's [a] with what contemporary philosophers call 'basic actions.' (See, for example, Arthur C. Danto, "Basic Actions," *American Philosophical Quarterly* 2 [1965]: 141–48.) Contemporary basic actions end where the human body ends, but Aristotle is certainly not limiting the actions whose oneness he is defining to actions that finish where the body finishes. "What moves or is moved" (as in [a]) might be a teacher, and his characteristic act finishes in his student (see chapter 2, section I). Aristotle does, however, speak of the moving of the limbs as in some sense basic; see *EN* iii,1, 1110a15–18: καὶ γὰρ ἡ ἀρχὴ τοῦ κινεῖν τὰ ὀργανικὰ μέρη ἐν ταῖς τοιαύταις πράξεσιν ἐν αὐτῷ ἐστίν· ὧν δ' ἐν αὐτῷ ἡ ἀρχή, ἐπ' αὐτῷ καὶ τὸ πράττειν καὶ μή. On these matters, see David Charles, *Aristotle's Philosophy of Action*, 70–84.

the per se–per accidens distinction, such an analysis would be impossible.

We see this same concern with pieces of intelligibility in what Aristotle says about (b) ('that in regard to which') and (c) ('the time at which'). Although presented as separate conditions (necessary but not sufficient) for the oneness of a movement, in fact the two are strictly connected. One sees this in Aristotle's answer to an objection that he considers regarding his own thesis. The objection maintains that, even if a movement occurs in two separate periods of time, that movement can be one, since recovering a state (a ἕξις) previously lost is simply a reactivation of one and the same movement. When a person rises in the morning healthy and that health continues throughout the day, that which continues is one and the same thing. When such a state is interrupted, why not, therefore, just say that that which reasserts itself (and therefore exists at separate times) is one and the same movement? For bodies that are in such states as health "move and flow" [*Phys.* v,4, 228a9], so clearly we are dealing with movements.

But it is precisely at this point that Aristotle attacks the objection. To be a state (a ἕξις) and to be an actualization (an ἐνέργεια) are quite different things. If there are distinct actualization-associated states, the associated actualizations must also be distinct (if a man is sick but also in love, these two states must involve separate actualizations); but a single state can be associated with more than one movement, "for when a walking man pauses, walking is no longer, but when he walks again it will be" [*Phys.* v,4, 228a16–17]. An actualization (which, as we saw in chapter 2, Aristotle associates closely with movement) is held together as what it is by its own continuity over time: if it stops—that is, genuinely comes to a halt—any similar actualization associated with it must be a different actualization. What are subject to oneness of time in the relevant sense are not *just any* phenomena but actualizations (or movements). A state that remains the same over a day or even reasserts itself after a period of remission may indeed be one, but it is not one actualization, so it is irrelevant to the question at hand.

The oneness of time that interests Aristotle is that bound up in the idea that an actualization began at this point in time and finished at that point in time. If process p begins at t^1 and finishes at t^n, and between these two times there is no break in the action, there is no need to explain anything: the compactness of the event is a mark of its intelligibility. But if there is a break, there is something to explain: something to be *made* intelligible. Aristotle would render it intelligible, as far as possible, by insisting first of all that we are dealing not with one unit of intelligibility but with two: that is, two actualizations. None of this should be understood, however, as Aristotle's denying that a human action might involve distinct stages: that Socrates's walking to Athens, for example, might involve a stay at a roadside inn. For one thing, Aristotle goes on to acknowledge that, although a movement might not be continuous, it can be regular—and regularity admits of degrees [*Phys.* v,4, 228b15–19, 229a1–3]. What is important is that the movement be specifically one [*Phys.* v,4, 229a3–6], and in human acts the species comes from the end (understood in a certain way). Since human action is so bound up in reason, and practical reason is about finding means to ends and means to those means (now regarded as ends) [*EN* iii,3, 1112b17–19], etc., the extent or scope of a line of intelligibility can be greater than that of a merely physical movement such as a cylinder's rolling to the bottom of an inclined plane. All that said, however, at the basis of any extended action (such as Socrates's walking to Athens), there are individual actualizations, each of which is potentially subject to moral evaluation. If Socrates's walking on day 2—but not his walking on days 1 and 3—is in violation of a ban on travelling, the walking of day 2 can and probably must be evaluated independently of its being part of the larger action, his three-day walk to Athens.

So then, according to Aristotle, we can establish criteria for saying that a movement is itself numerically one, and one of those criteria is the presence of a per se line of intelligibility within the movement. Moreover, as we saw above in considering *EN* v,8, 1135a23–28, this line of intelligibility must be understood by the agent, otherwise it will not be a constituent in the strict sense. Having established this criterion is no mean thing: since such lines of intelligibility are so basic, we know what sort of relationship or situation might constitute a genuine contribution to our comprehension of the intelligibility of a larger ethical system, such as a character type or a culture or a system of laws and customs. None of this is to say, however, that Aristotle thinks that we can gather up all the bits of intelligibility in individual actions and fit them into a deductively satisfying science that allows us finally to be rid of the contingency of human action. As we said earlier, Aristotle does not think that ethics admits of such a treatment. His method is rather to "keep his nose to the ground," examining the facts in order to see what sense can be made of them. Unlike Plato, he does find a great deal of intelligibility at the level of concrete moral phenomena; and, as he finds bits or units or layers of intelligibility, he works them into the account he sets out especially in the *Nicomachean* and the *Eudemian Ethics*.

III. To What End?

The second of the two "most important" constituents identified in *EN* iii,1, 1111a18–19 is the ἕνεκα τίνος, 'to what end.' In many ways, this is the most "ethical" of the constituents, providing an easy opening onto the moral assessment of particular acts. We saw in chapter 4 that this constituent has two faces: it can refer to the end that a particular piece of behavior has in itself, as when the action performed by the daughters of Pelias (dismemberment, not to mention boiling) ends up killing him, not saving him [*EE* ii,9, 1225b2–3], that being the natural result of dismembering someone; or it can refer to the agent's end *in* acting (the daughters' end was to restore Pelias's youth). Following *EN* v,8, 1135a23–28, only the second is per se a constituent, for constituents, in the strict sense, are understood by their agents: their agents know that they are part of what they are doing.

An action such as that of Pelias's daughters might involve a number of subsidiary actions, and these subsidiary actions might for various reasons be related to the overall action per se or per accidens. The daughters may purchase a whetstone, for instance, in order to sharpen the knife that will dismember the old man. Such a subsidiary action would be related per se to the end of the natural process which finishes in their father's death, which is the end of *their* action only per accidens, since they think they are restoring his youth. Also, although the end of such a subsidiary action might be per se (in the sense that the daughters know that and why they are purchasing the whetstone, that is, in order to sharpen the knife), the subsidiary action with its end is related per accidens to the per se end of restoring the youth of their father, since there is no intelligible connection between purchasing whetstones or sharpening knives (or, for that matter, dismemberment) and restoring youth. If, on the other hand, the daughters should *want* to kill their father, the subsidiary action, receiving as it does its species from its per se end, would be part of the larger action performed per se; and so the whole complex would be quite simply per se the action that it is. But even within such an action the per accidens might be present. In order to raise money to buy the whetstone the daughters might perform a song and dance routine, which, qua song and dance routine, is related only per accidens to dismemberment; or, after sharpening the knife, the daughters might flip a coin to decide whether to go ahead with the deed. In both these cases, the per accidens is included within the per se. Such inclusion is quite normal, since ethics does not do what the sciences proper are obliged to do: exclude the per accidens.

This is not to say that all of that which might be identified as per accidens with respect to the end intended (and understood) by an agent enters into the act in the moral sense. As Aristotle argues in *EE* ii,6–9, the defining characteristic of the voluntary is 'that which is according to thought.'[24] If some per accidens aspect of an act is not known to be part of an act—and provided such ignorance is not due to the agent's negligence (see chapter 4, section I)—it is not part of its moral content. In the Greek myth, the daughters of Pelias, deceived by Medea, do not know that they are killing their father; they do not, therefore, commit parricide. If, however, we suppose, as we did just above, that the daughters do know what they are doing and so act willingly, if accomplishing the murder involves a song and dance routine, since they know that they are performing the routine in order to buy the whetstone (in order to sharpen the knife, in order to dismember the old man), that per accidens segment of what they do is a morally significant part of their act of killing their father. In itself, performing such a routine is not immoral, but it takes on the immorality that characterizes the end for which they act.[25]

---

24 *EE* ii,9, 1225a37. *EE* ii,6–9 is translated in Appendix 2 and discussed in chapter 3.
25 See *Phys.* ii,2, 194b35–195a1, *EN* ii,4, 1105a28–33, and *EN* v,8, 1135b2–8. In the latter passage, Aristotle says that the man who performs a just act without the proper motivation (out of fear, for example) performs a just act only per accidens.

So, in the ethical sphere, the per se has to do with what is known and, in a particular way, with ends that are known. Indeed, Aristotle says at one point that, when something is done for the sake of something else, only the end is desired per se.[26] This all has a bearing not only upon the analysis of individual acts, such as that performed by the daughters of Pelias, but also upon the way in which individual acts fit into the moral lives of their agents—and so ultimately upon the analysis of character types.

In the passage (just mentioned) in which Aristotle makes the point about things desired for the sake of other things [*EN* vii,9, 1151a35–b2], he is in fact discussing two connected puzzles: (1) whether the term ἐγκρατής ('continent') is properly applied not only to someone who manages by dint of will power to do the right thing, correctly understood, but also to someone who manages by dint of will power to do what he *incorrectly* believes to be the right thing to do; and (2) whether the term ἀκρατής ('weak of will') is properly applied not only to someone who out of moral weakness and due to pleasure (although not the type of pleasure attaching to noble activities) acts contrary to what he correctly believes to be the right way of proceeding but also to someone who has an incorrect understanding of what is the right way of proceeding and acts contrary to that, again out of weakness and due to pleasure.

A modern example sometimes used to illustrate the latter case of ἀκρασία is that of Mark Twain's Huck Finn, who believes he should turn in to the authorities a slave, Jim, but fails to do so out of ἀκρασία. In Aristotle, this term ἀκρασία refers to a person who fails to do the right thing out of weakness. Indeed, in order to correspond to Aristotle's point in *EN* vii,9, where the person who falls prey to ἀκρασία does so due to pleasure of a baser sort, we should suppose that Huck fails to turn Jim in because he enjoys, for instance, drinking or gaming with him. We should also suppose that Huck genuinely believes that the right thing to do is to turn Jim in and that he is not negligently ignorant of the correct moral principle (e.g., "No one is to be enslaved"). The question then is whether we can

---

26 *EN* vii,9, 1151a35–b2. See also *EN* viii,8, 1159a17–21: "But it seems to be not for its own sake [δι' αὐτὸ] that people choose honor, but incidentally [κατὰ συμβεβηκὸς]. For most people enjoy being honored by those in positions of authority because of their hopes (for they think that if they want anything they will get it from them; and therefore they delight in honor as a token of favor to come) …."

say that Huck is ἀκρατής. The Aristotelian answer would be that, yes, he is ἀκρατής: he does think that one should pursue the good—even though he does think that the (in fact) wrong thing to do is the right thing to do— and he falls away from that good intention.[27] On the other hand, Aristotle acknowledges that the term applies strictly speaking [ἁπλῶς] to the non-anomalous ἀκρατής (i.e., the one who falls away from the true good), since the anomalous ἀκρατής (such as Huck) seeks as if it were the genuine good that which is good only per accidens.

The relevant passage runs as follows:

Is the man who abides, by whatever reasoning and whatever choice, continent [ἐγκρατής], or rather the man who abides by the right choice?[28] And is the man who does not abide, by whatever choice and whatever reasoning, weak of will [ἀκρατής], or rather the man who does not abide by the reasoning that is not false and the choice that is right, as was puzzled about earlier? Or does not the one abide, the other not abide per accidens to "whatever," per se to the true reasoning and the right choice? For if someone chooses or pursues this for the sake of that, per se he pursues and chooses the latter, per accidens the former—and we call the per se 'strictly speaking' [ἁπλῶς]. So, in a sense the one man abides by, the other departs from, whatever opinion; but, strictly speaking [ἁπλῶς], the true opinion.[29]

---

27 It is another issue—not addressed here by Aristotle—whether the agent is culpable for being in this state of ignorance. Aristotle touches upon this issue at *EE* ii,9, 1225b14–16. See above, chapter 4, section I.

28 Aspasius discusses Aristotle's use of the word 'choice' [προαίρεσις] here and suggests that he really means will (βούλησις)—or that perhaps he means choice that is in accord with will and reason (λόγος) [Aspasius, *In Ethica Nicomachea quae supersunt commentaria*, vol. 19.1 of *Commentaria in Aristotelem Graeca*, ed. Gustavus Heylbut (Berlin: Reimer, 1889), 137.24–28]. Since the present passage has to with the good and the apparent good, this suggestion is not unreasonable. It would also establish a connection with *EN* iii,4, to be considered just below.

29 τερον οὖν ἐγκρατής ἐστιν ὁ ὁποιῳοῦν λόγῳ καὶ ὁποιᾳοῦν προαιρέσει ἐμμένων ἢ ὁ τῇ ὀρθῇ, καὶ ἀκρατὴς δὲ ὁ ὁποιᾳοῦν μὴ ἐμμένων προαιρέσει καὶ ὁποιῳοῦν λόγῳ ἢ ὁ τῷ μὴ ψευδεῖ λόγῳ καὶ τῇ προαιρέσει τῇ ὀρθῇ, ὥσπερ ἠπορήθη πρότερον; ἢ κατὰ μὲν συμβεβηκὸς ὁποιᾳοῦν, καθ' αὑτὸ δὲ τῷ ἀληθεῖ λόγῳ καὶ τῇ ὀρθῇ προαιρέσει ὁ μὲν ἐμμένει ὁ δ' οὐκ ἐμμένει· εἰ γάρ τις τοδὶ διὰ τοδὶ αἱρεῖται ἢ διώκει, καθ' αὑτὸ μὲν τοῦτο διώκει καὶ αἱρεῖται, κατὰ συμβεβηκὸς δὲ τὸ πρότερον· ἁπλῶς δὲ λέγομεν τὸ καθ' αὑτό. ὥστε ἔστι μὲν ὡς ὁποιᾳοῦν δόξῃ ὁ μὲν ἐμμένει ὁ δ' ἐξίσταται, ἁπλῶς δὲ [ὁ] τῇ ἀληθεῖ [*EN* vii,9, 1151a29–b4]. The Bywater edition excises the ὁ in 1151b4, as does Susemihl-Apelt. I have repunctuated line 1151b2, using a semicolon rather than a period, on the grounds that ἁπλῶς δὲ λέγομεν τὸ καθ' αὑτό falls within the scope of the γάρ in line 1151a35; that is, it is part of Aristotle's explanation why the relevant terms apply καθ' αὑτό to those who correctly identify the good for man. The passage referred to in 1151a32–33 ("as was puzzled about earlier") seems to be *EN* vii,2, 1146a16–21. But note that Neop-

The most difficult remark in this most difficult passage is the one about seeking something for the sake of something else, for it seems to speak of a means-end relationship between the apparent good and the good for man.[30] A second difficulty in the same remark is that it seems to say that even the man who does not know what the good for man is and pursues some apparent good pursues per se *not* the apparent good but rather the genuine good, the good for man: "For if someone chooses or pursues this for the sake of that, per se he pursues and chooses the latter, per accidens the former" [1151a35–b2]. J. A. Stewart regards 1151a35–b2 as "merely a logical note introduced to explain the difference between καθ' αὑτὸ and κατὰ συμβεβηκὸς—which hardly needs explanation—and to enable the writer to wind up with the satisfactory formula ἔστι μὲν ὡς ... ἁπλῶς" [1151b3–4].[31] That, however, is little more than a wish that the remark would go away. In any case, there is a way of understanding the larger passage which makes of the remark a working part of Aristotle's argument and a principle in Aristotle's philosophical psychology.

One of the key terms in the argument is ὁποιοσοῦν, translated here as 'whatever.' Aristotle acknowledges that everyone involved—the anomalous and the non-anomalous ἐγκρατεῖς and ἀκρατεῖς—have their long-term sights fixed upon the apparent good. The latter could be *anything* ("whatever"), even the true good. When the apparent good coincides with the true good, obviously there is no conceptual distance between the two: they are the same thing; but when they do not coincide, the one (the apparent good) is sought for the sake of the other (the true good), even if the person is unaware of this.[32] In other words, the reason why we

---

tolemus (mentioned at 1146a19) is declared not ἀκρατής in 1151b17–22, while 1151a29–b4 is about the ἀκρατής (and the ἐγκρατής). I take it that, when Aristotle refers to what was "puzzled about earlier," he means just that the issues discussed in 1151b29–b4 were touched upon in an indirect way in *EN* vii,2, 1146a16–21. (On Neoptolemus, see below, note 58.)

30 The phrase 'the good for man' comes from *EN* i,2, 1094b7; I shall continue to use it in what follows, in order to avoid any confusion with "the Good" in the strictly Platonic sense.

31 Stewart, *Notes on the Nicomachean Ethics of Aristotle*, II, 208. Grant calls the remark "perfectly irrelevant" [Alexander Grant, *The Ethics of Aristotle: Illustrated with Notes and Essays* (London: Longmans, Green, and Co., 1885), 228].

32 The anonymous commentator on *EN* vii uses the example of a person who likes sweet wine because it is sweet. The wine is per accidens sweet and therefore not sought for itself (per se) [Anonymous, *In Ethica Nicomachea VII commentaria*, vol. 20 of *Commentaria in Aristotelem Graeca*, ed. Gustavus Heylbut (Berlin: Reimer, 1892), 440.34–441.1]. See also Aspasius, *In Ethica Nicomachea quae*

pursue even the apparent good is that we are so constructed as to pursue the true good—and, in fact, we always do, although we sometimes mistake the apparent good for it. Since that which all parties (the anomalous and non-anomalous alike) seek is the good per se, the relevant terms (ἐγκρατής, ἀκρατής) apply as appropriate to them all. When, for instance, Huck Finn fails to turn Jim over to the authorities, he is correctly called ἀκρατής. But strictly speaking (ἁπλῶς) the term ἀκρατής refers to the man who has a true grasp of the good for man (and how it relates to the action he is about to perform) but fails to pursue it. The same can be said of the ἐγκρατής: both the anomalous and the non-anomalous types are called ἐγκρατής, although the term applies strictly speaking to that man who, resisting pleasure, holds tenaciously to the genuine good. The reason why the term applies across the board in this way is that all parties do pursue the genuine good; the reason why strictly speaking the appropriate terms apply only to those who correctly identify the genuine good is that the 'strictly speaking' (the ἁπλῶς) is closely associated with the per se: "For if someone chooses or pursues this for the sake of that, per se he pursues and chooses the latter, per accidens the former—and we call the per se 'strictly speaking'" [1151a35–b3].[33]

---

supersunt commentaria 138.9 (who also mentions wine but not sweetness). The interpretation of *EN* vii,9, 1151a35–b4 presented here coincides with that of Aspasius (138.6–17). I would connect it also with Aristotle's remarks at *EN* iii,4, 1113a13–31, where he rejects the thesis that the object of the will is the genuine good *if* that means that those who do not choose the genuine good have no object of the will. His solution (1113a22ff.) in effect rejects the notion that the natural object of the will depends on what a person wills as the genuine good. The good man's apparent good coincides with the genuine good; the bad man's apparent good is whatever it is. But the object even of the latter's will is still (per se) the genuine good, *somewhat* in the way that a sick man seeks what normally would not be healthy (cauteries, blood-letting, etc.) in order to arrive at health or in the way that a sick man is unable to identify the truly sweet since the sweet tastes bitter to him. These latter two analogies limp fiercely; the first one, however, corresponds fairly closely—and limps in a manner similar to—Aristotle's remark at *EN* vii,9, 1151a35–b2 that, "if someone chooses or pursues this for the sake of that, per se he pursues and chooses the latter, per accidens the former."

33 Gauthier argues that Aristotle is speaking in the first part of this quotation about the ἐγκρατής who manages, by dint of strength, to follow a false rule (thinking it a true rule). This type of ἐγκρατής behaves well but only per accidens, "for he does not do it except in so far as he believes the rule to be true" [Gauthier and Jolif, *L'Éthique à Nicomaque*, 2.2 649]. This, I think, is quite near to being right. What, according to Gauthier, would be pursued καθ' αὑτό? The true rule. The wrong rule would be followed because of the right rule [τοδὶ διὰ τοδὶ αἱρεῖται ἢ διώκει—*EN* vii,9, 1151a35–b1]. But what about the ἀκρατής? He *fails* to act according to (even) the false rule. In his case, there is no active adhering to the false rule "for the sake of" (διὰ) the true. Aristotle must have in mind simply—that is,

In the case(s) of the anomalous ἐγκρατής and ἀκρατής there is a break in intelligibility between what they consciously choose or seek and that which is the true good for man. This type of break is not a good thing, for it means that the person involved *has something wrong*—rather than that there is a disconnect between two pieces of intelligibility, as happens, for instance, when a person performs a song and dance routine in order to buy a whetstone in order to carve the Sunday roast more efficiently (the song and dance being related only per accidens to carving). As one ascends the order of goods, and in particular when the issue is whether an agent understands and pursues the good for man, matters become more ethical. It is true that, if there is no way that Huck might have known that slaves ought not to be turned over to the authorities, then he would not act immorally in turning over Jim—and so the per accidens character of the good he seeks would have no moral significance.[34] But the fact that the merely apparent good is good only per accidens indicates that there is reason—indeed, moral reason—to set his thinking aright, if at all possible, for even Huck in his non-culpable ignorance pursues the genuine good per se.

What then about the difficulties identified above, that is, that Aristotle seems to be saying at *EN* vii,9, 1151a35–b3 that the apparent good is a means to the genuine good and that the anomalous ἐγκρατής and ἀκρατής seek the genuine good per se although they do not think that it *is* the genuine good? The latter idea seems especially difficult to reconcile with the passage we examined above, where Aristotle says that a constituent that is not known is not strictly speaking a constituent but a constituent per accidens [*EN* v,8, 1135a23–28].[35] But perhaps we have not wholly understood his position. Perhaps, that is, what makes a per se constituent per se is not strictly speaking its being known but rather its completing that particular piece of intelligibility. A constituent of a moral act is by definition known, so going beyond the known, presumably to something unknown, would be to leave the intelligibility of a moral constituent; such an object could

---

independently of any action at the moment in question—the relationship between the apparent good and the true good for man.

34 See chapter 4, section I.
35 See also *EE* ii,9, 1225b5.

not complete the intelligibility of 'constituent of a moral act.' But it is perfectly possible for an object to complete the intelligibility of a *nature* without that object's being known.

In *EN* iii,4, Aristotle argues along the same lines as in *EN* vii,9 but speaks more explicitly about human nature. In the chapter, the issue is whether the object of the will [βούλησις] can be the good, given that some people do not seek the good but seek only the apparent good (which seems to be the object of their wills):

> That will is for the end has been stated; but it seems to some that it is for the good, to others that it is for the apparent good. It turns out, for those (1) who say that the object of the will is the good, that for the man who does not choose correctly there is no object of the will which he wills (for, if there is to be an object of the will, it will also be good, but it was supposed that it could be bad); for those (2) who say that the object of the will is the apparent good, that there is no natural object of the will [φύσει βουλητόν], but for each man it is that which seems to him good, a different thing for each: it could even be contrary things. If, therefore, these things are unsatisfactory, ought we then to say that simply speaking [ἁπλῶς] and in truth the object of the will is the good, but for each person the apparent good—for the good man, therefore, that which is in truth good, for the bad man, whatever it might be ... ?[36]

Aristotle's implicit answer to this latter question is affirmative: yes, we ought to say that strictly speaking and in truth there is a natural object of the will, the good. The good man (the φρόνιμος and related types) knows this and straightforwardly seeks the good. The bad man, because he shares the same nature, also has this (the good) as the object of his will— we must say this, for the alternative is to say that his will *has* no object

---

36 Ἡ δὲ βούλησις ὅτι μὲν τοῦ τέλους ἐστὶν εἴρηται, δοκεῖ δὲ τοῖς μὲν τἀγαθοῦ εἶναι, τοῖς δὲ τοῦ φαινομένου ἀγαθοῦ. συμβαίνει δὲ τοῖς μὲν τὸ βουλητὸν τἀγαθὸν λέγουσι μὴ εἶναι βουλητὸν ὃ βούλεται ὁ μὴ ὀρθῶς αἱρούμενος (εἰ γὰρ ἔσται βουλητόν, καὶ ἀγαθόν· ἦν δ', εἰ οὕτως ἔτυχε, κακόν), τοῖς δ' αὖ τὸ φαινόμενον ἀγαθὸν βουλητὸν λέγουσι μὴ εἶναι φύσει βουλητόν, ἀλλ' ἑκάστῳ τὸ δοκοῦν· ἄλλο δ'ἄλλῳ φαίνεται, καὶ εἰ οὕτως ἔτυχε, τἀναντία. εἰ δὲ δὴ ταῦτα μὴ ἀρέσκει, ἆρα φατέον ἁπλῶς μὲν καὶ κατ' ἀλήθειαν βουλητὸν εἶναι τἀγαθόν, ἑκάστῳ δὲ τὸ φαινόμενον· τῷ μὲν οὖν σπουδαίῳ τὸ κατ' ἀλήθειαν εἶναι, τῷ δὲ φαύλῳ τὸ τυχόν ... ; [*EN* iii,4, 1113a14–26]. With Susemihl-Apelt, I shift the question mark to line 1113a29, after the word ἕκαστα. I understand τὸ κατ' ἀλήθειαν in 1113a25 by analogy with τὰ κατ' ἀλήθειαν τοιαῦτα [ὑγιεινὰ] in 1113a27, that is, in effect as τὸ κατ' ἀλήθειαν ἀγαθόν. The latter phrase appears at *EN* iii,5, 1114b7.

[1113a17–18]—but he wills it under the appearance of something else.[37] Assuming, as in *EN* vii,9, an equivalence between the ἁπλῶς and the per se, we can say again that the man who pursues the apparent good pursues the true good per se, the apparent good per accidens; he does this even while believing that the apparent good is the true good. Aristotle goes on to say [*EN* iii,4, 1113a25–29] that the good man knows what he is pursuing, just as the healthy man recognizes (tastes) the goodness of good food. The sick man, on the other hand, does not always perceive the goodness of good food; as healthy as some food may be, it tastes unpleasant to him. But it *is*—per se—good for him.

Aristotle's answer, therefore, to the second difficulty mentioned above —the difficulty, that is, that the anomalous character types are understood as seeking the genuine good per se even though they do not recognize it as the genuine good—would simply be to say that it is not a difficulty. The issue is not so much what a person has in mind as what, by nature, he pursues. Per se (or ἁπλῶς) he does pursue the true good, whether he recognizes this or not. This approach also helps us with the first difficulty mentioned above, the difficulty, that is, that on Aristotle's account, the apparent good turns out to be a means to an end (the end being the genuine good). By denying that ignorance of the true good prevents one from—stands in the way of—pursuing the true good, Aristotle in effect eliminates any distance the person who is attached to the apparent good has to travel in order to get to the true good. It is not a question of seeking the true good by *way* of a means but of pursuing the good *in* and *by* pursuing the apparent good.

At this point, we clearly have entered the realm of ethics, since, as Aristotle all but explicitly says in *EN* iii,4, consistency between the true good and one's conception of the good is better than inconsistency: it is a more "healthy" state, morally; consistency between one's actions and one's nature is better, morally, than inconsistency. The genuine good, the end of human nature itself, sheds its influence over the whole of the practical realm in a way similar to the way in which the end of any movement gives—or, at least, contributes to giving—species to the movement it

---

37 *EE* ii,10, 1227a18–30 might be expounded in a similar fashion. This passage concludes with the following sentence: ὁμοίως δὲ καὶ ἡ βούλησις φύσει μὲν τοῦ ἀγαθοῦ ἐστί, παρὰ φύσιν δὲ καὶ τοῦ κακοῦ, καὶ βούλεται φύσει μὲν τὸ ἀγαθόν, παρὰ φύσιν δὲ καὶ διαστροφὴν καὶ τὸ κακόν [*EE* ii,10, 1227a28–30].

completes. Not even the acts of the man who does not acknowledge the status of the genuine good escapes the latter's influence. For this reason, Aristotle can go on to say in *EN* iii,4 that the good man is the "norm and measure" [κανὼν καὶ μέτρον—1113a33] of all human action.

IV. Aiming, Hitting the Mark, and Acts "Bound up with Badness"

Although it can happen that a person is non-culpably ignorant that the good he pursues is an apparent good and not the per se object of his own will, strictly speaking leading a virtuous life is a matter of being oriented toward the true good known to be such. In speaking of this orientation toward the true good, Aristotle often employs the language of archery and other aiming sports. In *EN* ii,6, 1106b6–7, for example, he compares virtue to an art which seeks [ζητεῖ] and chooses [αἱρεῖται] the mean [τὸ μέσον], and then he says that, since, like nature, virtue is even better and more accurate than any craft, it too must aim at the mean. The word he eventually uses, στοχαστική [1106b15–16], comes from the word στόχος denoting an aim or an aiming.[38] For Aristotle, a virtuous act involves an endeavor, at which someone might or might not succeed. The person who succeeds hits the center of an extended target. (One might think of a foot ruler, with a line drawn at the six-inch mark.)[39] The shot of the person who fails hits to one side or the other of the center: either on the defect or on the excess side. In this connection, Aristotle refers favorably to the

---

38 See also *EN* viii,8, 1159b19–23, where Aristotle opposes the idea that opposites aim at opposites; on the contrary, natures aim per se at the mean where the good is found: ἴσως δὲ οὐδ' ἐφίεται τὸ ἐναντίον τοῦ ἐναντίου καθ' αὑτό, ἀλλὰ κατὰ συμβεβηκός, ἡ δ' ὄρεξις τοῦ μέσου ἐστίν· τοῦτο γὰρ ἀγαθόν, οἷον τῷ ξηρῷ οὐχ ὑγρῷ γενέσθαι ἀλλ' ἐπὶ τὸ μέσον ἐλθεῖν, καὶ τῷ θερμῷ καὶ τοῖς ἄλλοις ὁμοίως. Aspasius says that Aristotle speaks here of humidity and dryness because of the example given at *EN* viii,1, 1155b2–4: Εὐριπίδης μὲν φάσκων ἐρᾶν μὲν ὄμβρου γαῖαν ξηρανθεῖσαν, ἐρᾶν δὲ σεμνὸν οὐρανὸν πληρούμενον ὄμβρου πεσεῖν ἐς γαῖαν....

39 In introducing this section on the mean, Aristotle writes, "In everything that is continuous and divisible [συνεχεῖ καὶ διαιρετῷ] it is possible to take more, less, or an equal amount—and that, either in terms of the thing itself or relatively to us; and the equal is an intermediate between excess and defect. By the intermediate in the object I mean that which is equidistant from each of the extremes, which is one and the same for all men; by the intermediate relatively to us that which is neither too much nor too little—and this is not one, nor the same for all" [*EN* ii,6, 1106a26–32, Revised Oxford Translation].

Pythagorian view that evil is unlimited, the good limited, since "there are many ways to miss [ἁμαρτάνειν—1106b28]," just one way to hit, the center.[40] One hits the center in so far as one is a person who not only performs virtuous acts but performs them knowledgeably, steadily, and for their own sakes (that is to say, per se).[41] Why someone should want to be virtuous requires no explanation: that is intelligible in itself. What is not intelligible in itself is vice; vice effects a break in the path that constitutes virtue and that leads to the true good.

The fact that the moral character of actions depends not just on intrinsic characteristics (the constituents, with the possible exception of the end) but also on how well they are aimed at something outside themselves obviously contributes to the difficulty of analyzing them. In *EN* ix,2, Aristotle poses a number of questions, such as, "whether one ought to render service to a friend rather than to a good man, and ought to show gratitude to a benefactor rather than to oblige a friend, if both are not possible" [1164b25–27] or whether "a man who has been ransomed from pirates ought to ransom his ransomer in return, whoever he may be (or, if the other has not been captured, ought he to pay the other when he requests payment), or should he ransom his father?" [1164b34–65a1]. Required in order to answer these questions properly is good aim, that is to say, φρόνησις, a certain facility in weighing the factors that intersect at a moment of decision. As Aristotle explains in *EN* ii,9, one becomes adept at hitting the mean where virtue lies by training one's interior movements:

> But we must consider the things towards which we ourselves also are easily carried away; for some of us tend to one thing, some to another; and this will be recognizable from the pleasure and the pain we feel. We must drag ourselves away to the contrary extreme; for we shall get into the intermediate state by drawing well away from error, as people do in straightening sticks that are bent.[42]

But even once the training is completed, shooting well is a contingent and tentative affair. The hands of the well-trained archer will trace out paths in

---

40 Aristotle continues to speak about hitting a target in *EN* ii,9; at the beginning of *EN* i,2, he speaks of aiming at the highest good: "Will not, therefore, knowledge of it be a great advantage? And ought we not, like archers who have a target, be more likely to hit upon what we should?" [1094a22–24].

41 ὁ πράττων πῶς ἔχων πράττῃ, πρῶτον μὲν ἐὰν εἰδώς, ἔπειτ᾽ ἐὰν προαιρούμενος, καὶ προαιρούμενος δι᾽ αὐτά, τὸ δὲ τρίτον ἐὰν καὶ βεβαίως καὶ ἀμετακινήτως ἔχων πράττῃ [*EN* ii,4, 1105a30–33].

42 *EN* ii,9, 1109b1–7 [Revised Oxford Translation].

the air before he fixes upon the target and lets loose the arrow: taking aim is all about movements and counter-pressures or counter-inclinations.[43] As such, it cannot be captured by the fixed formulae of mechanics. A similar thing can be said of the φρόνιμος, the well-trained deliberator.[44]

Although this passage from *EN* ix,2 is useful for understanding the fluidity of ethics, it also provides information about that fluidity's limits: the formal banks of the river, so to speak. Having run through questions of the type already mentioned (whether to ransom one's ransomer, etc.), Aristotle remarks: "As has been said many times, therefore, reasonings about passions and actions have a definability corresponding to their subject matter."[45] Aristotle states any number of times in the *Nicomachean Ethics* that ethics is characterized by a certain imprecision proper to itself, most of these remarks coming in the early books.[46] Here in *EN* ix,2 he is telling us what he had in mind in making those statements: reasonings involved in decisions such as whether to ransom one's ransomer or rather one's father. But this means that we are free to find stability and precision with respect to other matters.

What might these other matters be? The *EN* ix,2 passage provides a fairly obvious clue. As we have just seen, when speaking about the definability that pertains to the subject matter of ethics, Aristotle refers to "reasonings about passions and actions" [οἱ περὶ τὰ πάθη καὶ τὰς πράξεις λόγοι—*EN* ix,2, 1165a12–13].[47] Passions and actions are paired up relatively few times in *EN*.[48] Most of these pairings are in *EN* ii, where Aristotle sets out his theory of virtue and the doctrine of the mean. (All of the pair-

43 See *EN* vi,1, 1138b22–23, where Aristotle says that the man who possesses right reason "tightens and relaxes": ... ἔστι τις σκοπὸς πρὸς ὃν ἀποβλέπων ὁ τὸν λόγον ἔχων ἐπιτείνει καὶ ἀνίησιν .... See Alfonso Gómez-Lobo, "Aristotle's Right Reason," in *Aristotle, Virtue and the Mean*, ed. Richard Bosley, Roger A. Shiner, and Janet D. Sisson (Edmonton, Alberta: Academic Printing & Publishing, 1996), 24–26. Gómez-Lobo points out that Grant "saw long ago" that the terms 'tightening' and 'relaxing' are taken from the field of music. "'Ἐπιτείνει καὶ ἀνίησιν is a metaphor from tuning the strings of a lyre" [Grant, *The Ethics of Aristotle*, ii,147].

44 On φρόνησις and the φρόνιμος, see below, chapter 7.

45 περ οὖν πολλάκις εἴρηται, οἱ περὶ τὰ πάθη καὶ τὰς πράξεις λόγοι ὁμοίως ἔχουσι τὸ ὡρισμένον τοῖς περὶ ἅ εἰσιν [1165a12–14].

46 See, for instance, *EN* i,3, 1094b11–27; i,4, 1095a30–b3; i,7, 1098a26–b8; ii,2, 1103b34–1104a10; and ii,9, 1109b20–26.

47 A similar phrase occurs at *EN* x,1, 1172a34.

48 *EN* ii,3, 1104b14; ii,3, 1105a3–4; ii,6, 1106b16; ii,6, 1106b24; ii,6, 1107a4; ii,6, 1107a8–9; ii,7, 1108a31; ii,8, 1108b18–19; ii,9, 1109a23; iii,1, 1109b30; iii,1, 1111b1–2; v,4, 1132a9; ix,2, 1165a13; x,1, 1172a34–35.

ings have something to do with virtue and the development of character.) In one of these passages (in *EN* ii,6), Aristotle makes a remark that has been controversial since ancient times.[49] It runs as follows:

> But not every action [πρᾶξις] nor every passion [πάθος] admits of a mean; for some as soon as they have been named are bound up with badness, e.g. spite, shamelessness, envy, and in the case of actions adultery, theft, murder; for all of these and such like things—and not the excesses or deficiencies of them—are called what they are called because they themselves are bad. It is not possible, therefore, ever to go right with regard to them; one must always go wrong.[50]

A slight over-translation of the last line, but one paying closer attention to the language Aristotle has employed just previously (i.e., at 1106b27–33: στοχαστική, ἁμαρτάνειν, κατορθοῦν, σκοποῦ), would run as follows: "It is not possible, therefore, ever to *shoot* straight with regard to them; one must always miss" [1107a14–15]. When in *EN* ix,2 Aristotle implicitly delimits ethics' inherent imprecision, it makes sense to connect that passage with this one in which such limits are explicitly discussed.

Aristotle's saying in this passage that the names of certain things are "bound up with badness" has sometimes been used to argue that he is saying that the badness of the things mentioned is solely a matter of naming, that there are no particular passions or actions which, independently of the names eventually used of them, can be characterized as bad. Murder, for instance, is just killing that has been assigned a name with a negative connotation. This issue is a complicated one, so we cannot go into it extensively here;[51] but it is clear, even from what we have just seen, that Aris-

---

49 See "the Old Scholiast": Anonymous, *In Ethica Nicomachea II–V commentaria*, vol. 20 of *Commentaria in Aristotelem Graeca*, ed. Gustavus Heylbut (Berlin: Reimer, 1892), 142.7–14. The latter is a comment on *EN* iii,1, 1110a19–23; but reference is made to adultery (τὸ μιγῆναι ἀλλοτρίᾳ γυναικί—142.11) and this would seem to be a reference to *EN* ii,6, 1107a11. See also W. F. R. Hardie, *Aristotle's Ethical Theory* (Oxford: Clarendon Press, 1968), 137.

50 πᾶσα δ' ἐπιδέχεται πρᾶξις οὐδὲ πᾶν πάθος τὴν μεσότητα· ἔνια γὰρ εὐθὺς ὠνόμασται συνειλημμένα μετὰ τῆς φαυλότητος, οἷον ἐπιχαιρεκακία ἀναισχυντία φθόνος, καὶ ἐπὶ τῶν πράξεων μοιχεία κλοπὴ ἀνδροφονία· πάντα γὰρ ταῦτα καὶ τὰ τοιαῦτα λέγεται τῷ αὐτὰ φαῦλα εἶναι, ἀλλ' οὐχ αἱ ὑπερβολαὶ αὐτῶν οὐδ' αἱ ἐλλείψεις. οὐκ ἔστιν οὖν οὐδέποτε περὶ αὐτὰ κατορθοῦν, ἀλλ' ἀεὶ ἁμαρτάνειν ... [*EN* ii,6, 1107a8–15]. There is a parallel passage at *EE* ii,3, 1221b18–26.

51 I go into the issue extensively elsewhere: see Kevin L. Flannery, "Moral Taxonomy and Moral Absolutes," in *Wisdom's Apprentice: Thomistic Essays in Honor of Lawrence Dewan, O.P.*, ed. Peter A. Kwasniewski (Washington, DC: The Catholic University of America Press, 2007), 237–59, especially 241–44.

totle's *concern* in *EN* ii,6 is not with the names of bad passions and actions but with how such things fit into the scheme he has set out just previously (with how such things fit, that is, into the scheme according to which a man is virtuous to the extent that his typical "shot" comes close to the mean). And Aristotle's point is that the passions and actions mentioned do not fit into the scheme at all.

When the 'that in which it consists' of an act is basically good—one's giving one's property to another, for instance—it is still an issue whether one "aims" that act well or badly. There are extravagant givers and there are those who are too stingy. But if the property one gives is not one's own, one cannot help but "miss" the mark, since such acts have not even the possibility of going forward to their corresponding good measure in ethical reality.[52] As Aristotle says at the beginning of our passage (1107a8–9), they do not admit of a mean; indeed, they do not even admit of a target. It is not as if a person shoots to the left, to the right, above or below the target; rather, the fundamental nature of such an act is such that it cannot even begin to go toward the target in its particular sector of ethics. The act has no intelligibility as a good act of that type, that is, an act aimed at the appropriate target. Think of an "arrow" that is so constituted that it cannot go toward a target. Aristotle would say that this is an arrow only by homonymy since arrows per se go toward targets.[53] The same might be said of the actions in Aristotle's list in the performance of which "one must always go wrong": qua things aimed at their respective means, they have no intelligibility, for they are *not* so aimed.

Aristotle connects all this with the constituents. Just after the remarks quoted above (i.e., the remarks about the impossibility of ever going right regarding certain things), Aristotle continues to expatiate upon things that are intrinsically bad: "Nor with respect to such things are 'the well and the not well' in the 'whom,' 'when' and 'how' one debauches, but sim-

---

52 Aristotle mentions the goods of others in such a context at *EN* iv,1, 1121b23–24. See also *Rhet.* i,9, 1366b7–11: " ... liberal people let their money go instead of fighting for it, whereas other people care more for money than for anything else. Justice is the excellence through which everybody enjoys his own possessions in accordance with the law; its opposite is injustice, through which men enjoy the possessions of others in defiance of the law" [Revised Oxford Translation].

53 On this sort of homonymy, see *Metaph.* vii,10, 1035b24–25; also *Generation of Animals* i,19, 726b22ff.

ply to do any of them is to go wrong."[54] Clearly, Aristotle has in mind here the constituents (which he will only introduce formally in the next book). The first of the constituents mentioned is 'whom' (or 'which woman': ἥν), which is associated, as we have argued, with the subject matter of the action.[55] In this case, the subject matter of the act is corrupted because of 'the whom,' for a man's act of sexual intercourse cannot be moral if its object is the wife of another. Since the subject matter of an action is one of the two "most important" constituents [*EN* iii,1, 1111a18–19], 'the what' (τί) that is done comes to so lack intelligibility that the act cannot possibly be the type of act that a φρόνιμος might aim (or shoot) at the appropriate target. So, talk of other more minor constituents, such as 'when' and 'how,' is beside the point.

But also beside the point, says Aristotle, is 'whom' (ἥν) the adulterer has intercourse with—that is, the *particular* object of his act—given that, whoever she is, she is the wife of another. If Russell commits adultery, it makes no difference whether she is the wife of Morrell or the wife of Malleson. This shows that the subject matter of a particular act of adultery, although made concrete by a particular object (the wife of some other man), brings into play the intelligibility of the type of act engaged in. The subject matter of an act of conjugal intercourse is 'wife,' which bears with itself all the intellectual and legal baggage of what it means to be a wife; and, of course, a man does not engage in conjugal intercourse in the absence of the appropriate object: his wife. But when Russell commits adultery, the fundamental problem is not the particular woman with whom he has intercourse (the wife of Morrell or the wife of Malleson), although she, bound up as she is in the subject matter, gives the act its species (εἶδος); the problem is that she, whoever she is, is the wife of another. This corrupts the act at its very heart. It is clear, then, that the analysis of such a human action has essentially to do with intelligibility, the intelligibility in this case coming from what we might call "actual wifeness" (that subject matter). When this very fundamental constituent is corrupted, 'the what' that is done is also corrupted. The act cannot have any of the intelligibility of aiming at the target of sexual temperance and propriety.

---

54 δ' ἔστι τὸ εὖ ἢ μὴ εὖ περὶ τὰ τοιαῦτα ἐν τῷ ἥν δεῖ καὶ ὅτε καὶ ὡς μοιχεύειν, ἀλλ' ἁπλῶς τὸ ποιεῖν ὁτιοῦν τούτων ἁμαρτάνειν ἐστίν [*EN* ii,6, 1107a15–17].

55 See chapter 4, section VII.

Another example of a type of act that goes irredeemably awry would be lying. In *EN* iv,7, Aristotle says that "falsehood is per se foul and reprehensible; the truth, [per se] noble and praiseworthy."[56] Although in this section Aristotle is speaking about the falsehoods involved in boasting or in mock-modesty, his point here has simply to do with telling falsehoods versus telling the truth.[57] The first (τὸ ψεῦδος: falsehood) lacks intelligibility—a person's ability to speak has as its natural object not falsehood but truth—and is therefore per se bad; the second (τὸ ἀληθὲς: truth) is perfectly intelligible in itself and is therefore per se good.[58]

V. Intelligible Decision

Toward the beginning of the previous section, we considered *EN* ix,2, where Aristotle identifies the type of imprecision he had in mind in the several passages where he says that ethics is subject to it. That passage pointed us to the passage in *EN* ii,6, where Aristotle says that certain actions—adultery, theft, murder—are always bad. The latter makes it apparent that, despite ethics' imprecision, we can say with perfect assurance that certain actions are always immoral. Aristotle, however, does not believe that the only clarity and precision available in ethics is that having to do with absolute moral prohibitions. So, before moving on to other matters, it will be best to say a brief word about *EN* ix,2, showing that, even

---

56 αθ' αὐτὸ δὲ τὸ μὲν ψεῦδος φαῦλον καὶ ψεκτόν, τὸ δ' ἀληθὲς καλὸν καὶ ἐπαινετόν [*EN* iv,7, 1127a28–30].

57 C. C. W. Taylor says that Aristotle in this chapter "restricts honesty to telling the truth about one's own merits" [C. C. W. Taylor, *Aristotle:* Nicomachean Ethics, *Books II–IV*, Clarendon Aristotle Series (Oxford: Clarendon, 2006), xviii]. I do not dispute this, although I do think that the statement at 1127a28–30 is not so restricted. See Kevin L. Flannery, "Being Truthful with (or Lying to) Others about Oneself," in *Thomas Aquinas and the Nicomachean Ethics*, ed. Tobias Hoffmann, Jörn Müller, and Matthias Perkams (Cambridge: Cambridge University Press, 2013).

58 At *EN* vii,2, 1146a18–21, Aristotle suggests that it is wrong to lie even in order to protect the interests of the Greeks and the life of Odysseus. He recalls that, in Sophocles's play *Philoctetes*, Odysseus asks Neoptolemus to lie to Philoctetes about his relationship with Greeks, saying that they had betrayed him (Neoptolemus). Neoptolemus replies, "What are you inciting me to do, except to tell a falseshood?" (Τί οὖν μ' ἄνωγας ἄλλο πλὴν ψευδῆ λέγειν; (*Philoctetes*, line 100; Paul Masqueray, ed. and trans., *Sophocle* [Paris: Société d'Édition 'Les Belles Lettres,' 1922–24], II,83). See also *EN* vi,2, 1139a26–29: αὕτη μὲν οὖν ἡ διάνοια καὶ ἡ ἀλήθεια πρακτική· τῆς δὲ θεωρητικῆς διανοίας καὶ μὴ πρακτικῆς μηδὲ ποιητικῆς τὸ εὖ καὶ κακῶς τἀληθές ἐστι καὶ ψεῦδος (τοῦτο γάρ ἐστι παντὸς διανοητικοῦ ἔργον).... See also *EN* vi,3, 1139b14–17 and *Metaph.* v,29, 1025a1–13. (The latter passage is discussed below, in chapter 7.)

there, and with respect to the very cases he says resist precision, Aristotle does not exclude genuine knowledge of the moral truth. We will come back to these issues in chapter 7, where we consider the φρόνιμος, who aims at and hits infallibly the target of virtuous action.

EN ix,2 begins with a series of three quite independent questions: whether one ought always to prefer and to obey one's father; whether, when ill, one should place one's confidence in a doctor; whether a city ought to choose as general someone with experience in battle. None of these questions seems intractably difficult. A bit further on, Aristotle poses some more difficult questions (the questions mentioned above): "whether one ought to render service to a friend rather than to a good man, and ought to show gratitude to a benefactor rather than to oblige a friend, if both are not possible" [1164b25–27]. Then Aristotle asks whether it is possible to decide [διορίσαι—1164b28] such matters with precision: "for this involves many and assorted differences of greatness and smallness [μεγέθει καὶ μικρότητι], nobility and necessity" [1164b28–29].

Aristotle clearly regards some of his questions as answerable, for he gives the answers himself. He says at EN ix,2, 1164b30–31: "That we ought not to give the preference to the same person always is not unclear." This is an answer to the first question in EN ix,2, whether one ought *always* to prefer and obey one's father.[59] Immediately afterwards, he says: "And we ought for the most part to reciprocate benefactions rather than to oblige friends ..." [1164b31–32]. Even the question whether a man who has been ransomed from pirates ought to ransom his ransomer or rather his father [1164b34–65a1] seems to admit of a definite answer for Aristotle: "For it would seem [he should prefer] his father even over himself" [1165a1–2]. It is not wholly clear what Aristotle means by this. The point seems to be that the man should ransom his father rather than ransom himself,[60] but that is not at issue: the man has already been ransomed. So, it would appear that Aristotle is saying that in this situation the man should prefer helping his father over helping himself by satisfying his benefactor. In either case, however, it is clear that Aristotle does not believe that, even in

---

59 The adverbial use of πάντα occurs both at 1164b23 and here at 1164b30.
60 Irwin translates 1165a1–2 [δόξειε γὰρ ἂν καὶ ἑαυτοῦ μᾶλλον τὸν πατέρα], "Here it seems that you should ransom your father, rather than even yourself."

such a difficult case, a correct answer to the moral question is beyond the realm of possibilities. Indeed, near the end of *EN* ix,2, following a series of similar questions about what is due to family members and close acquaintances, he remarks:

> The comparison is easier when the persons belong to the same class, and more laborious when they are different. Yet we must not on that account shrink from the task, but decide the question as best we can.[61]

At *EN* ix,2, 1165a7–10, Aristotle says that sometimes it is not necessary that one lend to someone who has lent to oneself in the past. "For one person lends to an upright man believing that he will be repaid; the other has no hope of being repaid (by an evil man)." In the case under consideration in the latter phrase ("the other has no hope ..."), a good man has paid back a presumably evil man who has lent money to him but feels no obligation to also lend to him since in that case repayment is unlikely. Aristotle then remarks: "If matters are truly thus, the request [to reciprocate] is not fair; if they are not thus but people *think* they are, to act in this way would not appear to be absurd" [1165a10–12]. The idea behind the second clause here would seem to be that, if one has reason to believe that the other is evil and therefore unreliable but this belief is not well founded—let us say that one has been fed lies about the other person—even still, refusing the loan would be justified.[62] Immediately after this example, Aristotle makes the remark we saw above: "As has been said many times, therefore, reasonings about passions and actions have a definability corresponding to their subject matter" [1165a12–14].

Aristotle's general position in this passage would seem, therefore, to be twofold: first, that, even if the information one has at one's disposal is inaccurate—it would indeed be impossible to have knowledge of all relevant factors before deciding a question—one can still decide well; secondly, that, if one does have all the relevant information, the φρόνιμος can and does make perfectly sound decisions.[63] That sometimes wise de-

---

61 *EN* ix,2, 1165a33–35 [Revised Oxford Translation].
62 Of course, one's ignorance of relevant factors must not be culpable ignorance; see above, chapter 4, section I.
63 At *EN* ii,6, 1106b14 Aristotle speaks of the aim of virtue as "more accurate than any craft."

cisions are the wrong decisions is due to the contingent nature of human affairs. The realm of ethics is fluid, but true statements can be made about it and wise decisions within it. We might add that, if in the world there exists the perfect φρόνιμος, his decisions and choices, even when they lead to undesirable consequences—that is to say, even when there is a break of intelligibility between what he had in mind and what transpires—will be consistent with the good for man. Ethically speaking, he will live in a wholly intelligible way. But these are matters to be discussed in chapter 7.

VI. Conclusion

The ethical analysis of human action involves, therefore, the many factors discussed previously in this work, especially in chapters 3 and 4, which dealt with how force and an agent's knowledge of his own action's constituents influence the voluntary. But ethical analysis proper begins when the scope of concern widens to include the correspondence (or lack of correspondence) between what an agent himself contributes to an action (his knowledge of its constituents, his way of conceiving the good pursued in performing such an action, etc.) and the true good, the end of human nature. The "properly ethical" concerns aiming well and hitting the target of good behavior, that is to say, behavior in accordance with human nature. There are certain actions, however, that do not admit of being aimed well; to perform them is always to go wrong.

Conceiving of the ethical in this way, in terms of aiming and hitting (or not hitting) the mark, is to conceive it along the lines depicted in chapter 2, where the "whence and the whither" of human movements was so prominent. But there is another side to ethics which is much less dynamic and directional. It has to do rather with the stabile structures of practical reason and of the ethical sphere. We turn to these matters in the next chapter (chapter 6).

Six

Action, Φρόνησις, and Pleasure

IN CHAPTER 5, especially in sections III and IV, we were concerned with an important aspect of Aristotle's philosophical psychology of action: the way in which behaving virtuously is very often a matter of taking aim at the target (the mean) determined by right reason. This approach is of a piece with ideas set out in chapter 2, where we argued that human acts share the basic structure of physical movements, as depicted in the *Physics*. A human act has, in some sense, "a whence and a whither": its intrinsic orientation is toward its own object and ultimately toward the good. But this same approach will not do as a complete account of what must be factored into the moral analysis of acts. Moral action cannot be reduced *simply* to aiming, which is essentially the act of the individual agent. If everything were reduced to aiming, it would be as if every time an agent performed a human act the moral universe was reinvented—and reinvented from within the agent.

To employ once again (as in chapter 5) the analogy of archery, aiming at a target is a matter of perceiving and internally counterbalancing pressures. Considered from this perspective, archery is certainly the archer's own activity: not the following of instructions written in a manual but rather doing something for which, through practice, the archer has acquired a personal proficiency. But acquiring such a proficiency presupposes a context. Archery, although an art and therefore an intellectual thing, is not completely free-floating but exists in a physical world governed by laws: the laws pertaining to gravity and air pressure, to the fatigue of muscles and bow strings, and so on. Also part of this context are sheer facts, such as the fact that the target is set up in a particular place relative to other objects, that the wind is of a certain force and from a certain direction, etc., etc. In an analogous way, human actions presuppose an objective moral universe. We acknowledged this to some extent in chapter 5, where we discussed Aristotle's assertion in *EN* ii,6 that certain actions—adultery, theft, and murder—are always bad; but that cannot be all there is to say about the moral context of human action, for deliberation about what is the moral thing to do is not only a matter of avoiding absolute prohibitions. The result of a good deliberation is an act (possibly an omission) that is in accordance with right reason. Actions can be unreasonable in this sense, and therefore immoral, even if they do not go against an absolute prohibition.

In section I of the present chapter, we return to *Metaph.* ix,6, where Aristotle draws the distinction between movements (κινήσεις) and actions (πράξεις). There are passages, especially in the *Nicomachean Ethics*, where he appears to ignore this distinction, thereby falling into apparent contradiction. But there is a way of reading the pertinent remarks in a consistent manner. What then is the point of the distinction in *Metaph.* ix,6? We suggest that Aristotle is calling attention there to the fact that genuine human acts involve knowledge—that which makes all the difference between genuinely human acts and the things that other animals do. In section II, we argue that this way of understanding the movement-action [κίνησις-πρᾶξις] distinction (which, for present purposes, is equivalent to the making-action [ποίησις-πρᾶξις] distinction) allows us to grasp how the city (the πόλις) holds together as a whole. As a moral entity, the city comprises actions pertaining to one regular pattern of human behavior or another. The various human crafts are especially important such patterns. As Aristotle says in any number of places, the actions proper to the crafts are makings: they are actions that find their completion in products. But such actions fit into the city not in so far as they are makings but in so far as they are understood.

In section III, we consider where in the physics of a movement knowledge might fit. Remarks in *Phys.* viii,5 and *Metaph.* ix,8 suggest that its place is in the first non-extended point from which a movement emerges. In section IV, we consider much the same problematic, but from within Aristotle's psychology, as set out especially in *de An.* ii,5. There Aristotle speaks of the housebuilder as unaltered "when he builds," the point being that he remains unaltered qua one in possession of the art of building. In effect, then, he shows us why even movements or makings, as long as they are effected by humans who know what they are doing, are actions. *De An.* ii,5 also connects this idea with human freedom. Knowledge, Aristotle says, is of universals, which are already in the soul, and so the person who knows is free to think "when he wills to."

In section V, we take a further step into properly ethical territory by depicting the way in which Aristotle distinguishes φρόνησις from crafts such as building. He maintains in *EN* vi that φρόνησις rules over the other human activities (such as crafts), not as an end rules over means to itself, but as an end might be intrinsic to—but also more extensive than—other ends. Distinctive about φρόνησις, however, is not just its generality but also its relationship with pleasure—or, more precisely, its connection with the higher or calmer pleasures. An appreciation for the calmer pleasures is a mark of the good man, as distinct from those character types who fall short of φρόνησις. The remainder of the present chapter (that is, sections VI and VII) is taken up, therefore, with a discussion of pleasure. The ideas presented in these sections will be useful in chapter 7, where we discuss the φρόνιμος, but especially in chapter 8, where we discuss some other character types.

I. *Ripresa variata:* Movement and Action

The matters before us concern, therefore, the relationship between knowledge (which, considered as such, does not move) and human action of the type readily analyzed according to the movement model. We encountered this juxtaposition of concepts in chapter 2, section IV, where we looked at *Metaph.* ix,6, 1048b18ff., a passage often interpreted as Aristotle's disqualification of movements as actions. The examples of movements used in *Metaph.* ix,6 are "making thin, learning, walking, building" [1048b29–30]. The ends of movements are not yet present while one is engaged in them: "... one journeys and has journeyed not at the same time, nor does one build and has built" [1048b30–33]. As Aristotle explains more fully in *Phys.* iii,3, learning (or teaching) is a movement that goes from the teacher to the student.[1] Actions, on the other hand, would include seeing, thinking, and understanding [1048b23–24], which are complete in themselves: "it is the same thing that at the same time has seen and sees, or thinks and has thought" [1048b33–34].[2]

One finds a similar idea in *EN* vi,5. Before this chapter, Aristotle has been concerned to show how human action and the pursuit of virtue fit into reason in its various forms. In *EN* vi,2, he excludes from the scope of his concerns the things that animals do; mere animals, he says, have sensation but have no share in action [πράξεως δὲ μὴ κοινωνεῖν—1139a20]. In *EN* vi,5, he discusses practical wisdom [φρόνησις], which, he says, participates in reason but is to be distinguished from scientific knowledge [ἐπιστήμη]. It is also, he says, to be distinguished from craft [τέχνη], "for the genus of action [πράξεως] is different from that of making [ποιήσεως] [1140b4–5]. At this point, Aristotle makes the remark reminiscent of *Metaph.* ix,6:

What is left, therefore, is that [φρόνησις] is a true state, accompanied by reason and ordered toward action, regarding the things that are good or bad for man. For making has an end other than itself, but action can have none such, since good conduct is itself an end. [*EN* vi,5, 1140b4–7]

Like the remarks in *Metaph.* ix,6, these remarks appear to distinguish sharply between action [πρᾶξις] strictly speaking and any sort of action (such as a "making" [ποίησις]) in which a distinct object might be discerned and about which, therefore, a person might deliberate, how to get *to* that object.

But there is a problem. In *EN* iii, and in other places, Aristotle recog-

---

1 See chapter 2, section I.
2 We also noted in chapter 2 (section III) that, while Aristotle somewhat reluctantly recognizes something like the movement-structure in phenomena such as seeing and thinking, he insists that the direction of the "movement" is from the object to the relevant faculty (the faculty of seeing or of thinking). See above, chapter 2, note 38.

nizes the place of deliberation in action, that is, the place of deliberation for distinct ends. He says, for example, as a partial conclusion to the argumentation of chapter *EN* iii,3, the following:

> It seems, therefore, as was said, that man is the first principle of actions. Deliberation is about the things to be done by an agent himself, and actions [πράξεις] are for the sake of things other than themselves. [*EN* iii,3, 1112b31–33]

This certainly sounds like a contradiction of the idea that actions are distinct from makings (and suchlike actions) in so far as they do not have ends other than themselves [*EN* vi,5, 1140b6–7]. This has led commentators to say that Aristotle is simply confused in this regard. Gauthier, for instance, says that in *EN* iii,3 Aristotle "maladroitly applies to moral action ideas developed earlier on in order to explicate productive activity."[3] Gauthier clearly prefers the idea that the moral has to do just with what is chosen for itself, to the exclusion of makings.[4]

There is a simple—and perfectly valid—way of resolving this controversy. In the *Metaph.* ix,6 passage—which is his most extensive discussion of the issue—Aristotle does not refuse to call movements (and such things) actions but says rather that they are *imperfect* actions. The opening line of the passage in question reads:

---

3 René-Antoine Gauthier and Jean Yves Jolif, *L'Éthique à Nicomaque*, 2.1 199. See also 2.1 203–4 (on *EN* iii,3, 1112b33), where Gauthier says that Aristotle risks compromising "l'originalité qu'il a ailleurs reconnue à l'action morale; il en arrive ici à se contredire formellement, en déniant expressément à l'action (πρᾶξις) l'immanence dans laquelle il avait reconnu sa caractéristique propre, et en lui attribuant une fin extérieure à elle-même, ce qui partout ailleurs est la caractéristique propre de la production (ποίησις) ...." (Charles discusses this remark at David Charles, *Aristotle's Philosophy of Action*, 65.)

4 In commenting upon *EN* vi,5, 1140b3–4, Gauthier explains how he understands Aristotle's development in this regard. Early on in his career, Aristotle developed the "artistic production" language ("... l'analyse aristotélicienne de l'action semble avoir été primitivement une analyse de la production artistique ..."), from which he never really freed himself [Gauthier and Jolif, *L'Éthique à Nicomaque*, 2.2 472]. See also René-Antoine Gauthier, *La morale d'Aristote* (Paris: Presses universitaires de France, 1958), 32–33, where Gauthier depicts Aristotle's distinction between πρᾶξις and ποίησις as a reaction to Plato and Prodicus, although he acknowledges that the distinction is found in one of the earliest Aristotelian works we have (see *Top.* vi,6, 145a15–18). So, although Gauthier recognizes that Aristotle made the πρᾶξις-ποίησις distinction early on, he maintains that he had the unfortunate tendency of slipping back into Platonic formulations. D. J. Allan tells a similar story about Aristotle's relationship with Plato in this regard, discussing especially *Phaedrus* 268A8ff. [Donald J. Allan, "The Practical Syllogism," in *Autour d'Aristote: Recueil d'études de philosophie ancienne et médiévale, offert à Monseigneur A. Mansion*, Bibliothèque Philosophique de Louvain, vol. 16 (Louvain: Publications universitaires de Louvain, 1955), 331–32].

Since (1) of the actions [τῶν πράξεων] which have a limit none is the end itself but all are relative to the end, e.g. of 'to thin,' 'making thin,' and since (2) the things themselves, when one is thinning in such a way that they are in movement, are not that at which the movement aims, *these* are not the action or at least not the complete one (for there is no end), but in *that* exists the end (that is, [in] the action).[5]

As we argued in chapter 2, section IV, the upshot of the larger argument in *Metaph*. ix,6 is that the intelligibility of a movement *as* an action is in its end rather than in the stages that lead to the end.[6] But, although this resolves the controversy regarding the seeming inconsistency between *EN* iii,3 and *EN* vi,5, to leave the matter thus would be to neglect the deeper issue. What is it that makes movements and makings to be actions? Why is it that, contrary to what Gauthier suggests, Aristotle is willing to associate movements and makings with actions proper and on what grounds does he make the association? Addressing such questions helps us to see how Aristotle manages to combine "whence and whither" analysis with the other more static characteristics of the moral universe.

Aristotle's basic idea in this regard is that, to the extent that an agent (including the artist and the "maker" [ὁ ποιῶν]) *understands* what he does while he is doing it—or we could even, making allusion to his remarks in *Metaph*. ix,6, speak of his "seeing" the sense of what he does while he is doing it—he is performing an action.[7] A housebuilder, for instance, although his house will be finished only next week, knows all the while he is building that he is building a house, how it is done, etc. Although (as we saw in

---

5 πεὶ δὲ τῶν πράξεων ὧν ἐστι πέρας οὐδεμία τέλος (ἀλλὰ τῶν περὶ τὸ τέλος, οἷον τοῦ ἰσχναίνειν ἡ ἰσχνασία) αὐτό, αὐτὰ δὲ ὅταν ἰσχναίνῃ οὕτως ἐστὶν ἐν κινήσει μὴ ὑπάρχοντα ὧν ἕνεκα ἡ κίνησις, οὐκ ἔστι ταῦτα πρᾶξις ἢ οὐ τελεία γε (οὐ γὰρ τέλος)· ἀλλ' ἐκείνῃ ἐνυπάρχει τὸ τέλος (καὶ ἡ πρᾶξις) [*Metaph*. ix,6, 1048b18–23]. On this piece of text, see Appendix 1 ("On the text of *Metaph*. ix,6, 1048b18–35").

6 At *EE* i,7, 1217a35–46, Aristotle also speaks of means as πράξεις; indeed, he is willing to extend the term also to the ends pursued by these means: "But since 'practicable' is ambiguous—for both the things for the sake of which we act and the things we do for their sake participate in action (thus we place among the practicables both health and wealth, as well as the things done for the sake of them: healthy actions and lucrative actions)—it is clear that we must consider happiness the best of human practicables" [ἐπειδὴ δὲ διχῶς λέγεται τὸ πρακτόν (καὶ γὰρ ὧν ἕνεκα πράττομεν καὶ ἃ τούτων ἕνεκα μετέχει πράξεως, οἷον καὶ τὴν ὑγίειαν καὶ τὸν πλοῦτον τίθεμεν τῶν πρακτῶν, καὶ τὰ τούτων πραττόμενα χάριν, τά θ' ὑγιεινὰ καὶ τὰ χρηματιστικά), δῆλον ὅτι καὶ τὴν εὐδαιμονίαν τῶν ἀνθρώπῳ πρακτῶν ἄριστον θετέον].

7 See on this point Mary Louise Gill, "Aristotle's Theory of Causal Action in *Physics* iii,3," 136.

chapter 2, section IV) the full intelligibility of building comes only at the end (with the completed house), the housebuilder has that idea in mind from the beginning—and that aspect of his action is never in motion.[8] It is this knowledge that allows him to say at any moment in the course of his building that he *has been* building, just as (according to *Metaph.* ix,6) the man who understands (or sees) can say that he has understood (or has seen). The builder cannot say that he has built—that is to say, that he has built a house—but he has certainly been engaged in building. Presumably an animal such as beaver, although he might build what we might call a 'house' for himself, could never say to himself any such thing, that is, that he has been building or that he has been building a house.

II. Crafts and the Organization of the City

The knowledge that an artisan, such as a housebuilder, has regarding his own activity qua practitioner of his proper craft makes him an integral part of the city. Aristotle's philosophical psychology is not just a psychology of individuals but also (as is Plato's *Republic*) a psychology of the city.[9] To use again the image used earlier, even if aiming is done by individual archers, their aiming is effected within a larger context that includes the physical world in which archers find themselves and also the art of archery itself. Similarly, according to Aristotle, any human act is performed within the context of the city. The city has physical properties and limits, of course, but even more important from an ethical point of view is the way in which it is organized.

The opening words of the *Nicomachean Ethics* run famously as follows: "Every craft and every inquiry, and similarly every action and choice, appears to aim at some good; and so with reason the good has been said to be that at which all things aim" [*EN* i,1, 1094a1–3]. Aristotle goes on then to say that all of these things—crafts and inquiries, actions and choices—

---

8 In saying that the builder "has that idea in mind," I do not mean to suggest that he is building only while 'building' or 'house' is held before his mind's eye; my point is only that his building is done knowingly. See G. E. M. Anscombe, *Intention* (Cambridge: Harvard University Press, 2000), passim.

9 See *R.* ii, 368C8–369A4; iv,435A6–436A3. See also Richard Robinson, "Plato's Separation of Reason and Desire," *Phronesis* 16 (1971): 38–48, and Kevin L. Flannery, "Robinson's Łukasiewiczian *Republic* IV,435–439," *Gregorianum* 77 (1996): 705–26.

fall under the science of politics, which "determines which of the sciences are required in the cities, and which sciences individuals should learn and up to what point; and we see also the most highly esteemed of capacities falling under this science, for instance, strategy, economics, and rhetoric ..." [*EN* i,2, 1094a28–b3]. So, for Aristotle, a city is not a random collection of acts aimed at individual—that is to say, individualistic—ends, but an assembly of acts defined by their ends (and their other relevant constituents), which themselves fall under the ends that define the sciences, crafts, etc., which in turn fall under the highest end, whatever that might be and however it might be pursued (see *EN* i,1, 1094a6–16).

How this system of interconnected actions and ends holds together is itself connected with the action-making distinction, as we have been expounding it. An individual action within a discipline may be a making (and therefore aimed at an end other than itself), but it is an action of that particular discipline in so far as, qua action of that discipline, it is pursued for its own sake.

In *Phys.* ii,8, Aristotle speaks of a relationship of imitation between crafts and nature. The relationship is reciprocal: craft ("art") imitates nature and nature imitates craft.[10] The latter idea is often deemed especially problematic. As long as one does not suggest that nature has ends it sets out to accomplish, it is all right to say that a craftsman sets out to do such things as nature "does"; but, it is objected, it is nonsense to suggest that nature, when it does what it does, sets out, like a craftsman, to accomplish what it would. This objection is subverted, however, by Aristotle's clarification that he is not talking about the craftsman but his craft—such as

---

10 "Moreover, where there is an end, that which came first and that which follows are for the sake of that. As in action, therefore, so in nature; and as in nature, so in each action, provided nothing interferes. But action is for some purpose; so also, therefore, is nature for some purpose. For instance, if a house were among the things coming to be by nature, it would have come to be in the same way as it does now by craft [τέχνη]; but if things coming to be by nature were to come to be not just by nature but also by craft, they would come to be in the same way as by nature. One thing is, therefore, for the sake of the other. In general, craft completes some things that nature cannot bring to completion; other things it imitates. If, therefore, things coming to be by craft are for the sake of something, it is clear that so also are things coming to be by nature, for in things by craft and in things by nature the relation of later to earlier stages is the same" [*Phys.* ii,8, 199a8–20]. Ross's comments on this passage include the following: "Art [τέχνη] partly completes and partly imitates the work of nature; therefore, if art is purposive, so is nature; for the later stages are related similarly to the earlier in art and in nature" [W. D. Ross, *Aristotle's Physics*, 357].

does not "set out" to do anything. "It is absurd to suppose that something comes about for no purpose because one does not see the mover deliberating. The fact is that even craft does not deliberate" [*Phys.* ii,8, 199b26–28].[11] For Aristotle, the reciprocal relationship of imitation between craft and nature has nothing to do with deliberating but with having a purpose: a proper end; so there is nothing preventing nature's imitating craft, as well as craft's imitating nature.

Since a craft itself does not deliberate, its end becomes difficult to distinguish from its form (that is to say, what the craft is). Indeed, Aristotle maintains that the presence of the end in both a craft and a natural kind *is* the presence of the form. "Since nature is twofold, as matter and as form, and the latter is the end, and everything else is for the sake of the end, form must be the cause, that is, the final cause" [*Phys.* ii,8, 199a30–32]. In either case—in nature and in craft—the end is not posited as something to be brought into existence; it is already there, as form. This is not to deny, of course, that a craft only eventually turns out a product or that the generation of an animal (for instance) occurs at the end of a process; the point is rather that the end of the craft that turns out the product and of the generation that finishes in an animal is present throughout either process. This is what makes building a house part of the craft of building and the generation of an animal *animal* generation.

In understanding the organization of a city, of crucial importance is this way in which crafts encompass—as form and as end—the actions that occur within them. Consider for example a medical procedure to straighten out a patient's leg, and let us presume too that medicine itself is defined by the end, 'the health of the patient.' Such an operation is clearly a making: its end, the straightened leg, is quite a different thing from the procedure itself, and the making is complete (fully present) only once the operation is finished. But, as we have just seen, all during the procedure the end 'the health of the patient' is present—which is just to say that all during

---

11 "The builder as such cannot want to build houses in any sense in which wanting to build houses could explain building by *the builder*" [Sarah Broadie, "Nature and Craft in Aristotelian Teleology," in *Biologie, logique et metaphysique chez Aristote*, ed. D. Devereux and P. Pellegrin (Paris: Éditions du Centre National de la Recherche Scientifique, 1990), 397 (emphasis hers); see also John M. Cooper, "Aristotle on Natural Teleology," in *Language and Logos: Studies in Ancient Greek Philosophy*, ed. M. Schofield and M. Nussbaum (Cambridge: Cambridge University Press, 1982), 197–222].

the procedure the surgeon can (or could) say truthfully, 'I am practicing medicine.' Presumably, years before this particular operation, the surgeon made a vocational choice to pursue 'the health of the patient.' This end, the object of a προαίρεσις, has moved into the background of his life as a doctor of medicine. But even still, that end gives species—form—to the medical acts he performs, while he is performing them.

The overall end of medicine, besides giving species (form) to individual medical acts, also holds the profession (the craft) together internally. The individual procedures found in the medical manual of a well-ordered medical profession are all "makings" (ποιήσεις), human movements given sense by the ends toward which they head: a repaired leg, a delivered baby, etc. But medicine is not simply a collection of such procedures. If this were the case, the procedures in the medical manual might just as well be procedures in some other discipline's manual or in no manual at all—and then it would not make sense to speak of 'medicine.' The whole of the medical manual is given sense by overarching good of health.

III. The Internal Structure of Self-Movement: *Phys.* viii,5 and *Metaph.* ix,8

There exists, therefore, in the action-movement (or action-making) distinction a passageway from the psychology of individual human acts to ethics itself. Before, however, entering into these more general—we might even say, political—considerations, it will be useful to take a step back in order to be more precise about just where and how knowledge fits into human acts. In the present section, we consider the first issue: where in a movement or a making knowledge might fit. In section IV, we consider how knowledge operates in that spot.

In *Phys.* viii,5 Aristotle argues that, in any action of a self-mover, there is an element that moves but is not moved. In that element, there is action but not movement. Just before the passage that interests us, he has argued that, in studying any complex movement effected by a self-mover, we must eventually come to two elements, one of which moves but is not moved, the other moved by the first but not necessarily moving anything else. Suppose, he says, there are three things: A, B, and C and that A moves B, which moves C. We can say that the whole complex, ABC, moves itself. If we take away C from the complex, we see that B *need* not move anything, although it is still moved by A—and AB is (like ABC) a self-mover. But AB does not move itself *as* a whole: there must be a part that moves (but is unmoved) and a part that is moved.

It is necessary, therefore, for that which moves itself to have a part that moves but is unmoved and a part that is moved but does not necessarily move anything else, both of these touching one another or just one touching the other. (If, therefore, the mover is continuous—for the moved *must* be continuous—each touches the other.)[12]

When Aristotle speaks here of that which is "continuous" [συνεχές], the issue is actually whether the things in question are bodies or not.[13] If both parts are bodies, each touches the other; if just one is a body—the other being a mind or a soul of some sort—the non-body touches the body but the body does not touch the non-body (which cannot be touched).[14] Aristotle's exposition is not especially clear here; but, in the end, there can be little doubt that he conceives of the relationship between the unmoved part and the moved in the second way he identifies, that is, as the mover touching but not being touched ("just one touching the other"). If the mover were a (continuous) body, it would be possible to take a part of *it* which would move the other part, and then a part of the new mover which would move the other part(s), and so on. Aristotle does not want "continuity" in the mover because this would be to allow into the mover movement, which is precisely what he wishes to exclude.[15]

---

12 ἄρα τὸ αὐτὸ ἑαυτὸ κινοῦν ἔχειν τὸ κινοῦν ἀκίνητον δέ, καὶ τὸ κινούμενον μηδὲν δὲ κινοῦν ἐξ ἀνάγκης, ἁπτόμενα ἤτοι ἄμφω ἀλλήλων ἢ θατέρου θάτερον. εἰ μὲν οὖν συνεχές ἐστι τὸ κινοῦν (τὸ μὲν γὰρ κινούμενον ἀναγκαῖον εἶναι συνεχές), ἅψεται ἑκάτερον ἑκατέρου [*Phys.* viii,5, 258a18–22].

13 See W. D. Ross, *Aristotle's Physics*, 703; see also *Phys.* vi,4, 234b10–20 and viii,5, 257a33–b1.

14 Ross speaks of the latter as "quasi-contact" on the part of the non-body [Ross, *Aristotle's Physics*, 703], and this seems right.

15 In the block quotation just above (*Phys.* viii,5, 258a18–22), that which I have placed in parentheses—the mover's being a body and therefore mover and moved touching one another—is, therefore, the excluded option. "[Aristotle] says, 'That which moves itself must contain something that causes motion but is unmoved and something that is moved but need not move anything else, and either both components are in contact with each other or one with the other' (258a18–21); in the next line he affirms the second alternative: between the unmoved mover and moved the contact is

But, although Aristotle wishes to exclude movement from the domain of the unmoved mover, that does not mean that he would exclude from there any sort of two-poled articulation. How this works he explains in *Metaph.* ix,8, two chapters after the chapter in which he insists upon the distinction between movements and actions or actualizations [ἐνέργειαι] (*Metaph.* ix,6). *Metaph.* ix,8 is about different senses of priority. One sense is that according to which an actualization is prior to its corresponding potency [δύναμις]. The corresponding potency, says Aristotle, need not be one that heads toward a distinct end or product:

> And I mean by potency not only (1) that definite kind which is said to be a principle of change in another thing or in the thing itself regarded as other, but in general (2) every principle of movement or of rest. For nature also is in the same genus as potency, for it is a principle of movement—not, however, in something else but in the thing itself qua itself.[16]

The first class (1) of potencies mentioned here would include not only the builder who eventually builds a house but also the "self-moving" doctor who eventually cures himself ("a principle of change ... in the thing itself regarded *as* other"); the second, more general class (2) would include also self-movement in which a splitting of that which is self-moved into that which moves and that which is moved is not possible, since the potency is in (or of) that which is already present in actuality—"the thing itself qua itself."

This additional type of potency Aristotle associates, at least temporarily, with nature [ἡ φύσις—1049b8]. He has in mind the sort of relationship spoken of in *Metaph.* ix,6, where the end is present as soon as and as long as the activity itself is present. Immediately after the passage just quoted, Aristotle remarks that, with respect to the latter type of potency, the corresponding actualization is prior in substance [τῇ οὐσίᾳ—

---

one-way (258a21–22)" [Mary Louise Gill, "Aristotle on Self-Motion," 26]. (In this section, I am much indebted to this essay by Gill, as well as to two other chapters in the same book: Christopher Shields, "Mind and Motion in Aristotle," 117–33, and Michael V. Wedin, "Aristotle and the Mind's Self-Motion," 81–116.)

16 δὲ δυνάμεως οὐ μόνον τῆς ὡρισμένης ἣ λέγεται ἀρχὴ μεταβλητικὴ ἐν ἄλλῳ ἢ ᾗ ἄλλο, ἀλλ' ὅλως πάσης ἀρχῆς κινητικῆς ἢ στατικῆς. καὶ γὰρ ἡ φύσις ἐν ταὐτῷ γένει τῇ δυνάμει· ἀρχὴ γὰρ κινητική, ἀλλ' οὐκ ἐν ἄλλῳ ἀλλ' ἐν αὐτῷ ᾗ αὐτό [*Metaph.* ix,8, 1049b5–10].

1049b11], a relationship he expounds only later (beginning at 1050a4). In this later section, he speaks of nature in the following manner: "For the product is the end and the actualization is the product, and so even the word 'actualization' [ἐνέργεια] comes from the product [τὸ ἔργον] and points to the fulfillment."[17] He immediately illustrates this idea by means of the *Metaph.* ix,6 distinction between seeing (where the thing "aimed at" is present from the beginning) and building (where the house is distinct from the building).[18] So nature, according to Aristotle, is similar in this respect to seeing: it is a potency that never needs to *get to* its end, since the end is present whenever the potency is present.

It is not easy to understand what Aristotle's point might be in mentioning nature as a proper action; but fortunately nature is not the only example he uses. Later in *Metaph.* ix,8, in a parallel argument, he again speaks of actualizations that are in the things moved [1050a34]; he then adds:

But where there is no "other thing," a product besides the actualization, the actualization is in the agents, for example, the seeing is in the one who sees and the theorizing in the one who theorizes and life is in the soul (and, therefore, happiness also, for it is a certain sort of life).[19]

These examples—seeing, theorizing, living, and even happy living [εὐδαιμονία]—are all instances in which, so to speak, there is no B: there is no moved thing, there is just A. This makes them different from building, in which there is a product besides the actualization [1050a28–30]. Nonetheless, we can speak of two poles, potency and actualization. Nature is, apparently, to be understood similarly: qua what it is in itself, it is just there; it does not have to get anywhere.

There is, however, a way in which building can be included among ac-

---

17 τὸ γὰρ ἔργον τέλος, ἡ δὲ ἐνέργεια τὸ ἔργον, διὸ καὶ τοὔνομα ἐνέργεια λέγεται κατὰ τὸ ἔργον καὶ συντείνει πρὸς τὴν ἐντελέχειαν [*Metaph.* ix,8, 1050a21–23].

18 It is interesting, however, that Aristotle suggests here that a product of the art of building is not just the house but also the act of building: ἀπὸ τῆς οἰκοδομικῆς οἰκία παρὰ τὴν οἰκοδόμησιν [*Metaph.* ix,8, 1050a26–27].

19 ὧν δὲ μὴ ἔστιν ἄλλο τι ἔργον παρὰ τὴν ἐνέργειαν, ἐν αὐτοῖς ὑπάρχει ἡ ἐνέργεια (οἷον ἡ ὅρασις ἐν τῷ ὁρῶντι καὶ ἡ θεωρία ἐν τῷ θεωροῦντι καὶ ἡ ζωὴ ἐν τῇ ψυχῇ, διὸ καὶ ἡ εὐδαιμονία· ζωὴ γὰρ ποιά τίς ἐστιν) [*Metaph.* ix,8, 1050a34–b2].

tivities such as seeing and theorizing. Although building moves toward a distinct product, the housebuilder's knowing that he is engaging in housebuilding is present—both the potency and the actualization—all the time that he is knowing that, just as the end of his seeing the construction materials in front of him is present all the while that he is seeing them.[20]

IV. The Psychology of Self-Movers: *de An.* ii,5

It will be worth our while to go more deeply into this matter of the type of activity found at the stabile, knowing end of human acts, for this is a pivotal aspect of Aristotle's philosophical psychology. An extremely rich (and pertinent) passage occurs in *de An.* ii,5, where Aristotle characterizes the special type of passivity ("suffering" [τὸ πάσχειν]) involved in (especially) thinking, in the end contrasting it with the passivity of sensation.[21]

But before getting to that passage, we must say something about the run-up to it. Aristotle introduces *de An.* ii,5 with an allusion to certain unnamed philosophers who maintain that the suffering involved in sensing is always a matter of like being affected by like: τὸ ὅμοιον ὑπὸ τοῦ ὁμοίου πάσχειν [416b35]. As we shall see, Aristotle is not wholly against this idea, for the type of suffering in which he is especially interested does involve likes, but he does note certain difficulties in this general approach. One such difficulty is the fact that the senses are never activated unless some sensible object comes to them, even though the senses have "within them"

---

20 See *de An.* ii,5, 417b8–9 (discussed also just below): "So, it is not quite right to say that the practically wise man, when he is being practically wise, is altered, just as neither is the housebuilder when he builds." Writes Christopher Shields: "A housebuilder does not change qua housebuilder precisely because he has a stable disposition (ἕξις), which permits him to engage in the activity of house building directly, and at will. By analogy, a thinker does not change, qua thinker, precisely because mastery over some body of knowledge is a stable state of the thinker himself" [Shields, "Mind and Motion in Aristotle," 131]. Cp. R. D. Hicks, *Aristotle, De Anima, with translation, introduction and notes* (Cambridge: Cambridge University Press, 1907), 356. Heinaman argues that, when in *de An.* ii,5 Aristotle says that the housebuilder is not altered, he means that the alteration is not in the housebuilder but in the house [Robert Heinaman, "Aristotle on Housebuilding," 154]. But it is not apparent on this interpretation what the point would be of the comparison with the practically wise man. The practically wise man would remain unaltered in a way quite different from the way that the housebuilder remains unaltered.

21 On *de An.* ii,5, see especially Heinaman, "Aristotle on Housebuilding," and Jean Christensen De Groot, "Philoponus on *De anima* ii,5, *Physics* iii,3, and the Propagation of Light," *Phronesis* 18 (1983): 177–96.

[417a4] physical elements, which are themselves objects of sensation. If sensation is a matter of like suffering like and if sensation is of the elements, it should make no difference whether the object of sensation comes from outside or is already present within. But the fact is, says Aristotle, sensation does not occur unless an external object "is present," just as a combustible thing does not burn unless fire "is present" [πυρὸς ὄντος—417a9]. The various concepts mentioned here—'being like' and 'being present'—are important for understanding the later passage (to be considered just below). Aristotle's conclusion in this earlier section is that suffering does, in a sense, involve a change due to something like and, in another sense, due to something unlike: "Hence it is that, as we have stated, in a sense, something suffers due to something like and, in a sense, due to something unlike; for an unlike suffers and, when it has suffered, it is like."[22]

Immediately after this remark, Aristotle notes that words such as 'potency' [δύναμις] have various senses. We might, for instance, call something (i.e., someone) a 'knower' either because he is a member of the species (e.g., the human species) that can know a science or because he is such a member who does in fact know a science. When we say that the first person has the potency to theorize, we are employing a different sense of potency than when we say that the second person has the potency to theorize. Aristotle then considers suffering:

Neither is 'to suffer' simple but it may indicate either a certain corruption under the influence of a contrary or alternatively the maintenance, due to a present actuality [ὑπὸ τοῦ ἐντελεχείᾳ ὄντος], of a present and similar potency [ὄντος τοῦ δυνάμει ὄντος καὶ ὁμοίου], even as a potency [5] stands with respect to an actuality. For something having knowledge becomes something theorizing and this is either not 'being altered' (for the progress is into itself, that is, into the actuality) or it is another type of alteration. So, it is not quite right to say that the practically wise man, when he is being practically wise, is altered, just as neither is the housebuilder when he builds. So, going [10] to actuality from a present potency in the case of thinking and being practically wise is not *teaching* but ought to have some other name. Something that from a present potency

---

22 διὸ ἔστι μὲν ὡς ὑπὸ τοῦ ὁμοίου πάσχει, ἔστι δὲ ὡς ὑπὸ τοῦ ἀνομοίου, καθάπερ εἴπομεν· πάσχει μὲν γὰρ τὸ ἀνόμοιον, πεπονθὸς δ' ὅμοιόν ἐστιν [de An. ii,5, 417a18–20].

"learns," that is, receives knowledge due to a present "teaching" actuality, either ought not to be said to suffer or there are two types of [15] alteration, the one a change to conditions of privation, the other to dispositions and to the nature.[23]

The first change of a sensing thing comes about due to the begetter. When it is born, it is as if it already *has* knowledge, and the sensing which is in act is said to be similar to theorizing. It differs, [20] however, in this: that in the one case the things that induce the actualization are from outside (the object of sight, the object of hearing, and similarly all the other sensibles). The reason is that sensation in act is of individuals but knowledge is of universals—and these latter are as if in the soul itself, so that to think depends upon the individual, when he wills to, [25] but to sense does not depend on him, for there must be a sensible object. The situation would be the same with respect to the branches of knowledge regarding sensible objects—and for the same reason: because sensible objects are of individuals which are outside. [*de An*. ii,5, 417b2–28][24]

In order to understand this argument, one must recall, first of all, that Aristotle does regard both seeing and thinking as (in some sense) passive, and so he treats them here together.[25] This position is bound up with the

---

23 Siwek says that these dispositions are positive dispositions [Paulus Siwek, ed. and trans., *Aristotelis Tractatus de Anima, Graece et Latine* (Rome: Desclée & C.i Editori Pontifici, 1965), ad 417b16]; see also Hicks, *Aristotle, De Anima*, ad 417b16, who cites *Metaph*. viii,5, 1044b30–34 to good effect.

24 οὐκ ἔστι δ' ἁπλοῦν οὐδὲ τὸ πάσχειν, ἀλλὰ τὸ μὲν φθορά τις ὑπὸ τοῦ ἐναντίου, τὸ δὲ σωτηρία μᾶλλον ὑπὸ τοῦ ἐντελεχείᾳ ὄντος τοῦ δυνάμει ὄντος καὶ ὁμοίου οὕτως ὡς δύν[5]αμις ἔχει πρὸς ἐντελέχειαν· θεωροῦν γὰρ γίνεται τὸ ἔχον τὴν ἐπιστήμην, ὅπερ ἢ οὐκ ἔστιν ἀλλοιοῦσθαι (εἰς αὑτὸ γὰρ ἡ ἐπίδοσις καὶ εἰς ἐντελέχειαν) ἢ ἕτερον γένος ἀλλοιώσεως. διὸ οὐ καλῶς ἔχει λέγειν τὸ φρονοῦν, ὅταν φρονῇ, ἀλλοιοῦσθαι, ὥσπερ οὐδὲ τὸν οἰκοδόμον ὅταν οἰκοδομῇ. τὸ μὲν οὖν [10] εἰς ἐντελέχειαν ἄγειν ἐκ δυνάμει ὄντος κατὰ τὸ νοοῦν καὶ φρονοῦν οὐ διδασκαλίαν ἀλλ' ἑτέραν ἐπωνυμίαν ἔχειν δίκαιον· τὸ δ' ἐκ δυνάμει ὄντος μανθάνον καὶ λαμβάνον ἐπιστήμην ὑπὸ τοῦ ἐντελεχείᾳ ὄντος καὶ διδασκαλικοῦ ἤτοι οὐδὲ πάσχειν φατέον, ἢ δύο τρόπους εἶναι ἀλ[15]λοιώσεως, τήν τε ἐπὶ τὰς στερητικὰς διαθέσεις μεταβολὴν καὶ τὴν ἐπὶ τὰς ἕξεις καὶ τὴν φύσιν.

τοῦ δ' αἰσθητικοῦ ἡ μὲν πρώτη μεταβολὴ γίνεται ὑπὸ τοῦ γεννῶντος· ὅταν δὲ γεννηθῇ, ἔχει ἤδη ὥσπερ ἐπιστήμην, καὶ τὸ αἰσθάνεσθαι τὸ κατ' ἐνέργειαν ὁμοίως λέγεται τῷ θεωρεῖν· διαφέρει [20] δέ, ὅτι τοῦ μὲν τὰ ποιητικὰ τῆς ἐνεργείας ἔξωθεν, τὸ ὁρατὸν καὶ τὸ ἀκουστόν, ὁμοίως δὲ καὶ τὰ λοιπὰ τῶν αἰσθητῶν. αἴτιον δ' ὅτι τῶν καθ' ἕκαστον ἡ κατ' ἐνέργειαν αἴσθησις, ἡ δ' ἐπιστήμη τῶν καθόλου· ταῦτα δ' ἐν αὐτῇ πώς ἐστι τῇ ψυχῇ. διὸ νοῆσαι μὲν ἐπ' αὐτῷ, ὁπόταν βούληται, αἰσθά[25]νεσθαι δ' οὐκ ἐπ' αὐτῷ· ἀναγκαῖον γὰρ ὑπάρχειν τὸ αἰσθητόν. ὁμοίως δὲ τοῦτο ἔχει κἀν ταῖς ἐπιστήμαις ταῖς τῶν αἰσθητῶν, καὶ διὰ τὴν αὐτὴν αἰτίαν, ὅτι τὰ αἰσθητὰ τῶν καθ' ἕκαστα καὶ τῶν ἔξωθεν [*de An*. ii,5, 417b2–28].

The text is basically from W. D. Ross, ed., *Aristotle: De anima, edited with introduction and commentary* (Oxford: Clarendon, 1961), except that in line 417b10 I have kept κατὰ; also, in 417b18 I have eliminated the sentence break and in 417b19 I have followed S and V in eliminating δὲ. In line 417b26, I understand ταῖς as presupposing αἰσθήσεσιν.

25 *De An*. iii,4, 429a13–15 [εἰ δή ἐστι τὸ νοεῖν ὥσπερ τὸ αἰσθάνεσθαι, ἢ πάσχειν τι ἂν εἴη ὑπὸ τοῦ νοητοῦ ἤ τι τοιοῦτον ἕτερον]; also iii,4, 429b24–25. See chapter 2, section III, at note 38.

Metaph. ix,6 idea that the ends of both are present as long as the activities are present. If either faculty had to *produce* its end, it would not be present until that process was completed; but if the end (in some sense) comes to the faculty, as is especially clear in the case of sight, the faculty does not have to get to its object: the object is already present and will be as long as that instance of seeing lasts. Aristotle has such ideas in mind in the passage translated: regarding knowledge, he is thinking not of a movement from a state of having knowledge (but not theorizing) to a state of having knowledge and actually theorizing but rather of the relationship between the potency (having knowledge) and its actualization (theorizing) *in* the second state. This is apparent from his repeated use of the present participle of εἶναι, translated in the passage as 'present,' and used, as we have seen, in the run-up to our passage [417a9], when Aristotle speaks of the requirement that fire be present in order for a combustible thing to burn.

Similar to what he says at *Metaph.* ix,8, 1049b10, where he speaks of something that is a potency in so far as it is a principle of motion not for "something else but in the thing itself qua itself," Aristotle speaks here of the "alteration" involved in knowledge as progress "into itself, that is, into the actuality." Because it is a progress into itself while both the potency and the actualization are present, it is not correct to speak of it as we speak of teaching [417b11], where the actualization is in another (the student):[26] it ought to have some other name (although Aristotle does not give it one). Continuing in this line, he speaks of something that "from a present potency 'learns,' that is, receives knowledge due to a present 'teaching' actuality" [417b12–13]. Obviously, Aristotle did not have at his linguistic disposal scare quotes such as we have used in the translation, but the sense of his remark calls for them. Since it is possible to speak of a potency and an actualization *in* an instance of thinking, the potency can be said to "learn"—but only by stretching the meaning of the term. For similar reasons, we might also have put within scare quotes the word 'to' [εἰς] in the earlier phrase "going *to* actuality from a present potency" [417b9–10]. In knowledge there is articulation—an active and a passive part—but no real movement.

This is what allows both movement and lack of movement to be com-

26 See chapter 2, section I.

bined in a builder. Building a house is indeed a movement, but knowing how to build a house, while building it, is not. Aristotle uses precisely that example here: "... it is not quite right to say that the practically wise man [φρονοῦν], when he is being practically wise [ὅταν φρονῇ], is altered, just as neither is the housebuilder when he builds" [417b8–9].[27] Building a house is a going from a certain state to its opposite (or condition of privation) [417b3, 15]; knowing how to build a house is a "maintenance" [σωτηρία] of the potency and actuality together or a going "to" positive dispositions and "the nature" [417b3, 16]. We saw Aristotle associating potency-actuality pairs with nature at the beginning of *Metaph.* ix,8 (at 1049b8–10) and, later in the same chapter, with theorizing, life, and even happiness [εὐδαιμονία—1050b1]. All of these involve the controlling intelligibility of that to which the relevant expression refers. Like the art of housebuilding or the idea of a house, a nature, qua nature, does not move but "regulates" by establishing what it is to be a thing of that sort.[28] We can say a similar thing not only of theorizing but also of life and happiness. (We shall consider these more extensively below.)

The second paragraph of the quotation draws a distinction between thinking and seeing (or sensation). The first sentence simply tells us what stages of sensing and knowledge Aristotle chooses here to regard as parallel: the capacity to sense that an animal has once it is born is parallel to the knowing subject's having knowledge (but not using it); an animal's actually sensing something is parallel to the knowing subject's actual theorizing. Then Aristotle goes into the differences: sensation is initiated by things "outside," thinking by things that are "as if [πώς] in the soul itself" [417b23]. That is, sensing is initiated by objects of sense, thinking is bound up with universals, and so sensing is not up to the sensing subject, but thinking is: he thinks "when he wills to" [ὁπόταν βούληται—417b24].

This association of freedom with universals raises issues we cannot go into here, except to draw attention to a connection with ideas set out earlier in the present work. We noted in chapter 1 that human acts, particularly when they are movements "from here to there," are worked out at the perceptual level, which is below the syllogistic level, the level of universals.

---

27 See above, note 20.
28 See Gill, "Aristotle on Self-Motion," 22–23.

We also noted there (in section I) that, in *Metaph.* i,1, Aristotle says that human beings share the lower level with the other animals—although, unlike the other animals, they are able to rise above that level.[29] Here in *de An.* ii,5 Aristotle associates this access to the higher level of universals with freedom of the will (βούλησις).[30] It is true that in *de An.* ii,5 Aristotle says only that, because thinking is of universals, one *thinks* when one wills to do so and not that the universal is involved in all exercises of freedom or in all human acts; but in *EN* vi he says that wisdom (σοφία), which is certainly of universals, stands above φρόνησις (practical wisdom), which, though an intellectual virtue, is bound up with human action and movement generally. So, in *EN* vi, the universal is in command of more than just its own thinking: it is in command of—it is the rule and measure of—the entire practical realm.[31] This same relationship is mirrored in the various subsidiary segments of the city's communal life: the builder, for instance, as the embodiment of the unmoving art of building, is in command of building, the movement.

According to *EN* vi, φρόνησις issues orders within the practical realm, but on behalf of wisdom, never to it.[32] Wisdom is like a sovereign, who *is* essentially the stabile understanding of the principles of the political life; φρόνησις, on the other hand, is like the city's general, actually issuing orders as he is pulled along by the course of the battle or by other exigencies of the military life. Although the sovereign thinks of whatever principle or course of action when he wills and, because of such exercises of the will, can be called the ultimate decision-maker, his making a decision involves no movement. A decision is an instance of a potency being "brought into" actuality, but that is no real movement. As Aristotle says in *de An.* ii,5, this is "either not 'being altered' (for the progress is into itself, that is, into the actuality) or it is another type of alteration" [417b6–7].

---

29 We also saw above, in section I of the present chapter, that in *EN* vi,2, Aristotle says that animals have sensation but no share in action [πράξεως δὲ μὴ κοινωνεῖν—1139a20]. Action requires genuine knowledge, that is, knowledge of universals.

30 Aristotle associates will (βούλησις) with reason at *de An.* ii,9, 432b5 and ii,10, 433a22–25.

31 Aristotle speaks of the good man (ὁ σπουδαῖος) as the "norm and measure" [κανὼν καὶ μέτρον: *EN* iii,4, 1113a33] of virtuous behavior and practical truth. In chapter 7, I associate this ethical type with the φρόνιμος.

32 *EN* vi,13, 1145a6–11; see also *EN* vi,12, 1143b33–35.

V. Φρόνησις and the End of Ends

Although the so-called "craft analogy" is very useful for coming to an understanding of the organization of the city and of Aristotelian ethics in general, it would be a grave mistake to conceive of φρόνησις (the predominant virtue of the practical realm) as simply a very general craft.[33] Although Aristotle certainly does recognize in φρόνησις a structure similar to that in the crafts, he is adamant in rejecting the thesis that φρόνησις *is* a craft [*EN* vi,4, 1140b2]. Understanding why will take us a further step into the properly ethical, for, although an act performed as part of a craft is a human act and therefore contained within the ethical, φρόνησις is immediately linked to the way things stand in—and the principles of—the moral universe.

An entry into Aristotle's thought in this regard is provided by a passage in *EN* vi,4. Says Aristotle:

> Making and action are different..., so that also the reasoned habit proper to action is different from the reasoned habit proper to making, nor is one included in the other, for an action is not a making and a making is not an action. [*EN* vi,4, 1140a2–6][34]

This remark—and, in fact, this whole chapter, *EN* vi,4—might serve as confirmation of the ideas put forward thus far in the present chapter, for here and throughout *EN* vi,4 Aristotle is clearly emphasizing the idea that both practices and makings involve reason ("the *reasoned* habit proper to action" ... "the *reasoned* habit proper to making"). Reason, as we have seen, in itself does not move, although it is the source of all practices (understood in the inclusive sense) [*EN* vi,2, 1139a19, 31]. Both practices and

---

33 The expression 'craft analogy' was introduced into contemporary philosophical discourse by Terence Irwin, especially in his *Plato's Moral Theory: The Early and Middle Dialogues* (Oxford: Clarendon, 1977).

34 τερον δ' ἐστὶ ποίησις καὶ πρᾶξις ...· ὥστε καὶ ἡ μετὰ λόγου ἕξις πρακτικὴ ἕτερόν ἐστι τῆς μετὰ λόγου ποιητικῆς ἕξεως. διὸ οὐδὲ περιέχεται ὑπ' ἀλλήλων· οὔτε γὰρ ἡ πρᾶξις ποίησις οὔτε ἡ ποίησις πρᾶξίς ἐστιν. The phrase translated 'reasoned' [μετὰ λόγου] might in other contexts be translated 'reasonable'; but, since later in *EN* vi,4 Aristotle speaks also of artlessness [ἡ ἀτεχνία—1140a21] as μετὰ λόγου, 'reasoned' seems more appropriate. See Gauthier and Jolif, *L'Éthique à Nicomaque*, 2.2 459.

makings are, therefore, human acts, since reason is the defining characteristic of the voluntary.[35] But what provides the entry into Aristotle's understanding of the difference between crafts and practical wisdom is the way in which the above passage has been interpreted, for, as has happened with other passages that draw a clear distinction between actions [πράξεις] and makings [ποιήσεις], this one has been held to be inconsistent with other Aristotelian remarks—in this case, remarks that come a mere two chapters earlier.

In *EN* vi,2, Aristotle says that makings fall under the practical intellect:

> Thought itself moves nothing, although thought that is for the sake of something and practical does, for this [that is, practical thought] also rules over making. For every maker makes for the sake of something and the makable [τὸ ποιητόν] is not an end simply speaking—only the practicable [τὸ πρακτόν] is that—but relatively, that is, as being *of* something. For good conduct [εὐπραξία] is an end and appetite is of this [*EN* vi,2, 1139a35–b4].[36]

But how, if making is different from action, so that neither is "included in the other" and "an action is not a making and a making is not an action" [*EN* vi,4, 1140a2–6], can making fall under—be ruled over by—practical thought? This objection to Aristotle's remarks has been posed by a number of commentators, including Ramsauer and Stewart.[37] They have received a reply from Greenwood:

> If 1140a5 is inconsistent with 1139b1, it must also be inconsistent with the whole of the latter part of this book, in which σοφία and the πρακτικὴ ἀρετὴ φρόνησις are in some sense or other admittedly asserted to cover the whole field of intellectual goodness, leaving no room for a ποιητικὴ ἀρετὴ distinct from either. But

---

35 See chapter 3, section III; also *de An.* ii,5, 417b22–23. Here in *EN* vi,4, he speaks of a craft as involving both the actual crafting and the thinking about how to do it: τὸ τεχνάζειν καὶ θεωρεῖν ὅπως ἂν γένηταί τι τῶν ἐνδεχομένων καὶ εἶναι καὶ μὴ εἶναι [1140a11–13].

36 διάνοια δ' αὐτὴ οὐθὲν κινεῖ, ἀλλ' ἡ ἕνεκά του καὶ πρακτική· αὕτη γὰρ καὶ τῆς ποιητικῆς ἄρχει· ἕνεκα γάρ του ποιεῖ πᾶς ὁ ποιῶν, καὶ οὐ τέλος ἁπλῶς (ἀλλὰ πρός τι καὶ τινός) τὸ ποιητόν, ἀλλὰ τὸ πρακτόν· ἡ γὰρ εὐπραξία τέλος, ἡ δ' ὄρεξις τούτου.

37 Ramsauer says that the ἄρχει (ἄρχειν) at 1139b1 means the same thing as the περιέχεται (περιέχειν) at 1140a5 and that the later passage carries on as if the former passage were not there ("Sed omnino inde a vs.1 ita agitur quasi illa 1139b1 sq. non praecessissent" [G. Ramsauer, *Aristotelis* Ethica Nicomachea, 383 (ad 1140a5)]. Stewart refers (and apparently defers) to Ramsauer [J. A. Stewart, *Notes on the Nicomachean Ethics of Aristotle*, ii,40 (ad 1140a5)].

there is no inconsistency. ποίησις can quite well be simply a means to πρᾶξις as 1139b1 asserts, and at the same time be a completely distinct thing from πρᾶξις as 1140a5 asserts. No more subtle distinction is intended in 1140a5 than lies in the fact that in ποίησις an external object is produced while in πρᾶξις it is not.[38]

Greenwood's point is a valid one: despite the all-encompassing character of φρόνησις, an action, qua action (in the limited sense), remains quite a different type of thing from a making, for, as Aristotle argues in *de An.* ii,5, it does not involve a movement-like structure in any robust sense. And, as Aristotle explains (among other places) here in *EN* vi, making is about generating something distinct from the maker [*EN* vi,4, 1140a10–12]; qua making, therefore, it is distinct from an action.[39] But we should hesitate before acquiescing to Greenwood's "ποίησις can quite well be simply a means to πρᾶξις as 1139b1 asserts," for 1139b1 (or, actually, 1139b1–4) never says that making is a means to action but only that, although a "makable" [ποιητόν] is an end but not an end simply speaking (τέλος ἁπλῶς), a "practicable" [πρακτὸν] is an end simply speaking. Saying that making is a means to action posits too much of a separation between the elements at issue here. Aristotle's remark that "the makable is not an end simply speaking ... but relatively, that is, as being *of* something [ἀλλὰ πρός τι καὶ τινός—1139b2–3]" suggests a closer— we might say, an internal—relationship.

The qualified end of 1139b1–4 is the makable; the "end simply speak-

38 L. H. G. Greenwood, *Aristotle: Nicomachean Ethics, Book Six, with essays, notes and translation* (Cambridge: Cambridge University Press, 1909), 182; Gauthier goes along with Greenwood in rejecting the understanding of Ramsauer and Stewart [Gauthier and Jolif, *L'Éthique à Nicomaque*, II.2 460].

39 Gauthier chastises Burnet for using *Metaph.* ii,1, 993b20–21 to support his thesis that "la science poétique rentrant dans la science pratique" [Gauthier and Jolif, *L'Éthique à Nicomaque*, 2.2 460]. (Gauthier refers to the Introduction, §§10–12, of John Burnet, *The Ethics of Aristotle*.) In that passage in *Metaph.* ii, Aristotle effects a bipartite division between theoretical and practical sciences, which would put ποίησις within the practical. Gauthier argues that "on s'accord aujourd'hui à regarder ce livre comme inauthentique." The consensus that Gauthier assumes, however, no longer exists: see Enrico Berti, "Note sulla tradizione dei primi due libri della *Metafisica* di Aristotele," *Elenchos* 3 (1982): 5–38. But we need not view the *Metaph.* ii,1 passage as an insuperable problem in any case. The crucial phrase in *Metaph.* ii,1 is the following: θεωρητικῆς μὲν γὰρ τέλος ἀλήθεια, πρακτικῆς δ' ἔργον [993b20–21]. We might understand any reference to πρᾶξις here as a reference to its wider sense. In *EN* vi,2, Aristotle refers to the ἔργον of virtue [1139a17] and even to truth as the ἔργον of theoretical thought [1139a29]. We need not assume that in *Metaph.* ii,1 Aristotle is using the word ἔργον in the sense applicable only to a ποίησις (that is, in the sense of a product that comes only at the end of a process). Moreover, πράξεις (in the strict sense) can still be distinct from ποιήσεις, even while both—in so far as they are types of human acts—fall within the practical (in the wider sense).

ing" is "good conduct" [ἡ εὐπραξία]. When a builder makes a house because he thinks that is a good thing to do (for the community, for instance, or for his family), this end simply speaking [τέλος ἁπλῶς] need not stand out from the activity of building as a distinct thing. We need not even speak of his building *because* he thinks doing so is a good thing, which suggests (although it does not entail) that he deliberately thinks about doing good things, identifies housebuilding as a good thing to do, and then sets out to do it. We might say simply that he builds a house knowing that this is a good thing to do.[40] There is no need to posit any distance at all here, since, as we have seen, at the one end of building there is the art of building and, although we can posit a quasi-whence and a quasi-whither there, in fact the end is present all the time that the activity of so thinking is there. Neither would it be to introduce means-to-end distance to "add in" the knowledge that this act of building is a good thing to do, for this type of knowledge does not work that way: it *informs* the activity in such a way that it becomes one with it, although it might also do the same for another activity (such as a "practicable"—1139b3). This is what allows Aristotle to say that the makable and good conduct are both ends, for it is *in* pursuing the makable that the maker pursues the good (or good conduct).

We find such "end of ends" talk elsewhere in the Aristotelian *corpus*. In the second chapter of *EN*, Aristotle speaks of "some end of practicable things, which we will for its own sake and the other ends for the sake of this" [τι τέλος ... τῶν πρακτῶν ὃ δι' αὑτὸ βουλόμεθα, τὰ ἄλλα δὲ διὰ τοῦτο—1094a18–19].[41] Not all translations render the expression τὰ

---

40 David Wiggins has shown that τὰ πρὸς τὸ τέλος (as at *EN* vi,13, 1145a6) can refer also to the component parts of an end (such as happiness) and not just means toward it [David Wiggins, "Deliberation and Practical Reason," in *Essays on Aristotle's Ethics*, ed. Amélie O. Rorty, 29–51 (Berkeley/Los Angeles/London: University of California Press, 1980), 221–40]. See also above, chapter 5, section III, where the anomalous ἀκρατής seeks per se the genuine good although he has something quite different (i.e., the apparent good) in mind.

41 See Stewart, *Notes on the Nicomachean Ethics of Aristotle*, I, 12–15; see also Alexander Grant, *The Ethics of Aristotle: Illustrated with notes and essays* (London: Longmans, Green, and Co., 1885), I, 424. The larger passage is a hypothetical statement and reads: Εἰ δή τι τέλος ἐστὶ τῶν πρακτῶν ὃ δι' αὑτὸ βουλόμεθα, τὰ ἄλλα δὲ διὰ τοῦτο, καὶ μὴ πάντα δι' ἕτερον αἱρούμεθα (πρόεισι γὰρ οὕτω γ' εἰς ἄπειρον, ὥστ' εἶναι κενὴν καὶ ματαίαν τὴν ὄρεξιν), δῆλον ὡς τοῦτ' ἂν εἴη τἀγαθὸν καὶ τὸ ἄριστον [1094a18–22]. A few lines later [1094a27–28], he suggests that the one end mentioned in the protasis is the end for which the political craft (μέθοδος—1094b11) is pursued, so he does hold what is stated in the apodosis, that is, that there is a best thing, which might also be called "the good." (A bit later in the same chapter, he says that the end of the political craft encompasses the ends of all the other sciences and pursuits: ...

ἄλλα here as "other ends"; the Revised Oxford Translation, for instance, speaks of "some end of the things we do, which we desire for its own sake (everything else [τὰ ἄλλα] being desired for the sake of this)." But "everything else" is not an especially close rendering of τὰ ἄλλα, which speaks in a more limited manner of things "other." If we regard these other things as the things one *does* for the sake of the ultimate end (and not as other ends), the logic of the sentence becomes awkwardly repetitious. Aristotle would be speaking first of "some end of practicable things" (which we will for no other reason) and then of things that are willed "for the sake of this"—but, since he has already said that practical things have this as their end, there is no need to go on to say that they are willed "for the sake of this" (that is, for the sake of the ultimate end). The logic of the phrase is rendered neat and crisp if we understand τὰ ἄλλα rather as referring to other ends: Aristotle would be speaking thus of an end of all practicables, which is willed for its own sake *and* which is the end of other ends.[42]

The consequence of all this is that an agent's moral understanding of what he does—such understanding being, as we have seen, an action [πρᾶξις] in the strict sense and no making—embraces all the things that he does (both actions and makings). The widest-scoped intellectual grasp of the practical is geared for moving (in some sense) toward other things;[43] but, since it enters into all such angles of the moral universe, it is in a position to judge them from a non-technical and properly ethical perspective. As we have seen, Aristotle says in *EN* vi,2 that practical thought "rules over making" [1139b1]. If, for instance, a pair of acts are in themselves perfectly in order, they may still be ill-advised in combination or even contradictory.

τὸ ταύτης τέλος περιέχοι ἂν τὰ τῶν ἄλλων ... [*EN* i,2, 1094b6].) That Aristotle would not reject outright the idea of a relationship, representable by means of the preposition διὰ, between things good in themselves and something else is apparent at *EN* i,6, 1096b18–19 where, speaking briefly in his own voice, he says that things sought for their own sake—things such as thinking, seeing, certain pleasures and honors—can also be sought on account of something else: ταῦτα γὰρ εἰ καὶ δι' ἄλλο τι διώκομεν, ὅμως τῶν καθ' αὑτὰ ἀγαθῶν θείη τις ἄν. Aspasius identifies this other thing as happiness: τούτων γὰρ ἕκαστον καὶ δι' αὑτὸ αἱρετὸν καὶ διὰ τὴν εὐδαιμονίαν [Aspasius, *In Ethica Nicomachea quae supersunt commentaria*, vol. 19.1 of *Commentaria in Aristotelem Graeca*, ed. Gustavus Heylbut (Berlin: Reimer, 1889), 15.28–29].

42 As mentioned above, in note 6, Aristotle allows that it is possible to speak of ends themselves as practicables; if that allowance is applicable here, the other ends could be among the practicables referred to in the first part of the phrase at *EN* i,2, 1094a18–19.

43 δὲ βουλὴ περὶ τῶν αὑτῷ πρακτῶν, αἱ δὲ πράξεις ἄλλων ἕνεκα [*EN* iii,3, 1112b32–33].

Determining (or understanding) this is the role of practical thought at its most general.

Aristotle insists on this general character of φρόνησις in *EN* vi,5, where he begins with a consideration of "particular φρονήσεις" in order to hone in on a definition of general—which, to his mind, is the only genuine—φρόνησις. Near the beginning of the chapter he says, "It seems to be characteristic of the φρόνιμος to be capable of deliberating well about the things that are good and expedient for himself, not in particular—for instance, not about what type of things lead to health or to strength—but about what type of things lead to living well generally" [*EN* vi,5, 1140a25–28]. A sign of this generality, he goes on to say, is the fact that, even when we say that someone is φρόνιμος regarding a more limited sector of the practical universe, being such is still a matter of reasoning well about "some good end of which there is no art."[44]

Aristotle's speaking of the φρόνιμος's concern for "the things that are good and expedient for himself" sounds at first as if φρόνησις comes down in the end to the ability to be intelligently selfish—but that that is not Aristotle's position becomes apparent later in the chapter where he says that Pericles and suchlike figures are called φρόνιμος because they can identify "the things that are good for themselves, that is, the things that are good for men."[45] So, when he speaks of the φρόνιμος as being practically wise regarding "the things that are good and expedient for himself," he means good and expedient for himself qua man.[46] The proper object of φρόνησις is the good toward which human nature as such is directed.

VI. The Relationship between Φρόνησις and Pleasure

At 1140b11, Aristotle introduces another—and a different type of—reason why φρόνησις is special. In effect, he gives us an explanation of how

---

44 σημεῖον δ' ὅτι καὶ τοὺς περί τι φρονίμους λέγομεν, ὅταν πρὸς τέλος τι σπουδαῖον εὖ λογίσωνται, ὧν μή ἐστι τέχνη [*EN* vi,5, 1140a28–30].

45 διὰ τοῦτο Περικλέα καὶ τοὺς τοιούτους φρονίμους οἰόμεθα εἶναι, ὅτι τὰ αὑτοῖς ἀγαθὰ καὶ τὰ τοῖς ἀνθρώποις δύνανται θεωρεῖν [*EN* vi,5, 1140b7–10].

46 See *EN* vi,5, 1140b5, i,2, 1094b6–7; also *EE* i,6, 1217a30–35.

man's capacity for φρόνησις can go awry. At *EN* vi,5, 1140b11ff., he draws a connection between the word φρόνησις and the word σωφροσύνη (often translated 'moderation' or 'prudence'), arguing that etymologically the latter has to do with preserving or maintaining φρόνησις: ... ὡς σῴζουσαν τὴν φρόνησιν [1140b12]. This language is reminiscent of *de An.* ii,5, where, as we have seen, Aristotle speaks of the "maintenance" [σωτηρία] of a "present and similar potency" [417b3-4] by the corresponding actuality, the idea being that (for instance) a particular instance of thinking is sustained as what it is all the while that it exists, rather than coming into existence by way of a progression from potency to act (see above, section IV). Here too, in *EN* vi,5, Aristotle says that σωφροσύνη preserves or maintains a certain manner of thinking or conception (ὑπόληψις—1140b13). The conception that remains as long as the intellectual virtue of φρόνησις is maintained is the very general conception of good conduct. This, as we have seen, is the "end simply speaking," the object of appetite [ὄρεξις—*EN* vi,2, 1139b4], so it is a practical conception: an orientation *toward* good conduct.

We need not assume that an actual idea of 'good conduct' stands always explicitly before the mind's eye of the φρόνιμος; what matters is that his understanding of the practical world is informed by his knowledge of it:[47] that he knows that what he does is part of good conduct. This general understanding of the importance of good conduct in one's life becomes corrupted because of pleasure—or, more precisely, because of the desire for pleasure and the aversion to pain. Pleasure and pain, Aristotle notes, do not have the same effect upon other, more limited knowledge: a person might forget, for example, this or that mathematical proof or even (by some freak accident) a large part of mathematics itself—and yet remain φρόνιμος, capable of deliberating well about "the things that are good or bad for man."

For the principles of the practicables are that for the sake of which they are practicables, but, when a person has been corrupted because of pleasure or pain, immediately the principle is not apparent, nor is it apparent that, for the sake of this or because of this, he ought to choose and do everything. (For vice is corruptive of the principle.)[48]

---

47 See above, at note 40.
48 αἱ μὲν γὰρ ἀρχαὶ τῶν πρακτῶν τὸ οὗ ἕνεκα τὰ πρακτά· τῷ δὲ διεφθαρμένῳ δι' ἡδονὴν ἢ λύπην

Why is it that φρόνησις is damaged because of pleasure but more particular knowledge is not—or, at least, not permanently?[49] It is important to note, first of all, that pleasure is not the ultimate cause of the corruption of φρόνησις. That is why Aristotle interjects the sentence, "For vice [κακία] is corruptive of the principle." As we have seen, he says in *de An.* ii,5, 417b22–24 that thought—including practical thought—is of universals, "so that to think depends upon the individual, when he wills to." The ultimate cause of the corruption is vice, and vice is voluntary; but pleasure (with which vice is bound up) is the cause of the corruption being *corruption* [διαφθορά], with its usual connotations: it is what makes the falling away from the good permanent, as death is permanent. Turning bad is not just a matter of changing one's mind from one general conception of what one should do to another in such a way that one could just as easily switch back to the former conception. Pleasure pushes along the thought of the person who has chosen to go down the wrong path in such a way that the *practical* conception 'good conduct' is no longer available to him.[50]

As Aristotle says in the above quotation, "immediately the principle is not apparent, nor is it apparent that, for the sake of this or because of this, he ought to choose and do everything." The fundamental deviation—which involves, as Aristotle says, "everything [πάντα—1140b19]"—is due to the practical intellect; the blindness (with respect to the good) is due to pleasure. That pleasure does not affect particular knowledge as it does affect φρόνησις is because pleasure is an accompaniment—although a very intimate accompaniment—of what primarily goes against φρόνησις: the choice to turn away from good conduct. When pleasure is attached to a choice of less scope, the choice to drink a beer, for instance, this may impede the ability to recall Euclid's proof of the fifth postulate (or whatever), but it brings about no such permanent or general blindness.

εὐθὺς οὐ φαίνεται ἀρχή, οὐδὲ δεῖν τούτου ἕνεκεν οὐδὲ διὰ τοῦθ' αἱρεῖσθαι πάντα καὶ πράττειν· ἔστι γὰρ ἡ κακία φθαρτικὴ ἀρχῆς [*EN* vi,5, 1140b16–22].

49 In the rest of this chapter, I speak of the influence of pleasure on human lives, ignoring (for the sake of simplicity) the issue of pain and its avoidance. What is said about pleasure is generally applicable also to the desire to avoid pain.

50 Aristotle speaks about this in *Metaph.* v,29; see below, chapter 7, section II.

VII. Pleasures Good and Bad

Much of what Aristotle says about pleasure is borrowed—often with changes—from Plato, especially from the *Philebus*. One idea that seems to have come over into Aristotle intact is the idea that pleasure is not a single thing, the term 'pleasure' referring rather to a phenomenon that—in a sense to be made precise below—"completes" individual human activities and therefore gets its proper sense from those activities.[51] There is no pleasure that is not pleasure *in* a particular activity; thus, although the pleasure of eating, the pleasure of sex, and the pleasure of doing philosophy are all pleasures, there is no such thing as pleasure *simpliciter*, that is to say, pleasure that is not either the pleasure of eating or the pleasure of sex or the pleasure of doing philosophy (or of whatever activity you wish).

The primary places where Aristotle expounds these ideas are *EN* vii,4 and 11–13, and *EN* x,1–5. (There are also a couple of pertinent remarks in *EN* i.) Pleasures, he says at the beginning of *EN* x,5, "differ in species":

> For we think that things different in species are completed by different things (both natural objects and things produced by art appear thus, for instance, animals, trees, a painting, a sculpture, a house, a vessel); and, similarly, that activities differing in species are completed by things differing in species. The activities of thought differ from those associated with the senses, and they themselves differ in species from one another. So also, therefore, do the pleasures that complete them. This is apparent also in the fact that each pleasure is paired with the activity which it completes. [*EN* x,5, 1175a22–30][52]

Against certain of his contemporaries who argued that pleasures could not be good, since they are spatio-temporally extended processes [γενέσεις] that *lead* to goods, Aristotle insists that

---

51 In the *Philebus*, see 12C1–13A5, 34e3–4. See also Kevin L. Flannery, "Homosexuality and Types of Dualism: A Platonico-Aristotelian Approach," *Gregorianum* 81 (2000): 355–59, Kevin L. Flannery, "Marriage, Mental Handicap, and Sexuality," *Studies in Christian Ethics* 17 (2004): 16–17.

52 In this passage, the word translated 'activity' is ἐνέργεια, which I have translated elsewhere—in particular, in chapters 2 and 3—'actualization,' actualization being distinguished from movement (see *Metaph*. ix,6, 1048b28). In the passages discussed in the present chapter, ἐνέργεια usually has this more general sense of 'activity.'

it is not necessary that there should be something *other* that is better than the pleasure, as some say the end is better than the process; pleasures are not processes nor are they all connected to a process, but they are activities *and* end. [*EN* vii,12, 1153a7–10][53]

Aristotle realizes that people do seek pleasure as an end; it is, therefore, in that sense, a distinct thing. But, when pursued in the proper way, a pleasure is so embedded in its proper activity as to be identified with it. An athletic young woman can say alternatively 'I run for the pleasure of it' or 'I just like running': they are nearly equivalent statements.

In *EN* x,4, Aristotle says that the pleasure of the highest activities perfects them, so that it is an end, but it does not perfect them "in the same way that a perceived object and perception, if they are good, do, just as health and the doctor are not in the same way cause of being healthy" [*EN* x,4, 1174b23–26]. In other words, just as there are different types of cause of the activity of being healthy—there is an efficient cause (a doctor) and a formal cause (health)—so also there are different types of perfection. The perfection of the activity of perceiving which is pleasure is different from the perfection of either the befitting perceived object or of the well-functioning faculty of perception—although the presence of these is indeed pleasurable.

Pleasure is not unlike health: like health, pleasure is present as long as the activity of being healthy is present. But pleasure is also a sort of final cause—without the separation characteristic especially of a perceived object. The relationship between pleasure and its proper activity is more like the relationship between a youth's being in the "bloom of youth" and the delight he takes in being in that state [*EN* x,4, 1174b33]: to be in that state *is*, in a sense, to take delight in it—just as 'the young woman's running joyfully' is nearly equivalent to 'the young woman's taking delight in running.'[54] Pleasure is, therefore, a sort of final cause, but it can also be

53 τι οὐκ ἀνάγκη ἕτερόν τι εἶναι βέλτιον τῆς ἡδονῆς, ὥσπερ τινές φασι τὸ τέλος τῆς γενέσεως· οὐ γὰρ γενέσεις εἰσὶν οὐδὲ μετὰ γενέσεως πᾶσαι, ἀλλ' ἐνέργειαι καὶ τέλος. Aristotle goes on immediately to say that an end need not be "something other" [ἕτερόν τι—1153a11].

54 Michael Pakaluk, commenting on the same passage, writes as follows: "The pleasure functions as a distinct goal not unlike beauty in relation to bodily fitness: we typically reach the peak of fitness through aiming to reach the peak of beauty" [Michael Pakaluk, *Aristotle's* Nicomachean ethics: *An Introduction*, Cambridge Introductions to Key Philosophical Texts (Cambridge: Cambridge University Press, 2005), 312].

viewed as a sort of formal cause. It arrives not at the end of the activity but is present at every moment that—and in so far as—the activity is present.

This close association between pleasures and their corresponding activities has a complex bearing upon such character types as the ἀκρατής (the incontinent man) and the ἀκόλαστος (the depraved man). Since human activities of whatever sort are movements that go from one point to a proper object, they can conflict. When this happens, the pleasures drive one another away, as pleasure in the music of flutes drives away the pleasure of study, if the former is stronger [1175b3–6]. This has no ill effects in itself, but when it happens frequently or characteristically it produces an ultimately dissatisfying cocktail of pleasure and pain. "For countervailing pleasures do pretty much what proper pains do," says Aristotle [EN x,5, 1175b16–17]. Moreover, a person finds his greatest pleasure in sustained activity of the type that most suits his nature;[55] if the pleasure to be derived, for instance, from study is constantly being countered by the pleasure of listening to the music of flutes, not only does this itself produce something akin to pain but it also deprives the person of the higher pleasure, which is sustained pleasure (see EN x,7, 1177a21–22).

Besides conflicting with one another, human activities (unlike mere animal activities) can also become perverted, aiming not at their proper object but at some object related to the proper object only by contrariety. Some of our natural activities can aim at one object alone; sight and hearing, for instance, have as their respective objects visible things and sounds. But once reason is involved, an activity will have its proper object but also the possibility of heading toward something quite contrary to that object, as a doctor can bring about either health or disease.[56] Such deviant objects are not disparate from the proper objects in any random way. A man who deviates from the virtue of truthfulness does not do so by eating too much but by lying. As Aristotle puts it in EE ii,10: "the corruption and

---

55 See EN x,5, 1176a15–26 and i,8, 1099a11–15. See also (in Plato) Phlb. 63D1–64A5.

56 The doctor who brings about disease does not do so, however, qua doctor, since a doctor takes his species from his proper object, health. See EE ii,10, 1227a25–35 and ii,11, 1227b19–38. As noted by von Arnim, these passages are closely related to Metaph. vii,7, 1032a25–b30 [Hans von Arnim, Eudemische Ethik und Metaphysik, Sitzungsberichte der Akademie der Wissenschaften in Wien: Philosophisch-historische Klasse, 207:5 (Vienna/Leipzig: Hölder-Pichler-Tempsky, 1928), 29–30]. See also Gauthier, La morale d'Aristote, 31–32. See below, chapter 7, section VII.

perversion [διαστροφὴ] of each thing heads not toward any chance thing but toward contraries and intermediates" [1227a31–32].[57] Pursuing such objects produces an especially feverish pleasure and not one that corresponds in any way to man's nature, for man's nature (if not disordered) pursues objects that are genuinely good for it.

Why is this? Why does pursuing the object contrary to the natural object produce an ultimately dissatisfying and unhealthy pleasure? Why could this pleasure not be as pleasant as that which corresponds to the activity naturally? As happens when any argument comes close to the principles of the field within which it is conducted, it is difficult to find a satisfying explanation of this fact. It is a matter of definition—although definition determining the essential features of the field, ethics, itself—that the pleasure attaching to natural activity is better and more pleasurable than that attaching to its contrary (unnatural activity), even though it may not be as strong. This is another idea that Aristotle takes over from Plato: the calm pleasures—which are all embedded in their respective natural activities—are better. They are better because they are natural and they are identifiable as natural because they are calm. But although non-circular explanations are wanting, phenomena in support of such principles are not. The sharp pleasure that the arrogant man finds in humiliating his neighbor, we know—and he *should* know—will not ultimately bring him happiness. The pleasure that is part of moderate eating and drinking with friends is superior—even *as* pleasure—to the pleasure experienced in imbibing food and drink simply for the bodily pleasures they bring. The one is also healthy, the other not: the one brings happiness, the other its opposite.

Once pleasures become detached from their proper activities, they are free to conflict with one another, and they inevitably do so. Aristotle associates this phenomenon especially with the hoi polloi, whom he contrasts with the virtuous:

For the masses, pleasures fight against each other because such are not by nature pleasant, but the things that are by nature pleasant are pleasant for the lovers of what is noble. Such are actions according to virtue, so that these are both

---

57 In the previous sentence Aristotle says that such objects are chosen παρὰ φύσιν and διὰ στροφὴν [*EE* ii,10, 1227a30].

pleasant to these persons and pleasant in themselves. Their life, therefore, has no additional need of pleasure as if of some ornament [περιάπτου τινός], but it has its pleasure in itself. [*EN* i,8, 1099a11–16]

The idea here is that the virtuous life, since it has its pleasure in itself, has no need of any pleasure that would lie like a necklace on top of its own beauty. But this latter is precisely the sort of thing that the non-virtuous or the less-than-virtuous (to the extent that they are less than virtuous) find attractive. Since there is no essential connection between an ornament and the beauty upon which its lies, it is all too easy for the ornament itself rather than the proper object of the practice to become the object of pursuit—and this allows for conflicts.

Although the ἀκόλαστος, who (as we shall see in chapter 8) has made a deliberate choice to pursue what he pursues, is not necessarily thrown about, as are the hoi polloi, by multitudinous conflicting pleasures, the concept of pleasure as an ornament—a treasure—pursued independently of its corresponding natural practice is central to his characterization. The ἀκόλαστος lacks the distance from the object of his particular desires required for reasonable, wholly rational, behavior in their regard. His objective is to *have* the relevant pleasures, rather than to engage in their corresponding activities and to accept what pleasure might be attached to them.

At one point Aristotle actually suggests that the highest pleasures involve no desire (ἐπιθυμία) at all and that the pleasure is just the activity itself. He speaks of pleasure that accompanies restoration to a natural state, noting that such pleasure can only be pleasure *per accidens* since "there are also pleasures that involve no pain or desire—for instance, the activities of theorizing, its nature wanting nothing" [1152b35–1153a2].[58] It would seem

---

[58] ὅτι δ' ἡ ἐνέργεια ἐν ταῖς ἐπιθυμίαις τῆς ὑπολοίπου ἕξεως καὶ φύσεως, ἐπεὶ καὶ ἄνευ λύπης καὶ ἐπιθυμίας εἰσὶν ἡδοναί, οἷον αἱ τοῦ θεωρεῖν ἐνέργειαι, τῆς φύσεως οὐκ ἐνδεοῦς οὔσης [*EN* vii,12, 1152b35–1153a2]. Bywater follows Aspasius and brackets ἐνέργειαι in 1153a1; I follow Susemihl-Apelt and leave it in. K[b] has ἡ τοῦ θεωρεῖν ἐνέργεια instead of αἱ τοῦ θεωρεῖν ἐνέργειαι in line 1153a1, which would be a bit easier to reconcile with the singular that follows (τῆς φύσεως οὐκ ἐνδεοῦς οὔσης). (One does wonder whether there *are* plural activities of theorizing.) In 1152b35, ὑπολοίπου is one of three possibilities offered by the MSS, the others being ἐπιλοίπου (found in L[b] and O[b], although Bywater does not mention O[b]) and ὑπολύπου (found in M[b]). None makes easy sense, although a conjecture by Obertus Gifanius (sixteenth/seventeenth century)—ἐπιλύπου—would makes sense, especially in so far as it introduces the issue of λύπη, which plays a part in the explanatory clause that follows (ἐπεὶ καὶ ἄνευ λύπης καὶ ἐπιθυμίας εἰσὶν ἡδοναί [1152b36–1153a1]).

to be relevant that, in this remark, the words 'the activities of theorizing' are in apposition to the words 'pleasures that involve no pain or desire.' It is as if he were saying that, in such cases, the pleasure just is the activity (although the activity is not the pleasure). The idea is that such pleasures do not involve the satisfying of a *felt* need, as when food satisfies hunger.[59] Since desire and pain (in this sense) are not present in activities such as theorizing, pleasure cannot involve desire and pain essentially. Why one would want to pursue such pleasures would be beyond the comprehension of the ἀκόλαστος.

Since the ἀκόλαστος is fixed upon having certain objects and what pleasure they afford, this weighting of his preferences (or desires) in one direction will inevitably pull against any desires he might have for more reasonable pleasures. Or, if his disordered preferences involve more than one ignoble pleasure, the desires for these will come into conflict, one or the other inevitably being left unsatisfied. A carpenter whose delight is in building good cabinets and whose other delights are similarly calm does not have this difficulty. If he enjoys a beer with his friends after work, that does not impede the pleasure he takes in building cabinets. It is true, as we shall be arguing in chapter 8, the ἀκόλαστος does not pursue every possible pleasure that presents itself, but the pleasure or pleasures he wants to have at all costs are for him the decisive object of pursuit. His life will be marked by conflicts between life's typical activities (with their attendant pleasures) and his particular obsession; and he will not have the moral wherewithal to pull himself away from the latter. And this not because he will not have the strength to pull away but rather because he has rejected in advance the ideas that would permit his own reformation.

VIII. Conclusion

This characterization of the less than practically wise characters as pursuing pleasure (at least occasionally) as such and not as part of a natural human practice is connected with Aristotle's understanding of actions (πράξεις) and makings (ποιήσεις): activities, that is, that have their ends

---

59 He goes on to deny that pleasure is a "perceived becoming": a γένεσις αἰσθητή [1153a13]. See also 1152b13.

in themselves and activities whose ends come only once the activity as such has terminated. If that was all there was to the latter activities—if they were just movements or makings finishing at particular spots—they would be inhuman: mere physical events or (at best) the activities of brute animals. What "domesticates" them is their reasonability, their connection with genuine action. As emerging from reason, they have a place in the city, whose only authentic inhabitants are rational animals, those who have a "share in action" [*EN* vi,2, 1139a20]. Although the house is a distinct product of the process of building, knowledge of the craft of building—which has its end present for as long as that knowledge itself is present—ensures that the making of the house is a human making (a human act). When, by contrast, pleasure is pursued for its own sake, this domesticating influence—reason—is excluded. Pleasure pursued for its own sake is not capable of organizing a life, since, *as* pursued for its own sake, it stands outside the intelligible activities to which it properly belongs. It might be regarded then as a sort of product: an ornament, but an ornament pursued by one who does not understand the relationship—the just proportion—between the ornament and that which it adorns.

Seven

Φρόνησις and the Φρόνιμος

A MAJOR IMPEDIMENT to understanding the character type called by Aristotle the φρόνιμος is the sheer difficulty of the first chapter of the eighth book of the *Eudemian Ethics*.[1] The difficulty stems from what has to be called the *weirdness* of Aristotle's argument. At one point, for instance, he says that φρόνησις—the quality that characterizes the φρόνιμος—cannot be understood as dancing girls using their hands for feet are understood; and then he conducts a fairly complicated argument in which he hypothesizes that parts of the human soul might perform similar contortions with one another. Understandably failing to understand what Aristotle is doing by means of these examples and strategies, later scholars and scribes attempted to bring sense to the text of *EE* viii,1 by supposing corruptions and by making emendations, thereby introducing—or, in some

1 As mentioned in the Introduction to the present work, the three chapters of the eighth book of *EE* are sometimes put at the end of the seventh book (an eighth book not being recognized). Pavlos Kontos has kindly pointed out to me that, since φρόνησις is not a moral but a dianoetic virtue, calling the φρόνιμος a *character* type might be misleading. Aristotle does maintain that the φρόνιμος is morally virtuous [*EN* vi,12, 1144a36–37; vii,2, 1146a8–9]; but the issue raised by Kontos is whether the φρόνιμος qua φρόνιμος is a moral character type, and I acknowledge that qua φρόνιμος he is not. The word 'character,' however, need not have moral significance (as when we say, "he was a meticulous character"), so I stipulate that the term 'character' here does not necessarily imply that the habit characterizing the type is a moral virtue. Nor should the word 'type' be understood in a Platonic manner as an immutable, supra-human, fully defined ideal. Aristotle's φρόνιμος is an ideal, but he is also human and mutable.

cases, adding to—the textual corruption. The present chapter is, for the most part, an attempt to get back to the original Aristotelian argument.

In section I, we examine the little-studied Platonic dialogue *Hippias Minor* [*Hp. Mi.*], which, fortunately for us, contains versions of a number of the curious examples Aristotle employs in *EE* viii,1. This is fortunate because it allows us to say with some level of assurance that this is the particular piece of Aristotle's philosophical background against which he develops the argument of *EE* viii,1; this in turn allows us to make more reasoned judgments about which of the various readings of the text ought to be adopted. The argument of Socrates in *Hp. Mi.* is to the effect that the character type that commits injustices voluntarily is the same as the character type that commits justices voluntarily, since they both, unlike the person who is constrained from so acting due to ignorance, are capable of doing the same things. It is unlikely that Plato actually held this position or even attributed it to the historical Socrates, for the dialogue ends with the standard declarations on the part of Socrates of his own ignorance in these matters; it is interesting for us simply as the argumentative background to Aristotle's *EE* viii,1.

Section II is an exegesis of the penultimate chapter (chapter 29) of *Metaph.* v (Aristotle's dictionary of philosophical terms), that chapter (or entry) being dedicated to "the false." *Metaph.* v,29 confirms the link between *Hp. Mi.* and *EE* viii,1, for it both cites *Hp. Mi.* (showing that Aristotle was interested in its argument) and makes mention of the φρόνιμος. Among the senses of "the false" discussed in *Metaph.* v,29 is that pertaining to the false man, who is the opposite of the φρόνιμος (or truthful man). Aristotle is primarily interested in depicting the character type of the false man as deriving its intelligibility from the false man's decided propensity to tell lies. This proves to be important in the interpretation of *EE* viii,1, where Aristotle suggests that the φρόνιμος cannot act in a way incompatible with φρόνησις. His point there has to do not so much with human liberty as with what it means to be φρόνιμος. To be φρόνιμος means to act with φρόνησις, which (contrary to the *Hp. Mi.* argument) excludes acting in the opposite manner, as the false man acts. Besides shedding light upon *EE* viii,1, *Metaph.* v,29 also helps us to understand Aristotle's much-discussed remarks in *EN* vi on practical truth (discussed in section VIII of the present chapter).

Sections III to VI offer a detailed exegesis of *EE* viii,1, which is divided into parts (five parts). In section III, we look at the first two parts, where the dancing girls are compared to scientists (or scholars) who can use their science in a similar way, that is, in a way that is (in a sense) unnatural but also indicative of their expertise. Aristotle argues that the impossibility of using φρόνησις similarly shows that, contrary to the thesis of the Socrates—that is to say, of the historical Socrates—φρόνησις is not a science. In section IV, we look at the third part of *EE* viii,1, the text of which has been subject to much emendation. The basic idea is that any attempt to explain failures of the supposed φρόνιμος to behave in a manner consistent with φρόνησις by positing divisions in the soul inevitably runs up against the Socratic principle that reason is never "dragged about as a slave," which Aristotle too maintains is a sound principle (when it is properly understood). Aristotle is clearly interested in undermining the *Hp. Mi.* position that the φρόνιμος has in his soul that which is characteristic of his opposite.

In section V, we look at the fourth part of *EE* viii,1, where Aristotle puts forward a number of explanations of why the "soul-splitting" hypothesis of the previous part does not go through. He says that the most obvious absurdity lies in the idea, to which soul-splitting leads, that one might out of ignorance behave in a manner incompatible with φρόνησις. This is absurd, since (as Aristotle maintains in *EN* vi) φρόνησις is an intellectual (or "dianoetic") virtue; it, therefore, as such, does not admit of ignorance. In section VI, we consider the conclusion (or fifth part) of *EE* viii,1, showing in particular that it espouses a position contrary to the position argued for by the character Socrates in *Hp. Mi.*, for it maintains that the φρόνιμος, qua φρόνιμος, is not possessed of the propensities of his opposite, except in a very minimal sense that would still exclude behaving qua φρόνιμος in a non-virtuous manner. Aristotle finishes off *EE* viii,1 with a brief remark in which he expresses qualified agreement with the historical Socrates regarding the dominance of reason.

In section VII, we use the ideas garnered from *Hp. Mi.*, *Metaph.* v,29, and *EE* viii,1, in order to fill out the analysis of the φρόνιμος begun in chapter 5, section III, where we discussed the per se and the per accidens as they pertain to a character type's orientation toward either the true good or the apparent good. The central idea here is that the soul of the φρόνιμος is united and one and consistent with his own nature. It is his orientation toward the good defining human nature that makes the idea of contorting φρόνησις in order to demonstrate φρόνησις an absurd one. One can use contortion only in order to demonstrate a proficiency that is superior to (and, therefore, essentially distinct from) the demonstration itself—as one might demonstrate one's mastery of a language by using it as would a person who has not mastered it. Since φρόνησις *is* the master capacity (or virtue) in the practical sphere, one cannot "misuse" it (contort it) in order to demonstrate one's mastery of φρόνησις: φρόνησις is not superior to itself. There is a passage earlier in the *Eudemian Ethics* (in *EE* ii,10) where Aristotle does speak of pursuing the merely apparent good by way of contortion; but this is a different type of contortion: one that demonstrates no proficiency but is simply and straightforwardly a misuse of the human capacity to act voluntarily for the sake of the true good for man.

We conclude, in section VIII, with a consideration of an issue that has vexed interpreters of Aristotle in recent years: the relationship between φρόνησις and truth. Does not being φρόνιμος have to do essentially with acting correctly, and does not acting correctly emerge from *inclinations* so to act? Then why should φρόνησις have any connection at all with truth, the object of speculative (and non-practical) reason? Our response to this challenge is simply to point out that for Aristotle, as is clear from *Metaph.* v,29, to be a φρόνιμος is to be a truthful man. That is what Aristotle means by the term. But the φρόνιμος is not simply an honest private individual; his honesty has to do with making deliberations and decisions regarding a larger enterprise of some sort: a household or a state. Indeed, in the most proper understanding of the term, the φρόνιμος has as his object the broad field of ethics itself. He is characteristically good at aiming well at what ought to be done in the moral sense.

I. *Hippias Minor*

A useful entry into Aristotle's understanding of the φρόνιμος is Plato's short but endlessly fascinating dialogue *Hippias minor*. The dialogue is useful because, in *Metaph.* v,29, Aristotle criticizes one of its central ideas and, in *EE* viii,1, develops this criticism into a full-blown account of the logical structure of the φρόνιμος. Although *Metaph.* v,29 is about 'the false' [τὸ ψεῦδος], including 'the false man,' the analysis of the latter also serves—with the appropriate adjustments—as an analysis of 'the true man,' who, as we shall see, is equivalent to the φρόνιμος.

Hp. Mi. is a dialectical exchange between Socrates and the sophist Hippias, whom Plato portrays as very proud of his own multifaceted knowledge. Just before the dialogue begins, Hippias has been speaking about Homer, and so Socrates is eager to know whether he regards Achilles or Odysseus as the better man. Hippias replies that Achilles is the better, since he is "true and straightforward" [ἀληθής τε καὶ ἁπλοῦς—365B4], whereas Odysseus is "wily and false" [πολύτροπός τε καὶ ψευδής—365B5]; indeed, he says, they are two quite different types of men [365C3-4]. Socrates gets Hippias to acknowledge that false men are capable, φρόνιμοι, knowledgeable, and wise regarding that with respect to which they are false [366A3-4]. Unlike the ignorant, who do not know whether they are telling the truth or not (and sometimes involuntarily tell the truth [367A3]), false men know when they are lying and therefore they are also capable of telling the truth. This makes them like Hippias himself, says Socrates, taking an ironical jab at his interlocutor, for he too, being knowledgeable, is capable like few others of lying voluntarily [367E1-369A2]. Since virtue is the capacity to do something and since the true man and the false are equally capable of telling the truth and lying, they are equally virtuous with respect to truth and falsehood.[2]

Socrates also mounts an attack against Hippias's idea that Achilles is "true and straightforward," thereby weakening the thesis that Achilles and Odysseus are distinct types [369B3-7]. Achilles proclaims at one point in the *Iliad* that he is not one to "harbor one thing in his mind but to say another."[3] But in fact, argues Socrates, he does just this, lying to Odysseus about preparing his ships to leave. "In an entirely noble manner [πάνυ γενναίως]," says Socrates, "he makes small account of speaking the truth."[4] These remarks are interesting on a pair of counts. First, they give

---

2 One finds similar ideas in the first book of Plato's *Republic*: *R.* i, 333E6-334B6.
3 τερον μὲν κεύθῃ ἐνὶ φρεσίν, ἄλλο δὲ εἴπῃ—*Il.* 9.313; *Hp. Mi.* 365B1, 370A5.
4 *Hp. Mi.* 370D5-6.

us a definition of lying, a definition with which Plato apparently agrees, for it goes unchallenged: lying is knowing something and yet saying to another something incompatible with it. Secondly, the remarks suggest that the character Socrates—and apparently Plato himself—are not entirely against lying. The language employed at *Hp. Mi.* 370D5–6 is very similar to the language employed in the infamous passage in the *Republic* where Plato speaks favorably of the noble lie [γενναῖόν τι ἓν ψευδομένους],[5] propagated for reasons of political expediency. At the end of *Hp. Mi.*, however, Socrates acknowledges that he is not sure of his own arguments. "I do not find it in me to agree with you in these matters," says Hippias. Says Socrates: "Nor I with myself, Hippias. But so it must necessarily appear to us, given the argument. As I said earlier, however, regarding these things I drift up and down and they never seem the same to me" [376B7–C3].

II. *Metaph.* v,29

As mentioned, Aristotle's reaction to all of this comes in the penultimate chapter of his analytical dictionary, *Metaph.* v, the entry dedicated to "the false" [τὸ ψεῦδος]. The entry is divided into three parts: the first {1} pertaining to falsehood as present (or, one might prefer to say, not present) at the level of τὸ πρᾶγμα (the thing); the second {2} to falsehood as attributed to a λόγος (an account or definition); the third {3} to falsehood as attributed to a man. In the first section of the first part {1a}, he says that we speak of a falsehood at the level of the thing (or of things) when {1a'} we refer either to something that cannot be (the diagonal of a square commensurate with a side) or {1a"} to something that could be but is not (you

---

5 Besides *R.* iii, 414B9–C1, see also ii, 382C7–D7. *Hp. Mi.* is usually considered to be an early dialogue and so written before *R.* Later in his life, Plato appears to have become more negative about lying: see, for instance, *Lg.* v, 730C1–6: "Truth heads the list of all things good, for gods and men alike. Let anyone who intends to be happy and blessed be its partner from the start, so that he may live as much of his life as possible a man of truth. You can trust a man like that, but not the man who is fond of telling deliberate lies (and anyone who is happy to go on producing falsehoods in ignorance of the truth is an idiot)" [translation by Trevor Saunders in John M. Cooper, *Plato: Complete Works* (Indianapolis: Hackett, 1997)]. But later in the same work, he set limits to (at least) prosecutable lying: *Lg.* xi, 916D2–917B7. One should not, he says, lie to the gods or to others superior to oneself. "Now the 'superiors' of bad men are the good, and of the young their elders (usually)—which means that parents are the superiors of their offspring, men are (of course) the superiors of women and children, and rulers of their subjects" [917A4–6; translation again by Trevor Saunders].

sitting, when you are standing); in the second section of the same part {1b}, he says that we speak too of falsehood when the thing *is* but either {1b'} appears to be but is not another thing that *is* (as a theatrical backdrop in Athens might appear to represent the walls of Thebes) or {1b"} when the thing appears to be something that is *not* (such as are visions that come in sleep).

In introducing the second part {2}, Aristotle says that a false account, "qua false" [1024b27], is about something different from that which the true account is about. He uses the example of the account (the definition) of a circle as applied to a triangle, as when someone says of a triangle that it is a plane figure whose center is equidistant from all points on the figure's periphery. Aristotle is saying something about the false account that he has not said about falsehoods at the level of things in part {1}. Important is the phrase "qua false": qua false such accounts refer to that which is not, but qua what they are, that is, qua accounts, they are true. It is true that the person saying that a triangle is 'a plane figure whose center is equidistant from all points on the figure's periphery,' utters a falsehood, but the account does refer to something (the circle).

Aristotle adds that there are true accounts that are not accounts of a thing's essence and yet truly describe their subject (for we can say both that Socrates is a rational animal and that he is musical), but then he says: "a false account, however, is strictly speaking an account of nothing."[6] We see here again a concern to acknowledge a certain connection with true accounts but also a desire to be clear: falsehood has to do with what is not. He goes on: "For this reason, Antisthenes simple-mindedly maintained that nothing proper is said except by means of its own account: one thing of one thing—from which it follows that there is no contradiction and practically no false-speaking."[7] In other words, Antisthenes was right at

---

6 δὲ ψευδὴς λόγος οὐθενός ἐστιν ἁπλῶς λόγος [*Metaph.* v,29, 1024b31–32]. Both Jaeger and Ross put this remark within parentheses. This, however, has the effect of separating it from the remark about Antisthenes that follows, with which it is certainly connected logically. (See note 7.)

7 διὸ Ἀντισθένης ᾤετο εὐήθως μηθὲν ἀξιῶν λέγεσθαι πλὴν τῷ οἰκείῳ λόγῳ, ἓν ἐφ' ἑνός· ἐξ ὧν συνέβαινε μὴ εἶναι ἀντιλέγειν, σχεδὸν δὲ μηδὲ ψεύδεσθαι [*Metaph.* v,29, 1024b32–34]. Aristotle understands how one might hold what Antisthenes holds (see *Top.* i,11, 104b19–24), for he too holds that a *proper* account is of that of which it is (qua instance of truth-telling). The fact is, however, that some people do employ accounts improperly.

It is not impossible that a μὴ has dropped out of line 1024b32 (so that we should read διὸ

least in this: he saw that false accounts are about nothing, although he was wrong to deduce from this that the person employing such an account "says nothing" and thereby avoids contradiction with the true account. Antisthenes failed to understand that, although a false account, qua false, refers to nothing, qua account it does refer to something. Its having direction toward something (toward the circle) but being aimed at that which is not a circle is what causes the problem, the problem of contradiction. What such a person says conflicts with what the truth-telling person says, because both accounts—which have sense and a certain reference qua accounts—cannot hold of the thing of which the true account speaks (truly). As we might put it, both accounts cannot get into the same logical spot.[8]

Part {3}, about the false man, is the most important part for present purposes, for in it Aristotle mentions both *Hp. Mi.* and the φρόνιμος. (As suggested above, the false man is the mirror image of 'the true man,' that is, of the φρόνιμος.) The general argument is that for the false man we must use not the analysis set out in {2} but the one set out in {1b}, where Aristotle speaks of the theatrical backdrop and the dream vision. If (as in {2}) false accounts are basically true accounts misused, false men on the other hand are simply false. Someone might be inclined to quibble, arguing that using a theatrical backdrop in Athens to represent the walls of Thebes is not unlike applying the definition of the circle to the triangle. But Aristotle can respond that a backdrop—or, literally, a shadow painting: σκιαγραφία [1024b23]—unlike a definition applied to the wrong object, was never meant to fix its audience's thoughts on (for instance) the walls of Thebes but is merely suggestive—and in that sense deceiving: it might serve next month to represent the walls of Sparta.[9] "The false man," says Aristotle, "is one who is heedless and decided regarding such [false] accounts [ὁ εὐχερὴς καὶ προαιρετικὸς τῶν τοιούτων λόγων], not for any other reason but for its

---

Ἀντισθένης ᾤετο μὴ εὐήθως μηθὲν ἀξιῶν λέγεσθαι), for in *Top.* i,11 Aristotle says that genuinely philosophical puzzles such as that of Antisthenes (as opposed to the sophistical puzzles mentioned at 104b24–28) are not the utterances of any chance person, which it would be simple-minded [εὔηθες—104b24] to take seriously. A presentation of the theory of Antisthenes can be found in Plato's *Euthydemus* at 285D7–286C8. There the theory is being exploited by the sophist Dionysodorus, although it is attributed to certain other philosophers (286B8–C3). See also *Metaph.* viii,3, 1043b23–32.

8 See chapter 2, section I.

9 Similarly, Aristotle says at *de Insomniis* 461b5–7 that dreams "do not generally seem real, unless the seat of judgment is restrained or does not activate its proper movement."

own sake."[10] Such a man is so constituted as to introduce false accounts into the minds of others, "just as we said also of false things such as introduce a false impression" [1025a5–6]. His being false is not simply a matter of something's being fundamentally true but used in a false manner. The man *is* false—although what he uses (false accounts) are false only in their use, that is, "qua false" [1024b27], and not in themselves.

"For this reason," continues Aristotle, "the argument in the *Hippias* throws one off track when it suggests that one and the same man is false and true" [1025a6–7]. Contrary to what Socrates suggests (although very ambiguously) in *Hp. Mi.* [376A2–B6], being a false or a true man is not simply a matter of being capable of telling both truth and falsehood voluntarily; rather, it is having a settled disposition toward one or the other. As we have just seen, one of the words that Aristotle uses in this regard is προαιρετικὸς [1025a2–4]—very literally, "possessed of the disposition of one who has made a choice." It is choices—in the particularly strong Aristotelian sense of something voluntary issuing from deliberation [*EN* iii,2, 1111b6–8, iii,3, 1113a9–12]—that determine the extreme character types: the true man and the false man.[11]

Aristotle concludes *Metaph.* v,29 with what appears to be a genial criticism of Plato.[12] As we have just seen, Aristotle says that the account in *Hp. Mi.* "throws one off track" (παρακρούεται) when it argues that "the same man is both false and true." "It assumes," he says,

that he who is able to lie is false *and* that he is the knowledgeable man or the φρόνιμος; it assumes, moreover, that he who voluntarily performs bad things is better.[13] But it arrives at this falsehood by induction, [adducing the idea] that

---

10 *Metaph.* v,29, 1025a2–4; see also *EN* iv,7, 1127b14–17. In chapter 8, we discuss "the liar" [ὁ ψεύστης] (see there, note 28). The character type referred to in *Metaph.* v,29 is a more thoroughly corrupted man, closer to (perhaps identical with) the ἀκόλαστος (see again chapter 8, sections I and VIII). Aristotle does not use the expression ὁ ψεύστης in *Metaph.* v,29, referring to this character type rather as the ἄνθρωπος ψευδής. That he is "heedless and decided [regarding false accounts] not for any other reason but for its own sake" is what picks him out; the liar lies for the sake of money, reputation, etc. On the word προαιρετικὸς (or προαίρεσις), see chapter 8, especially sections I and VIII.

11 That is to say, the φρόνιμος and, as we shall see more clearly in chapter 8, the ἀκόλαστος.

12 One notes, however, that he speaks throughout only about the account (λόγος) of *Hp. Mi.*, never mentioning either Plato or Socrates.

13 Following Jaeger's reading: ἔτι τὸν ἑκόντα <πράττοντα> τὰ φαῦλα βελτίω [*Metaph.* v,29, 1025a9].

the voluntary lame man is better than the involuntary, *meaning* 'to simulate being lame' [is better]—for if a man is a voluntary lame man he is probably worse, as he is so also ethically.[14]

This argument about being lame or limping is one of a number of examples that Socrates uses in order to convince Hippias ("by induction") that the voluntarily false man is a good and virtuous man: just as he who voluntarily limps ("is lame") is virtuous with respect to the use of the legs, so also is he who voluntarily lies with respect to the use of language. So, Aristotle's main point here at the end of *Metaph.* v,29 is that Socrates's argument is not a good one, since it includes this ambiguous reference to the voluntary lame man. When Socrates says that the voluntary lame man is better than the involuntary one, he *means* that the man who simulates being lame is in the better state, correctly predicting that his interlocutor will not pick up the equivocation on 'being lame' and 'simulating being lame.' Aristotle is in effect saying that Socrates is doing something not dissimilar to what he (Socrates) says Achilles does in the *Iliad*: having one thing in mind but saying another.[15] Had Hippias challenged Socrates at that point and elicited from him a clarification and had Socrates said that he meant 'being lame,' Hippias could have responded that, no, just as one who is voluntarily lame is worse off than the involuntarily lame, so the person given over to falsehood is worse off than the one who involuntarily utters a falsehood since 'false' characterizes who (or what) he is.[16]

---

14 τοῦτο δὲ ψεῦδος λαμβάνει διὰ τῆς ἐπαγωγῆς–ὁ γὰρ ἑκὼν χωλαίνων τοῦ ἄκοντος κρείττων–τὸ χωλαίνειν τὸ μιμεῖσθαι λέγων, ἐπεὶ εἴ γε χωλὸς ἑκών, χείρων ἴσως, ὥσπερ ἐπὶ τοῦ ἤθους, καὶ οὗτος [*Metaph.* v,29, 1025a9–13]. The word χωλαίνω can mean either to *be* lame (someone who must limp) or simply to limp (which would include simulating being a lame person). To be a voluntary lame man probably means to make oneself lame (in order, perhaps, to avoid military service). The relevant exchange in Plato is at *Hp. Mi.* 374C5–D2: {–ΣΩ.} Δέξαιο δ' ἂν πότερον τἀγαθὰ κεκτῆσθαι ἢ τὰ κακά; {–ΙΠ.} Τἀγαθά. {–ΣΩ.} Πότερον οὖν ἂν δέξαιο πόδας κεκτῆσθαι ἑκουσίως χωλαίνοντας ἢ ἀκουσίως; {–ΙΠ.} Ἑκουσίως. {–ΣΩ.} Χωλεία δὲ ποδῶν οὐχὶ πονηρία καὶ ἀσχημοσύνη ἐστίν; {–ΙΠ.} Ναί. Immediately after this exchange, Socrates mentions the case that figures prominently in *EE* viii,1: that of seeing double voluntarily.

15 See above, note 4.

16 The exchange about the "lame" man is probably an instance of Socratic irony. Elsewhere Aristotle criticizes the ironical man who in dialectical exchange denies the facts or makes light of them: see *EN* ii,7, 1108a19–23 and iv,7, 1127a22–23. But Aristotle's attitude toward irony (and specifically toward Socratic irony) is not severe: see *EN* iv,7, 1127b22–26. He says that the great-souled man will speak the truth, except when he's being ironical with the vulgar [*EN* iv,3, 1124b30–31].

It is interesting that, in making this criticism of Socrates's argument as he concludes this chapter about 'the false,' Aristotle employs an example of being false—or, at least, of being not entirely straightforward. Indeed, he mentions two such instances: Socrates's suggestion that he means 'being lame' (and not 'simulating being lame') and the limper's suggestion that he is lame (when, in fact, he is not). Neither example satisfies the criteria for being a false account as set out in {2}—understood in a certain way, the words or actions involved do correspond to something in realty—but, in each, that which the agent hopes will be communicated does not correspond to what he has in mind.

III. *EE* viii,1, parts I and II

That brings us to *EE* viii,1, a chapter fraught with textual difficulties, caused originally, no doubt, by the strangeness of Aristotle's examples and argumentation, especially for copyists who did not know *Hp. Mi.*[17] The chapter divides in a fairly easy manner into the following parts:

I. 1246a26–b4: distinctions: natural-unnatural; per se–per accidens;

II. 1246b4–12: the willing person in command;

III. 1246b12–19: a possible response: split the soul (but this would mean that reason is dragged about like a slave);

IV. 1246b19–28: more reasons why the response is absurd;

V. 1246b28–36 (conclusion): in contrast with the ideas put forward earlier, the analysis of an excellence includes potencies with respect to which that excellence is incapable; the φρόνιμος is committed, with a united soul, to pursuing the good; and so Socrates was both right and wrong.

In part I, Aristotle draws a distinction between using something in its natural way and using it in an unnatural way; he distinguishes this dis-

---

17 On *EE* viii,1, see Henry Jackson, "*Eudemian Ethics* Θ i, ii (H xiii, xiv), 1246a26–1248b7," *Journal of Philology* 32 (1913): 170–221; Anthony Kenny, *The Aristotelian Ethics*, 1978), 184–89; Paul Moraux, "Das Fragment VIII 1: Text und Interpretation," in *Untersuchungen zur* Eudemischen Ethik*: Akten des 5. Symposiums Aristotelicum (Oosterbeek, Niederlande, 21–29. August 1969)*, ed. Paul Moraux and Dieter Harlfinger (Berlin: De Gruyter, 1971), 253–84; Michael Woods, *Aristotle: 'Eudemian Ethics,' books I, II and VIII*, 158–64, and Franz Dirlmeier, *Aristoteles* Eudemische Ethik, 471–78.

tinction from the per se–per accidens distinction. One can use the eye in order to see in the natural way or, by "contorting" [διαστρέψαντα] it, to see double. This is quite different from using an eye per accidens, as one does if one sells it or eats it—as opposed to using it qua eye or for its per se purpose: to see, whether normally or double. This example is evidence that the arguments of *EE* viii,1 arise from Aristotle's consideration the arguments in *Hp. Mi.*, for the example of the eye occurs there.[18] In *Hp. Mi.*, it serves much the same purpose as the limping example. Socrates argues that, if one who knows enough about seeing to vary its use in this way is better than the person who cannot do so, then the person who can both tell the truth and lie is better than the person who, not knowing the truth, cannot do this. This leads eventually to the conclusion that, since both the knowledgeable truth-teller and the knowledgeable false man are equally capable, they are really just the same character type. Aristotle also uses the example of someone who deliberately writes something incorrectly (in order, presumably, to instruct someone in the proper way to write) and the example of dancing girls who dance on their hands (using their hands as if feet). The writing example also appears in *Hp. Mi.* (at 366C2).

Although, as we shall see, it is significant that Aristotle distinguishes the natural-unnatural distinction from the per se–per accidens one, in the argumentation of *EE* viii,1, he is primarily interested in the phenomenon of using something unnaturally, beginning the chapter with the question whether it is always possible to use something in this way. He tacitly grants that we can always use a science (ἐπιστήμη) or a technique (τέχνη) in this manner—a mathematician might deliberately draw a wrong conclusion in order to see whether his students catch the error—but Aristotle asks whether the moral virtues can always be so used. If they are all sciences, as Socrates maintains,[19] it will be possible to be using justice while seeming to be doing injustice; it will be possible, that is, to act unjustly

---

18 {-ΣΩ.} Τί δέ; ἀμβλυωπία οὐ πονηρία ὀφθαλμῶν; {-ΙΠ.} Ναί. {-ΣΩ.} Ποτέρους οὖν ἂν βούλοιο ὀφθαλμοὺς κεκτῆσθαι καὶ ποτέροις συνεῖναι; οἷς ἑκὼν ἄν τις ἀμβλυώττοι καὶ παρορῴη ἢ οἷς ἄκων; {-ΙΠ.} Οἷς ἑκών. [*Hp. Mi.* 374D3–7]. This example comes just after the limping example: see above, note 14.

19 That is, the historical Socrates, not the Socrates who, in *Hp. Mi.*, attempts to confound Hippias. See *EN* vi,13, 1144b28–30.

"by doing unjust things"—but from justice.[20] One thinks immediately of Plato's noble lie.[21]

As is stated in part V, Aristotle rejects the Socratic thesis that the moral virtues are sciences (or techniques); the proof presented here is that they cannot be used unnaturally (although per se) as can be the eye or one's knowledge of writing. This is not to say, however, that even in this respect a moral virtue is wholly different from a science. Someone who knows arithmetic can, relying on this knowledge, deliberately make an error in computation, but he cannot "*be* ignorant from science" [ἀγνοεῖν ἀπὸ ἐπιστήμης—1246b2], just as no one can really commit injustices *from* justice.[22]

In part II, it becomes apparent that Aristotle's concern in *EE* viii,1 is φρόνησις (and the φρόνιμος), for he mentions this virtue—this intellectual virtue—in its first line.[23] This does not make *Metaph.* v,29, with its analysis of the decided false man, any less relevant, for, as mentioned, the φρόνιμος is the mirror image of that character type. Aristotle says here again that, if the use of φρόνησις must be single [ἁπλῆ]—if, that is, it cannot involve a "contortion" [στροφή] as when one deliberately sees double—then one acts in a wise manner [φρονίμως] only when doing morally upright and genuinely wise things.[24] Why must this be? Because, he explains, when one uses one's knowledge in order to make errors (for the sake of one's students, for example), there is something standing above the relevant science as "commander" [κυρία—1246b9] which effects the contortion. But such a commander cannot be in command of φρόνησις.

What is this commander? Aristotle does not answer (or even address)

---

20 ... ἀδικήσει ἄρα ἀπὸ δικαιοσύνης τὰ ἄδικα πράττων ... [*EE* viii,1, 1246a37]. See also *EN* vi,5, 1140b22–24: καὶ ἐν μὲν τέχνῃ ὁ ἑκὼν ἁμαρτάνων αἱρετώτερος, περὶ δὲ φρόνησιν ἧττον, ὥσπερ καὶ περὶ τὰς ἀρετάς.

21 See above, note 5.

22 At 1246a38, Aristotle speaks of doing τὰ ἀγνοητικὰ ἀπὸ ἐπιστήμης. This does not mean that one is *ignorant* from science (or knowledge)—which is impossible—but that one does "ignorant things" from science. Aristotle did not have scare quotes at his disposal.

23 See also *EE* viii,1, 1246b33 and viii,2, 1246b37.

24 In order to avoid awkward phrases, we employ in this chapter the word 'wise' (instead of what might be considered the more properly Aristotelian 'practically wise') in reference to actions which the φρόνιμος qua φρόνιμος would perform or counsel. The intellectual virtue of wisdom (σοφία)—to be discussed below—has as its proper object not wise actions but truths.

this question, but it must be the φρόνιμος. The intellectual virtue φρόνησις attaches so directly to the φρόνιμος that there cannot be between him and the actions he performs (qua φρόνιμος) the distance that would make it possible ever to say truly that he misuses φρόνησις out of φρόνησις. As we have seen, a knowledgeable man can use a science in an unnatural way in order to show that he is knowledgeable, but he cannot use ignorance itself in this way in order to show the same thing. Similarly, the φρόνιμος cannot use real folly in order to show that he is φρόνιμος.[25]

IV. *EE* viii,1, part III

Part III is also—indeed, especially—difficult. The Greek text as we have it contains at least one lacuna and several variant readings; the argument appears to have been formulated in a very compressed manner in any case. The best way of grasping at least its thrust is to bear in mind: (1) Aristotle's argument in *Metaph.* v,29 against the ideas articulated by Socrates in *Hp. Mi.*, for we know that the argumentation up to this point in *EE* viii,1 has come out of that discussion; (2) one other place, *EN* vii,2, where Aristotle discusses issues related to the issues discussed in part III; (3) the conclusions drawn in part V, toward which (of course) this argument is moving.

As to (1), we know that Aristotle does not share the conclusions to which Socrates's argumentation in *Hp. Mi.* leads. That is, he does not think that the φρόνιμος can be defined as a character type who might just as well perform actions incompatible with φρόνησις. As we have seen in parts I and II, Aristotle holds that, although some capacities (such as the capacity to see by means of the eye) can be used in either a natural or an unnatural manner and still be used as what they are per se, φρόνησις does not work like that. Just as the false man (as opposed to the weak false man) is "heedless and decided" [εὐχερὴς καὶ προαιρετικὸς] with respect to falsehood [*Metaph.* v,29, 1025a2–3], so the φρόνιμος is decided (if not heedless) with

---

25 As Aristotle indicates at 1246b29, he does not have a word (like 'folly') to serve as the opposite of φρόνησις, so he uses instead ignorance (ἄγνοια), the opposite of knowledge or knowing (γνῶσις) (mentioned in the last line of the chapter: 1246b36). Since φρόνησις is an intellectual virtue, this is not unreasonable; but it does not make his argumentation any clearer!

respect to truth in practical matters. He is what he is with respect to wise actions.

As to (2), Aristotle discusses in *EN* vii,2 both the ἀκρατής and the φρόνιμος; the relationship between these two—that is to say, the differences between them—is also clearly under discussion in *EE* viii,1, part III. In *EN* vii,2, Aristotle also discusses the Socratic principle that reason cannot be "dragged about like a slave" [1145b24]—a principle with which he agrees, provided it is correctly understood and applied.[26] Here in *EE* viii,1, part III, the principle plays an important role.

In *EN* vii,2, Aristotle first mentions that some thinkers have argued that the problem of ἀκρασία—the problem of how someone who knows what he ought to do can do something quite different—can be solved by saying that the ἀκρατής has not knowledge of what he ought to do but only opinion. Aristotle replies that such an argument simply sidesteps the issue of ἀκρασία, for the ἀκρατής (at least as centrally conceived) is not the man who is not sure what he should do but the man who knows full well and yet succumbs to his lower inclinations [1145b31–1146a4]. So, suggests Aristotle [1146a4–5], let us say that the opposing force is not mere opinion but φρόνησις—which is the strongest thing [ἰσχυρότατον]—and let us say too that the ἀκρατής possesses this. "But this is absurd," he says, "for the same man will be both φρόνιμος and ἀκρατής and no one would say that it belongs to the φρόνιμος to perform willingly the foulest things."[27] The absurdity that Aristotle rejects here is the absurdity argued for in *Hp. Mi.* by Socrates. "Besides these things," adds Aristotle, "it was demonstrated earlier that in any case the φρόνιμος is *practical*—he has to do with ultimate things [i.e., actions]—and he possesses also the other virtues" [1146a7–9].[28] There is a direct line of intelligibility between the φρόνιμος and his actions: to the extent that this line is broken, he is not φρόνιμος.

---

26 See *EN* vii,2, 1145b21–24 and 1146a4–5, and *EN* vii,3, 1147b13–17. In Plato, see, for instance, *R.* ix, 588E3–599A4 and *Protagoras* 352A8–C7.

27 ' ἄτοπον· ἔσται γὰρ ὁ αὐτὸς ἅμα φρόνιμος καὶ ἀκρατής, φήσειε δ' οὐδ' ἂν εἷς φρονίμου εἶναι τὸ πράττειν ἑκόντα τὰ φαυλότατα [*EN* vii,2, 1146a5–7]. The language used here is very similar to that found at *Metaph.* v,29, 1025a9: ἔτι τὸν ἑκόντα <πράττοντα> τὰ φαῦλα βελτίω (see above, note 13).

28 The back reference is to *EN* vi,7, 1141b14–23; note especially the language at 1141b21–23: ἡ δὲ φρόνησις πρακτική· ὥστε δεῖ ἄμφω ἔχειν, ἢ ταύτην μᾶλλον. εἴη δ' ἄν τις καὶ ἐνταῦθα ἀρχιτεκτονική. In this passage too φρόνησις is supreme.

As to (3), the conclusion to *EE* viii,1 (part V) is also corrupt but it is apparent that it involves the idea that being φρόνιμος and having good habits in the irrational part of the soul go together [ἅμα—1246b33]. Again, this is consistent with what we have seen in Aristotle's reaction to the *Hp. Mi.* arguments: φρόνησις, says Aristotle, takes over the whole of the subject; one cannot have at the same time both φρόνησις and its opposite. Aristotle also maintains in this conclusion that Socrates was right in holding that nothing is stronger than φρόνησις (although he went wrong in believing that φρόνησις is a science [ἐπιστήμη]).[29] In other words (and to repeat), Aristotle agrees that knowledge (in this case φρόνησις) cannot be dragged around like a slave.

So then, as we have seen, in the run-up to part III of *EE* viii,1 Aristotle has been discussing the possibility that φρόνησις might be used to perform acts not characteristic of the φρόνιμος. He now asks:

Who then will be [the φρόνιμος]? Will it not be as if to say that ἀκρασία is a wickedness of the irrational part of the soul and that somehow the ἀκρατής, having reason, is ἀκόλαστος? But if this were the case, and should desire be stronger, it will contort [reason?] and will reckon the opposite.[30] Or is it not clear that, should virtue be in the one part and ignorance in the rational, they, being diverse, typically change character? So justice will be used both justly and wickedly and φρόνησις unwisely—as also in the opposite manner. [*EE* viii,1, 1246b12–19][31]

Regarding the initial two sentences here, one wonders why the ἀκρατής has suddenly become ἀκόλαστος—a different character type altogether (for the soul of the ἀκρατής is divided, that of the ἀκόλαστος de-

---

29 ὅτε δῆλον ὅτι ἅμα φρόνιμοι καὶ ἀγαθαὶ ἐκείνων αἱ <τοῦ> ἀλόγου ἕξεις, καὶ ὀρθῶς τὸ Σωκρατικόν, ὅτι οὐδὲν ἰσχυρότερον φρονήσεως [*EE* viii,1, 1246b32–34]. This is the Walzer-Mingay text, which seems to make more sense than what Susmihl gives.

30 I use the archaic 'reckon' in order to indicate that Aristotle is speaking here (at least indirectly) about the λογιστικόν, often translated 'reckoning part'—i.e., the part of the soul which considers what should be done. (See *EN* vi,1, 1139a12.)

31 τίς οὖν ἐστίν; ἢ ὥσπερ λέγεται ἀκρασία κακία τοῦ ἀλόγου τῆς ψυχῆς, καί πως ἀκόλαστος ὁ ἀκρατὴς ἔχων νοῦν; ἀλλ' εἰ δή, ἂν ἰσχυρὰ ᾖ ἡ ἐπιθυμία, στρέψει καὶ λογιεῖται τἀναντία. ἢ ἔστι δῆλον ὅτι, κἂν ἐν μὲν τούτῳ ἀρετή, ἐν δὲ τῷ λόγῳ ἄγνοια ᾖ, ἕτεραι μεταποιοῦνται; ὥστε ἔσται δικαιοσύνη τὸ δικαίως χρῆσθαι καὶ κακῶς καὶ φρονήσει ἀφρόνως, ὥστε καὶ τἀναντία [*EE* viii,1, 1246b12–19]. This version of the text borrows readings from both the Walzer-Mingay and the Susemihl editions. In dealing with the lacuna at 1246b15 (and also with other details), I follow Jackson [Jackson, "*Eudemian Ethics* Θ i, ii,*" 177, 205].

cided).³² The answer is that Aristotle is here suggesting that the φρόνιμος who acts in a non-φρόνιμος manner might be like the ἀκρατής—which is to say that a *part* of the soul might be bad (ἀκόλαστος) and another part might have reason (or act reasonably). In other words, the supposed ἀκρατής does not himself become ἀκόλαστος but a part of him does, which—due to its combination with the part that acts reasonably—makes the soul itself ἀκρατής.

Henry Jackson, whose reading of the next bit (1246b15–16) we follow here, makes 'desire' [ἡ ἐπιθυμία] the subject of both the verb 'contort' [στρέψει] and the verb 'reckon' [λογιεῖται].³³ The contortion Aristotle hypothesizes would be analogous to the contortion deliberately effected by the man who sees double. Aristotle is trying to portray the way in which the characteristics of both the φρόνιμος and his opposite might belong to the same soul in such a way that the φρόνιμος "might just as well" perform unwise acts, and so he supposes that the soul can somehow achieve the distance necessary for contortion within itself, by playing the irrational part of the soul off against the rational (see *EN* vi,1, 1139a 4–5). According to this hypothesis, desire would move into the role of initiator of action.³⁴ Similarly, if the Jackson reading is correct, Aristotle would be suggesting in the same line that desire might "reckon." From an Aristotelian point of view, it is difficult to conceive of desire as doing reasoning of any sort, but Aristotle never presents this whole conception of how the soul works as coherent, and he eventually says that the conception is all quite absurd— in particular, the idea that the soul, truly led by desire, might contort itself in such a way as to perform unwise acts but without forfeiting φρόνησις. This would be for reason to be dragged about like a slave. At 1246b16–17 ("Or is it not clear ... "), Aristotle in effect acknowledges that the ideas put forward just previously are difficult—indeed, ultimately impossible— to make sense of. He acknowledges, that is, that when the parts of the soul (the rational and the irrational) assume unaccustomed roles, they change character.

32 These types are to be discussed more extensively in chapter 8, where the unity of the ἀκόλαστος's soul is subject to qualification. On the positing of parts within the soul, see chapter 8, note 21.
33 See above, note 31.
34 Note that in lines 1246b19–20 Aristotle similarly makes μοχθηρία the agent that contorts (στρέψει) the virtue of the λογιστικόν.

Doubtless, the initial strangeness of all this was a contributing cause of the corruption and chronic emendation of the Greek text.

V. *EE* viii,1, part IV

If the present interpretation is correct, the interpretation (and readings) of part IV of *EE* viii,1 ought obviously to be consistent with it; also, the interpretation ought not to introduce ideas wholly absent from parts I–III, since part IV clearly comprises comments upon the ideas set out in parts I–III. (At 1246b19 we read the words, "For it would be absurd if … [ἄτοπον γὰρ εἰ …]"—and then Aristotle offers three (inadequate) accounts of the divided soul hypothesized in part III; and at 1246b26 we read the words, "But these things are absurd … [ἔστι δὲ ταῦτα ἄτοπα]," referring to the accounts presented just previously.)

Part IV lists three accounts of the hypothesized soul-splitting of part III. The first two are more central to Aristotle's argument than the third, which is introduced by the words καὶ πάλιν ("and conversely") and is appropriately placed in parentheses in the Walzer-Mingay edition [1246b23–25]. The first account [1246b19–21] suggests that vice [μοχθηρία] in the irrational part might contort [στρέψει] virtue in the rational. One reasonably asks how such a contortion might represent doing unwise things out of φρόνησις, the analogue of making writing errors out of knowledge of writing or seeing unnaturally out of (by means of) good vision. But such an objection does not take into consideration that giving a convincing account of *that* (doing unwise things out of φρόνησις) is impossible, for the idea is manifestly incoherent, just as the idea of actually being ignorant out of being knowledgeable is manifestly incoherent. Aware of this, Aristotle offers more circumscribed accounts—of states of soul themselves in which a break of intelligibility affords to the "φρόνιμος" the leverage that would be required in order to do, qua φρόνιμος, things incompatible with φρόνησις.

This might happen, the first account suggests, when vice in the irrational part contorts the virtue in the rational part. But this is impossible for a number of sound Aristotelian reasons. First of all, it would mean that reason is being dragged about like a slave. The irrational part dragging about the rational might at first seem plausible, until one realizes that that would make the irrational part an agent. The agent—the human person himself—is found not in his irrational but in his rational part: indeed, the person *is* essentially his rational part (although that rational part is just a part of the whole rational animal).[35] Even if that agent is hopelessly ensnared by concupiscence, it is still intellect that has the lead in his actions. As we have seen repeatedly in the present work, but especially in the analysis in chapter 3 of *EE* ii,6–9, if a person does not know what he is doing (and provided that ignorance is itself non-culpable), he is not culpable for what he does. Also, as we saw in chapter 6 (section III), the origin of self-movement (such as the movement of a rational soul) is the non-extended point Aristotle identifies as the intellect.

The idea that a φρόνιμος might perform vicious acts because of tension within his soul is also impossible, according to Aristotle, because the φρόνιμος is a character type quite distinct from the ἀκρατής (who is so conflicted). In a sense, then, the argument would be that the character type of the φρόνιμος excludes by definition the capacity to perform vicious acts: if a person does perform such acts, he is not φρόνιμος. But the argument is not just an analytic one. Φρόνησις truly exists in the moral universe and its essence is to be incompatible with vicious action. Its intelligibility lies in that and not (as Socrates suggests, perhaps ironically, in *Hp. Mi.*) in the capacity to perform virtuous *and* vicious acts.

The second inadequate account mentioned in part IV [1246b21–23] is the reverse of the first: in the first, a vicious irrational part contorts the virtuous rational part; in the second, a virtuous irrational part contorts an ignorant rational part, causing it to judge wisely the proper things to do.[36] Says Aristotle (after the parenthesis which contains the third account), "in

---

35 See *EN* ix,4, 1166a14–19: καὶ βούλεται δὴ ἑαυτῷ τἀγαθὰ καὶ τὰ φαινόμενα καὶ πράττει (τοῦ γὰρ ἀγαθοῦ τἀγαθὸν διαπονεῖν) καὶ ἑαυτοῦ ἕνεκα (τοῦ γὰρ διανοητικοῦ χάριν, ὅπερ ἕκαστος εἶναι δοκεῖ) καὶ ζῆν δὲ βούλεται ἑαυτὸν καὶ σῴζεσθαι, καὶ μάλιστα τοῦτο ᾧ φρονεῖ. See also *EN* ix,8, 1168b28–34, x,7, 1178a2–3.

36 Here is the piece of part IV containing the first two anomalies: ἄτοπον γὰρ εἰ τὴν μὲν ἐν τῷ λογιστικῷ ἀρετὴν μοχθηρία ποτὲ ἐγγενομένη ἐν τῷ ἀλόγῳ στρέψει καὶ ποιήσει ἀγνοεῖν· ἡ δ' ἀρετὴ ἐν τῷ ἀλόγῳ <ἐν τῷ λογιστικῷ> ἀγνοίας ἐνούσης οὐ στρέψει ταύτην, καὶ ποιήσει φρονίμως κρίνειν καὶ τὰ δέοντα [1246b19–23 (in Susemihl, 1246b19–22)]. This is identical to the Walzer-Mingay text, except for a change of punctuation in line 1246b21 (which allows one to make better sense of the οὐ in line 1246b22).

this way there will be acting wisely from ignorance."[37] Again, the point of the hypothesized contortion is to give an account of someone's being disunified within (and thereby having the leverage that allows contortion) and yet acting wisely [φρονίμως]; Aristotle's objection is that such a situation constitutes reason's being dragged about like a slave. In the parenthesis, Aristotle mentions the converse of this second account: that is, instead of a virtuous irrational part contorting an ignorant rational part, a rational part which is φρόνιμος overpowers a depraved irrational part [τὴν ἐν τῷ ἀλόγῳ ἀκολασίαν—1246b24], resulting in virtuous action. This is the third inadequate account. Aristotle does not deny that such might happen—indeed, this makes more sense than the other possibilities mentioned, since the intellect is here clearly the agent—but this is not, he says, φρόνησις but rather ἐγκράτεια [1246b24–25].

Part IV has its own sub-conclusion, in which Aristotle says again that the three accounts are all non-starters, but especially absurd, he says, is the idea of behaving wisely from ignorance,[38] by which Aristotle apparently means the second account.

These things are all absurd, especially the idea that [the φρόνιμος] might behave wisely from ignorance. For we see this in no other branch of knowledge—that, for example, depravity [ἀκολασία] contorts medicine or grammar. [1246b25–28]

Of course, as Aristotle argues in part I, a *person* in possession of the appropriate knowledge might contort medicine or grammar in order to make a didactical point, but depravity [ἀκολασία] has no power with respect to one's knowledge of such sciences or disciplines.[39]

VI. *EE* viii,1, part V

That brings us to part V:

Well, in any case,[40] it is not ignorance [that contorts φρόνησις] (supposing this to be the opposite),[41] the reason being that the dominant quality is not included

---

37 ὅτ' ἔσται καὶ ἀπὸ ἀγνοίας φρονίμως [1246b25].
38 ὅτι δὲ ταῦτα ἄτοπα, ἄλλως τε καὶ ἀπὸ ἀγνοίας χρῆσθαι φρονίμως [1246b25–26].
39 See *EN* vi,5, 1140b13–16; see also chapter 6, section VI.
40 See J. D. Denniston, *The Greek Particles*, 2d ed. (Oxford: Clarendon Press, 1987), 443 (4).
41 See above, note 25.

Φρόνησις and the Φρόνιμος 227

in [something else] but it is the virtue that invariably stands in that relation with respect to the vice. For everything that the unjust man does the just man *could* do, that is, the impotence is invariably included in the potency. So it is clear that the φρόνιμοι are good together with those states of the irrational part—and the Socratic doctrine says correctly that there is nothing stronger than φρόνησις. But when he said that [φρόνησις] is a science, this was not correct, for φρόνησις is a virtue and not a science but another type of knowing. [1246b28–36][42]

The key idea of this conclusion is the contrary of the thesis argued for by Socrates in *Hp. Mi.*: that is, contrary to the suggestion that the soul of the φρόνιμος can be contorted in the manner of an eye made to see double. Conceiving of things in this latter way, the ability to go wrong—or, as Aristotle puts it in part I, the ability to act unnaturally—includes in itself the ability to go right: to act in accordance with nature. But no, says Aristotle, the direction of the relation is rather the reverse: and, indeed, the two elements are not on an even footing. Rather than the negative capacity including the positive, the positive includes the negative—and not as a capacity on a par with itself (in which case the honest man would also be a false man) but as an incapacity, for qua φρόνιμος the φρόνιμος cannot be unwise. Truth-telling is included in lying only in the sense that the intelligibility of lying depends on that of truth-telling, and not vice-versa: if we had no idea of truth-telling, we could have no idea of lying, but truth-telling has its own intelligibility in itself. Speaking falsely means *not* telling the truth. Even if telling the truth might be defined as not speaking falsely, it has a positive sense all its own.[43] To use the definition of lying mentioned in *Hp. Mi.*,[44] if lying is deliberately saying something contrary

---

42 'οὖν οὐ τὴν ἄγνοιαν, ἐὰν ᾖ ἐναντία, διὸ τὸ μὴ ἐνεῖναι τὴν ὑπεροχὴν ἀλλὰ τὴν ἀρετὴν ὅλως μᾶλλον εἶναι πρὸς τὴν κακίαν οὕτως ἔχουσαν. καὶ γὰρ <ἃ> ὁ ἄδικος πάντα ὁ δίκαιος δύναται, καὶ ὅλως ἔνεστιν ἐν τῇ δυνάμει ἡ ἀδυναμία. ὥστε δῆλον ὅτι ἅμα φρόνιμοι καὶ ἀγαθοί, ἐκεῖναι δ'ἄλλου ἕξεις, καὶ ὀρθῶς τὸ Σωκρατικόν, ὅτι οὐδὲν ἰσχυρότερον φρονήσεως. ἀλλ' ὅτι ἐπιστήμην ἔφη, οὐκ ὀρθόν· ἀρετὴ γάρ ἐστι καὶ οὐκ ἐπιστήμη, ἀλλὰ γένος ἄλλο γνώς <εως ἡ φρόνησις>. This is the text proposed by Jackson [Jackson, "*Eudemian Ethics* Θ i, ii," 179].

43 τὸ μὲν γὰρ λέγειν τὸ ὂν μὴ εἶναι ἢ τὸ μὴ ὂν εἶναι ψεῦδος, τὸ δὲ τὸ ὂν εἶναι καὶ τὸ μὴ ὂν μὴ εἶναι ἀληθές, ὥστε καὶ ὁ λέγων εἶναι ἢ μὴ ἀληθεύσει ἢ ψεύσεται ... [*Metaph.* iv,7, 1011b26–28]; ἔτι τὸ εἶναι σημαίνει καὶ τὸ ἔστιν ὅτι ἀληθές, τὸ δὲ μὴ εἶναι ὅτι οὐκ ἀληθὲς ἀλλὰ ψεῦδος, ὁμοίως ἐπὶ καταφάσεως καὶ ἀποφάσεως, οἷον ὅτι ἔστι Σωκράτης μουσικός, ὅτι ἀληθὲς τοῦτο, ἢ ὅτι ἔστι Σωκράτης οὐ λευκός, ὅτι ἀληθές· τὸ δ' οὐκ ἔστιν ἡ διάμετρος σύμμετρος, ὅτι ψεῦδος [*Metaph.* v,7, 1017a31–35]; λόγος δὲ ψευδὴς ὁ τῶν μὴ ὄντων, ᾗ ψευδής, διὸ πᾶς λόγος ψευδὴς ἑτέρου ἢ οὗ ἐστὶν ἀληθής [*Metaph.* v,29, 1024b26–28].

44 See above, note 3.

to what one thinks, that definition depends on the corresponding positive idea: saying what one does think. The basic intelligibility comes always from the positive element.

"So it is clear that the φρόνιμοι are good together with those states of the irrational part—and the Socratic doctrine says correctly that there is nothing stronger than φρόνησις" [1246b32–34]. Aristotle's here restates, in converse form, something we encountered in his *Metaph.* v,29 polemic against *Hp. Mi.*—and then says his position is consistent with what Socrates says about the predominance of knowledge over appetite. In *Metaph.* v,29, he says that the false man of whom he speaks "is one who is heedless and decided regarding such [false] accounts, not for any other reason but for its own sake."[45] Note that he does not say that the false man is heedless and decided regarding false accounts for *their* own sake. He can still make a true statement, but what he has decided to make a career of is lying and deception. Conversely, the true man is committed to telling the truth: this is a character trait that takes in not just his intellect, which knows both the truth and (by logical necessity) the corresponding falsehood, but also the irrational part of his soul. In neither analysis is it permissible to set one part of the soul off against the other, as Aristotle does in a hypothetical manner in parts III and IV. But this latter point is just the Socratic principle that reason is never dragged about like a slave.

The final sentence of the conclusion distinguishes this position—that reason is not dragged about like a slave—from that attacked especially in parts I and II: that φρόνησις is a science. We can contort a science, even in the name of that science and in order to promote that science; a similar thing can never be done with φρόνησις. This is not to say, however, that φρόνησις is knowledge, that is, γνῶσις. Φρόνησις is not a system of thought, with principles, theorems and demonstrations, that might be taught in lectures. It is just as wide ranging as science [ἐπιστήμη]—if not more so—but it not only characterizes the (singular) person who possesses it himself but also concerns matters that cannot be demonstrated in a scientific (apodeictic) manner.

---

45 πος δὲ ψευδὴς ὁ εὐχερὴς καὶ προαιρετικὸς τῶν τοιούτων λόγων, μὴ δι' ἕτερόν τι ἀλλὰ δι' αὐτό [*Metaph.* v,29, 1025a2–4].

VII. The Φρόνιμος and Human Nature

Our final task in this chapter is to state in a synthetic manner what it is to be φρόνιμος—what are the characteristics, for Aristotle, of that very central character type. One characteristic that has become apparent in this present chapter is the φρόνιμος's truth—or his honesty. There are clear indications in *Metaph.* v,29 that for Aristotle the φρόνιμος is simply the opposite of the false man (see 1025a8). The truth at issue here is practical truth or truth bound up with getting *to* things.[46] Just as the false man is the man who is decided in favor of the false in such a way that also the irrational part of his soul is given over to deception, so the desires of the φρόνιμος are ordered toward truth in a stabile manner.[47] This does not mean that the φρόνιμος cannot possibly behave in an unwise manner; it means that he desires the good in the free manner proper to those who know and are therefore possessed of the distance from possible objects of desire that allows them to deliberate wisely.[48]

At one point, speaking of the φρόνιμος, Aristotle says that "of his past actions, sweet are the recollections; of his future actions, his hopes are good—and, as such, pleasant."[49] This way of putting things makes it apparent that to say that the φρόνιμος always does things compatible with φρόνησις and that, when he does otherwise, he is not acting qua φρόνιμος is not simply the statement of an analytic truth (as when someone says, 'unjust acts are those that violate justice'). It is true that, if in the future

---

46 Although, as we saw in chapter 6, section IV, any knowledge is itself not a "getting to" anything but an "already being there."

47 See chapter 6, section VI.

48 See chapter 6, section IV.

49 τῶν τε γὰρ πεπραγμένων ἐπιτερπεῖς αἱ μνῆμαι, καὶ τῶν μελλόντων ἐλπίδες ἀγαθαί, αἱ τοιαῦται δ' ἡδεῖαι [*EN* ix,4, 1166a24–26]. Gauthier's translation of this passage suggests that the φρόνιμος *knows* his future actions will be good: "De ses actions passées, douces sont les souvenances, et ses actions futures, il sait qu'elles seront bonnes, perspective qui elle aussi est plaisante" [René-Antoine Gauthier, *La morale d'Aristote*, 74]. Gauthier and Jolif offer a more sober translation: "La traduction littérale: 'De ses actions futures, les espérances qu'il a sont bonnes ... et pareilles espérances sont plaisantes" [René-Antoine Gauthier and Jean Yves Jolif, *L'Éthique à Nicomaque*, 2.2 730–31]; but they interpret Aristotle's words as *meaning* that the virtuous man knows his actions will be good. They refer to their own argument at 2.1 232–33; that argument, however, does not succeed in demonstrating that in Aristotle the word ἐλπίς means knowledge that something good will occur.

the φρόνιμος behaves in a non-φρόνιμος manner, he necessarily does so not qua φρόνιμος; but even now we can recognize a quality in him that makes him φρόνιμος—that is to say, without waiting for the future we can recognize now his φρόνησις. We can also recognize that this quality in its core intelligibility is incompatible with bad acts (or bad counseling). As Aristotle says, the hopes of the φρόνιμος are good: he has the reasonable expectation that he will continue to make good and moral decisions, for his previously disciplined desires pull him in that direction. But they pull him in that direction because he is "decided" [προαιρετικὸς] in that direction,[50] which one cannot be unless there is at least the possibility that one might do something incompatible with going in that direction. One disciplines oneself *lest* one commit undesirable acts. One can arrive at a point where one is confident that one will not commit the undesirable acts, but even then one knows that it is a matter of deliberately holding to that course (which one finds most reasonable and most natural).

We shall come back to the issue of practical truth in the next section; for the moment, however, we must delve further into the characteristic of the φρόνιμος we have just now touched upon: his orientation toward the good. We saw in chapter 5 (section III) that even the man who pursues the apparent good can be said to pursue per se the true good, since man is defined with respect to the true good and not the apparent good.[51] This is tied up with the idea, argued for in the first two parts of *EE* viii,1, that it is impossible to act in a non-φρόνιμος manner out of φρόνησις. As we have seen, one of the distinctive ideas in that argument is that of effecting a contortion (a στροφή): says Aristotle, one can contort a science and thereby demonstrate one's expertise, but one cannot do the same with φρόνησις. The reason for this is that the bits of knowledge one "misuses" in performing the contortion fall *under* the capacity the agent demonstrates that he possesses by means of the contortion. Since φρόνησις, like 'being knowledgeable' itself, is a general capacity—that is, a capacity bound up with what it is to be human itself—there is nothing outside of itself which might serve as the capacity its contortion demonstrates.

---

50 See *Metaph.* v,29, 1025a3.
51 *EN* vii,9, 1151a35–b2.

Now, if the defining object of human nature *were* the apparent good, none of this would make any sense. There would be no limit to the contortions that one might perform, for there would be no general capacity to not admit of contortion—but then there would also be no reason to perform the contortions in the first place, for they could never demonstrate the possession of a capacity admirable because bound up with what it is to be human and with doing well what humans, by nature, have the capacity to do.[52] Any attempt to define a capacity in terms of an apparent good is doomed to failure from the outset. As shown by the non-tenability of Socrates's position in *Hp. Mi.*, definitions are in terms of the positive member of the pair of possibilities that are present in whatever capacity; the negative member is the shadow of the positive, being only the possibility of *not* exercising the virtue proper to the capacity in question. One cannot demonstrate one's mastery of man's core practically oriented virtue, φρόνησις, by pursuing that which is misapprehended or misconstrued as the good, for that is not to demonstrate the relevant virtue.

To sum up this part of the argument, therefore, since man's practical nature is defined in terms of the true good, one can demonstrate one's mastery of man's core practically oriented virtue, φρόνησις, only by pursuing this genuine good. If there were some sense to performing foolish actions out of φρόνησις as a demonstration of a virtue defined (as it must be) as the capacity to behave in a way that corresponds to the good for man, the person so acting would have to be "performing foolish actions out of φρόνησις" *out* of this capacity to behave in accordance with the good for man; but to *this* capacity (or virtue) we must assign the term φρόνησις. This virtue is defined as being (qua that virtue) incompatible with performing actions that are not in accordance with the good for man; so, if someone should claim to be performing foolish actions out of φρόνησις, he would be misusing the term φρόνησις.

Aristotle addresses these issues in a passage in *Eudemian Ethics* ii,10. In the passage that interests us, he has just made the point that those who deliberate, deliberate not about the end with respect to which they deliberate but about the means of getting to that end. And then he says:

---

52 See *EN* i,7, 1098a7–18, where Aristotle connects virtue with exercising a capacity *well* (εὖ).

The end is always something good by nature; it is that about which men deliberate in a partial manner. For instance, the doctor deliberates about whether he should give a drug and the general about where he should pitch camp: for them, the end which is absolutely the best is good. Contrary to nature, however, and by contortion [the end] is not the good but the apparent good. The cause of this is that some things are such that they cannot be used in a manner other than that which is natural for them, for instance, sight, for it is not possible to see what is not visible or to hear what is not audible. But it is possible to do "from a science" that which does not belong to the science, for one and the same science is not related similarly to health and to disease, but according to nature to the former, contrary to nature to the latter. Similarly, will [βούλησις] is by nature of the good but contrary to nature also of the bad; one wills by nature the good but contrary to nature and by contortion also the bad.[53]

We find here again the idea that the man who pursues even the apparent good pursues (per se) the true good. Aristotle begins by saying that the end is "*always* [ἀεί] something good by nature," but then he acknowledges that the end can be the merely apparent good when its pursuit involves a certain category of contortion. This is a different type of contortion than that involved when a teacher makes an error as part of a lesson. The contortion involved in pursuing the apparent good is *simply* a contortion and not one that demonstrates the capacity to exercise the science to which it belongs. An example of what Aristotle has in mind would be a teacher who teaches an error out of ignorance or even in order that a student might do poorly in an interview. There is a break of intelligibility here, for the act makes no sense *as* an act of teaching.

It is significant that Aristotle uses as a parallel to the contortion involved in pursuing the apparent good the unnatural use of medicine. A

---

53 τὸ δὲ τέλος ἐστὶ φύσει μὲν ἀεὶ ἀγαθόν, καὶ περὶ οὗ κατὰ μέρος βουλεύονται, οἷον ἰατρὸς βουλεύσαιτο ἂν εἰ δῴη φάρμακον, καὶ στρατηγὸς ποῦ στρατοπεδεύσηται, οἷς ἀγαθὸν τὸ τέλος τὸ ἁπλῶς ἄριστον ἐστίν· παρὰ φύσιν δὲ καὶ διὰ στροφὴν οὐ τὸ ἀγαθόν, ἀλλὰ τὸ φαινόμενον ἀγαθόν. αἴτιον δ'ὅτι τῶν ὄντων τὰ μὲν οὐκ ἔστιν ἐπ' ἄλλῳ χρήσασθαι ἢ πρὸς ἃ πέφυκεν, οἷον ὄψει· οὐ γὰρ οἷόν τ' ἰδεῖν οὐ μὴ ἔστιν ὄψις, οὐδ' ἀκοῦσαι οὐ μή ἐστιν ἀκοή· ἀλλ' ἀπὸ ἐπιστήμης ποιῆσαι καὶ οὐ μή ἐστιν ἡ ἐπιστήμη. οὐ γὰρ ὁμοίως τῆς ὑγιείας ἡ αὐτὴ ἐπιστήμη καὶ νόσου, ἀλλὰ τῆς μὲν κατὰ φύσιν τῆς δὲ παρὰ φύσιν. ὁμοίως δὲ καὶ ἡ βούλησις φύσει μὲν τοῦ ἀγαθοῦ ἐστι, παρὰ φύσιν δὲ καὶ τοῦ κακοῦ, καὶ βούλεται φύσει μὲν τὸ ἀγαθόν, παρὰ φύσιν δὲ καὶ διὰ στροφὴν καὶ τὸ κακόν [*EE* ii,10, 1227a18–31]. The text is the Walzer-Mingay text, which is identical to the Susemihl text, except that the latter's two instances of διαστροφὴν are changed to διὰ στροφὴν (see *EE* viii,1, 1246b9).

doctor cannot be pursuing health, acting truly as a doctor, while pursuing disease—which is quite different from realizing that a person will walk with greater difficulty without a leg but amputating it in order to save the person's life (and health). The doctor is capable of doing genuine harm to a patient; but, when he does so, that contortion of medicine contradicts its very nature. If teaching an error can be a good thing because it remains within the capacity to teach (one makes the error in order to teach), no contortion of medicine itself can remain within medicine. Aristotle says in the above quotation that knowledge of a science is unlike natural faculties such as sight or hearing, "for it is not possible to see what is not visible or to hear what is not audible" but it is possible to use medicine to pursue disease. But when this is done one is still acting "contrary to nature" (as Aristotle says), since medicine receives its intelligibility not from disease but from health. The same can be said of the will (βούλησις): it pursues the merely apparent good only contrary to nature and by undesirable contortion.

What allows it to be the case that deliberately contorting one's vision is not a bad use of vision is the fact that vision (qua vision) can only be used in order to see, whereas a science (or discipline) like medicine can be used in such a way that it heads toward that which is incompatible with medicine: toward, that is, the privation of health. The vision of even the contorted eye still heads toward the good (the end) of vision: the visible. A medical act that mistakenly heads toward the privation of health is heading not toward the good that defines medicine (health) but toward an apparent good in the same genus. Supposing (as we are at the moment) that the doctor genuinely believes that he is promoting the health of his patient, we would still say that his act is a medical act, since per se he is pursuing health, per accidens the privation of health. The real intelligibility of his act lies in the per se relationship between his will (qua doctor) and the end he seeks (health of the patient).[54]

When, however, a doctor deliberately pursues disease and death, he is

---

54 Aristotle does not explicitly address the issue, when an act can be called an act of a particular discipline. It seems reasonable, however, to say that, as acts done, for example, in order to promote health become more and more incompetent, they forfeit the right to be called medical acts—even if their agent genuinely believes he is pursuing the health of his patient. Medical acts are acts performed by medical persons; medical persons are legitimately identified as such in so far as they possess medical knowledge, as understood by the particular culture making use of the term 'medical.'

no longer pursuing health in any sense.⁵⁵ As we saw in chapter 5, section III, he continues to pursue per se the good for man, for a human being can never escape human nature; but this doctor's pursuit of an apparent good (money, for instance, or "the health of the race" as distinct from the health of his patient) causes him to act contrary to the good that defines medicine, that is, the health of the patient. This case must involve an apparent general good, for this doctor knows that he is not pursuing the health of his patient, that is, he is not simply making a mistake, which would allow him still to be pursuing the genuine good of medicine and thereby also the genuine good for man. The doctor in question must have some overall good in mind, since otherwise he would not go on with the procedure. He believes that in behaving as he does he is pursuing the true good: what Aristotle calls in the above passage, that which is "absolutely the best." But he is mistaken, for pursuing the true good for man entails avoiding actions of this type, that is, actions that purport to be actions of a particular discipline natural to man but go contrary to its nature.⁵⁶ He is, therefore, pursuing a mistaken understanding of the true good for man; he is pursuing a merely apparent good.

The φρόνιμος has none of these problems: he is neither innocently erring nor bad-willed; his actions are never such as to entail a per se ultimate good distinct from an apparent good. For him the per se (natural) good sought in any instance coincides with the apparent good: what appears good to him is the good in accordance with nature. Presuming that the political structure (the πόλις) within which he lives is a just one, he is not one to act contrary to the goods that define its natural practices—the procedures of the various disciplines and the laws legitimately established—for he could do this only by seeking a merely apparent good at a higher level.

VIII. Practical Truth

That brings us finally to the issue of practical truth, a solid grasp of which—and inclination toward—is part of the φρόνιμος's character.⁵⁷

---

55 Someone might argue that, if in pursuing disease a doctor actually brings about health, he does pursue health, although per accidens. But the word 'pursue' here would have to be placed in scare quotes.

56 See above, chapter 6, section II and VII.

57 The nature of the practical truth that pertains to the φρόνιμος has been a source of con-

This is apparent from *Metaph*. v,29, 1025a8, where the φρόνιμος is identified as the opposite of the false man. Although Aristotelians tend (with good reason) to associate truth with theoretical rather than with practical reason, to be a truth-teller is certainly a moral (or practical) attribute rather than a purely intellectual one. We do not say of a good physicist or a mathematician that he is a truthful man—or, at least, if we do, we do not say this of him qua physicist or mathematician. Just as the false man is decidedly inclined to deceive, the φρόνιμος is decidedly inclined to tell the truth. This is part of his character as one who finds "good and noble acts" pleasant [*EE* vii,2, 1236a3–6].[58]

And yet the φρόνιμος's being truthful cannot be solely a matter of his not lying. As we have seen, φρόνησις is not a private virtue.[59] Aristotle acknowledges that the Greeks of his day called people like Pericles φρόνιμοι "because they can see what is good for themselves and what is good for men in general; we consider that those can do this who are good at managing households or states."[60] A lowly craftsman or even a slave can be truthful; when Aristotle speaks of the φρόνιμος, however, he has in mind someone who is in charge of some larger enterprise and is able to "deliberate well about what is good and expedient" [*EN* vi,5, 1140a25–27] with respect to that enterprise. Indeed, since Aristotle's central discussion of φρόνησις is included in his ethical writings (*EN* vi, which is identical to *EE* v), it is clear that, in the proper sense of the term, φρόνησις has to do with deliberations regarding (or within) the whole field of ethics. This

---

troversy among contemporary commentators. See, for instance, G. E. M. Anscombe, "Thought and Action in Aristotle: What Is Practical Truth?" in *From Parmenides to Wittgenstein*, vol. 1 of *Collected Philosophical Papers* (Minneapolis/Oxford: University of Minnesota Press/Basil Blackwell, 1981), 66–77; G. E. M. Anscombe, "Practical Truth," in *Human Life, Action and Ethics: Essays by G. E. M. Anscombe*, ed. Mary Geach and Luke Gormally, St. Andrews Studies in Philosophy and Public Affairs (Exeter: Imprint Academic, 2005), 149–58; Stephen L. Brock, "Realistic Practical Truth," *Doctor Communis* (2008): 62–75; Michael Pakaluk, "The Great Question of Practical Truth—and a Diminutive Answer," *Acta Philosophica* 19 (2010): 145–60; Hermann Weidemann, "Überlegungen zum Begriff der praktischen Wahrheit bei Aristoteles," *Zeitschrift für philosophische Forschung* 59 (2005): 345–57; Andreas Graeser, "Aristotle on Practical Truth: Coherence vs. Correspondence?" *Bochumer philosophisches Jahrbuch für Antike und Mittelalter* 9 (2004): 191–200; Carlo Natali, *The Wisdom of Aristotle*, SUNY Series in Ancient Greek Philosophy (Albany: State University of New York Press, 2001), 12–19.

58 See also chapter 6, section VI.
59 See the end of chapter 6, section V.
60 διὰ τοῦτο Περικλέα καὶ τοὺς τοιούτους φρονίμους οἰόμεθα εἶναι, ὅτι τὰ αὑτοῖς ἀγαθὰ καὶ τὰ τοῖς ἀνθρώποις δύνανται θεωρεῖν· εἶναι δὲ τοιούτους ἡγούμεθα τοὺς οἰκονομικοὺς καὶ τοὺς πολιτικούς [*EN* vi,5, 1140b7–11]. One notices especially the word θεωρεῖν.

is by no means to exclude simple truth-telling as a characteristic of the φρόνιμος—Aristotle would not call φρόνιμος a politician or philosopher who tells lies—but the "straight talk" of the φρόνιμος pertains to a field of larger scope than that which concerns the honest private citizen, craftsman, or slave.

Since practical truth has to do with deliberating, it has to do also with "aiming," as discussed in chapter 5. We saw in that chapter (section IV) that the ethical aiming of acts has its limits. Aristotle says of adultery, theft, murder that "it is not possible ... ever to go right with regard to them, one must always go wrong" [EN ii,6, 1107a14–15]. We can be sure, therefore, that for Aristotle it is *true* that an act of adultery, theft, or murder is immoral and that his φρόνιμος will be not unwilling to say this. But φρόνησις and practical truth are not just about such delimiting cases.

At the beginning of EN vi, Aristotle makes it clear that he is interested in understanding the type of knowledge involved when a man takes aim in the proper way with respect to what should be done in whatever situation [vi,1, 1138b21–25]. Such knowledge belongs to a part of the soul that is intellectual (as opposed to sensual) but not purely intellectual, since it is by virtue of this part that action occurs, and the intellect, considered in itself, "moves nothing" [EN vi,2, 1139a35–36]. In EN vi,2, he sets out to identify the best or perfect state of soul with respect to such practical knowledge; this would be the respective virtue [EN vi,2, 1139a15–17]. The best state of the purely intellectual part is that in accordance with which it never errs about its proper objects, which are the things that can never be otherwise than how they are; the best state of the other part is that in accordance with which it never errs about *its* proper objects, which are things that can be otherwise. It is this difference of object and also the different limits of the infallibility of the best states that require the positing of two parts: one having to do just with knowledge (in the strict sense), the other having to do with doing things (or not doing them). Aristotle calls this latter "the reckoning part" [τὸ λογιστικόν—EN vi,1, 1139a12]. Each state can be called infallible because each is the virtue of its respective part; if either erred regarding its proper objects, to that extent it would not possess the virtue.

The reckoning part of the soul, since it both points forward and also has the capacity of arriving at truth, has two facets: desire (ὄρεξις) and reason (λόγος or νοῦς). These always operate together, so that, when the reckoning part is in its best state, its desire is correct and its reasoning is true [*EN* vi,2, 1139a24]. The desires and sensibilities of the good man's soul are such that he hits the target aimed at; that target is the target of both desire and reason, since the reckoning part is a single part (defined in terms of its proper object). "This, therefore, is the thought and the truth that is practical," says Aristotle; and then he draws the comparison between the "well-functioning" of the purely intellectual part and that of the reckoning part:

'The well and the ill' of thought that is theoretical and not practical or productive is truth and falsehood (for this is the task of everything intellectual); the truth of that which is practical and intellectual stands in a similar relation with right desire.[61]

Just as the purely intellectual part is operating well when what it affirms corresponds to the truth (about necessary things), so the reckoning part is operating well when what it affirms corresponds to right desire.[62]

This might sound at first as if the measure of the reckoning part were wholly subjective; but that cannot be, for Aristotle is speaking throughout this passage about truth, which is not wholly subjective.[63] Achieving truth, says Aristotle, "is the task of *everything* intellectual," not just the purely intellectual part. Truth enters into the practical in so far as the reckoning part lines up with right desire, that is to say, in so far as the desire of the reckoning part, which is inseparable from its reason, hits the mean on the extended target.[64] When the reckoning part is operating well, it hits this mean infallibly. What the φρόνιμος takes aim with are acts with their

---

61 αὕτη μὲν οὖν ἡ διάνοια καὶ ἡ ἀλήθεια πρακτική· τῆς δὲ θεωρητικῆς διανοίας καὶ μὴ πρακτικῆς μηδὲ ποιητικῆς τὸ εὖ καὶ κακῶς τἀληθές ἐστι καὶ ψεῦδος (τοῦτο γάρ ἐστι παντὸς διανοητικοῦ ἔργον)· τοῦ δὲ πρακτικοῦ καὶ διανοητικοῦ ἀλήθεια ὁμολόγως ἔχουσα τῇ ὀρέξει τῇ ὀρθῇ [*EN* vi,2, 1139a26–31].

62 For such a "correspondence theory" of practical truth, see Weidemann, "Überlegungen zum Begriff der praktischen Wahrheit bei Aristoteles." Writes Weidemann, in connection with *EN* vi,2, 1139a21–31: "In order to be true in the practical sense, the judgment issuing from my deliberation must, in short, be true in the sense that the means that I choose in order to arrive at a particular end is the right *means* for arriving at the *right end*" (p. 353, emphases Weidemann's).

63 "It is not because we think that you are white, that you are white, but because you are white we who say this have the truth" [*Metaph.* ix,10, 1051b6–9].

64 Aristotle mentions at *EN* ii,9, 1109a14–26 that to hit the "center of the circle is not for anyone but for the one who knows."

own structure of intelligibility, which depends upon their constituents. An act that involves breaks of intelligibility such as indicate incompatibility with the good for man cannot be an act of a φρόνιμος. On the more positive side, the acts of the φρόνιμος are those best suited to bring the φρόνιμος—and those who follow his counsel—toward the good for man.

This does not mean that, when a practically wise man makes a decision, everything following from that decision will necessarily turn out well. If, for instance, a practically wise man decides to fight intruders, reckoning that by doing so he has a greater chance of protecting his property, he may in fact lose it all in a close fight; but that does not mean that his decision was not the correct one. Given that he is practically wise—and that he employs practical wisdom regarding this decision—his aim is infallible. That *in fact* things did not turn out well was due to the contingent nature of the matter with which the reckoning part deals. The truth, however, of the reckoning part does not have to do with these contingent facts but with his *aim*'s being at the mean; this can be called practical *truth*, since the reckoning part involves not only desire but also reason, which sees—and allows one to hit—the mean. Near the beginning of the *Nicomachean Ethics*, Aristotle says famously that "it is the mark of an educated man to look for precision in each class of things just so far as the nature of the subject admits" [*EN* i,2, 1094b23–25]. A couple of lines before this remark, he speaks of men who have been harmed "by reason of their courage" [*EN* i,1, 1094b19]; he regards this as an instance of the imprecision that characterizes ethics. He does not mean that these men are harmed because they are too rash, for that is not to be courageous. Courage is the mean between cowardice and rashness; it is the target, the center point, along the relevant measure [*EN* ii,7, 1107a33–b4]. He means that even when a man makes the correct and moral decision and makes it knowingly, things can go wrong.

IX. Conclusion

To conclude, then, a great aid in understanding what Aristotle is saying in *EE* viii,1 about the φρόνιμος is Plato's *Hippias Minor*, in which the dramatic character Socrates suggests that that which makes a false man a false man also makes him a φρόνιμος. We are able to link *EE* viii,1 with *Hp. Mi.*, not only because similar examples are used in each, but also because Aristotle takes issue with the *Hp. Mi.* argument in another passage, *Metaph.* v,29, where he also mentions the φρόνιμος. A close examination of the argument of *EE* viii,1 shows that Aristotle understands the φρόνιμος to be a character whose soul is without internal divisions: the φρόνιμος is univocally decided in favor of the pursuit of the good for man. We also know (again, from *Metaph.* v,29) that the φρόνιμος is truthful. The truth so referred to is practical truth, which is to say that it pertains not to the non-contingent subject matter of the proper sciences but to the contingent subject matter of ethics and to the application of the more general precepts that set the limits of good behavior within that field.

Eight

Some Other Character Types

ARISTOTLE EMPLOYS IN his ethical writings a veritable menagerie of character types, most of whom we have already met. They include the φρόνιμος (the practically wise man), the σπουδαῖος (the good man), the ἀκρατής (the incontinent man), the ἀκόλαστος (the depraved man), and the ἐγκρατής (the self-constrained man). Aristotle's analysis of these character types exploits many of the ideas we have seen in previous chapters of this book, especially the principle of non-contradiction and the distinction between the per se and the per accidens, although he brings in also other logical principles we have not yet seen.

The present chapter begins (in section I) with some brief descriptions, employing concepts set out in earlier chapters, of the major character types discussed by Aristotle. These are preliminary sketches, to be filled out later in the chapter. Section II is about the role of the principle of non-contradiction in the practical realm. Again, this section employs ideas we have already seen, although here special attention is drawn to Plato's analysis of the soul in *Republic* [R.] iv, where he maintains that, even in the soul divided by conflicting inclinations, there is a core unit that goes forward toward just one of a number of incompatible alternatives. This idea is important for understanding the psychological structure of the ἀκρατής.

Some Other Character Types   241

This is followed (in sections III to VII) by a detailed examination of a passage in *EE* vii,6 where Aristotle sets out a logical analysis of the ἀκρατής and other related character types. Section III looks at the first three sentences of the passage, which are considerably less difficult than what follows. The idea in these sentences is that (as Plato suggests in *R*. iv) even the divided soul has a core unit that remains indivisible. This means that even the man with a divided soul can (given the satisfaction of other conditions) be held responsible for his actions: his core unity can be reduced to the more pervasive unity of the good man (who is the knowing agent *par excellence*).

In the next three sentences of the *EE* vii,6, passage Aristotle says some—at first glance—strange things about a certain "Coriscus." His remarks appear less strange once one understands that Aristotle is employing the sophistic method of hypostatizing ideas one might have about an individual as if the ideas too were individuals. As explained in section IV, employing this method (while rejecting the sophists' ontological claims), Aristotle is able to analyze in terms of temporal units, besides the ἀκρατής, the character type called "the repenter" and the one called "the liar."

In section V, we offer an explanation of why in the fifth sentence of the *EE* vii,6 passage Aristotle speaks of Coriscus and of aspects (or parts) of his soul as quantities. We derive this explanation from Aristotle's very elastic concept of 'quantity,' which includes not only numbers and distances but also (as he says in *Metaph*. v,13) qualities such as being musical. Aristotle says that such qualities are called quantities not because of what they are in themselves but because of what they apply to; they apply, that is, to extended things, such as admit of quantity. He also says that, when the things to which these qualities apply are substances—such as are indivisible—the quantitative analysis applies to them not as indivisible but as moving through space and time.

The final sentence in the *EE* vii,6 passage reads: "For when they accuse themselves, they kill themselves; but each seems to himself good." In section VI, we argue that the "they" who accuse and kill themselves are internally conflicted character types such as the ἀκρατής. Aristotle appears to be worried that his audience, having heard him say that within all these types there is a central part that considers itself good and therefore wants to do good for itself, will wonder how it is that such types occasionally kill themselves. This is not the only possible reading of the sentence, but it does correspond to a remark in a parallel passage in *EN* ix,4. Showing that the two passages are parallel is not difficult to do, although there does appear to be a discrepancy between the two having to do, in fact, with the love that conflicted character types feel toward themselves. We offer a solution to this latter difficulty.

The solution offered helps us, in section VII, to resolve another problem in *EE* vii,6, identified earlier and having to do with Aristotle's way of analyzing the various conflicted souls in terms of temporal quantities. The problem is that the ἀκρατής is apparently conflicted at one and the same time, and so conflicting *extended* temporal quantities seem to be excluded. The solution is to interpret Aristotle's talk of "at the same time" [ἅμα] as including a number of independent moments.

In section VIII, we offer an analysis of the ἀκόλαστος as one who is not a conflicted soul in the way the other character types are, although he is not entirely whole or psychologically healthy either. Especially useful here are some remarks by Elizabeth Anscombe. A question here is whether the ἀκόλαστος actually believes that his way of behaving is the right (that is, the moral) way of behaving. Anscombe maintains that he may very well say that his way is the right and moral way but in doing so he does not speak honestly. Section IX discusses some minor character types who might be thought similar to the ἀκόλαστος; in fact, however, they are quite different from him because they do not make the evil προαίρεσις that he makes.

I. Character Sketches

We have already (especially in chapters 6 and 7) given a good deal of attention to the φρόνιμος; but, since most of the other character types are defined in terms of the φρόνιμος—as falling short of being φρόνιμος in some way—a few more words about him (and a bit of repetition) might be appropriate here. In *EN* vi,5, Aristotle offers a description of the φρόνιμος: "Now it is thought to be a mark of the φρόνιμος to be able to deliberate [βουλεύσασθαι] well about what is good and expedient for himself, not in some particular respect, e.g. about what sorts of things conduce to health or to strength, but about what sorts of things conduce to the good life in general" [1140a25–28]. Aristotle's point in the words "what is good and expedient for himself" [τὰ αὑτῷ ἀγαθὰ καὶ συμφέροντα] is not that the φρόνιμος is selfish but that his concern is with getting (or getting to) rather than with knowing things. If anything, the things he gets are beneficial to the city (the πόλις): they are conducive to "the good life in general." For this reason the corresponding virtue, φρόνησις, is especially associated with politics: the good politician, as opposed to the citizen, says Aristotle, needs to be φρόνιμος.[1] But the φρόνιμος is not simply clever at getting to whatever ends might be posited [vi,12, 1144a27–29], for it is impossible, says Aristotle, to be φρόνιμος without being good (ἀγαθόν), that is, without being oriented toward the good and proper end(s) of human action.[2] The φρόνιμος has himself under control but he is not opposed to human pleasures. He seeks "tranquil freedom" [ἀλυπία] from the more violent varieties of pleasure, that is, "those which imply appetite and pain" and with respect to which, according to Aristotle, the ἀκόλαστος (to be discussed shortly) is ἀκόλαστος [*EN* vii,12, 1153a29–34].

The σπουδαῖος is not very different from the φρόνιμος, and in certain contexts he appears to be the identical character type. At *EN* iii,4, 1113a33, for instance, he is called the "norm and measure" [κανὼν καὶ μέτρον] toward which society looks when asking questions about good and bad actions.[3] At *Rhet.* i,9, 1367b22–23 Aristotle says that the particular characteristic of the σπουδαῖος is his acting according to προαίρεσις (to be discussed shortly). If there is a difference between the σπουδαῖος and the φρόνιμος, it is one of conceptual emphasis: with the φρόνιμος, the concept of practice is to the fore; with the σπουδαῖος, the good is—that is, *being* good (ἀγαθός) [*Metaph.* v,16, 1021b14–24].

The ἀκρατής and the ἀκόλαστος are best expounded together.[4] The

---

1 *Pol.* iii,4, 1277a14–16; see also *EN* vi,7, 1141a20–3.

2 *EN* vi,12, 1144a3–b1; vii,2, 1146a8–9.

3 See also *EN* ix,4, 1166a12–13 and x,6, 1176b24–27. See also above chapter 5, section III, and chapter 6, section IV.

4 My characterization of the ἀκρατής and the ἀκόλαστος and my understanding of προαίρεσις are much indebted to: G. E. M. Anscombe, "Thought and Action in Aristotle, 66–77; David Charles, *Aristotle's Philosophy of Action*, 151; and Terence H. Irwin, "Vice and Reason," *Journal of Ethics* (2001):

difference between these two character types is tied up with what Aristotle calls προαίρεσις. Especially as used by Aristotle, this word is notoriously difficult to translate. Often it is rendered as 'choice,' but for Aristotle a person makes a προαίρεσις only when his choice (in our terms) involves deliberation with respect to a person's long-term goals, so that 'choice' has too wide a meaning to serve as the translation of προαίρεσις: every προαίρεσις is a choice but not every choice is a προαίρεσις. But since the alternatives to 'choice' (and its cognates) also bear with them difficulties, in this chapter, when we do translate it, we translate προαίρεσις (and cognates) as 'choice' (and cognates). The frequent appearance of the untranslated word will serve to remind the reader that Aristotle's understanding of προαίρεσις word is not the same as our understanding of 'choice.'

The most succinct statement of the difference between the ἀκρατής and the ἀκόλαστος comes in EN vii,3, where Aristotle acknowledges that the subject matter [περὶ ποῖα—1146b9] is one and the same for the two character types, although they come *at* this subject matter in different ways. They are both concerned with pleasurable things, but the character of ἀκόλαστος is fixed by his προαίρεσις, which is to the effect that "one ought always to pursue the present pleasure." The ἀκρατής is characterized by no such προαίρεσις, but, moved by desire, he does pursue the same thing (or things).[5]

The phrase translated 'the present pleasure' is τὸ παρὸν ἡδὺ [1146b23]. This should not be interpreted as meaning that the ἀκόλαστος can show no restraint or cannot use deliberation in pursuing what he seeks. In the sentence in which he is described as pursuing τὸ παρὸν ἡδὺ, he is characterized also as acting with προαίρεσις: "he is led on, having made a προαίρεσις, believing that he ought always to pursue the present pleasure" [EN vii,3, 1146b22–23]. As we have seen, a προαίρεσις presupposes deliberation.

80–84. See Kevin L. Flannery, "Anscombe and Aristotle on Corrupt Minds," *Christian Bioethics* 14 (2008): 151–64. Aristotle devotes a chapter of the *Eudemian Ethics* to the ἀκόλαστος (EE iii,2), recognizing that the term ἀκόλαστος has many meanings (λέγεται δ' ὁ ἀκόλαστος πολλαχῶς—1230a37). The meaning of the term that predominates, both here (see 1230b6–7) and in Aristotle's ethical writings generally, picks out the person who is not just unchastised but is "unchastisable." In the present book, when I refer to the ἀκόλαστος, I mean this ethical type. On ἀκολασία, see also Pavlos Kontos, *Aristotle's Moral Realism Reconsidered*, 64–72.

5 EN vii,3, 1146b19–24, vii,8, 1151a20–26; see also iii,2, 1111b14.

At *EN* iii,10, 1118a23–26, Aristotle says at first that ἀκολασία is concerned with touch and tastes but then corrects himself. The ἀκόλαστος has none of the distance from his object of desire that the connoisseur has; he simply wants to *have* it, whether it be food or wine or other naked bodies. "This is why a certain gourmand prayed that his throat might become longer than a crane's, implying that it was the contact that he took pleasure in" [*EN* iii,10, 1118a32–b1; see also *EE* iii,2, 1231a6–17]. It is better to say, therefore, that the characterizing sense of the ἀκόλαστος is touch: the desire to make contact. Thus, the fact that the ἀκόλαστος characteristically pursues τὸ παρὸν ἡδὺ has not so much to do with his pursuing whatever pleasure presents itself at any one moment but with his attitude toward the particular pleasure (or pleasures) to which he is attached: he wants them *present*.

Aristotle also mentions in *EN* iii,11, that the favorite pleasures of the ἀκόλαστος control everything he does: "The ἀκόλαστος, therefore, desires all the pleasures or the most prominent, and he is impelled by desire to choose these rather than others" [1119a1–3]. This irrational favoring of some pleasures over others subverts the order of his life and ultimately finishes in pain [1119a4–5].

Although a mark of the ἀκόλαστος would be his προαίρεσις of his overall end, that is, his "believing that one ought always to pursue the present pleasure," it would be a mistake to say that the ἀκόλαστος makes a deliberated choice to pursue evil every time he performs an act proper to his character type. In *EN* vii,8, Aristotle says, in effect, that the ἀκόλαστος eventually fails to advert to the evil of the things he performs [1150b36], so the προαίρεσις that distinguishes the ἀκόλαστος does not necessarily occur while his bad actions are being performed. When Aristotle says that, having made a προαίρεσις, the ἀκόλαστος pursues the present pleasure, he is referring to a certain "decisiveness" in his personal orientation toward the wrong end—as opposed to the ἀκρατής, whose character is not so set and who, indeed, at least believes that one ought not to pursue the present pleasure always. Aristotle speaks of ἀκολασία as a chronic and ever-present disease like "dropsy" [ὕδερος = peripheral edema] or consumption, as opposed to a problem that might manifest itself intermittently, like epilepsy, to which Aristotle compares ἀκρασία [*EN* vii,8, 1150b31–34]. A few lines later, he compares the ἀκρατής to a person who gets drunk easily: he does sometimes get drunk, but his overall disposition is not that of a drunk [1151a3–5]. By contrast, the ἀκόλαστος is (often literally) given over to drink.

Since what distinguishes a προαίρεσις from a merely voluntary act is deliberation [*EN* iii,2], in some sense the ἀκόλαστος's being ἀκόλαστος is connected with deliberation, and the ἀκρατής's being ἀκρατής with an absence of the same. But it would be a mistake to say that the ἀκρατής does not deliberate at all. While discussing deliberation in *EN* vi,9, Aristotle says that the ἀκρατής "will reach as a result of his calculation what he sets himself to do, so that he will have deliberated correctly, but he will have got for himself a great evil."[6] The difference, therefore, between the ἀκρατής and the ἀκόλαστος is not that the former does not deliberate at all but that certain human acts he performs do not correspond to that toward which he has deliberately directed his character.

The last major character type, the ἐγκρατής or continent man, does not figure a great deal in the passages we shall be discussing below; still, in order to complete the schema, it is good to know something about him. Aristotle acknowledges that some people do not distinguish the ἐγκρατής from the simply good man, but Aristotle sees in him a certain tenseness that is not present in the φρόνιμος or the σπουδαῖος, who pursue the good and are not tempted to pursue anything less than the good. Unlike the ἐγκρατής, the φρόνιμος is not constantly pushing away possibly wayward desires.

The ἐγκρατής is also interestingly different from the ἀκρατής. One obvious (and, therefore, less interesting) difference is that the ἀκρατής goes for what he believes is bad and the ἐγκρατής does not; but Aristotle also says that their concerns are different. "The ἀκρατής, knowing that the things he is contemplating are bad, due to passion, performs them nonetheless; the ἐγκρατής, knowing that his *desires* are bad, due to reason, does not follow them."[7] The ἀκρατής is not preoccupied with his desires. This is not what distinguishes him (the ἀκρατής) from the φρόνιμος (or

---

6 γὰρ ἀκρατὴς καὶ ὁ φαῦλος ὃ προτίθεται δεῖν ἐκ τοῦ λογισμοῦ τεύξεται, ὥστε ὀρθῶς ἔσται βεβουλευμένος, κακὸν δὲ μέγα εἰληφώς [1142b18–20]. The translation is from the Revised Oxford Translation, which reads δεῖν for ἰδεῖν.

7 *EN* vii,1, 1145b12–14; but see also vii,4, 1148a13–17.

σπουδαῖος), for neither does the φρόνιμος worry about controlling his desires, but it does distinguish him from the ἐγκρατής. The ἐγκρατής does not experience remorse, since what he eventually does corresponds to his overall end and character, but he does not have his life and character entirely "together." In terms that will becomes more clear below, he is not entirely friends with himself.

II. Practical Contradiction

I argue below that what generates Aristotle's analysis of the ἀκρατής (especially in *EE* vii,6) is a concern to maintain the unity of the ἀκρατής (and other similar character types) despite his (their) having contradictory beliefs, desires, and attitudes. So, before getting to the analysis of that and other passages, it would be good to say something about the principle of non-contradiction (the PNC) as it applies to the issues we shall be considering.

As we saw in chapter 2 (section III), Aristotle's first formulation of the principle in the book of the *Metaphysics* largely dedicated to it runs as follows: "the same attribute cannot at the same time belong and not belong to the same subject in the same respect" [*Metaph.* iv,3, 1005b19–20]. Here Aristotle clearly has in mind the way that things stand—and/or can stand—in the world; he has in mind, that is, theoretical rather than practical reason. But the way in which he understands the principle—as being about attributes that belong or not to some other thing—makes it easily applicable also in the practical realm, where one either heads or does not head toward some other point (or object). Thus, in arguing for the PNC Aristotle can remark, "Why does a man, who thinks he ought to, walk to Megara and not remain inactive?" [*Metaph.* iv,4, 1008b14–15]. And immediately afterwards: "Why does [a man] not walk early some morning into a well or over a precipice, if one happens to be in his way? Why do we observe him guarding against this, evidently not thinking that falling in is alike good and not good?" [*Metaph.* iv,4, 1008b15–17]. What is not possible *logically* here is both to apply and not to apply the same attribute—such as, 'I want to (x)'—to the same object, in the same respect, and at the same time.

Recognition of a role for the PNC in the practical sphere is not new with Aristotle but is found also in his teacher Plato; indeed, Plato's approach sheds a good deal of light on Aristotle's.[8] In the fourth book of *Republic*, in a context that is wholly practical, Plato writes:

> It is clear that the same thing will not wish at the same time to do or to suffer opposites, with respect to the same thing—or, in any case, with respect to the same object—so that, should we ever discover in them that these have come about, we will know that it was not the same thing but more.[9]

The "PNC language" in this passage is apparent. Imagine a single entity that has a wish with respect to a single thing. One must think of a wish as having a *terminus ad quem*: either doing something or suffering something, e.g. throwing oneself into a well or being thrown into it. If the partition of the wish does not occur at the *terminus ad quem*, it is forced to occur—as a matter of logical principle—at the other end: the *terminus ab quo*. Plato would be saying then that a single thing ("the same thing") cannot have a wish for true contraries at the same time: both to go into the well and not to do so.[10] If in a single soul there are found wishes for contrary things, we must posit, therefore, separate entities in the soul that have these contrary wishes.

And not only that, but we would also have to say that the wishes of these parts are, at least in certain circumstances, separate in time. Even if we posit two "parts" in a person's soul, one pursuing something incompatible with what the other pursues, these cannot be at the same time in the fully active mode that leads to action, since ultimately there is just one thing—one person—who acts. When one or the other desire comes to action, the other must necessarily recede.

---

8 See Christopher Shields, "Unified Agency and *akrasia* in Plato's *Republic*," in Akrasia *in Ancient Philosophy: From Socrate to Plotinus*, ed. C. Bobonich and P. Destrée (Leiden: Brill, 2007), 61–86. See also Kevin L. Flannery, "Robinson's Łukasiewiczian *Republic* IV, 435–39," 705–26.

9 ὅτι ταὐτὸν τἀναντία ποιεῖν ἢ πάσχειν κατὰ ταὐτόν γε καὶ πρὸς ταὐτὸν οὐκ ἐθελήσει ἅμα, ὥστε ἄν που εὑρίσκωμεν ἐν αὐτοῖς ταῦτα γιγνόμενα, εἰσόμεθα ὅτι οὐ ταὐτὸν ἦν ἀλλὰ πλείω [*R*. iv, 436B8–11]. The "in them" of the translation (here ἐν αὐτοῖς) refers to parts of the soul posited just previously.

10 Or to be thrown into the well and not to be thrown; but we can safely ignore for the moment this other option: i.e., that the wish might be to suffer rather than to do something.

III. *EE* vii,6: Unity of Soul

The problem (or puzzle) of ἀκρασία is well known. It presupposes a certain definition of the phenomenon at issue: ἀκρασία is equivalent to knowing what one ought to do and not doing it.[11] Plato's Socrates argues in the *Protagoras* and elsewhere that, since no one acts to one's own disadvantage and since doing what one ought to do is to one's own greatest advantage, if one knows what one ought to do, when faced with the choice of either doing it or not, one cannot but choose to do it. So, when people do not do what they ought to do, they cannot know what they ought to do—since otherwise they would do it. But, as stated, the definition of ἀκρασία includes the idea that one knows what one ought to do; so, ἀκρασία is impossible.

The problem with this argument is, of course, that ἀκρασία does exist—indeed, it is widespread. The challenge, then, is to explain in as philosophically perspicuous a manner as possible how this can be. Plato solves the problem of ἀκρασία in book four of the *Republic*, where he argues that a person can know in one part of his soul that something ought (or ought not) to be done but not know the same thing in another part. When the moment to act arrives, the person follows the lead of the non-knowing part.[12] Aristotle's solution to the problem of ἀκρασία seems at times to differ little from Plato's (see, for instance, *EN* v, 11, 1138b5–13). Without a doubt, his solution is related to Plato's; but a close examination of the pertinent passages reveals a more elaborate approach with interesting connections to other sectors of Aristotle's philosophy, especially his physics and his metaphysics.[13]

---

[11] As discussed in chapter 5, section III, ἀκρασία is also present, although in a secondary sense, when a person erringly thinks that something is the right thing to do and fails out of weakness to do that.

[12] See Terence H. Irwin, *Plato's Moral Theory*, 191–200, 293 n.5; John Gould, *The Development of Plato's Ethics* (Cambridge: Cambridge University Press, 1955), chapter 2; Richard Robinson, "Plato's Separation of Reason and Desire," 38–48. See also Flannery, "Robinson's Łukasiewiczian *Republic* IV, 435–39".

[13] There are also hints in Plato that he recognized that the solution to the Socratic puzzle regarding ἀκρασία requires a more finely calibrated division of the soul than that provided by the three-part (λογιστικὸν-θυμοειδὴς-ἐπιθυμητικὸν) division of (for instance) *R.* iv, 436A8–b3. See *R.* iv,

An important passage in this regard appears in *EE* vii,6, where Aristotle discusses the possibility of a man's friendship with himself. At the beginning of the chapter, Aristotle issues a caveat to the effect that, strictly speaking, friendship requires two persons; but then he acknowledges that one can speak of a man's friendship with himself if one posits parts of his soul in relationship with one another [*EE* vii,6, 1240a17]. He then speaks of three marks of friendship: wishing for good things—or, at least, apparently good things—for the other, wishing that the other might exist, and wishing to live together with the other [1240a24–30]. (This list will become important below.) Next, Aristotle says that the characteristics of friendship can be referred—or applied—to the interior state of a single individual [ἄπαντα ταῦτα ἐπαναφέρεται πρὸς τὸν ἕνα—1240b4–5]. And then comes our passage (into which I have inserted numerical markers):

{1} All these characteristics belong to the good man in relation to himself since, in the bad man—in the incontinent [ἐν τῷ ἀκρατεῖ], for instance—there is conflict. {2} And for this reason it appears even to be possible for a man to be an enemy to himself—although qua one and indivisible, he is an object of desire to himself. {3} The good man is such, that is, the man who is a friend with respect to virtue (for, in any case, the wretched man [μοχθηρὸς] is not one but many and in the same day other than himself and inconstant, so that also his friendship toward himself is led up to the friendship of the good man[14]—for in so far as he is similar, that is, single and good to himself, so far is he a friend and object of desire to himself);[15] and he is thus by nature, but the bad man is thus against nature.

{4} The good man does not revile himself at one and the same time, as does the incontinent man [ὁ ἀκρατής], nor does the later revile the earlier as does the

---

443D5–7: ... ὥσπερ ὅρους τρεῖς ἁρμονίας ἀτεχνῶς, νεάτης τε καὶ ὑπάτης καὶ μέσης, καὶ εἰ ἄλλα ἄττα μεταξὺ τυγχάνει ὄντα ... .

14 Dirlmeier gives here "So läßt sich denn auch die Freundschaft des Menschen mit sich selbst zurückführen auf die des Guten (mit sich selbst)" [Franz Dirlmeier, *Aristoteles* Eudemische Ethik, 78] which at least acknowledges the τὴν in 1240b18 (πρὸς τὴν τοῦ ἀγαθοῦ). The Revised Oxford Translation gives: "So that a man's friendship for himself is at bottom friendship towards the good."

15 τι γάρ πῃ ὁμοιοῖ καὶ εἷς καὶ αὐτὸς αὑτῷ ἀγαθός, ταύτῃ αὐτὸς αὑτῷ φίλος καὶ ὀρεκτός [1240b19–20]. This is the Susemihl text. The word given here as ὁμοιοῖ has been a source of difficulties. The codices have ὅμοιοι; Susemihl, following Fritzsche, writes ὁμοιοῖ; Walzer and Mingay, following Bekker, write ὅμοιος. Whatever is the correct reading, the general sense of the passage suggests that the bad man is similar to the good man in being at least minimally unified.

repenter [ὁ μεταμελητικός],[16] nor does the earlier revile the later as does the liar [ὁ ψεύστης]. {5} In general, if we must define things as the sophists do, it is as if 'Coriscus' was also good Coriscus, for it is clear that the same quantity of them all is good. {6} For when they accuse themselves, they kill themselves; but each seems to himself good. [*EE* vii,6, 1240b11–28][17]

Obviously, there is a lot going on in this passage and it raises a plethora of questions. What, for instance, is the role of time in this passage? And the role of quantity? Why does Aristotle say both that "each seems to himself good" and that, "when they accuse themselves, they kill themselves"? A point-by-point exegesis of this passage will prove a useful vehicle for an appreciation of the manifold connections Aristotle's solution to the problem of ἀκρασία has with other aspects of his philosophical system. (We go into these connections in subsequent sections of the present chapter.)

The argument of the first section (sentences {1} through {3}) is fairly clear. Unlike the good man, the ἀκρατής (mentioned as only an example of a bad man: οἷον, 1240b13) is not internally unified. It appears indeed that he can be an enemy [ἐχθρὸν] to himself, although even in this case there is some core unit of himself that cannot be so considered. This core

---

16 It is common to translate μεταμέλεια as 'regret'—which would make the μεταμελητικός 'the regretter.' But, as we shall see below, there is reason to distinguish between μεταμέλεια and regret. According to Aristotle, the ἀκόλαστος does not experience μεταμέλεια, but there is no reason to say that he does not or cannot regret his unhappy state. So, instead of translating μεταμελητικός as 'the regretter,' we employ the somewhat artificial term 'the repenter.' Unlike a man who experiences mere regret, a man who repents of what he has done still perceives himself as "trying to be good." Although less so than 'penitent,' the word 'repent' can bear in English a religious—even Christian—connotation; our translations of μεταμελητικός as 'repenter' should not be understood to bear any such a connotation. The word 'repentance' might seem the appropriate word to render that which the repenter has, i.e., μεταμέλεια; but the religious connotation is very prominent in that word. Fortunately, we have another that is not so freighted, 'remorse.'

17 πάντα δὲ ταῦτα τῷ ἀγαθῷ ὑπάρχει πρὸς αὐτόν. ἐν γὰρ τῷ πονηρῷ διαφωνεῖ, οἷον ἐν τῷ ἀκρατεῖ. καὶ διὰ τοῦτο δοκεῖ καὶ ἐχθρὸν ἐνδέχεσθαι αὐτὸν αὑτῷ εἶναι· ᾗ δ' εἷς καὶ ἀδιαίρετος, ὀρεκτὸς αὐτὸς αὑτοῦ. τοιοῦτος ὁ ἀγαθὸς καὶ ὁ κατ' ἀρετὴν φίλος, ἐπεὶ ὅ γε μοχθηρὸς οὐχ εἷς ἀλλὰ πολλοί, καὶ τῆς αὐτῆς ἡμέρας ἕτερος καὶ ἔμπληκτος. ὥστε καὶ ἡ αὐτοῦ πρὸς αὑτὸν φιλία ἀνάγεται πρὸς τὴν τοῦ ἀγαθοῦ. ὅτι γάρ πῃ ὁμοιοῖ καὶ εἷς καὶ αὐτὸς αὑτῷ ἀγαθός, ταύτῃ αὐτὸς αὑτῷ φίλος καὶ ὀρεκτός· φύσει δὲ τοιοῦτος, ἀλλ' ὁ πονηρὸς παρὰ φύσιν. ὁ δ' ἀγαθὸς οὔθ' ἅμα λοιδορεῖται ἑαυτῷ, ὥσπερ ὁ ἀκρατής, οὔτε ὁ ὕστερος τῷ προτέρῳ, ὥσπερ ὁ μεταμελητικός, οὔτε ὁ ἔμπροσθεν τῷ ὑστέρῳ, ὥσπερ ὁ ψεύστης. ὅλως τε εἰ δεῖ ὥσπερ οἱ σοφισταὶ διορίζουσιν, ὥσπερ τὸ Κορίσκος καὶ Κορίσκος σπουδαῖος. δῆλον γὰρ ὡς τὸ αὐτὸ πόσον σπουδαῖον αὐτῶν, ἐπεὶ ὅταν ἐγκαλέσωσιν αὐτοῖς, ἀποκτιννύασιν αὐτούς· ἀλλὰ δοκεῖ πᾶς αὐτὸς αὑτῷ ἀγαθός. Walzer and Mingay put ὅλως τε ... σπουδαῖον αὐτῶν in parentheses. I do not think this helps to make sense of the passage at all. Plato uses the word λοιδορέω in a very similar context at *R*. iv, 440B1.

unit in the soul is one and indivisible [ἀδιαίρετος]. This idea is connected with the point made in chapter 2 (sections I and III) and also just above about a person's not being able to go toward true contraries at the same time. The self is an indivisible unit "moving" through time, moment by moment.[18] At any one moment, the person cannot want contradictory things (to go into the well and to remain out). Even in the extreme case in which the person's preference changes in alternating moments, the person at the present moment (that "moves" through time) always goes indivisibly toward *one* of the alternatives.

In sentences {2} and {3} Aristotle is focusing in on this one indivisible unit in the soul of even the akratic person. Even if, because of the fractured general state of the ἀκρατής, he is in that respect unlike the good man, there is still a core unit in him that possesses the unity of the good man: that is, the unit that looks out upon any particular present moment. This, says Aristotle, is "led up"—or reduced [ἀνάγεται—1240b18]—to the friendship that the good man has with himself (sentence {3}). The difference between the good man and "wretched" men like the ἀκρατής is that the unity of the good man's core unit is spread also throughout his soul. The bad man is like Plato's tyrant in book nine of the *Republic*: full of internal fears and desires, he is condemned to living "for the most part, like a woman, in the house" (as opposed to the city).[19] As we shall see below, Aristotle associates this core unit of any person with the intellect.

Sentence {3} finishes with the remark that the good man is unified by nature [φύσει], the bad man [πονηρὸς] against nature [παρὰ φύσιν]. I take this to mean that, by seeking, as he does the merely apparent good,[20] the bad man has been and is on a trajectory toward disunity—although this can never finish in *utter* disunity, since the core unit will always be one. Thus, the bad man does maintain as much unity as his character will allow, although this happens despite himself (that is, despite what characterizes him as a bad man); the good man's soul is united in accordance with his nature as good.

---

18 See Ursula Coope, *Time for Aristotle: Physics IV.10–14*, Oxford Aristotle Studies (Oxford: Clarendon, 2005), 132–39.

19 *R.* ix, 579B8. I am grateful to Christopher Shields for this reference. See also *Lg.* 781C2–D1 and *Gorgias* 485D3–E2.

20 See above chapter 5, section III, and chapter 7, section VII.

IV. *EE* vii,6: The Many Faces of Coriscus

Sentences {4} through {6} are considerably more obscure. Let us begin with {5}, "In general, if we must define things as the sophists do, it is as if 'Coriscus' was also good Coriscus, for it is clear that the same quantity of them all is good." 'Coriscus' in Aristotle means basically 'John Smith': some individual.[21] Aristotle is exploiting here the sophists' way of dividing up an individual 'Coriscus' into various thoughts that one might have about him. In effect, what they do is to hypostatize the various things that might be said of Coriscus, treating them each as if they were subsistent entities: 'musical Coriscus' becomes as much a concrete individual as Coriscus himself.[22] The sophists do adopt a strange way of proceeding, but it is not without sense. When thoughts about Coriscus run through one's mind, they are all—qua thoughts—of an equal standing: the thought of Coriscus is as much a distinct thought as the thought of Coriscus himself. So, if all we know is what goes through our minds and if each thought is independent of any other, it would seem to be impossible to know (for instance) that Coriscus has become musical, for that would be to know that he has become musical Coriscus, who is distinct from all other "Coriscuses," including Coriscus himself.[23]

We hear of this same approach in a passage in the *Sophistici elenchi* [*SE*], chapter 22, where Aristotle alludes to the Platonic "third man" argument, according to which, in order to account for the resemblance of two (or more) men as men, one must posit a "third man" similar to the first

[21] Certain sophists would apparently split the individual up into accidental aspects and derive paradoxes by referring to the aspects as if they were the persons themselves. Aristotle speaks of "Coriscus himself" as opposed to "musical Coriscus" at *Metaph.* vi,2, 1026b16–18. See also *APr.* i,33, 47b29–32 and *SE* v, 166b32–33. (In the *SE* passages, Coriscus is actually mentioned.) In Plato, see *Phlb.* 14C11–E4 and *Lg.* v, 731D6–732B4.

[22] "They say, not that Coriscus is both musical and unmusical, but that *this* Coriscus is musical and *this* Coriscus unmusical" [*SE* xvii,175b19–21].

[23] In *SE* v, Aristotle writes as follows: "Fallacies, then, that depend on accident occur whenever any attribute is claimed to belong in a like manner to a thing and to its accident. For since the same thing has many accidents there is no necessity that all the same attributes should belong to all of a thing's predicates and to their subject as well. Thus (e.g.), if Coriscus is different from a man, he is different from himself: for he is a man; or if he is different from Socrates, and Socrates is a man, then, they say, you have admitted that Coriscus is different from a man, because it is an accident of the person from whom you said that he is different that he is a man" [*SE* v,166b28–166b36].

two (or however many concrete men there are).²⁴ Aristotle is explaining why a "third man" is thought to be necessary; he says:

> Again, there is the argument that there is a third man above and beyond the man himself and individual men. For 'man' or any commonality signifies not a concrete individual [τόδε τι], but some quality [τοιόνδε], or quantity [ποσὸν] or relation [πρός τι], or something of that sort. So also in the case of 'Coriscus' and 'musical Coriscus' and the question whether they are the same or different.²⁵

Aristotle's point is that any "commonality"—whether it be the universal 'man' or a commonality of the type assigned to the second category (quality) or to the third (quantity) or to any of the categories—typically holds *of* a concrete entity; the commonality itself, however, is not a concrete entity. In positing a third man, Plato (or certain Platonists) make the same error that the sophists do, according to Aristotle.

So, it is apparent that, when in *EE* vii,6 Aristotle alludes to the sophists' methods, he is alluding to their way of hypostatizing attributes of Coriscus, treating them as if they were concrete entities.²⁶ He is willing to do this, but only up to a point: ultimately we must acknowledge that these things are attributes of the only thing (in this context) that is truly a concrete entity or substance: Coriscus. In *EE* vii,6, the attributes that Aristotle speaks of in this way are all moral attributes. He speaks, that is, not of musical Coriscus (as at *APo*. i,24, 85a24–25) or of "Coriscus in the marketplace" (as at *Phys*. iv,11, 219b21), but rather of the ἀκρατής, the repenter [ὁ μεταμελητικός], and the liar [ὁ ψεύστης]. The idea, therefore, is to isolate (for the sake of exposition) Coriscus the ἀκρατής, Coriscus the repenter, and Coriscus the liar, *as if* each of these was distinct from Coriscus himself, but to do so in such a way that Coriscus remains the substratum of any such predications.

It is apparent also that in the *EE* vii,6 passage Aristotle has in mind

---

24 We have already considered this passage, that is, in chapter 1. I do not wish to enter into the dispute about whether the third-man argument is genuinely Platonic or whether Aristotle correctly sets out the Platonic position; on such matters, see Gail Fine, *On Ideas: Aristotle's Criticism of Plato's Theory of Forms*, 203–41.

25 αἱ ὅτι ἔστι τις τρίτος ἄνθρωπος παρ' αὐτὸν καὶ τοὺς καθ' ἕκαστον· τὸ γὰρ ἄνθρωπος καὶ ἅπαν τὸ κοινὸν οὐ τόδε τι ἀλλὰ τοιόνδε τι ἢ ποσὸν ἤ πρός τι ἤ τῶν τοιούτων τι σημαίνει. ὁμοίως δὲ καὶ ἐπὶ τοῦ Κορίσκος καὶ Κορίσκος μουσικός, πότερον ταὐτὸν ἢ ἕτερον; [*SE* xxii,178b36–179a1].

26 See *Metaph*. vi,2, 1026b14–21, also Coope, *Time for Aristotle*, 135–36.

temporal attributes of some sort: the ἀκρατής accuses himself of inconsistency "at one and the same time"; in other words, even as he performs the bad act, he knows (although, perhaps, not in the most active sense) that he ought not to do so.[27] The repenter may have had an easy conscience when he did what he did, but later he repents what he has done. And the liar knows that his present statements or boasts are inconsistent with what he will be able to perform in the future—but he is not worried about that now.[28]

One might have supposed that "the repenter" would be categorized by Aristotle as ἀκρατής. In the present schema, however, he is distinct from the ἀκρατής who, as we have seen, does repent of what he does. As conceived of in the present chapter, the liar would also repent. It may be, therefore, that the repenter represent a phenomenon rather than a character type. Or (and I think this the more likely explanation) it could be that

---

27 See also EE ii,8, 1224b16–21, where Aristotle speaks of the ἀκρατής and the ἐγκρατής in terms of their attitudes toward the future: "[T]he continent feels pain now in acting against his appetite, but has the pleasure of hope, i.e. that he will be presently benefited, or even the pleasure of being actually at present benefited because he is in health; while the incontinent is pleased at getting, through his incontinency, what he desires, but has a pain of expectation, thinking that he is doing ill" [καὶ γὰρ ὁ ἐγκρατευόμενος λυπεῖται παρὰ τὴν ἐπιθυμίαν πράττων ἤδη, καὶ χαίρει τὴν ἀπ' ἐλπίδος ἡδονήν, ὅτι ὕστερον ὠφεληθήσεται, ἢ καὶ ἤδη ὠφελεῖται ὑγιαίνων· καὶ ὁ ἀκρατὴς χαίρει μὲν τυγχάνων ἀκρατευόμενος οὗ ἐπιθυμεῖ, λυπεῖται δὲ τὴν ἀπ' ἐλπίδος λύπην, οἴεται γὰρ κακὸν πράττειν].

28 In EN iv,7 Aristotle discusses the "false-sayer" [ὁ ψευδόμενος: 1127a19] or the liar [ὁ ψεύστης: 1127b16]. (This character type is different from the "false man" of Metaph. v,29: see chapter 7, note 10.) Under the general type 'liar,' there are two subtypes: the boaster (ὁ ἀλαζών) and the self-underestimating person (ὁ εἴρων), although the title of liar attaches more to the boaster, since he is the more despicable character. (Socrates, for instance, is singled out as a self-underestimating person, i.e., as employing irony [εἰρωνία], but his way of downplaying his own praiseworthy qualities is regarded as pleasing [1127b22–26].) There are boasters who lie about themselves simply for the sake of lying; more common, however, and culpable, are those who lie about themselves for the sake of reputation and honor and gain. Those who lie for the sake of gain, says Aristotle, "claim qualities which are of value to one's neighbors and one's lack of which is not easily detected, e.g. the powers of a seer, a sage, or a physician" [1127b19–20]. It is this subtype that Aristotle seems to have especially in mind in EE vii,6, when he says that the liar [ὁ ψεύστης] reviles his later self. Such behavior depends on a sort of "disconnect" between an act of boasting now and what will or might be accomplished in the future. In fully reasonable (i.e., ethical) behavior, there would be no such disconnect and no need to posit a fragmentation of the soul—of the history—of the person in question. At Lg. xi,921A6, Plato speaks of as lying the craftsman who fails to produce a product in the time agreed to with a buyer. See also Sophocles's Antigone (1191–95): Ἐγώ, φίλη δέσποινα, καὶ παρὼν ἐρῶ οὐδὲν παρήσω τῆς ἀληθείας ἔπος· τί γάρ σε μαλθάσσοιμ' ἂν ὧν ἐς ὕστερον ψεῦσται φανούμεθ'; ὀρθὸν ἀληθεῖ' ἀεί. On EN iv,7, see Kevin L. Flannery, "Being Truthful with (or Lying to) Others about Oneself," in Thomas Aquinas and the Nicomachean Ethics, ed. Tobias Hoffmann, Jörn Müller, and Matthias Perkams (Cambridge: Cambridge University Press, 2013), forthcoming.

Aristotle thinks that we might isolate various character types within a single person ("Coriscus") without being obliged to say that one character type excludes another, just as accident can be predicated of an accident.[29]

V. *EE* vii,6: Quantities, Subjects, and Actions

Aristotle uses in {5} also some different—and fairly technical—language to say much the same thing; he speaks, that is, of quantities. He says that, however the sophists choose to speak, Coriscus is also good Coriscus, "for it is clear that the same *quantity* [τὸ αὐτὸ πόσον] of them all is good."[30] It is true that Aristotle uses the word 'quantity' [πόσον] only of "the same quantity of them all [which] is good," that is, "basic Coriscus," but it is reasonable to extend the term to the other hypostatizations. In the first place, this gives us an explanation of how Aristotle can introduce the concept of quantity so suddenly: we must assume that his listeners would have already understood that 'incontinent Coriscus,' 'repenting Coriscus,' and 'lying Coriscus' (like 'musical Coriscus' and 'Coriscus in the marketplace') were quantities; speaking, therefore, of Coriscus (or good Coriscus) as a quantity would not have come to them as a surprise, as it does to us.

Moreover, it seems not unreasonable to use the term 'quantity' of the line of intelligibility between the liar at the present moment (let us call it t_o) and at t_s when he fails to measure up to his attitudes or claims at t_o, or the line of intelligibility between the repenter at t_s and the same man at t_o with respect to which (whom?) he reviles himself. It *is* a problem for this type of analysis that the incontinent man reviles himself at one and the same time [ἅμα: 1240b21]; but let us set that problem to one side for the moment.

In fact, it is less difficult to understand how Aristotle might speak of Coriscus's "temporal parts" as quantities than it is to understand how he could refer to Coriscus as a quantity. But exploration of this idea gives us insight into the role of Aristotle's physical and metaphysical ideas in his

---

29 In 'the bird was bright red,' 'bright' qualifies red and not the bird. See *Cat.* viii, 10b26–27; also *Metaph.* vii,4, 1030a17–27.

30 δῆλον γὰρ ὡς τὸ αὐτὸ πόσον σπουδαῖον αὐτῶν [1240b25–26]. I take it that the αὐτῶν refers to the various hypostases: Coriscus the ἀκρατής, Coriscus, the liar, and Coriscus the repenter.

philosophical psychology. *Metaph.* v,13 opens with a definition of sorts: "We call a quantity [ποσόν] that which is divisible into two or more constituent parts of which each is by nature a one and a 'this'" [*Metaph.* v,13, 1020a7–8].[31] It is apparent here that Aristotle's basic conception of quantity is quite a broad one: it is not limited, for instance, to mathematics; all one needs in order to have a quantity is divisibility. "Some things," he says, "are called quantities in virtue of their own nature, others accidentally, e.g. the line is a quantity by its own nature, the musical is one accidentally" [*Metaph.* v,13, 1020a14–17]. If Aristotle is willing to speak of being musical as a quantity, it would not be out of philosophical character for him to refer to "akratic" Coriscus as a quantity.

Aristotle goes on in *Metaph.* v,13 to say:

Of things that are quantities accidentally, some are so called in the sense in which it was said that musical and white were quantities, viz. because that to which they belong is a quantity. [1020a26–28]

So, the attributes 'musical' and 'white' are called quantities at all because that to which each belongs is a quantity. In the case of 'musical' what else could that to which it belongs be but a man, such as Coriscus? So, also here, Coriscus would in some sense be a quantity. And yet, as Aristotle certainly realizes, this too is not quite accurate—or, at least, not the whole story. A man belongs properly to the category of substance and not to that of quantity. Appropriately, then, just after discussing accidental quantities such as musical and white, Aristotle discusses a second type:

... others [are accidental quantities] in the way in which movement [κίνησις] and time are so; for these are called quantities and extended [συνεχῆ] because the things of which these are attributes are divisible. I mean not that which is moved, but the space through which it is moved; for, because that is a quantity, movement also is a quantity; and, because this is a quantity, time is so. [*Metaph.* v,13, 1020a28–32]

Here again the substances of which these other accidental quantities hold are identified, only to be pushed (although not wholly) into the back-

---

31 This definition would take in even numbers such as 3, 4, 5, etc., conceived in the traditional Greek manner: as groups of objects. According to this approach, 1 is not a number (or quantity).

ground. Movement and time are called accidental quantities because "the things of which [they] are attributes are divisible." But, of course, substances, qua substances, are not divisible, so movements and times must get their character as quantities from such substances qua (in some secondary sense) divisible. It is for this reason that Aristotle immediately issues a clarification: "I mean not that which is moved, but the space through which it is moved [ὃ ἐκινήθη: 1020a31]...." This "space" (or, more literally, "that which it is moved") is not just any space but that through which *it* (the substance) is moved: its progress through space and time. Similarly, the quantity of which the further quantity 'Coriscus the ἀκρατής' is attributed is not strictly speaking Coriscus, but Coriscus *as* moving through space and time.

Aristotle's use of the term 'extended quantity' in *Metaph.* v,13 also establishes a link with the more extensive—and somewhat different—treatment of quantity in the *Categories*. He explains there that an extended quantity is different from a discrete quantity [ποσόν διωρισμένον: vi, 4b20] in so far as it stretches over a distance of some sort: this is the difference between a point and a line, between the number 5 and the distance 5 feet.[32] Among the extended quantities—although not in the primary sense—are, he says, movements and actions. Extended quantities in the primary sense include lines and times; other things are called this "accidentally" [κατὰ συμβεβηκός: vi, 5a39]: "for it is to [lines, times, etc.] that we look when we call the others quantities. For example, we speak of a large amount of white because the surface is large, and an action [πρᾶξις: vi, 5b2] or a change [κίνησις: vi, 5b3] is called long because the time is long." So, even if movements and actions are not quantities in the primary sense, they can still be so analyzed, as long as they are associated with something that traverses space over time.

---

32 Aristotle makes the difference between discrete and extended quantity precise by means of the concept of a common boundary [κοινὸς ὅρος]. A point does not share a boundary with another point, otherwise they would not be points; but a line, he says, is an extended quantity, since "it is possible to find a common boundary at which its parts join together: a point" [5a1–2]. Similarly "present time [ὁ νῦν χρόνος] joins on to both past time and future time" [5a7–8], functioning there as a boundary.

VI. Suicide and the Core Unit
(*EE* vii,6 and *EN* ix,4)

That brings us to the final sentence in the *EE* vii,6 passage {6}: "For when they accuse themselves, they kill themselves; but each seems to himself good" [1240b26–28]. It has been suggested to the present author that Aristotle is still characterizing here the different hypostatizations of Coriscus: since they do not agree with one another, they somehow kill each other off, leaving just good Coriscus. This reading gives to the plurals "*they* accuse themselves, *they* kill themselves" a clear reference from within the same sentence.[33] But a comparison of *EE* vii,6 with its parallel in the *Nicomachean Ethics* strongly suggests that with the plurals in sentence {6} Aristotle is referring to the akratic types (including also the repenter and the liar), who constitute the more general topic of the chapter and is saying very briefly—certainly too briefly—that, although they think themselves good enough at least to rise up and accuse other parts of themselves of being bad, they do sometimes kill themselves. This would correspond to the remark at *EN* ix,4, 1166b11–13: "And those who have done many terrible deeds and are hated for their wickedness even shrink from life and destroy themselves."[34]

The parallels between *EE* vii,6 and *EN* ix,4 are unmistakable. Both chapters are about friendship with oneself and both discuss (among other similar unspecified character types) the ἀκρατής, who is said to be at variance with himself (see *EN* ix,4, 1166b7–9). The good man, by contrast, says *EN* ix,4, desires always the same things "with all his soul" [κατὰ πᾶσαν τὴν ψυχήν—1166a14]. (As we have seen, in {3} of *EE* vii,6, Aristotle says of any man that, "so far as he is similar, that is, single and good to himself, so far is he a friend and object of desire to himself.") Both chapters connect unity or disunity of soul with the "history" of the individual in

---

33 *EE* vii,6, 1240b25–27: δῆλον γὰρ ὡς τὸ αὐτὸ πόσον σπουδαῖον αὐτῶν, ἐπεὶ ὅταν ἐγκαλέσωσιν αὑτοῖς, ἀποκτιννύασιν αὑτούς....

34 δὲ πολλὰ καὶ δεινὰ πέπρακται καὶ διὰ τὴν μοχθηρίαν μισοῦνται, καὶ φεύγουσι τὸ ζῆν καὶ ἀναιροῦσιν ἑαυτούς. Irwin would read διὰ τὴν μοχθηρίαν μισοῦσί τε καὶ φεύγουσι τὸ ζῆν with L[b] [Irwin, "Vice and Reason," 90 n.28] and that may be preferable.

question both past and future (see *EN* ix,4, 1166a24–26 and 1166b15–16) and both speak of each person's considering himself in some sense good (see *EN* ix,4, 1166a11–12, 1166b3–4). But most importantly, in both chapters Aristotle lists the three marks of friendship: wishing good—or apparently good—things for the other, wishing that the other might exist or live, wishing to live together with the other.[35] Indeed, *EN* ix,4 is explicitly structured around these three marks.[36] Here, therefore, we see not just parallel themes but a deliberate single *approach* to the same themes.

So, how should we interpret {6} ("For when they accuse themselves, they kill themselves")? As mentioned, one solution would be to say that Aristotle is still speaking about the hypostatizations of Coriscus. But so understood, it is not at all clear what point the remark would then be intended to convey; and, in any case, that solution would make it the lone operative idea in *EE* vii,6 without a parallel in *EN* ix,4. Furthermore, we expect to find Aristotle saying something about suicide at this point in his exposition in *EE* vii,6 (i.e., at 1240b26–27), since the argument at 1240b17–20 (that there is a core element of unity and self-friendship even in the bad man) would seem to suggest that no one could (or would) commit suicide. In order to dispel that impression, Aristotle feels that he must at least

---

35 Julia Annas speaks of five marks [Julia Annas, "Plato and Aristotle on Friendship and Altruism," *Mind* 86 (1977): 540], but her last two are clearly part of what is considered here the third mark (see *EN* ix,4, 1166a6–8).

36 *EN* ix,4 divides evenly into two parts: the first (1166a1–b2) having to do with a good man's friendship toward himself, the second (1166b2–29) with whether certain bad individuals, the φαῦλοι, can be similarly disposed. This second group is introduced in the first part, at 1166a11–12, as "the others" [οἱ λοιποί], and described as regarding themselves as good (ἐπιεικεῖς); it is only later that they are spoken of as the φαῦλοι. (That the λοιποί and the φαῦλοι are the same group is apparent in the words used to describe them originally—ἢ τοιοῦτοι [i.e., ἐπιεικεῖς] ὑπολαμβάνουσιν εἶναι [1166a11]—and when they are re-introduced at the beginning of the second part: ἀρέσκουσιν ἑαυτοῖς καὶ ὑπολαμβάνουσιν ἐπιεικεῖς εἶναι [1166b3–4].) The chapter begins with a list of "amicable properties" [τὰ φιλικά] that can be ascribed not only to distinct friends but to good men in relation to themselves (conceived as other): (a) wishing and bringing about good things—or, at least, apparently good things—for the other [1166a3–4]; (b) wishing the other "to be and to live" [1166a4–5]; (c) wishing to live together with the other: rejoicing together at the same good things, being pained together at the same bad things [1166a6–8]. Aristotle goes through these amicable properties twice in order, showing first that they pertain to the good man, then that they do not pertain to the φαῦλοι. In the *EE* vii,6, the three things are discussed most explicitly in lines 1240a23–30; they do not shape the structure of the chapter in the same way that they do in *EN* ix,4. A form of the list also appears in *MM* ii,11: καὶ γὰρ συζῆν μεθ' ἡμῶν αὐτῶν βουλόμεθα (ἴσως δὲ τοῦτο καὶ ἀναγκαῖον) καὶ τὸ εὖ ζῆν καὶ τὸ ζῆν καὶ τὸ βούλεσθαι τἀγαθόν, οὐκ ἄλλῳ τινί [1210b35–37].

mention—what is, in any case, obvious—that akratic types do sometimes kill themselves. If we do understand 1240b26–27 as the expected remark about suicide, we are left with the full complement of operative ideas in both of the parallel passages, *EE* vii,6 and *EN* ix,4; if we do not, *EE* vii,6 lacks one.

This is not to say that there are not problems with what Aristotle says in *EN* ix,4 about suicide or that there is no difference between what he says there and what he says in *EE* vii,6. The main issue is whether he has maintained in the *EN* account the idea that there will always be a core unit in a person that is friendly with itself. When in *EN* ix,4 he first mentions such matters, he makes an allusion to the idea we have already seen (in examining *EE* vii,6, 1240b17–18) that even the bad person's limited self-love can be reduced ("led up") to the love of the good man. Speaking of the three marks he says:

Now each of these is true of the good man's relation to himself (and of all other men in so far as they think themselves good; excellence and the good man seem, as has been said, to be the measure of every class of things).[37]

But one wonders what Aristotle means by the phrase, applied to other men, "*in so far* as they think themselves good." Does he mean that any person's self-love might be limited to a very narrow ambit (to recall the passage in *R.* ix, one's house, as opposed to the city)[38] but still be self-love, as in *EE* vii,6? Or does he think that love of self might become completely obliterated and that men are friends with themselves only *as long as* they think themselves good? A few lines later, again speaking of the marks of friendship, he employs similar phraseology: "Are we to say then that in so far as they are satisfied with themselves and think they are good, they share in these attributes?"[39]

The passage that most suggests that Aristotle has changed his mind on

---

37 πρὸς ἑαυτὸν δὲ τούτων ἕκαστον τῷ ἐπιεικεῖ ὑπάρχει (τοῖς δὲ λοιποῖς, ᾗ τοιοῦτοι ὑπολαμβάνουσιν εἶναι· ἔοικε δέ, καθάπερ εἴρηται, μέτρον ἑκάστων ἡ ἀρετὴ καὶ ὁ σπουδαῖος εἶναι) ... [*EN* ix,4, 1166a10–13]. As the back reference, Gauthier proposes *EN* iii,4, 1113a33.

38 See above, at note 19.

39 ' οὖν ᾗ τ' ἀρέσκουσιν ἑαυτοῖς καὶ ὑπολαμβάνουσιν ἐπιεικεῖς εἶναι, ταύτῃ μετέχουσιν αὐτῶν; [*EN* ix,4, 1166b3–4]. The word μετέχουσιν could itself be associated with the reduction mentioned at *EE* vii,6, 1240b17–18.

self-love comes just after his remark about extremely evil persons shrinking from life and destroying themselves:

> And wicked men seek for people with whom to spend their days, and shun themselves; for they remember many a grievous deed and anticipate others like them when they are by themselves, but when they are with others they forget. And having nothing lovable in them they have no feeling of love toward themselves. [*EN* ix,4, 1166b13–18]

The last sentence certainly appears to contradict the doctrine of *EE* vii,6.

There is a way of escaping this conclusion. Since here in *EN* ix,4 Aristotle does not emphasize the core unit which considers itself good, he could simply be offering a generic explanation of why people kill themselves: that is, because they find nothing good in themselves. Strictly speaking, this is not incompatible with the remark in *EE* vii,6, "when they accuse themselves, they kill themselves," for, even if some part of the soul still considers itself superior enough to make an accusation, it is still *accusing* and it could be accusing every other part but itself. While accusing itself it would find no element in itself that is good, since the active accusing part does not *find* itself as an object.

There is also another brief remark in which one might descry an escape route. Aristotle says at *EN* ix,4, 1166a17–21 that the good man

> wishes himself to live and be preserved, and especially the element by virtue of which he thinks. For existence is good to the good man, and each man wishes himself what is good, while no one chooses to possess the whole world if he has first to become someone else....[40]

Here Aristotle is clearly referring to the intellect, which, as we have seen, is the core unit of the person, which cannot go toward contrary prospects in the same sense and at the same time. Aristotle is obviously speaking in the passage about preserving oneself in being; he argues, in effect, that no one ever forfeits the last kernel, perhaps we cannot say of "self-regard," but

---

40 The passage continues: "(for that matter, even now God possesses the good); he wishes for this only on condition of being whatever he is; and the element that thinks would seem to be the individual man, or to be so more than any other element in him" [*EN* ix,4, 1166a17–23]. I am not at all sure what the remark about God means.

at least of self-preference.[41] Those who kill themselves do not want death for anyone else but for themselves. Of course, they accuse all the other "quantities" of themselves, and perhaps even a moment before killing themselves they accuse that quantity that would do such a foul thing as to kill itself, but in—and at—the end they do want something *for* themselves. Very near the conclusion of *EN* ix,4 Aristotle envisions just such a moment-by-moment self-accusation. Still speaking of the type of person who, having done very foul things, might kill himself, he says: "If a man cannot at the same time [ἅμα—1166b22] be pained and pleased, at all events after a short time he is pained because he was pleased, and he could have wished that these things had not been pleasant to him; for bad men are filled with remorse" [*EN* ix,4, 1166b22–25].

VII. A Problem Earlier in the *EE* vii,6 Passage Resolved

The remark just quoted serves also as a solution to the small difficulty in *EE* vii,6, alluded to above (in section V). There, as we have seen, Aristotle offers an analysis of three character types in terms of quantities and time: the repenter reviles his earlier self, the liar reviles his later self, but the ἀκρατής reviles himself at one and the same time [ἅμα—1240b21].

Bearing in mind *EN* ix,4, 1166b22–25 and also the idea that the part that is reviling cannot include itself in its reviling while that reviling is being done (since a reviling part necessarily places itself in a position of moral superiority with respect to the reviled part), we probably have to interpret in a loose sense Aristotle's saying in *EE* vii,6 that the ἀκρατής reviles himself at one and the same time, understanding it to mean that, relative to the repenter and the liar, he reviles himself over a much shorter span of time than they. The ἀκρατής who consumes an unhealthy dessert could be reviling himself even while he eats (but not at the very moment he commits to the next morsel); the reviling of the repenter and the liar

---

41 As we have seen, Aristotle says at *EE* vii,6, 1240b19–20 that even the divided man, "in so far as he is similar, i.e., single and good to himself, so far is he a friend and object of desire to himself" [ὅτι γάρ πῃ ὁμοιοῖ καὶ εἷς καὶ αὐτὸς αὑτῷ ἀγαθός, ταύτῃ αὐτὸς αὑτῷ φίλος καὶ ὀρεκτός].

occurs over a larger time frame. Aristotle is certainly as aware in *EE*, as he is in *EN* ix,4, of the impossibility of a single agent engaging in contrary movements at one and the same time;[42] in *EE* vii,6, therefore, he would be speaking informally, as we do when we say, for instance, that "at the moment he is conflicted whether to go or not."

At the tail end of the passage we have been examining (and near the end of *EN* ix,4), Aristotle says, "for bad men are filled with remorse" [1166b24-25]. This remark shows, incidentally, that Aristotle has in mind throughout *EN* ix,4 an akratic character type, for this person has remorse for what he has done—indeed, it is this which pushes him toward suicide. Aristotle never mentions in *EN* ix,4 the ἀκόλαστος. Indeed, it is hard to imagine the ἀκόλαστος committing suicide—except, perhaps, for reasons of perceived personal advantage, in order to avoid pain or disgrace or whatever. He would certainly not be among those described here, who, tossed to and fro and pulled to pieces psychologically [1166b21-22], kill themselves.

VIII. The Ἀκόλαστος

At this point, having examined in some detail *EE* vii,6, we have a fairly clear idea of the logical properties of ἀκρασία (and related moral failings). In order to round off our account of how Aristotle conceives of character types, it will be useful to say a few words about the character type just mentioned, that is, the ἀκόλαστος, whose logical properties are significantly different from those of the ἀκρατής.

We saw in section I of the present chapter that, according to the contrast set out in *EN* vii,3, the primary difference between the ἀκρατής and the ἀκόλαστος is that the latter's behavior is due to a προαίρεσις in favor of the idea that "one ought always to pursue the present pleasure" [1146b23],

---

42 "For what a man does voluntarily [ἑκών] he wishes [βουλόμενος πράττει], and what he wishes to do he does voluntarily. But no one wishes what he thinks to be bad; but surely the man who acts incontinently [ὁ ἀκρατευόμενος] does not do what he wishes, for to act incontinently is to act through appetite contrary to what the man thinks best; whence it results that the same man acts at the same time both voluntarily and involuntarily; but this is impossible [ὥστε ἅμα συμβήσεται τὸν αὐτὸν ἑκόντα καὶ ἄκοντα πράττειν· τοῦτο δ' ἀδύνατον]" [*EE* ii,7, 1223b5-10]. See also a bit later: ἅμα ἄρα ὁ αὐτὸς τὸ αὐτὸ πράξει ἑκὼν καὶ ἄκων [*EE* ii,7, 1223b17].

the former's is not. The practical reasoning of the ἀκόλαστος is straightforward: he always heads toward that which he wants. By contrast, the προαίρεσις of the ἀκρατής would be to pursue something other than what in fact he does pursue, and so his soul is riven; and, once he has performed the action that he would rather not have performed, he repents of having done so.[43] In *EN* vii,8, Aristotle, again contrasting the ἀκρατής and the ἀκόλαστος, says that the latter is firm in his resolution to pursue pleasure and is not carried away by passion [ἄλλος δ' ἐναντίος, ὁ ἐμμενετικὸς καὶ οὐκ ἐκστατικὸς διά γε τὸ πάθος—1151a26–27]. Unlike the ἀκρατής, he does pursue pleasure "without restraint" [ἀνέδην—1151a23], but this does not mean that he lacks self-mastery but rather that he is unselfconsciously rapacious.[44]

The soul of the ἀκόλαστος is not unlike that of the σπουδαῖος (the upright man).[45] There is a certain simplicity about both these character types: the σπουδαῖος is habituated to doing the right thing and he does it; the ἀκόλαστος is habituated to pursuing the present pleasure and he does that, come what may. Like that of the σπουδαῖος, the practical reasoning of the ἀκόλαστος enjoys a certain per se intelligibility: once we understand what his overall principle is, it is easy to understand why he does what he does. The practical reasoning of the ἀκρατής, by contrast with both that of the σπουδαῖος and that of the ἀκόλαστος, involves breaks of intelligibility. Often even he cannot explain fully why he does what he does.

But it would be a mistake to conceive of the soul of ἀκόλαστος as a unity in the way that the soul of the σπουδαῖος is a unity.[46] The reason for this is that the ἀκόλαστος—like any human being—must live and operate

---

43 See above, note 16.

44 See also *EN* vii,6, 1149b27–1150a8, which finishes with the statement that "the evil man would perform a thousand times more evil than the beast." This is so because he has reason [νοῦς—1150a5]. In *EN* iii,10, Aristotle does say that both temperance [σωφροσύνη] and ἀκολασία are concerned with the type of things that concern the other animals (actually *eating*, for instance, as opposed to delighting to see that which might be eaten) [1118a18–26]. This is not to deny, however, that human beings pursue such objects in a characteristic way.

45 As mentioned above, the σπουδαῖος and the φρόνιμος are quite nearly synonymous; for the sake of simplicity, I will refer just to the σπουδαῖος.

46 Julia Annas maintains that "Aristotle's bad man is like his good man in so far as both display unity of thought and feeling when they act" [Annas, "Plato and Aristotle on Friendship and Altruism," 554], but this is contested by Broadie: "I know of no passage that says this about vicious people in general" [Sarah Broadie, *Ethics with Aristotle* (New York: Oxford University Press, 1991), 177 n. 41].

in the human moral universe with its component institutions and practices, many of which come naturally to men. Important in this universe are truth-telling and honesty, which constitute in fact the background logic of its institutions and practices. (The very idea of modelling a political entity and assigning primacy to falsehood and dishonesty is an absurd one.) A person who tells the truth and deals honestly with others ensures that at least his part in that universe—his life—is without contradictions. Of course, contradictions might come from without: an honest man might be opposed by others for one reason or another; but, even still, the life he leads will be consistent and, in that respect, tranquil. Such tranquility is not available to the ἀκόλαστος, for his overall προαίρεσις in favor of the pursuit of the present pleasure must inevitably defy the strictures of truth-telling and honesty; and then he cannot fail to see—and to feel—the disparity between his life and the moral universe with which his life is bound up.

At one point (*EN* iii,12, 1119a27–32), Aristotle notes that the individual acts characteristic of the ἀκόλαστος are more voluntary than the acts characteristic (for instance) of the coward. But that does not mean, he says, that the state of soul that results from these acts is desirable, "for no one desires to be ἀκόλαστος" [1119a32–33]—presumably, not even the ἀκόλαστος himself. The ἀκόλαστος, says Aristotle

> desires all pleasant things—or, at least, those that are especially pleasant—and is led by desire to cling to these in preference to all else; and so he is distressed both in failing to get what he wants and in desiring (for the desire comes with pain). [*EN* iii,11, 1119a1–4]

Lacking in the overall object of the ἀκόλαστος's desiring is the orderliness that gives tranquility to the σπουδαῖος.

Aristotle says in a couple of places that the ἀκόλαστος is pursuaded that he *ought* to pursue pleasure. But this does not mean that he believes that this is the most ethical way of proceeding. The "ought" here [δεῖν—*EN* vii,3, 1146b23, vii,8, 1151a23] has to do with pursuing pleasure within limited contexts. Regarding this point, Elizabeth Anscombe remarks:

> [T]he uncontrolled man [the ἀκρατής] is not prepared to say: "This is my idea of good work (εὐπραξία), this is the kind of life I want." Whereas, of course,

that is the attitude of the licentious man, the ἀκόλαστος: a life spent doing such things is his idea of a well-spent life—and a fig for moral virtue. It is not that the licentious man thinks licentiousness is moral virtue; what he thinks is rather that this is a good way to carry on. "One should pursue the present pleasure," δεῖν τὸ παρὸν ἡδὺ διώκειν, doesn't mean: it's virtuous, or morally obligatory, to do that—but: that's the thing to do!⁴⁷

Later in the same essay, she acknowledges that the man who acts in accordance with an evil προαίρεσις will sometimes say that that was the just thing to do; but, she says, "his description 'justice performed' of what he has done will be a lie."⁴⁸ This is consistent with what we saw at the end of chapter 1 (section VII), where we considered Aristotle's presupposition in *APr.* ii,21 that even the ἀκόλαστος cannot actually *believe* that to be good is to be bad. To lie is to assert as true what one believes to be false.⁴⁹

So, it is not as if the ἀκόλαστος were simply another theorist of the good life who happens to come up with the wrong theory. He may indeed have a theory, but what is ultimately determinative for him is his own desires. If the ἀκόλαστος is a theorist of some sort—a journalist, for instance, or a politician—that which governs whatever theorizing he does will not be the way things are but the way he wants his conclusions to come out. If he is not a theorist—if he is a businessman, for instance—in justifying his self-serving actions, he will invoke whatever principles come to mind and

---

47 Anscombe, "Thought and Action in Aristotle," 70. On "the present pleasure," see above, section I.

48 Anscombe, "Thought and Action in Aristotle," 77. In her essay "Modern Moral Philosophy," Anscombe famously accuses certain modern philosophers—those who would, for example, favor the occasional judicial condemnation of persons whom everyone knows to be innocent—of having corrupt minds (her way of saying that they are ἀκόλαστοι). Such a thinker *knows* that he is favoring unjust acts [G. E. M. Anscombe, "Modern Moral Philosophy," in *Ethics, Religion and Politics*, vol. 3 of *Collected Philosophical Papers* (Minneapolis/Oxford: University of Minnesota Press/Basil Blackwell, 1981), 40–41]. In an essay that has only recently become generally available, entitled "Practical Truth," Anscombe remarks: "At some level of characterization of his action, the wicked man's will be false. The falsehood may be in an earlier identification—for example, helping your neighbors *is* doing well, but killing someone for them is not helping them" [G. E. M. Anscombe, "Practical Truth," 153, emphasis hers]. It is possible to conceive of a situation in which this would be a non-culpable mistake: some extremely primitive culture, where the murder of family enemies is not considered immoral. But that is not what Anscombe has in mind here. As the murderer murders, he tells himself a story about helping his neighbor or the family or whatever; but that is a lie: his judgment and his wanting do not correspond to the truth.

49 As suggested in chapter 7 (section II), the ἀκόλαστος, as a character type, is close to the character type of the false man of *Metaph.* v,29. In chapter 7, see note 10.

appear likely to convince himself or (at least) to convince others that he is acting properly.

The primary logical difference between the soul of the ἀκρατής and the soul of the ἀκόλαστος is not that the former is beset by internal conflicts, the latter not, but rather that the former's conflicts are conflicts of desire having to do with the prospect of being good or not. The ἀκρατής really does want to do the right thing (or, at least, what he believes is the right thing), but there is also a part of himself that wants to do otherwise. This conflict causes him to repent of that which, in his weakness, he does. As for the ἀκόλαστος, because he is not interested emotionally in whether or not he is living morally, he is not torn in the way the ἀκρατής is, although inevitably his life does involve unpleasant contradictions.

Although the ἀκόλαστος does what he wants, he can never be happy, since happiness, says Aristotle, consists in activity that is "according to virtue."[50] The ἀκόλαστος might occasionally do something that is according to virtue; but, as we saw in chapter 5, he would do so only per accidens, since, per se, virtuous activity requires performing the act as the virtuous man would perform it.[51] In other words, virtuous activity would require that the ἀκόλαστος perform the act, not in a per accidens way, as when a con artist performs an honest act in order to gain the trust of a victim, but because it is the right thing to do. The ἀκόλαστος cannot do such a thing, since, as Aristotle explains at *EN* vii,8, 1151a11–17, the first principle (the ἀρχὴ) of ethical action has been destroyed in him. Since he has given himself over to the "present pleasure," the motivation for noble acts done for their own sake is simply not there. The ἀκρατής is not in this state—or, at least, not yet. He is still capable of heeding the criticisms of others or of his own better self.

IX. Some Minor (and Unfortunate) Character Types

It is not the case, however, that every person in whom the first principle for ethical action has been destroyed is ἀκόλαστος. In *EN* vii,5 Ar-

---

50 *EN* i,10, 1101a14–16, i,13, 1102a5, x,7, 1177a12; *EE* ii,1, 1219a38–39; *Pol.* iv,11, 1295a36–37.
51 *EN* v,8, 1135b2–8; also vii,9, 1151a35–b3; in chapter 5, see section II.

istotle conducts a division of certain ethical types who cannot be called ἀκρατεῖς in the strict sense. The chapter begins by distinguishing things pleasant by nature from things pleasant not by nature, which would include things pleasant because those who enjoy them have natures of a certain type [1148b18]—which shows that Aristotle is willing to separate talk of "natures," some of which are bad, from talk of *nature*, which is the measure of that which is good. He then says that corresponding to such unnaturally pleasant things are certain states (or ἕξεις). Some of these are bestial (such as cannibalism), some are "due to diseases" [1148b25-27], and some are termed νοσηματώδεις [1148b27], which we might translate 'disease-like'.[52] These latter include states inclining a person to bite nails, to eat coal or dirt, and to have sexual relations with men (that is to say, homosexual relations).[53] Regarding this latter, for some the problem occurs "by nature" [φύσει—1148b29] (although not nature in the positive, normative sense); for others it occurs "by habituation [ἐξ ἔθους], for instance, in those abused from childhood" [1148b30-31].

Aristotle asserts that we do not say that those who have disease-like tendencies by nature are subject to ἀκρασία, in the sense of falling away from one's better inclinations, since their inclinations are disordered in the first place. (Neither, he says, do we say that a woman's inclination to be passive in sexual relations is a falling away, for she is that way inclined naturally). The same can be said of those who have such tendencies by habituation: it becomes so ingrained in them that it becomes a second—albeit disordered—nature. Their souls are pointed inexorably toward the wrong end—we might even say, toward the present pleasure—and yet they have not made a προαίρεσις in that regard, so they cannot be called ἀκόλαστοι.

EN vii,5 concludes with the remark that the term ἀκρασία qualified by such adjectives as 'bestial' and 'disease-like' must be distinguished from

---

52 I take the translation from K. J. Dover, *Greek Homosexuality* (Cambridge: Harvard University Press, 1978), 168.

53 τῶν ἀφροδισίων τοῖς ἄρρεσιν [1148b29]. K. J. Dover argues that Aristotle's later mention of the passive sexual attitude of women [EN vii,5, 1148b32-33] is indication that his "mind is running on the moral evaluation of sexual passivity" [Dover, *Greek Homosexuality*, 169]. This would go along with Dover's more general thesis that there is no sign in Aristotle that "a genital response to the bodily beauty of a younger male was regarded as a defect or impairment of male nature, no matter what view was taken of the duty of the law to prevent gratification of the desire aroused by this response" [Dover, *Greek Homosexuality*, 170]. I do not believe that EN vii,5 provides any evidence against this thesis— for the reason that Dover gives.

ἀκρασία in the strict sense (ἁπλῶς). The latter includes only ἀκρασία which is "with respect to human ἀκολασία" [ἡ κατὰ τὴν ἀνθρωπίνην ἀκολασίαν μόνη—1149a20]. Aristotle has in mind human actions in the strict sense: acts that are voluntary and therefore the moral responsibility of the agent. No one is either ἀκρατής or ἀκόλαστος unless he has the capability of performing human acts. The acts that make the ἀκρατής ἀκρατής are about the same things as are the acts that make the ἀκόλαστος ἀκόλαστος. But these two character types come *at* this subject matter differently.[54]

X. Conclusion

To conclude, then, a close study of *EE* vii,6 reveals that Aristotle's analysis of character types depends upon a conception of the unity (or disunity) of the human soul. In performing this analysis, Aristotle exploits a device employed by sophists of his day in which aspects of a person (things that might be said of the person) are each treated as if they *were* individual persons; he also makes use of an expanded signification of the term 'quantity.' This all allows him (and us) an understanding not only of the ἀκρατής and the ἀκόλαστος but also of a number of other minor character types.

54 It might seem that the expression ἡ κατὰ τὴν ἀνθρωπίνην ἀκολασίαν μόνη [1149a20] shows that Aristotle was capable of using the word ἀκολασία as the equivalent of ἀκρασία. But the very next lines make it apparent that the 'κατὰ + accusative' construction is decisive here. Aristotle writes : Ὅτι μὲν οὖν ἀκρασία καὶ ἐγκράτειά ἐστι μόνον περὶ ἅπερ ἀκολασία καὶ σωφροσύνη ... [1149a21–22]. The relevant point is that ἀκρασία is only *about* that which ἀκολασία is about. (The word μόνον is parallel to the μόνη at 1149a20.)

Conclusion

I STATED in the Introduction that the overall movement of this book is from the consideration of individual acts to the consideration of ethics itself and ethical character types. The earlier chapters (chapters 1 through 4) had to do primarily with acts, the later (chapters 5 through 8) with matters of larger scope. But there has also been evident right from the beginning a particular orientation of the larger argument. Although, as its subtitle suggests, the book itself has to do with logic ("The Logic of the Moral Life"), chapter 1 turns our attention immediately away from formal logic as set out in Aristotle's syllogistic and toward the realm of particular acts, the realm of the practical. It is from the logic discoverable—although never wholly formalizable—at that level that the principles governing character eventually emerge. It was necessary to push off the argumentative vehicle in this way so that the reader might understand that the realm of the practical is subject to logical principles—and especially to the principle of non-contradiction—but not in a manner that prescinds from the infinite variety and fluidity of human action.

Aristotle certainly recognizes—in fact, he insists upon—the fact that ethics is so bound up in the contingent that a fully developed science of ethics is out of the question. And yet he also recognizes that we can know a great deal about morally relevant behavior and can organize this knowledge in such a way that we can speak to one another intelligently about the acts that we and others perform. As we have seen in chapter 2, we can identify, for instance, the basic movement-like structure of a human action. The act of teaching, for instance, "moves toward" its object, the student who learns. If a near-sighted teacher is led before a manikin who appears to him to be a student and begins to expound the Pythagorean theorem, no matter what he thinks he is doing, he is not teaching. Thus Aristotle proves that the full analysis of a human action often involves factors outside the agent himself.

But the structure of the human act gets much more complicated than this: much more complicated, that is, than beginning at a point and finishing at another. As we have seen in chapter 3, Aristotle, in an extremely convoluted section of his *Eudemian Ethics* (ii,6–9), discusses one of the two major influences upon the moral character of human acts: force. It is quite obvious that a movement that is wholly forced upon a person is not that person's moral action; but it is also possible to identify *within* an individual moral act (which is by definition not forced) aspects subject to force. All this helps us to understand eventually not only individual actions but also the character types of those who perform them.

The second major influence upon the moral character of human acts is ignorance, especially of their constituents (classically referred to as "circumstances"), which were treated in chapter 4. As in the previous chapter, where we saw Aristotle recognizing that force might have a bearing not only upon an entire movement but also upon aspects within a human act, so here his identification of the constituents of a human act allows him to speak intelligibly of the internal articulation of acts. In other words, Aristotle maintains that, when giving an account of what an agent does, we are not limited to acknowledging that the agent knows (or does not know) that he performs a particular act considered as a whole, but we can also identify constituent parts of the act of which the agent is aware or not aware.

One of the most important results of this study of the constituents is that, in the most definitive list of the constituents (the list in *EN* iii,1), what in other lists appears as 'whom' [ὅν] becomes 'that about which' [περὶ τί] an action is and/or 'that in which' [ἐν τίνι] an action consists. This not only broadens the relevant concept so that it might refer not just to the human object of an act (*whom* a man shoots, for example); it also tells us that the object of an act must be understood within its intelligible context:

the type of action for which it serves as object. The object is bound up with 'that in which' the action consists. This idea goes to the heart of contemporary controversies, especially among scholars invoking Aquinas, regarding the extent to which the physical, such as a physical object, might enter into the correct analysis of a moral act. According to Aristotle, even the analysis of a purely physical movement must take into consideration the type of movement for which the object serves as object. In a parallel way, when we move into the realm of human actions, an object, while possibly physical, can enter into the analysis of an act only *as* completing an action with particular intelligible characteristics, not excluding that of having been caused by an act of the will. In brief, the objects of moral acts can indeed be physical, but they can never be merely physical. To use language developed especially by Aquinas, the object of an act of theft might be a physical thing, but it cannot, qua physical thing, give the act its *species*; it does so rather qua belonging to another person—and, indeed, qua being taken unjustly—which is an intelligible context of a different order from that of a merely physical movement.

So, the first four chapters of this book have looked primarily at the internal structure of particular acts. We can indicate this structure to the person who performs the action, and elicit from him acknowledgment that that is indeed what he has done. Similarly, we can identify various components of acts and elicit, not just from their agents but from all reasonable people, the acknowledgment that such are indeed the typical components of a human acts. Such knowledge and ability to categorize do not allow us to predict what a person will do next or even to conduct an exhaustive analysis of a person's character, but they do allow us to converse intelligently about what people do and to formulate principles or even laws about what constitutes, for instance, being culpable for doing what one ought not to do.

We can use our ability to identify the smaller components of human behavior in order to construct models of various human character types. We can also identify lines of intelligibility in a person's life having to do with the person's relationship to or attitude toward the laws and mores of the society in which he lives or having to do with the person's attachment to pleasures, as distinct from the human practices that pleasures inform in a natural way. We can also speak intelligibly about whether a person characteristically pursues the true good for man rather than some apparent good, even while recognizing that pursuing this good occurs in radically different types of lives: radically disparate ways of seeking and achieving happiness. Such investigations were conducted in the second half of the present work, although, as cautioned in the Introduction, it was not always possible or even desirable to sequester these more macroscopic issues from the microscopic ones.

In chapter 5, we have seen that Aristotle's major linguistic means of indicating pieces of intelligibility, the per se–per accidens distinction, can be a source of confusion. Aristotle is perfectly capable of picking out an aspect of human behavior and dismissing it as per accidens with respect to a contrasting aspect and then turning around and speaking of the same aspect as not per accidens but per se. Occasionally too he will speak of a larger complex of ideas as per se—which might suggest that it is per se intelligible "all the way down"—but then he will identify within the complex, as integral parts, things that are related only per accidens. All this becomes easier to understand once one realizes that, for Aristotle, the per se–per accidens distinction is simply a tool for pointing at things he finds interesting and/or important in the practical realm and distinguishing them from others.

This method of Aristotle's is especially adapted to the study of human behavior, since, unlike the properly scientific realm, the practical makes no effort to exclude the "accidental." Indeed it cannot exclude it, since human action so very often involves the joining together of otherwise unrelated pieces of intelligibility into intelligible units. The results of the next chapter (chapter 6) were closely related to this understanding of practical activity as the "joining together" of pieces, for it concerned the interrelationship between knowledge [ἐπιστήμη] and craft [τέχνη]. In the practical realm, we are all "joiners" (in the British sense of woodworkers), but this does not mean that one engaged in a practical activity can comprehend no more than what is involved in bringing together one piece of a final product with another. A craft is an intellectual system and, as such, not only comprehends the final product in its entirety (its form) but does so throughout the making of the product. It is here that we see the interrelationship—or intertwining—just mentioned between knowledge and craft. The making of a chair is fully present (accomplished) only once the chair is complete, but the craft of making chairs is present at the very beginning of the process and throughout; and yet, as Aristotle insists, learning a craft is never just an intellectual activity.

Responsible for gathering together in an orderly way all practical activities—all makings and doings—is an intellectual virtue, φρόνησις, although, even as such, φρόνησις is part of the moral sphere. One sees this especially in its relationship with pleasure, as we have seen at the end of chapter 6. According to Aristotle, the first casualty of an attachment to pleasure is always φρόνησις: pleasure draws a person's attention away from the comprehension of—and appreciation for—reasonable activity and toward itself. This leads to the *intellectual* corruption of the person, whose capacity to understand is now less than it might have been, but this is obviously also a moral corruption. The φρόνιμος has a "feel" for the good in activity and a desire to pursue it; the person who falls away from φρόνησις or who never achieves it (even vicariously) will only ever strike upon the good by chance: per accidens and not per se, as in this context Aristotle might put it.

Along these same lines, we have seen in chapter 7 that the φρόνιμος is given over "heart and soul" to the pursuit of the good. In this connection, we examined Aristotle's remarks in *Metaph.* v about Plato's *Hippias Minor* and his (at first blush) very weird remarks at the beginning of *EE* viii about girls dancing on their hands and teachers making deliberate errors in order to teach. What emerged from this examination was the idea that the φρόνιμος's being so unequivocally oriented toward the good is not simply a matter of a decision on his part to head in that direction but concerns the very logic of the practical sphere itself. Since the φρόνιμος, because of his intrinsic ordering to the good for man, in effect defines the practical sphere, he cannot (as can the teacher with respect to his own discipline) stand outside φρόνησις in order to choose to misuse it for the sake of the good. Such would be contradictory: the φρόνιμος would not be φρόνιμος and φρόνησις would not be φρόνησις. As we saw in chapter 1, although the practical sphere eludes the systematizing reach of the syllogistic, it is very much subject to the principle of non-contradiction.

This brings us finally to the last chapter, chapter 8, in which were considered a handful of character types that fall short of φρόνησις. What is common to these types is their lack of unity: they can (and do) harbor within themselves contradictions, since, unlike the φρόνιμος, their definitions do not link them intrinsically to moral order. But their internal contradictions are of different sorts. As Tolstoy says in the opening lines of *Anna Karenina*, happy persons are all alike, but every unhappy person is unhappy in his own way.

Aristotle's means of analyzing these various flawed character types is the device (invented by certain unnamed sophists) of speaking of various states of a person as if they were distinct persons: good Coriscus, for instance, musical Coriscus, and Coriscus in the marketplace. Aristotle insists, however, that even imperfect moral characters maintain a certain unity, for otherwise they could not be criticized as imperfect. If they had maintained no unity whatsoever, they would be utterly (and literally) schizophrenic and so not morally responsible. There would be nothing immoral about the behavior of the individual "persons" into which these flawed characters would be split: each pursues a particular good in a consistent manner. What goes wrong in truly morally flawed individuals is that they pursue goods that are incompatible. They do not organize their moral lives in the reasonable and consistent manner of the φρόνιμος.

APPENDIX 1

On the Text of *Metaph.* ix,6, 1048b18–35

Metaph. ix,6, 1048b18–35, discussed in chapter 2, section IV, is extremely difficult from a textual point of view, incorporating apparently an unusual number of marginal notes or afterthoughts (perhaps by Aristotle himself). It does not appear in some manuscripts and was unknown to most Latin writers, including Thomas Aquinas and William of Moerbeke. More recently, the text has been heavily emended, notably by Bonitz and Bywater, whose emendations have been accepted by later editors of *Metaph.*—in particular, by Ross and Jaeger.[1] The text that the modern editors come up with is not inconsistent philosophically with the text I propose, but the latter, as difficult as it is, puts into relief important aspects of Aristotle's conception of human action which the emended text obscures.

The text runs as follows:

Ἐπεὶ δὲ τῶν πράξεων ὧν ἔστι πέρας οὐδεμία τέλος
(ἀλλὰ τῶν περὶ τὸ τέλος, οἷον τοῦ ἰσχναίνειν ἡ ἰσχνασία)
[20] αὐτό, αὐτὰ δὲ ὅταν ἰσχναίνῃ οὕτως ἐστὶν ἐν κινήσει μὴ
ὑπάρχοντα ὧν ἕνεκα ἡ κίνησις, οὐκ ἔστι ταῦτα πρᾶξις ἢ
οὐ τελεία γε (οὐ γὰρ τέλος)· ἀλλ' ἐκείνη ἐνυπάρχει τὸ
τέλος (καὶ ἡ πρᾶξις). οἷον ὁρᾷ (ἀλλὰ καὶ φρονεῖ) καὶ νοεῖ
καὶ νενόηκεν, ἀλλ' οὐ μανθάνει καὶ μεμάθηκεν οὐδ' ὑγιά-
[25]ζεται καὶ ὑγίασται· εὖ ζῇ καὶ εὖ ἔζηκεν· ἀλλὰ καὶ

---

[1] Bonitz's emended text is in his commentary: Hermann Bonitz, *Aristotelis* Metaphysica: *Rcognovit et enarravit Hermannus Bonitz* [Bonn: A. Marcus, 1848–49 [2 vols.]], v.2 397–98. The text which I propose here corresponds closely to what is found in the major manuscripts. I take it from Bonitz, *Aristotelis* Metaphysica: *Recognovit et enarravit Hermannus Bonitz*, v.1 168–69, although I occasionally introduce round brackets in order to sort out what appear to be interpolations.

εὐδαιμονεῖ καὶ εὐδαιμόνηκεν. εἰ δὲ μή, ἔδει ἄν ποτε παύεσθαι ὥσπερ ὅταν ἰσχναίνῃ, νῦν δ' οὔ, ἀλλὰ ζῇ καὶ ἔζηκεν.
   τούτων δὴ τὰς μὲν κινήσεις λέγειν, τὰς δ' ἐνεργείας. πᾶσα
γὰρ κίνησις ἀτελής, ἰσχνασία μάθησις βάδισις οἰκοδό-
[30]μησις· αὗται δὲ κινήσεις, καὶ ἀτελεῖς γε. οὐ γὰρ ἅμα
βαδίζει καὶ βεβάδικεν, οὐδ' οἰκοδομεῖ καὶ ᾠκοδόμηκεν, οὐδὲ
γίγνεται καὶ γέγονεν ἢ κινεῖται καὶ κεκίνηκεν, ἀλλ' ἕτερον (καὶ κινεῖ καὶ κεκίνηκεν)· ἑώρακε δὲ καὶ ὁρᾷ ἅμα τὸ
αὐτό, καὶ νοεῖ καὶ νενόηκεν. τὴν μὲν οὖν τοιαύτην ἐνέργειαν
[35]λέγω, ἐκείνην δὲ κίνησιν.

At 1048b19–20, Ross has οἷον τὸ ἰσχναίνειν ἡ ἰσχνασία [αὐτό]; Jaeger, regarding ἡ ἰσχνασία (perhaps ἡ ἰσχνασία) as a marginal note, has οἷον τὸ ἰσχναίνειν [ἡ ἰσχνασία] [αὐτό]. Jaeger rejects the τοῦ ἰσχναίνειν ἡ ἰσχνασία of the MSS on the grounds that ἰσχνασία is a κίνησις (and understanding the MSS to be saying that τοῦ ἰσχναίνειν ἡ ἰσχνασία πέρας ἐστί); he argues moreover that ἰσχνασία is not τὸ τέλος τοῦ ἰσχναίνειν but its synonym. As argued in chapter 2 and as represented in the translation given there, I understand τὸ (τοῦ) ἰσχναίνειν to be the τέλος, ἡ ἰσχνασία the κίνησις. (At *Metaph.* v,2, 1013b1 ἡ ἰσχνασία is spoken of as a means to the end of health; see also *Phys.* ii,3, 194b35–195a3.) As to the αὐτό in 1048b20, bracketed out by both Jaeger and Ross, perhaps that is the best solution; but sense can just be made of it by associating it with τέλος in 1048b18. (Bonitz too in his emended text associates αὐτό with the end.) There are other differences between this and the modern editions.

Ross reports that what he calls Γ (and which he says is a very literal Latin translation that "may with comparative certainty be ascribed to William of Moerbeke")[2] reads at 1048b23 not ἡ πρᾶξις but τῇ πράξει. This gives the correct sense of the text, but this is not much evidence for τῇ πράξει. The word is (or would be) in the nominative case apparently because it is picking up on πρᾶξις in 1048b21 (καὶ ἡ πρᾶξις may, therefore, be a marginal note). The earlier πρᾶξις is the antecedent of ἐκείνη [1048b22], so a scribe (or a translator), finding καὶ ἡ πρᾶξις, would have had good reason to change (actually or in effect) ἡ πρᾶξις in 1048b23 to τῇ πράξει. (In the 1995 edition of Moerbeke's translation of *Metaph.*, lines 1048b18–35 are absent.)[3]

---

2 W. D. Ross, *Aristotle's* Metaphysics: *A Revised Text with Introduction and Commentary*, 2d ed. [Oxford: Clarendon, 1953], vol. 1 clxiv.

3 Gundrun Vuillemin-Diem, ed., *Metaphysica: Lib. I–XIV, Recensio et Translatio Guillelmi Moerbeka*, Aristoteles Latinus, 25.3 (1–2) (Leiden: E. J. Brill, 1995), pt. 2 186.

Appendix 1

At 1048b23–24, both Ross and Jaeger introduce a number of illuminating emendations. The phrase οἷον ὁρᾷ (ἀλλὰ καὶ φρονεῖ) καὶ νοεῖ καὶ νενόηκεν becomes οἷον ὁρᾷ ἅμα <καὶ ἑώρακε,> καὶ φρονεῖ <καὶ πεφρόνηκε> καὶ νοεῖ καὶ νενόηκεν... ("E.g. at the same time we are seeing and have seen, are understanding and have understood, are thinking and have thought ... " [Revised Oxford Translation]). This is certainly the sense that should be given to the phrase, but, given the apparently "under construction" character of the general passage (1048b18–35), it is not difficult to imagine Aristotle's simply expressing himself here very elliptically.

APPENDIX 2

Eudemian Ethics ii,6–9

I. Setting the Agenda

[*EE* ii,6, 1222b15] Let us take up, then, another starting point for the subsequent investigation. So, all substances are by nature principles of sorts, and so each is also capable of generating many more such as itself: a man men, or, generally, an animal animals, and a plant plants. But in addition to these things, man, alone [20] among animals, is the principle of certain actions, for we would not say that any of the others *act*. Of these principles, such as are the first sources of movements are called sovereign principles, and most properly so called are the sources of necessity—over which perhaps God rules. Among immobile things, among mathematical entities, for example, there is no sovereign principle. In any case, however, this is meant [25] as an analogy, for also here, if the principle is altered, all the things demonstrated from it would certainly change but the things demonstrated do not change one another, one destroyed by the other—except in the case of the destruction of an assumption, by means of which something is demonstrated.¹ Man, however, is the principle of a certain move-

---

1 J. Solomon explains this latter remark ("except in the case of the destruction of an assumption, by means of which something is demonstrated" [1222b27–28]) in the following manner: "e.g. if ἀρχή A led to B and C, of which C was absurd, then C by refuting A would refute the other consequence B" [J. Solomon, *Ethica Eudemia*, vol. 9.2 of *The Works of Aristotle*, ed. W. D. Ross (Oxford: Clarendon, 1915), ad loc]. Not incompatibly, I understand the larger passage (1225b25–28) as Aristotle's acknowledging that the analogy with mathematical principles limps somewhat. It is true that mathematical principles have a direct bearing upon the propositions that are derived from them and so (in a sense) they are ἀρχαί κύρια, but, as Solomon explains, a denied derived proposition can also influence another derived proposition, as in a *reductio ad impossibile* ("the destruction of an assumption, by means of which something is demonstrated"). Such a thing does not happen with human actions: their voluntary character depends just upon the will (and intellect) of the agent and not on

ment, for action is movement. Since [30] as in other things the principle is the cause of the things that are or come about because of it, it is necessary to understand it as in the case of demonstrations. For if, a triangle having angles equal to two right angles, a quadrilateral figure must have angles equal to four right angles, it is clear that the cause of this is the triangle's having angles equal to two right angles. But if the triangle should change, [35] the quadrilateral must change, for instance, if the one has angles equal to three, the other must have angles equal to six, if four, eight. But if the one should not change, as the one is, so must the other be. That what we are attempting to show here is necessary is apparent from the *Analytics*, although at the moment it is not possible to deny or to affirm precisely more than this; for, if there is no other reason [40] for the triangle's being the way it is, it would be a principle of sorts and the cause of the things that come later.

Just so, if it is possible for some entities to be in contrary states, it is necessary that their principles be also such. [1223a1] For, from things that hold of necessity, a necessary conclusion follows, but from these might come about opposites—and many such things are up to men themselves and they are also the principles of such things. So it is clear that, of the acts of which man is [5] the principle and sovereign, these might both come about and not and it is up to him whether they come about or not—in any case those of which he is master of their being or not being. As many, however, as it is up to him to or not to do, he is the cause of these; and, of as many as he is the cause, they are up to him. Since virtue and vice and [10] their works are some praisable, some blamable (for blamed and praised are not those things that come about due to necessity or chance or nature but those of which we are the causes, for of things of which there is another cause this latter receives the blame or praise), it is clear that both virtue and vice have to do with those actions of which a man himself is [15] cause and principle. To be taken up now, therefore, is, of which actions is a man cause and principle. So, we all agree that, of as many things as are voluntary and according to choice of each man, he is the cause of these; but, of as many as are involuntary, he is not the cause. That everything he has chosen is

---

one another. Michael Woods comments on this passage as follows: "The point seems to be that if a starting-point A has consequences B and C, then, if A had not been the case, B and C would have been different also. To this, it is natural to object that it assumes that B and C each entail A rather than conversely" [Michael Woods, *Aristotle: 'Eudemian Ethics,' Books I, II and VIII*, 117]. The point is well taken, but it merely points to another way in which the relationship between mathematical principles and their consequences is different from that between a sovereign principle such as the will and its acts.

also voluntary is clear; it is clear, therefore, that virtue and [20] vice would be of voluntary things.

II. The Preliminary Argument

(a) [*EE* ii,7] To be taken up now, therefore, is what is the voluntary and what the involuntary, and also what is choice, since virtue and vice are defined by these. First to be examined is the voluntary and the involuntary. It would seem to be one of three things: either that which is according to appetite, according to [25] choice, or according to thought: the voluntary is according to one of these, the involuntary against. But appetite is divided into three: into will and desire and aggression, so that these need to be distinguished; and the first of them is 'according to desire.'

(b) [P1] It would seem that everything that is according to desire is voluntary, for the [30] involuntary appears all to be forced and the forced is painful, as is all that which those who are coerced do or suffer, as also Evenus says, "for every coerced action is by nature unpleasant." So, if something is painful, it is forced, and if it is forced, it painful. That, however, which is against desire is all painful (for desire is for the pleasant), so it is [35] forced and involuntary. That which is according to desire is, therefore, voluntary, for they are contraries of one another.

[P2] Moreover, all wickedness makes a person more unjust and incontinence appears to be wickedness. The incontinent man is such a one as acts according to desire and against reason; he behaves incontinently when he acts according to desire. But to act unjustly is voluntary, so the [1223b1] incontinent man acts unjustly by acting according to desire; he will, therefore, act voluntarily and that which is according to desire is voluntary. For it would be strange if, those who become incontinent should become more just.

Given these things, it would seem that that which is according to desire is voluntary; but from the [5] following things, the opposite. [N1] All that a man does voluntarily, he wills, and what he wills he does voluntarily; no one, however, wills that which he thinks is bad. However, the incontinent man does things that he does not want to do, for, to act incontinently is to do, on account of desire, that which one thinks is not best. So, it will follow that the same man acts at the same time both voluntarily and involuntarily; but that is impossible. [N2] Moreover, [10] the continent man acts justly, that is, more than incontinence, for continence is a virtue and virtue makes men more just. A man acts

Appendix 2   283

continently when he acts according to reason, against desire. So, if acting justly is voluntary, as is [15] acting unjustly (for both seem to be voluntary and, necessarily, if the one voluntary, so is the other) but acting against desire is involuntary, then the same man at the same time does the same thing voluntarily and involuntarily.

(c) The same argument can be made also with respect to aggression, for there seem to be incontinence and continence also of aggression, just as of desire, and [20] what goes against aggression is painful and its repression is forced, so, if the forced is involuntary, everything that goes against aggression would be voluntary. And it seems that Heraclitus is speaking about the strength of aggression when he sees that its suppression is painful, "for it is difficult," he says, "to fight against aggression since it hazards its life." But if it is impossible for [25] the same man voluntarily and involuntarily at the same time to do the same thing and with respect to the same aspect of the act, then that which is according to the will is more voluntary than that which is according to appetite or aggression; and a proof of this is that we do many things voluntarily without anger or desire.[2]

(d) It remains, therefore, to be investigated whether the willed and the voluntary are the same thing. [30] But also this appears impossible. For we assumed, and it seems to be the case, that wickedness makes men more unjust, and incontinence appears to be a type of wickedness; but the opposite will follow. For no one wills things he thinks are bad; he does them, however, when he becomes incontinent; if, therefore, to act unjustly is voluntary and the voluntary is that which is according to will, when [35] a man becomes incontinent, he no longer acts unjustly but is more just than he was previously to becoming

---

[2] εἰ δ' ἀδύνατον τὸ αὐτὸν ἑκόντα καὶ ἄκοντα πράττειν ἅμα τὸ <αὐτὸ> κατὰ τὸ αὐτὸ τοῦ πράγματος, μᾶλλον ἑκούσιον τὸ κατὰ βούλησιν τοῦ κατ' ἐπιθυμίαν καὶ θυμόν. τεκμήριον δέ· πολλὰ γὰρ πράττομεν ἑκόντες ἄνευ ὀργῆς καὶ ἐπιθυμίας [*EE* ii,7,1223b24–28]. Although in this book I generally use the Susemihl Greek text [Franciscus Susemihl, ed., [*Aristotelis: Ethica Eudemia*] *Eudemi Rhodii Ethica* (Teubner: Leipzig, 1884)], occasionally (as here) I follow the Walzer-Mingay text [R. R. Walzer and J. M. Mingay, *Aristotelis: Ethica Eudemia*, Oxford Classical Texts (Oxford: Clarendon, 1991)]. I also follow Woods in identifying "the same" [τὸ αὐτὸ] as an aspect [Woods, *Aristotle: 'Eudemian Ethics,' Books I, II and VIII*, 24] and not (as in the Revised Oxford Translation) as "the same part of the act." In his translation, Woods suggest that the aspect is "of the situation" and, in his note on the passage, he rather tentatively suggests that what is being qualified is the voluntariness or involuntariness of the act in question. But, as he acknowledges, if that were Aristotle's meaning, "the argument of this chapter would be undermined" [Woods, *Aristotle: 'Eudemian Ethics,' Books I, II and VIII*, 126]; so I prefer to attach the "same aspect" to the act. This is also gives us a closer parallel to the principle of non-contradiction as formulated at *Metaph*. iv,3.

incontinent. But this is impossible. That, therefore, the voluntary is not to act according to appetite (nor the involuntary to act against appetite) is clear.

(e) [*EE* ii,8] That it is not that which is according to choice is clear again from the following considerations: for it has been demonstrated that that which is according to will is [1224a1] not involuntary but rather that all that is willed is also voluntary (but it has only been shown that one can do voluntarily even what one does not will). But we willingly do many things suddenly; no one, however, chooses anything suddenly.[3]

[5] But if necessarily the voluntary was one of these three—either that which is according to appetite or according to choice or according to thought—and it is not two of these, all that is left is that the voluntary consists in somehow doing that which is thought.

III. The Force and Compulsion Argument

(a) Moreover, advancing the argument a bit further, let us put a cap on the definition with respect to the voluntary and the involuntary.[4] It seems that doing something due to force and [10] not due to force are germane to the things discussed thus far, for we say that the forced is involuntary and that all the involuntary is forced. So, we must look first at that which is due to force: what it is and how it is related to the voluntary and the involuntary. It seems, therefore, that the forced and the compelled (and force and compulsion) are opposed to the voluntary and convinced preference, [15] in the case of acts performed. We speak generally of the forced and compulsion also with respect to inanimate things, for we say that a stone is carried upwards and fire downwards due to

---

3 τι δ' οὐδὲ κατὰ προαίρεσιν, πάλιν ἐκ τῶνδε δῆλον. τὸ μὲν γὰρ κατὰ βούλησιν ὡς οὐκ ἀκούσιον ἀπεδείχθη, ἀλλὰ μᾶλλον πᾶν ὃ βούλεται καὶ ἑκούσιον (ἀλλ' ὅτι καὶ μὴ βουλόμενον ἐνδέχεται πράττειν ἑκόντα, τοῦτο δέδεικται μόνον)· πολλὰ δὲ βουλόμενοι πράττομεν ἐξαίφνης, προαιρεῖται δ' οὐδεὶς οὐδὲν ἐξαίφνης. This is the Susemihl text; the Walzer-Mingay text punctuates the remark somewhat differently, closing the parenthesis after ἐξαίφνης. (See note 2.)

4 πιθῶμεν τέλος τῷ περὶ τοῦ ἑκουσίου καὶ ἀκουσίου διορισμῷ. δοκεῖ γὰρ τὸ βίᾳ καὶ μὴ βίᾳ τι ποιεῖν οἰκεῖα τοῖς εἰρημένοις εἶναι [*EE* ii,8,1224a8–10]. At 1224b6, these lines are referred back to as a διορισμὸς and at *EE* ii,9,1225a36–b1, Aristotle again speaks in this connection of defining. Dirlmeier (citing Hermannus Bonitz, *Index Aristotelicus*, vol. 5 of *Aristotelis Opera* [Berlin: De Gruyter, 1961], 200b15) argues that the διορισμὸς at 1224b6 ought not to be translated 'definition' but rather (in Bonitz's Latin) *quaestio* or *disputatio* [Franz Dirlmeier, *Aristoteles* Eudemische Ethik (Berlin: Akademie, 1962), 279]. The fact that this διορισμὸς is said at 1224a9 to be περὶ τοῦ ἑκουσίου καὶ ἀκουσίου seems to support this thesis and suggests that the διορισμῷ at 1224a9 might be translated 'defining discourse' (a sort of *disputatio*); but such a translation would be awkward in English. See also *EE* ii,9, 1225b17.

Appendix 2

force and compulsion. When these things are carried in accordance with the tendency naturally within them (the tendency that belongs to them per se), they are not said to be subject to force—but neither are they said to be voluntary [agents]; rather, [20] the antithesis is without a name. When, however, they are carried against this tendency, we say that this is due to force. Similarly, with respect to animate things and animals, we see them both suffer and perform many things due to force when, against the tendency within them, something moves them from without. In inanimate things, the principle is simple, but in <some> animate things it is multiplex, for appetite and reason [25] are not always in agreement. Whereas with other animals force is simple just as with inanimate things (for they do not have reason and opposing appetite but they live by appetite), in man there is present both, that is, at a certain age when we acknowledge acting, for we do not say that the child acts, nor the animal, but only the man who [30] acts from reason.[5]

So, it seems that all force is painful and no one acts due to force with pleasure, and, therefore, regarding the continent man and the incontinent, there is much debate, for each acts spurred on by tendencies contrary to himself, so that the continent man, they say, draws himself away from the pleasurable [35] desires by force (for he is pained as he fights against countervailing appetite), but the incontinent man acts due to force against reason. It seems, however, that he is pained less, for his desire is for the pleasant, after which he follows gladly, so that the incontinent acts voluntarily rather than due to force because there is no pain in his acting. Convinced preference is opposed to both force and compulsion. The continent man [1224b1] goes toward that of which he is convinced and he proceeds not due to force but voluntarily. But desire leads on not having convinced, for it does not partake of reason.

That, therefore, these seem to act only due to force and involuntarily and why this is so (because they act according to a likeness of acting due to force, according to which likeness [5] we say the same also of inanimate things) has been stated; but if someone appends to the definition the addendum, also then

---

5 Aristotle seems to be saying in 1224a23–30 both that in all the animated "there is more than one principle" *and* that some of them have a single principle (desire). I have suggested elsewhere that this might be fixed by emending τοῖς in 1224a24 to τισι, giving ἐν μὲν τοῖς ἀψύχοις ἁπλῆ ἡ ἀρχή, ἐν δὲ τισι ἐμψύχοις πλεονάζει. (Kevin L. Flannery, "Force and Compulsion in Aristotle's Ethics," 44). Aristotle would be saying then that in inanimate things the moving principle [ἀρχή] is simple, but in some animated things (i.e., man) it is complex. Or, as I have translated the pertinent passage at 1224a23–24, "In inanimate things, the principle is simple, but in <some> animate things it is multiplex."

the contention is dealt with.[6] For, when something from without and contrary to the internal tendency moves or causes not to move, we say that this occurs due to force; when not, it is not due to force. In the incontinent and the continent, the man's per se internal tendency leads him forward [10] (for he has both tendencies), so that neither acts due to force and neither is compelled but (in any case, according to these arguments) he would act voluntarily. For the external principle—the principle that either impedes or moves contrary to tendency—we call 'compulsion,' just as if someone, grabbing the hand of one who resists and neither wills nor desires this, should strike someone. When, [15] however, the principle is internal, the action is not due to force.

(b) Moreover, pleasure and pain is present in both, for the continent man feels pain at the moment in acting against his desire and is pleased with respect to expected pleasure, for later he will benefit—or he benefits even now, for he is healthy. And the incontinent is pleased in so far as he attains that which, as incontinent, [20] he desires; but he is pained because of expected pain, for he believes he is doing something wrong. So, to say that each acts due to force is reasonable: each at some point acts involuntarily due to appetite and due to reason, for these, being separated, are dominated one by the other. Thus, these terms [25] are applied to the whole soul because people see some such thing among the parts of the soul. With respect to the parts, therefore, one can say this, but the whole soul of both the incontinent man and the continent acts voluntarily; neither acts due to force, but something *in* each does, for even by nature we have both.

For reason exists by nature for, [30] once genesis is allowed and not impeded, it is present; and so is desire, for it follows immediately upon birth and is then present. It is practically as if by these two we define that which is by nature: on the one hand, such things as pertain to all the moment they are gener-

---

6 τι μὲν οὖν δοκοῦσιν οὗτοι μόνον βίᾳ καὶ ἄκοντες ποιεῖν, καὶ διὰ τίν' αἰτίαν, ὅτι καθ' ὁμοιότητά τινα τοῦ βίᾳ, καθ' ἣν καὶ ἐπὶ τῶν ἀψύχων λέγομεν, εἴρηται· οὐ μὴν ἀλλ' εἴ τις προσθῇ τὸ ἐν τῷ διορισμῷ προσκείμενον, κἀκεῖ λύεται τὸ λεχθέν [*EE* ii,8, 1224b2–7]. The codices have ὅτι μὲν οὖν δοκοῦσιν οὗτοι μόνοι βίᾳ καὶ ἄκοντες ποιεῖν κτλ. Most commentators acknowledge that μόνοι in line 3 cannot be right: Aristotle presents no argument to the effect that the ἐγκρατής and the ἀκρατής *alone* act under force. Harris Rackham [*Aristotle: The Athenian Constitution, the Eudemian Ethics, On Virtues and Vices* (Cambridge, MA/London: Harvard University Press/William Heinemann, 1981), 276] suggests replacing μόνοι with μόνον and I have adopted this solution, as reflected in the translation ("these seem to act only due to force and involuntarily"). The μόνον can also be understood as picking up on the argument at *EE* ii,7, 1223b5–17, where Aristotle also puts both the ἐγκρατής and the ἀκρατής in the "forced and involuntary" column (*only*), thereby generating contradiction with the immediately preceding arguments (*EE* ii,7, 1223a29–b3) to the effect that all action according to desire is voluntary.

ated, on the other, such things as, generation allowed to proceed regularly, happen to us, such as greying and old age and other [35] such things. So that each acts *not* according to nature and, simply speaking, *according* to nature, although not the same nature. The puzzles then about the incontinent and continent man—about whether both or one of them act due to force, so that, acting either not voluntarily or at the same time due to force *and* voluntarily, supposing that force is involuntary, they act at the same time voluntarily and involuntarily [1225a1]—how these are to be addressed is reasonably clear from what has been said.[7]

(c) [i] In another way, too, men are said to act due to force and to be compelled to act, without any disagreement between reason and appetite in them, that is, when they do what they consider both painful and bad, [5] but should they not do it, there would be lashings or chains or deaths. For they say that they acted having been compelled. Or is that not right but all do the thing itself voluntarily? For they had it in them not to act and to endure the alternative affliction.

[ii] Moreover, perhaps someone might say that, of these acts, some are voluntary, some not. For of the things that depend on a man [10] whether they come about or not, those which he does without willing them he always does voluntarily and not due to force; but those that do not depend on him, he in a sense does due to force but not simply speaking, for he does not choose that itself which he does but he does choose the end for which it is done (since also among these there is a certain difference).

[iii] For, if in order not to be seized someone groping about were to slay another, [15] it would be ridiculous if he were to say that he acted due to force, that is, that he was compelled, but there must always be some greater and more painful evil which will befall the one not acting (for in this way one *is* compelled and acts not due to force, or not by nature, when he does something evil for the sake of good, or for the sake of release from some greater evil); in any case, he acts involuntarily, for these things do not depend upon him.[8] So, [20]

---

7 αἱ μὲν οὖν περὶ τὸν ἀκρατῆ καὶ ἐγκρατῆ ἀπορίαι—περὶ τοῦ βίᾳ πράττειν ἢ ἀμφοτέρους ἢ τὸν ἕτερον, ὥστε ἢ μὴ ἑκόντας ἢ ἅμα βίᾳ καὶ ἑκόντας, εἰ δὲ τὸ βίᾳ ἀκούσιον, ἅμα ἑκόντας καὶ ἄκοντας πράττειν—σχεδὸν δὲ ἐκ τῶν εἰρημένων δῆλον ἡμῖν ὡς ἀπαντητέον [*EE* ii,8, 1224b36–1225a1]. This is basically the Susemihl text, although I have repunctuated it and eliminated his conjectured αὖται in line 37 as unnecessary.

8 This involves repunctuation of 1225a14–19, as follows: εἰ γὰρ ἵνα μὴ λάβῃ ψηλαφῶν ἀποκτείνοι, γελοῖος ἂν εἴη, εἰ λέγοι ὅτι βίᾳ καὶ ἀναγκαζόμενος, ἀλλὰ δεῖ μεῖζον κακὸν καὶ λυπηρότερον εἶναι, ὃ πείσεται μὴ ποιήσας (οὕτω γὰρ ἀναγκαζόμενος καὶ μὴ βίᾳ πράξει, ἢ οὐ φύσει, ὅταν κακὸν ἀγαθοῦ ἕνεκα ἢ

many regard love and some outbursts of aggression—that is, natural things—as involuntary because stronger even than nature; these admit of forgiveness as they are things by nature capable of forcing nature.

[iv] A man would seem *more* to act from force and involuntarily if he acts in order not to experience strong than in order not to experience light pain, and if in order not to experience pain generally than in order [25] not to take pleasure.[9] For that which depends on him—and everything comes down ultimately to this—is the following: what his nature is able to bear. What it cannot bear, nor pertains by nature to his appetite or reason, does not depend on him. Therefore those who are inspired and prophesy, although they perform a work of reason, even still we do not say that it depends on them not to say what they said, [30] not to do what they did. Nor do they act due to desire. So, some thoughts and affections—or the acts performed according to such thoughts and reasonings—also do not depend on us, but, as Philolaus said, some arguments are stronger than we are.

So, if the voluntary and the involuntary have to be considered also with respect to that which is due to force, [35] let it be defined thus. Those especially impeding the voluntary ... acting as if due to force but voluntarily ....[10]

IV. The Constituents of Action

[*EE* ii,9] Since this argument is finished and the voluntary is not defined by either appetite or choice, all that is left [1225b1] as defining characteristic is 'that which is according to thought.' The voluntary, therefore, seems to be the contrary of the involuntary and one's having known either 'whom,' 'by what means,' or 'to what end' (for sometimes one knows that that *was* one's father but acted not in order to kill but in order to save, as in the case of the daughters of Pelias, or that that there was a drink but containing [5] a love charm or wine and not hemlock) to one's being ignorant—*due* to ignorance and not *per accidens*—of 'whom,' 'by what means,' and 'what.' That which is due to ignorance ('what,' 'by what means,' and 'whom') is involuntary; its opposite is voluntary.

So, whatever a man, in whose power it is not to act, does not unknowingly

---

μείζονος κακοῦ ἀπολύσεως πράττῃ), καὶ ἄκων γε, οὐ γὰρ ἐφ' αὑτῷ ταῦτα. In line 1225a17, Susemihl puts the μὴ in square brackets; for reasons explained in chapter 3, section IV, I would leave the μὴ in.

9 Again, Susemihl puts μὴ in square brackets: καὶ ὅλως ἵνα μὴ ἀλγῇ ἢ ἵνα [μὴ] χαίρῃ [1225a24–25]; as argued in chapter 3, section IV, I think that its presence is consistent with Aristotle's general approach in the force and compulsion argument.

10 The text of the last few words in this chapter is corrupt.

and *due to himself*, this must needs be voluntary, for [10] this is what the voluntary is; but whatever he does unknowingly and *due to the ignorance* is involuntary. Since, however, 'to understand' or 'to know' has two meanings: one being 'to have' knowledge, the other 'to use' it, the man who has but does not use would in a sense justly, in a sense not justly, be called 'unknowing,' for instance, if it is *due to* negligence that he does not use it. Similarly, the man who does not even have knowledge would be blamed if he has not knowledge that was easy or necessary to have *due to* negligence [15] or pleasure or pain. So, these things must be added to the definition.

So, let this be our way of speaking, by way of definition, of the voluntary and the involuntary.

BIBLIOGRAPHY

Works by Ancient Commentators on Aristotle

Alexander of Aphrodisias. *In Aristotelis Analyticorum Priorum Librum I Commentarium* [*in APr.*]. Vol. 2.1 of *Commentaria in Aristotelem Graeca*. Edited by Maximilian Wallies, 1–418. Berlin: Reimer, 1883.

———. *Quaestiones* [*Quaest.*]. Vol. 2.2 <supplement> of *Commentaria in Aristotelem Graeca*. Edited by Ivo Bruns and I. Bruns, 1–163. Berlin: Reimer, 1892.

Anonymous. *In Ethica Nicomachea II–V commentaria* [*in EN*]. Vol. 20 of *Commentaria in Aristotelem Graeca*. Edited by Gustavus Heylbut, 122–255. Berlin: Reimer, 1892.

———. *In Ethica Nicomachea VII commentaria* [*in EN*]. Vol. 20 of *Commentaria in Aristotelem Graeca*. Edited by Gustavus Heylbut, 407–60. Berlin: Reimer, 1892.

Aspasius. *In Ethica Nicomachea quae supersunt commentaria* [*in EN*]. Vol. 19.1 of *Commentaria in Aristotelem Graeca*. Edited by Gustavus Heylbut, 1–186. Berlin: Reimer, 1889.

Heliodorus. *In Ethica Nicomachea paraphrasis* [*in EN*]. Vol. 19.2 of *Commentaria in Aristotelem Graeca*. Edited by Gustavus Heylbut, 1–233. Berlin: G. Reimer, 1889.

Philoponus [= John Philoponus]. *In Aristotelis Analytica Priora Librum I Commentarium* [*in APr.*]. Vol. 13.2 of *Commentaria in Aristotelem Graeca*. Edited by Maximilian Wallies, 1–386. Berlin: Reimer, 1905.

———. *In Aristotelis Physicorum Libros Octo Commentaria* [*in Ph.*]. Vol. 16–17 of *Commentaria in Aristotelem Graeca*. Edited by Hieronymus Vitelli, 1–495, 496–908. Berlin: Reimer, 1887–88.

Simplicius. *In Aristotelis Physicorum Libros Quattuor Priores Commentaria* [*in Ph.*]. Vol. 9 of *Commentaria in Aristotelem Graeca*. Edited by Hermannus Diels, 1–800. Berlin: Reimer, 1882.

Themistius. *In Aristotelis Physica Paraphrasis* [*in Ph.*]. Vol. 5.2 of *Commentaria in Aristotelem Graeca*. Edited by Henricus Schenkl, 1–236. Berlin: Reimer, 1900.

Works by Modern Authors (including editions and translations of works by Aristotle)

Ackrill, J. L. "Aristotle's Distinction between *energeia* and *kinēsis*." In *New Essays on Plato and Aristotle*, edited by R. Bambrough, 121–41. New York: Humanities Press, 1965.

Allan, Donald J. "The Practical Syllogism." In *Autour d'Aristote: Recueil d'études de philoso-*

phie ancienne et médiévale, offert à Monseigneur A. Mansion, 325–40. Louvain: Publications universitaires de Louvain, 1955.

Annas, Julia. "Plato and Aristotle on Friendship and Altruism." *Mind* 86 (1977): 532–54.

Anscombe, G. E. M. "Causality and Determination." In *Metaphysics and the Philosophy of Mind*. Vol. 3 of *Collected Philosophical Papers*, 133–47. Minneapolis/Oxford: University of Minnesota Press/Basil Blackwell, 1981.

———. *Intention*. Cambridge: Harvard University Press, 2000.

———. "Modern Moral Philosophy." In *Ethics, Religion and Politics*. Vol. 3 of *Collected Philosophical Papers*, 26–42. Minneapolis/Oxford: University of Minnesota Press/Basil Blackwell, 1981.

———. "Practical Truth." In *Human Life, Action and Ethics: Essays by G. E. M. Anscombe*, edited by Mary Geach and Luke Gormally, 149–58. Exeter: Imprint Academic, 2005.

———. "Thought and Action in Aristotle: What Is Practical Truth?" In *From Parmenides to Wittgenstein*. Vol. 1 of *Collected Philosophical Papers*, 66–77. Minneapolis/Oxford: University of Minnesota Press/Basil Blackwell, 1981.

Balme, D. M. "Aristotle's Use of Division and Differentiae." In *Philosophical Issues in Aristotle's Biology*, edited by Allan Gotthelf and James G. Lennox, 69–89. Cambridge: Cambridge University Press, 1987.

———. "The Snub." In *Philosophical Issues in Aristotle's Biology*, edited by Allan Gotthelf and James G. Lennox, 306–12. Cambridge: Cambridge University Press, 1987.

Barnes, Jonathan. "Aristotle and the Method of Ethics." *Revue Internationale de Philosophie* 34 (1980): 490–511.

———. "Logical Form and Logical Matter." In *Logica, mente e persona*, edited by A. Alberti, 7–119. Florence: Leo S. Olschki, 1990.

———. *Truth, etc.: Six Lectures on Ancient Philosophy*. Oxford: Clarendon, 2007.

———, ed. *The Complete Works of Aristotle: The Revised Oxford Translation*. Princeton: Princeton University Press, 1984.

———, translator and commentator. *Aristotle: Posterior Analytics*. Oxford: Clarendon, 1994.

Berti, Enrico. "Note sulla tradizione dei primi due libri della *Metafisica* di Aristotele." *Elenchos* 3 (1982): 5–38.

Bonitz, Hermann. *Aristotelis* Metaphysica: *Recognovit et enarravit Hermannus Bonitz*. Bonn: A. Marcus, 1848–49 [2 vols.].

Bonitz, Hermannus. *Index Aristotelicus*. Vol. 5 of *Aristotelis Opera*. Berlin: De Gruyter, 1961.

Broadie, Sarah. *Ethics with Aristotle*. New York: Oxford University Press, 1991.

———. "Nature and Craft in Aristotelian Teleology." In *Biologie, logique et metaphysique chez Aristote*, edited by Daniel Devereux and Pierre Pellegrin, 389–403. Paris: Éditions du Centre National de la Recherche Scientifique, 1990.

Brock, Stephen L. "Causality and Necessity in Thomas Aquinas." *Quaestio* 2 (2002): 217–40.

———. "Realistic Practical Truth." *Doctor Communis* (2008), 62–75.

Burnet, John. *The Ethics of Aristotle: Illustrated with essays and notes*. London: Longmans, Green, and Co., 1895.

Bywater, Ingram, ed. *Aristotelis Ethica Nicomachea*. Oxford: Clarendon, 1894.

Charles, David. *Aristotle's Philosophy of Action*. London: Duckworth, 1984.

Coope, Ursula. *Time for Aristotle: Physics IV.10–14*. Oxford: Clarendon, 2005.

Cooper, John M. "Aristotle on Natural Teleology." In *Language and Logos: Studies in Ancient Greek Philosophy*, edited by M. Schofield and M. Nussbaum, 197–222. Cambridge: Cambridge University Press, 1982.

———. "The *Magna Moralia* and Aristotle's Moral Philosophy." *American Journal of Philology* 94 (1973): 327–49.

———. Review of *The Aristotelian Ethics* by Anthony Kenny. *Noûs* 15 (1981): 381–92.

———, ed. *Plato: Complete Works*. Indianapolis/Cambridge: Hackett, 1997.

Crivelli, Paolo. *Aristotle on Truth*. Cambridge: Cambridge University Press, 2004.

Dancy, R. M. *Sense and Contradiction: A Study in Aristotle*. Dordrecht: D. Reidel, 1975.

Danto, Arthur C. "Basic Actions." *American Philosophical Quarterly* 2 (1965): 141–48.

De Groot, Jean Christensen. "Philoponus on *De anima* ii,5, *Physics* iii,3, and the Propagation of Light." *Phronesis* 18 (1983): 177–96.

Denniston, J. D. *The Greek Particles*. 2d ed. Oxford: Clarendon Press, 1987.

Deslauriers, Marguerite. *Aristotle on Definition*. Leiden: Brill, 2007.

Diels, H., and W. Kranz, eds. and trans. *Die Fragmente der Vorsokratiker*. 6th ed. Dublin/Zurich: Weidmann, 1951.

Dirlmeier, Franz. *Aristoteles* Eudemische Ethik. Berlin: Akademie, 1962.

———. *Aristoteles,* Magna Moralia. Berlin: Akademie, 1958.

———. *Aristoteles,* Nikomakische Ethik. Berlin: Akademie, 1967.

Dover, K. J. *Greek Homosexuality*. Cambridge: Harvard University Press, 1978.

Fine, Gail. *On Ideas: Aristotle's Criticism of Plato's Theory of Forms*. Oxford: Clarendon.

Finnis, John. "Allocating Risks and Suffering: Some Hidden Traps." *Cleveland State Law Review* 38 (1990): 193–207.

Flannery, Kevin L. *Acts Amid Precepts: The Aristotelian Logical Structure of Thomas Aquinas's Moral Theory*. Washington, DC / Edinburgh: The Catholic University of America Press / T & T Clark, 2001.

———. "Anscombe and Aristotle on Corrupt Minds." *Christian Bioethics* 14 (2008): 151–64.

———. "The Aristotelian First Principle of Practical Reason." *Thomist* 59 (1995): 441–64.

———. "Aristotle and Human Movements." *Nova et Vetera* 6 (2008): 113–38.

———. "Aristotle's Infallible Φρόνιμος." In *Studies in Practical Reason*, edited by Bradley Lewis. Washington, DC: The Catholic University of America Press, forthcoming.

———. "Being Truthful with (or Lying to) Others about Oneself." In *Thomas Aquinas and the Nicomachean Ethics*, edited by Tobias Hoffmann, Jörn Müller, and Matthias Perkams. Cambridge: Cambridge University Press, 2013.

———. "Capital Punishment and the Law." *Ave Maria Law Review* 5 (2008): 399–427.

———. "Due sensi della logica in Aristotele." In *L'Attualità di Aristotele*, edited by Stephen L. Brock, 73–84. Rome: Armando Editore, 2000.

———. "Ethical Force in Aristotle." *Vera Lex* 6 (2005): 147–62.

———. "Force and Compulsion in Aristotle's Ethics." In *Proceedings of the Boston Area Colloquium in Ancient Philosophy*, vol. 22 (2006), edited by John Cleary and Gary Gurtler, 41–60. Leiden: E. J. Brill, 2007.

———. "Homosexuality and Types of Dualism: A Platonico-Aristotelian Approach." *Gregorianum* 81 (2000): 335–72.

———. "Logic and Ontology in Alexander of Aphrodisias's Commentary on *Metaphysics*, book IV / Logica e significato nel commento di Alessandro di Afrodisia alla *Me-*

tafisica, libro IV." In *Alessandro di Afrodisia e la «Metafisica» di Aristotele*, edited by Giancarlo Movia, 117–52. Milan: Vita e Pensiero, 2003.

———. "Marriage, Mental Handicap, and Sexuality." *Studies in Christian Ethics* 17 (2004): 11–26.

———. "Moral Taxonomy and Moral Absolutes." In *Wisdom's Apprentice: Thomistic Essays in Honor of Lawrence Dewan, O.P.*, edited by Peter A. Kwasniewski, 237–59. Washington, DC: The Catholic University of America Press, 2007.

———. "Robinson's Łukasiewiczian *Republic* IV, 435–439." *Gregorianum* 77 (1996): 705–26.

———. *Ways into the Logic of Alexander of Aphrodisias*. Leiden: Brill, 1995.

Freeland, Cynthia A. "Aristotelian Actions." *Nous* 19 (1985): 397–414.

Gauthier, René-Antoine. *La morale d'Aristote*. Paris: Presses universitaires de France, 1958.

Gauthier, René-Antoine, and Jean Yves Jolif. *L'Éthique à Nicomaque: Introduction, traduction et commentaire*. 2d ed. Louvain-la-neuve: Éditions Peeters, 2002.

Geach, Peter. "History of the Corruptions of Logic." In *Logic Matters*, 44–61. Oxford: Basil Blackwell, 1972.

Gill, Kathleen. "On the Metaphysical Distinction between Processes and Events." *Canadian Journal of Philosophy* 23 (1993): 365–84.

Gill, Mary Louise. "Aristotle on Self-Motion." In *Self-Motion: From Aristotle to Newton*, edited by Mary Louise Gill and James G. Lennox, 15–34. Princeton: Princeton University Press, 1994.

———. "Aristotle's Distinction between Change and Activity." *Axiomates* 14 (2004): 3–22.

———. "Aristotle's Theory of Causal Action in *Physics* iii,3." *Phronesis* 25 (1980): 129–47.

Gould, John. *The Development of Plato's Ethics*. Cambridge: Cambridge University Press, 1955.

Gómez-Lobo, Alfonso. "Aristotle's Right Reason." In *Aristotle, Virtue and the Mean*, edited by Richard Bosley, Roger A. Shiner, and Janet D. Sisson, 15–34. Edmonton, Alberta: Academic Printing & Publishing, 1996.

Graeser, Andreas. "Aristotle on Practical Truth: Coherence vs. Correspondence?" *Bochumer philosophisches Jahrbuch für Antike und Mittelalter* 9 (2004): 191–200.

Graham, Daniel W. "States and Performances: Aristotle's Test." *Philosophical Quarterly* 30 (1980): 117–30.

Grant, Alexander. *The Ethics of Aristotle: Illustrated with notes and essays*. London: Longmans, Green, and Co., 1885.

Greenwood, L. H. G. *Aristotle: Nicomachean Ethics, Book Six, with Essays, Notes and Translation*. Cambridge: Cambridge University Press, 1909.

Hardie, R. P., and R. K. Gaye, trans. "Physica." In *The Works of Aristotle*, vol. 2, edited by W. D. Ross. Oxford: Clarendon, 1930.

Hardie, W. F. R. *Aristotle's Ethical Theory*. Oxford: Clarendon Press, 1968.

Heinaman, Robert. "Aristotle on Housebuilding." *History of Philosophy Quarterly* 2 (1985): 145–62.

———. "Compulsion and Voluntary Action in the *Eudemian Ethics*." *Nous* 22 (1988): 253–81.

———. "The *Eudemian Ethics* on Knowledge and Voluntary Action." *Phronesis* 30 (1986): 128–47.

———. "Frede and Patzig on Definition in *Metaphysics* Z.10 and 11." *Phronesis* 42 (1997): 283–98.

Hicks, R. D. *Aristotle, De Anima, with translation, introduction and notes.* Cambridge: Cambridge University Press, 1907.

Husik, Isaac. "Aristotle on the Law of Contradiction and the Basis of the Syllogism." *Mind* 15 (1906): 215–22.

Inciarte, Fernando. "Aristotle's Defense of the Principle of Non-contradiction." *Archiv für Geschichte der Philosophie* 76 (1994): 129–50.

Irwin, Terence H. "Aristotelian Actions." *Phronesis* 31 (1986): 68–89.

———. *Aristotle: Nicomachean Ethics.* Hackett: Indianapolis, Cambridge, 1985.

———. *Plato's Moral Theory: The Early and Middle Dialogues.* Oxford: Clarendon, 1977.

———. "Reason and Responsibility in Aristotle." In *Essays on Aristotle's Ethics*, edited by Amélie O. Rorty, 117–55. Berkeley: University of California Press, 1980.

———. Review of *The Aristotelian Ethics* and *Aristotle's Theory of the Will*, both by Anthony Kenny. *The Journal of Philosophy* 77, no. 6 (June 1980): 338–54.

———. "Vice and Reason." *Journal of Ethics* (2001): 73–97.

———. "Who Discovered the Will?" *Philosophical Perspectives* 6 (1992): 453–73.

Jackson, Henry, ed. *The Fifth Book of the* Nicomachean Ethics *of Aristotle.* Cambridge: Cambridge University Press, 1879.

———. "Eudemian Ethics Θ i, ii (H xiii, xiv), 1246a26–1248b7." *Journal of Philology* 32 (1913): 170–221.

Jaeger, Werner, ed. *Aristotelis Metaphysica.* Oxford Classical Texts. Oxford: Clarendon, 1957.

Kenny, Anthony. *The Aristotelian Ethics: A Study of the Relationship between the* Eudemian *and* Nicomachean Ethics *of Aristotle.* Oxford: Clarendon Press, 1978.

———. *Aristotle's Theory of the Will.* London: Duckworth, 1979.

Kontos, Pavlos. *Aristotle's Moral Realism Reconsidered: Phenomenological Ethics.* New York: Routledge, 2011.

Lear, Jonathan. *Aristotle and Logical Theory.* Cambridge: Cambridge University Press, 1980.

Le Blond, Jean Marie. "Aristotle on Definition." In *Articles on Aristotle: 3. Metaphysics*, edited by Jonathan Barnes, Malcolm Schofield, and Richard Sorabji, 63–79. London: Duckworth, 1979.

Łukasiewicz, Jan. "Aristotle on the Law of Contradiction." Translated by Jonathan Barnes. In *Articles on Aristotle, vol. 3: Metaphysics*, edited by J. Barnes, M. Schofield, and R. Sorabji, 50–62. London: Duckworth, 1975.

MacIntyre, Alasdair. *Dependent Rational Animals: Why Human Beings Need the Virtues.* Chicago: Open Court, 1999.

Maier, Heinrich. *Die Syllogistik des Aristoteles.* Leipzig: K. F. Koehler, 1896–1900.

Mansion, Augustin. "Étude critique sur le texte de la *Physique* d'Aristote (L.I-IV)." *Revue de philologie, de littérature et d'histoire anciennes* 47 (1923): 5–41.

Masqueray, Paul, editor and translator. *Sophocle.* Paris: Société d'Édition 'Les Belles Lettres', 1922–24.

Meyer, Susan Sauvé. *Aristotle on Moral Responsibility: Character and Cause.* Oxford: Blackwell, 1993.

Mignucci, Mario. *Aristotele, Gli analitici primi: Traduzione, introduzione, commento.* Naples: Loffredo, 1969.

Moraux, Paul. "Das Fragment VIII 1: Text und Interpretation." In *Untersuchungen zur*

Eudemischen Ethik: Akten des 5. Symposiums Aristotelicum (Oosterbeek, Niederlande, 21–29. August 1969), edited by Paul Moraux and Dieter Harlfinger, 253–84. Berlin: De Gruyter, 1971.

Mourelatos, Alexander P. D. "Aristotle's kinēsis/energeia Distinction: A Marginal Note on Kathleen Gill's Paper." Canadian Journal of Philosophy 23 (1993): 385–88.

Natali, Carlo. L'action efficace: Études sur la philosophie de l'action d'Aristote. Leuven: Peeters, 2004.

———. The Wisdom of Aristotle. Albany, NY: State University of New York Press, 2001.

Nussbaum, Martha. Aristotle's De motu animalium. Princeton: Princeton University Press, 1978.

Pakaluk, Michael. Aristotle's Nicomachean Ethics: An Introduction. Cambridge: Cambridge University Press, 2005.

———. "The Egalitarianism of the Eudemian Ethics." Classical Quarterly 48 (1998): 411–32.

———. "The Great Question of Practical Truth—and a Diminutive Answer." Acta Philosophica 19 (2010): 145–60.

Pauly, August Friedrich, Georg Wissowa, and others, eds. Paulys Real-Encyclopädie der classischen Altertumswissenschaft: Neue Bearbeitung. Stuttgart: Metzler, 1893.

Penner, Terry. "Verbs and the Identity of Actions: A Philosophical Exercise in the Interpretation of Aristotle." In Ryle: A Collection of Critical Essays, edited by O. Wood and G. Pitcher, 393–460. New York: Anchor Books (Doubleday), 1970.

Rackham, Harris. Aristotle: The Athenian Constitution, the Eudemian Ethics, On Virtues and Vices. Cambridge, MA/London: Harvard University Press/William Heinemann, 1981.

Radt, Stefan. Tragicorum graecorum fragmenta, vol. 3, Aeschylus. Göttingen: Vandenhoeck & Ruprecht, 1985.

Ramsauer, Gottfried, ed. Aristotelis Ethica Nicomachea: Edidit et commentario continuo instruxit. Leipzig: Teubner, 1878.

Richards, Herbert Paul. Aristotelica. London: G. Richards, 1915.

Robinson, Richard. "Plato's Separation of Reason and Desire." Phronesis 16 (1971): 38–48.

Ross, W. D., ed. Aristotle: De anima, Edited with Introduction and Commentary. Oxford: Clarendon, 1961.

———, ed. Aristotle's Metaphysics: A Revised Text with Introduction and Commentary. 2d ed. Oxford: Clarendon, 1953.

———, ed. Aristotle's Physics: A Revised Text with Introduction and Commentary. Oxford: Clarendon, 1936.

———, ed. Aristotle's Prior and Posterior Analytics. Oxford: Clarendon, 1949.

Rowe, C. J. The Eudemian and Nicomachean Ethics: A Study in the Development of Aristotle's Thought. In Proceedings of the Cambridge Philological Society, supplement no. 3. Cambridge: Cambridge Philological Society, 1971.

———. "A Reply to John Cooper on the Magna Moralia." American Journal of Philology 96 (1975): 160–72.

———. Review of Aristotle's Theory of the Will by A. Kenny. Journal of Hellenic Studies 102 (1982): 250–53.

Schiaparelli, Annamaria. "Aspetti della critica di Jan Lukasiewicz al principio aristotelico di non-contraddizione." Elenchos 15 (1994): 43–77.

Shields, Christopher. "Mind and Motion in Aristotle." In Self-Motion: From Aristotle to

Newton, edited by Mary Louise Gill and James G. Lennox, 117–33. Princeton: Princeton University Press, 1994.

———. "Unified Agency and *akrasia* in Plato's *Republic*." In Akrasia *in Ancient Philosophy: From Socrate to Plotinus*, edited by C. Bobonich and P. Destrée, 61–86. Leiden: Brill, 2007.

Siwek, Paulus, editor and translator. *Aristotelis Tractatus de Anima, Graece et Latine*. Rome: Desclée & C.ⁱ Editori Pontifici, 1965.

Smith, Robin, trans. *Aristotle: Prior Analytics*. Indianapolis: Hackett, 1989.

Solomon, J. *Ethica Eudemia*. In *The Works of Aristotle*, vol. 9.2, edited by W. D. Ross. Oxford: Clarendon, 1915.

Sorabji, Richard. *Animal Minds and Human Morals: The Origins of the Western Debate*. London: Duckworth, 1993.

Stewart, J. A. *Notes on the Nicomachean Ethics of Aristotle*. Oxford: Clarendon Press, 1892.

Susemihl, Franciscus, ed. *Aristotelis Ethica Eudemia (Eudemi Rhodii Ethica)*. Teubner: Leipzig, 1884.

———, ed. *Aristotelis quae feruntur Magna moralia*. Teubner: Leipzig, 1883.

Susemihl, Franciscus, and Otto Apelt, eds. *Aristotelis Ethica Nicomachea*. Teubner: Leipzig, 1912.

Taylor, C. C. W. *Aristotle:* Nicomachean Ethics*, books II–IV*. Oxford: Clarendon, 2006.

von Arnim, Hans. *Eudemische Ethik und Metaphysik*. Vienna: Hölder-Pichler-Tempsky, 1928.

Vuillemin-Diem, Gundrun, ed. *Metaphysica: Lib. I-XIV, Recensio et Translatio Guillelmi Moerbeka*. Leiden: E. J. Brill, 1995.

Waitz, Theodor, ed. *Aristotelis Organon Graece: Novis codicum auxiliis adiutus recognovit, scholiis ineditis et commentario instruxit Theodorus Waitz*. Leipzig: Hahn, 1844–46.

Walzer, R. R., and J. M. Mingay. *Aristotelis: Ethica Eudemia*. Oxford: Clarendon, 1991.

Waterlow, Sarah. *Nature, Change and Agency in Aristotle's* Physics: *A Philosophical Study*. Oxford: Clarendon, 1982.

Wedin, Michael V. "Aristotle and the Mind's Self-Motion." In *Self-Motion: From Aristotle to Newton*, edited by Mary Louise Gill and James G. Lennox, 81–116. Princeton: Princeton University Press, 1994.

Weidemann, Hermann. "Überlegungen zum Begriff der praktischen Wahrheit bei Aristoteles." *Zeitschrift für philosophische Forschung* 59 (2005): 345–57.

Wiggins, David. "Deliberation and Practical Reason." In *Essays on Aristotle's Ethics*, edited by Amélie O. Rorty. 29–51, 221–40. Berkeley: University of California Press, 1980.

Woods, Michael. *Aristotle: 'Eudemian Ethics,' books I, II and VIII*. 2d ed. Oxford: Clarendon, 1992.

INDEX OF NAMES

Achilles, xxvi, 211, 216
Ackrill, 65, 68, 291
Alexander of Aphrodisias, 2, 7n12, 9n16, 10–12n22, 16n30, 33n68, 102, 291
Allan, 177n4, 291
Annas, 260n35, 265n46, 292
Anonymous, 128, 291
Anscombe, xxix, 143n4, 242, 266, 292
Apelt, xxix–xxx, 19n39, 106n62, 146n9, 148n12, 157n29, 161n36, 204n58, 297
Aquinas, ix–xii, xx–xxi, 273, 277
Aspasius, 121, 124, 128, 146n9, 157n28, 158n32, 163n38, 195n41, 204n58, 291
Aspasius, 195n41

Balme, 75n2, 292
Barnes, xxixn8, 11n21, 16n31, 57n31, 75n2, 77n7, 92n38, 96n46, 105n60, 145n6, 292, 295
Berti, 194n39, 292
Bobonich, 248n8, 297
Bonitz, 66, 277–78, 284n4, 292
Bosley, 165n43, 294
Broadie, 181n11, 265n46, 292
Brock, 33n68, 143n4, 234n57, 292
Burnet, 107, 128, 194n39, 292
Bywater, xxixn3, xxx, 19n39, 26n57, 120n13, 146n9, 148n12, 157n29, 204n58, 277, 292

Charles, 26n57, 39n1, 41n3, 42n6, 47n15, 50n22, 65n44, 66n45, 151n23, 177n3, 243n4, 292
Coope, 252n18, 254n26, 292
Cooper, xxix, 97n50, 103n57, 181n11, 212n5, 293, 296
Crivelli, 124n21, 293

Dancy, 33n68, 293
Danto, 151n23, 293
De Groot, 186n21, 293
Denniston, 226n40, 293
Deslauriers, 75n2, 89n30, 293
Destrée, 248n8, 297
Diels, 100n53, 293
Dirlmeier, 72n1, 96n46, 98n51, 128, 217n17, 250n14, 284n4, 293
Dover, 269nn52–53, 293

Fine, 12n24, 254n24, 293
Finnis, 103n56, 293
Flannery, 1n2, 7n12, 9n16, 16n30, 24n52, 33n68, 77n9, 95n45, 103n56, 166n51, 169n57, 179n9, 200n51, 243n4, 248n8, 249n12, 255n28, 285n5, 293
Freeland, 65n44, 135n39, 294

Gauthier, xiv, xxx, 18–20, 21n42, 22n45, 23–25, 26n56, 96n48, 102, 112–13, 120nn13–14, 121n17, 123n20, 125–26n26, 128–29n30, 130n32, 135, 159n33, 177–78, 192n34, 194nn38–39, 202n56, 229n49, 261n37, 294
Gaye, 43n9
Geach, M., 234n57, 267n48
Geach, P., 21n44, 294
Gill, K., 65n44, 294, 296
Gill, M. L., 39n1, 45n12, 67n48, 178n7, 183n15, 190n28, 294, 297
Gormally, 234n57, 267n48, 292
Gotthelf, 75n2, 292
Gould, 249n12, 294
Gómez-Lobo, 165n43, 294
Graeser, 234n57, 294

299

Graham, 65n44, 294
Grant, 128, 158n31, 165n43, 195n41, 294
Greenwood, 19n39, 193–94n38, 294

Hardie, R. P., 43n9, 294
Hardie, W. F. R., 166n49, 294
Harlfinger, 217n17, 296
Heinaman, 65n44, 75n2, 76n4, 90n31, 186nn20–21, 294
Heliodorus, 125n23
Heylbut, 125n23, 157n28, 158n32, 166n49, 195n41, 291
Hicks, 186n20, 188n23, 295
Husik, 57n31, 295

Inciarte, 57n31, 295
Irwin, 50n20, 76n4, 77n11, 103n57, 105n60, 170n60, 192n33, 243n4, 249n12, 259n34, 295

Jackson, 96n46, 105n61, 217n17, 222n31, 223, 227n42, 295
Jaeger, xxixn1, 213n6, 215n13, 277–79, 295
Jolif, xxx, 18n37, 19n39, 21n42, 23nn49–50, 24n51, 96n48, 102n55, 120nn13–14, 121n17, 123n20, 125n23, 126n24, 126n26, 128n29, 129n30, 130n32, 135n38, 159n33, 177nn3–4, 192n34, 194nn38–39, 229n49, 294

Kenny, 80, 98n51, 103n57, 107, 115n2, 121n16, 131n33, 135n38, 148n12, 217n17, 293, 295–96
Kontos, 5n8, 207n1, 243n4, 295
Kranz, 100n53, 293

Lear, 38n80, 295
Le Blond, 75n2, 295
Lennox, 45n12, 75n2, 183n15, 292, 294, 297
Łukasiewicz, 33n68, 57n31, 179n9, 248n8, 249n12, 294–96

MacIntyre, 4n6, 295
Maier, 11n20, 35n75, 295
Mansion, 45n13, 177n4, 292, 295
Masqueray, 169n58, 295
Meyer, 72n1, 295
Mignucci, 11n20, 295
Mingay, xxixn2, 98n51, 222n29, 222n31, 224, 225n36, 232n53, 250n15, 251n17, 283n2, 284n3, 297
Moerbeke (William of), 277–78, 297

Moraux, 217n17, 295–96
Mourelatos, 65n44, 296

Natali, 65n44, 234n57, 296
Neoptolemus, 169n58
Nussbaum, xxix, 181n11, 293, 296

Odysseus, xxvi, 169n58, 211

Pakaluk, 103n57, 201n54, 234n57, 296
Pauly, 96n46, 296
Penner, 296
Philoctetes, 169n58
Pitcher, 296
Plato, xxvi, xxix–xxx, 12n24, 13n26, 14, 34nn70–71, 41n2, 46, 142, 154, 158n30, 177n4, 179, 192n33, 200, 202n55, 203, 207n1, 208, 210–12n5, 213n7, 215, 216n14, 219, 221n26, 238, 240–41, 248–49n13, 251n17, 252–54n24, 255n28, 275, 293

Ramsauer, 19n39, 26n57, 120n12, 193, 194n38, 296
Richards, 120n13, 128, 130–31, 296
Robinson, 179n9, 248n8, 249n12, 294, 296
Rorty, 76n4, 195n40, 295, 297
Ross, xxixn1, 12, 13n26, 19n39, 21n42, 37n79, 43nn8–9, 47n16, 77n7, 120n12, 128, 130, 150n20, 183nn13–14, 188n24, 213n6, 277–79, 280n1, 294, 296–97
Rowe, 97n50, 103n57, 296

Schiaparelli, 33n68, 57n31, 296
Shields, 183n15, 186n20, 248n8, 252n19, 296
Shiner, 165n43, 294
Sisson, 165n43, 294
Siwek, 188n23, 297
Smith, 11n20, 34n71, 35n75, 297
Socrates, xxvi–xxvii, 30, 126n24, 208–9, 211–12, 215–18, 220–22, 225, 227–28, 231, 238, 249, 255n28
Solomon, J., 280n1, 297
Sophocles, 169n58, 255n28
Sorabji, 4n6, 57n31, 75n2, 295, 297
Stewart, 19n39, 30n63, 128, 143n3, 158, 193, 194n38, 195n41, 297
Susemihl, xxix–xxx, 19n39, 97n49, 98n51, 106n62, 146n9, 148n12, 157n29, 161n36, 204n58, 222n31, 225n36, 232n53, 250n15, 283n2, 284n3, 287nn7–8, 288n9, 297

Taylor, 169n57, 297

von Arnim, 202n56, 297
Vuillemin-Diem, 297

Waitz, 13n26, 35n74, 297
Walzer, xxixn2, 98n51, 222n29, 222n31, 224, 225n36, 232n53, 250n15, 251n17, 283n2, 284n3, 297

Wedin, 183n15, 297
Weidemann, 234n57, 237n62, 297
Wiggins, 195n40, 297
Wissowa, 96n46, 296
Wood, 296
Woods, 76nn4, 6, 79, 81n18, 84n22, 90n32, 96n46, 98n51, 103n57, 217n17, 280n1, 283n2, 297

INDEX OF ARISTOTELIAN PASSAGES CITED

Note: Aristotle's works are listed in their traditional order, so that the "Bekker numbers" are in sequence. A title in {curly brackets} signifies that the work is of doubtful authenticity.

Categoriae [*Cat.*]
  vi: 4n5, xxviii
    4b20: 258
    5a1–2: 258n32
    5a7–8: 258n32
    5a39: 258
    5b2: 258
    5b3: 258
  viii
    10b26–27: 256n29

de Interpretatione [*Int.*]
  i
    16a12–16: 59n33
  vii
    17b14–16: 21n44

Analytica priora [*APr.*]
  i,1
    24a19–22: 36n77
    24b26–28: 21n44
  i,2
    25a14–17: 7n12
  i,6
    28a22–23: 7
  i,8
    30a6–14: 2, 7–9n15
    30a11–13: 9n17
    30a12–13: 14
  i,10: 11n19
    30b31–35: 11n19
  i,11: 11n19

i,21: 3
i,27
  43b17–21: 21n44
i,33
  47b21–26: 16
  47b27: 16
  47b29–32: 253n21
i,39
  49b6: 11n19
i,40
  49b11: 11n19
i,41: 9n17, 11, 14
  49b14–32: 11
  49b17: 9n17
  49b33–50a4: 10–11
  49b37–50a1: 11n20, 12
  50a1: 9n17
  50a3–4: 9n17
ii,2–4: 31n67
ii,15: 3, 31, 33, 37
  63b40–64a19: 31n66
  64b7–10: 32
ii,21: 33–34, 37
  67a14: 33
  67a16–19: 34n69
  67a21–26: 34n70
  67b10–11: 34n72
  67b12–13: 35n73, 36n78
  67b12–26: 35
  67b15: 36n78
  67b17–22: 36
ii,22: 36n76

Analytica posteriora [*APo.*]
  i,4: xxii, 144, 146
    73a34–b24: 144n5
    73b11–13: 145
    73b13–16: 145n6, 146n9
  i,10
    76b39–77a3: 10n18
  i,24
    85a24–25: 254
  ii,6
    92a21–23: 77n7
  ii,8: 89n30
  ii,19: 6
    100a12–13: 5
    100a13: 5n7
    100a14–b5: 5
    100a15: 6n11
    100b2: 6n11
    100b10: 6n10

Topica 14 [*Top.*]
  i,4: 89n30
  i,11
    104b19–24: 213n7
    104b24: 213n7
    104b24–28: 213n7
  ii,7
    113a27: 14
    113a31–32: 14
  vi,4–6: 89n30
  vi,6
    145a15–18: 177n4

Topica 14 [*Top.*] (cont.)
  vi,9
    147a29–b25: 77n7
  vi,10
    148a14–18: 14n28
  vii,3
    153a26–b24: 77n7

Sophistici Elenchi [*SE*]
  v
    166b28–166b36: 253n23
    166b32–33: 253n21
  xvii
    175b19–21: 253n22
  xxii: 2, 253
    178b36–179a1: 254n25
    178b36–179a10: 12, 13n27, 14

Physica [*Phys.*]
  i,7
    190b24–25: 150
    190b24–27: 151n21
  i,8
    191b22: 60
  ii,2
    194b35–195a1: 155n25
  ii,3
    194b34: 64n41
    194b35–195a3: 278
    194b36: 64n41
  ii,8
    199a30–32: 181
    199b26–28: 181
  iii,1
    201a29–201b2: 49n19
  iii,2
    202a9–12: 46
  iii,3: 39, 42–43, 45–51, 61, 63, 71
    202a14–15: 40
    202a18: 42, 48
    202a19–20: 42n5
    202a20–21: 43
    202a21–22: 43
    202a21–b5: 45
    202a22–23: 44n10
    202a22–24: 43n9
    202a22–36: 43

    202a22–b5: 43–44
    202a25: 44n10
    202a34–35: 46, 47n16
    202a35–36: 47
    202a36: 44nn10–11, 47
    202a36–b2: 44n10
    202a36–b5: 43
    202b4–5: 48
    202b5: 48n17
    202b5–14: 48
    202b5–22: 43
    202b6–8: 51
    202b8–9: 42n7
    202b9: 61n36
    202b12: 42
    202b13–14: 42n5
    202b14: 48n17
    202b14–15: 50n22
    202b14–22: 51
    202b16: 61n36
    202b18–20: 48n18
    202b19–21: 50n22
    202b21: 50n22
  iii,5
    204b4: 21n42
    204b10: 21n42
  iv,9
    217a5: 132n35
  iv,11
    219b21: 254
  v,1
    224a35: 150n20
    224b7: 127n27
    224b7–8: 41n3, 127n27, 132n36
    224b8–10: 132n36
  v,4: 122, 133–34, 150
    227b14–18: 133
    227b14–20: 127n27
    227b15–16: 133
    227b19: 48n17
    227b21–22: 150n19
    227b23: 151n23
    227b23–24: 122n18, 150n20
    227b25: 150
    227b27–30: 150n20
    227b29–30: 127n27, 134
    227b31–33: 151n22

    228a1–3: 151
    228a9: 152
    228a16–17: 152
    228b1–3: 150n20
    228b15–19: 153
    228b26: 150n20
    229a1–3: 153
    229a3–6: 153
    229a22–27: 132n36
  v,5
    229a22–27: 127n27
    229a25: 127n27
  vi,1
    231b30–232a1: 42n5
  vi,4
    234b10–20: 183n13
  vi,5
    236b3: 150n20
  vi,7: 70
  vii,1
    242b71–72: 46n14
  viii: 40
  viii,5: xxv, 42n4, 52, 54–56, 175, 182
    256b7–27: 56n29
    256b27–34: 54
    256b27–257a14: 55n28
    256b33–34: 55n27
    256b34: 54
    256b34–257a3: 54n25
    257a3–6: 55n27
    257a7: 56
    257a11: 55n28
    257a12–14: 42n4, 56
    257a33–b1: 183n13
    258a18–21: 183n15
    258a18–22: 182, 183nn12, 15
    258a21–22: 183n15

de Anima [*de An.*]
  i,1
    402b15: 60n34, 127n27
  i,5
    411a4: 127n27
  ii,4
    415a20: 60n34
    415a20–22: 127n27
  ii,5: xxv, 175, 186, 191, 194

Index of Aristotelian Passages Cited

416b35: 186
417a4: 186
417a9: 187, 189
417a12–14: 63n39
417a18–20: 187
417b3: 190
417b3–4: 198
417b6–7: 191
417b8–9: 186n20, 190
417b9–10: 189
417b10: 188n24
417b11: 189
417b12–13: 189
417b15: 190
417b16: 188n23, 190
417b18: 188n24
417b19: 188n24
417b2–28: 187–88n24
417b22–23: 193n35
417b22–24: 199
417b23: 190
417b24: 190
417b26: 188n24
ii,6
    418a12: 127n27
ii,8
    419b18–22: 91n35
ii,9
    432b5: 191n30
ii,10
    433a22–25: 191n30
iii,2
    426a2–3: 57n30
    426a2–6: 62n38
    426a12: 61n35
    426a15–19: 42n7, 61
    426a17–18: 61n35
    427a4–5: 61n36
    427a8–9: 61
iii,3
    428a13: 127n27
    428b25: 127n27
iii,4: xvi, 63n39
    429a13–15: 62n38, 188n25
    429a14–15: 62n38
    429a17–18: 57n30
    429b24–25: 62n38, 188n25
iii,5: 63n39
    430a23–25: 63n39

iii,6
    430a26: 127n27
iii,9
    432b3–7: 91n37
    432b5–7: 16n32
    432b26–29: 25n53
    433a1–3: 26n57
iii,10
    433a23–25: 91n37
iii,11: 18n34
    434a5–7: 20n40
    434a5–15: 16n32, 29n60
    434a16: 25n53
    434a17–19: 21n44
    434a18–19: 24n51

de Insomnias [*Insomnia.*]
    461b5–7: 214n9

de Motu animalium [*MA*]: xxix
    vii: 2n4, 18n34, 28
    701a15–16: 23n50, 29n61
    701a26–28: 24
    701a29–b1: 29

de Generatione Animalium [*GA*]
i,19
    726b22ff: 167n53

{*Mechanica*} [{*Mech.*}]
    proem.
    847b15–16: 106n62

Metaphysica [*Metaph.*]
i,1: 3–4, 7, 10, 18, 191
    980a21–26: 65n42
i,2
    982b20–21: 65n42
ii,1
    993b20–21: 194n39
    993b28–31: 80n15
iv: 57, 59
iv,3: 283n2
    1005b19–20: 57, 77n10, 79, 247
    1005b19–22: 58
iv,4: xvi, 32, 40
    1006a21: 33

    1006b7–10: 62n37
    1008b14–15: 247
    1008b15–17: 247
iv,6
    1011b13–14: 58n32
iv,7
    1011b26–27: 124
    1011b26–28: 227n43
iv,4
    1008b14–15: 59
v,2
    1013b1: 64n41, 278
    1013b34–1014a1: 145, 146n9
v,6: 144n5
v,7
    1017a31–35: 227n43
v,12
    1019a15–20: 67
v,13: 241, 258
    1020a7–8: 257
    1020a14–17: 257
    1020a26–28: 257
    1020a28–32: 257
    1020a31: 258
v,16
    1021b14–24: 243
v,18: 144n5
v,29: xxvi–xxvii, 199n50, 208–12, 214–17, 219–20, 228–29, 239, 255n28, 267n49, 275
    1024b23: 214
    1024b26–28: 227n43
    1024b27: 213, 215
    1024b31–32: 213n6
    1024b32: 213n7
    1024b32–34: 213n7
    1025a1–13: 169n58
    1025a2–3: 220
    1025a2–4: 215, 228n45
    1025a3: 230n50
    1025a5–6: 215
    1025a6–7: 215
    1025a8: 229, 235
    1025a9: 215n13, 221n27
    1025a9–13: 216n14
v,30: 144n5, 146
    1025a16: 146

***Metaphysica* [*Metaph.*]** *(cont.)*
    1025a25–27: 102
    1025a25–30: 146
    1025a28–30: 146
  vi,2
    1026b14–21: 254n26
    1026b16–18: 253n21
  vi,4
    1027b18–34: 59n33
  vii,4
    1029b13: 21n42
    1030a17–27: 256n29
  vii,7
    1032a25–b30: 202n56
  vii,10
    1035b24–25: 167n53
  vii,12: 89n30
  viii,1
    1042a13–21: 89n30
  viii, 2
    1043a19–21: 89n30
  viii,3
    1043b23–32: 213n7
  viii,5
    1044b30–34: 188n23
  viii,6: 89n30
  ix,2
    1046b4: 54n26
  ix,6: xvi, xxiv–xxv, 40,
    42n4, 65, 68, 139, 174,
    177–79, 184–85, 189
    1048b18: 278
    1048b18–23: 175, 177,
      178n5
    1048b18–35: 63, 64nn40–
      41, 65, 67, 175,
      277–79
    1048b19: 67n49
    1048b19–20: 278
    1048b20: 66, 278
    1048b21: 278
    1048b22: 278
    1048b23: 278
    1048b23–24: 176,
      279
    1048b26–2: 68n52
    1048b28: 200n52
    1048b29–30: 176
    1048b30–33: 176

    1048b33–34: 176
    1048b34: 67
  ix,8: xxv, 67, 175, 182, 184
    1049b5: 68n51
    1049b5–10: 184
    1049b8: 184
    1049b8–10: 190
    1049b10: 189
    1049b11: 184
    1050a4: 67, 185
    1050a7–8: 67
    1050a14: 67
    1050a21–23: 185
    1050a23–1050a29: 67
    1050a24: 67n49
    1050a26–27: 185n18
    1050a28–30: 185
    1050a34: 185
    1050a34–b2: 185
    1050b1: 190
  ix,10
    1051b6–9: 237n63
  xiii,2: 14n29
  xiii,3
    1078a14–21: 10n18

***Ethica Nicomachea* [*EN*]**
103n57
  i 200
  i,1
    1094a1–3: 179
    1094a6–16: 180
    1094a14–16: 150
    1094b19: 238
  i,2: 195
    1094a18–19: 195,
      196n42
    1094a18–22: 195n41
    1094a22–24: 164n40
    1094a27–28: 195n41
    1094a28–b3: 180
    1094b6: 195n41
    1094b6–7: 197n46
    1094b7: 158n30
    1094b11: 195n41
    1094b23–25: 238
  i,3
    1094b11–27: 1n1,
      165n46

  i,4
    1095a30–b3: 1n1, 165n46
    1095b4–8: 143n3
  i,6
    1096b13–14: 65n42
    1096b18–19: 195n41
  i,7
    1098a7–18: 231n52
    1098a26–b8: 1n1,
      165n46
    1098a33–b3: 143n3
  i,8
    1099a11–15: 202n55
    1099a11–16: 204
  i,10
    1101a14–16: 268n50
  i,13
    1102a5: 268n50
  ii: 165
  ii,2
    1103b34–1104a10: 1n1,
      165n46
  ii,3
    1104b14: 165n48
    1105a3–4: 165n48
  ii,4
    1105a28–33: 155n25
    1105a30–33: 164n41
    1105b5–12: 149
  ii,6: xxiv, 142, 166–67, 169,
    174
    1106a26–32: 163n39
    1106b14: 171n63
    1106b15–16: 163
    1106b16: 165n48
    1106b24: 165n48
    1106b27–33: 166
    1106b28: 164
    1106b6–7: 163
    1107a4: 165n48
    1107a8–9: 165n48, 167
    1107a8–15: 166n50
    1107a11: 166n49
    1107a14–15: 166, 236
    1107a15–17: 168n54
  ii,7
    1107a33–b4: 238
    1108a19–23: 216n16
    1108a31: 165n48

Index of Aristotelian Passages Cited

ii,8
 1108b18–19: 165n48
ii,9: 164n40
 1109a14–26: 237n64
 1109a23: 165n48
 1109b1–7: 164
 1109b20–26: 1n1, 165n46
iii: 176
iii,1: xvii, xix–xx, 71, 94,
  101–4, 106, 111–13,
  115–22, 124, 132–34,
  272
 1109b30: 165n48
 1109b31–32: 107
 1109b35–1110a14: 101
 1110a2–3: 101
 1110a8–12: 77n8
 1110a9–10: 103
 1110a12–14: 103
 1110a13–14: 103
 1110a15–18: 151n23
 1110a19–23: 166n49
 1110a24–26: 107
 1110b18: 115
 1110b18–1111a2: 114
 1110b19–20: 115
 1110b22–23: 136
 1110b23: 115n2
 1110b26: 106n64
 1110b33: 128
 1110b33–1111a1: 120–21,
  127–31
 1111a3: 118
 1111a3–5: 149n17
 1111a3–6: 119n10, 120n14,
  128n28, 131
 1111a3–21: 113
 1111a4: 112, 128, 129n31,
  133n37
 1111a5: 135, 136n41
 1111a6 :136–37
 1111a6–7: 122
 1111a6–8: 135
 1111a7–8: 132
 1111a8: 120n13, 125
 1111a8–11: 120n13, 124
 1111a9: 120n12
 1111a10–11: 126n25,
  148

 1111a11–12: 127n27
 1111a12–13: 134
 1111a15–17: 130
 1111a16: 120, 128, 131
 1111a18: 120, 128, 131,
  133n37, 140
 1111a18–19: 112, 120n13,
  130, 131n33, 145,
  149, 154, 168
 1111a19–21: 136
 1111a24: 120, 128
 1111a25–26: 85
 1111b1–2: 165n48
iii,2: 106, 246
 1111b6–8: 215
 1111b14: 244n5
 1118a18–26: 265n44
iii,3: 177–78
 1112b17–19: 150, 153
 1112b31–33: 177
 1112b32–33: 196n43
 1112b33: 177n3
 1113a9–12: 215
iii,4: 141, 157n28, 162–63
 1113a13–31: 158n32
 1113a14–26: 161
 1113a17–18: 162
 1113a25: 161n36
 1113a25–29: 162
 1113a29: 161n36
 1113a33: 163, 191n31, 243,
  261n37
iii,5
 1113b33–1114a3: 116n6
 1114b26–30: 146n9
 1114b7: 161n36
 1114b27: 146n9
iii,10
 1118a23–26: 245
 1118a32–b1: 245
iii,11
 1119a1–3: 245
 1119a1–4: 266
 1119a4–5: 245
iii,12
 1119a27–32: 266
 1119a32–33: 266
iv,1
 1121b23–24: 167n52

iv,2
 1122a25–26: 123n20
 1122b23–26: 123n20
iv,3
 1124b30–31: 216n16
iv,7: 169, 255n28
 1127a22–23: 216n16
 1127a28–30: 169nn56–57
 1127b14–17: 215n10
 1127b16: 255n28
 1127b22–26: 216n16
v: 103–4, 147n11
v–vii: 119
v,4
 1132a9: 165n48
v,8: xxii, 103–4, 107–8, 113,
  116n4, 119, 131–32,
  134–35, 140–41,
  147–48
 1135a23: 103
 1135a23–28: 148, 153–54,
  160
 1135a24: 148n12
 1135a24–28: 148n12
 1135a25: 119, 127n27,
  131–32
 1135a26: 117n7, 148
 1135a27–28: 104
 1135a28–30: 132
 1135a31: 104
 1135b2–8: 155n25, 268n51
 1135b4–6: 149
 1135b7–8: 149
 1135b8: 104
 1135b8–11: 104
 1135b11: 105n58
 1135b11ff: 105
 1135b12: 105n58
 1135b13: 119, 131
 1135b13–16: 135
 1135b14–16: 132, 131n33
 1135b15–16: 119
 1135b16: 105n58
 1135b17: 105
 1135b17–18: 105
 1135b18: 105
 1135b18–19: 105n59, 116n4
 1135b19: 105
 1135b20: 106

308 Index of Aristotelian Passages Cited

Ethica Nicomachea [EN]
103n57 *(cont.)*
   1135b25–27: 106n63
   1136a5–9: 107–8n67,
      114n1
   1136a8–9: 107
v,11
   1138b5–13: 249
vi: xxvii, 175, 191, 194, 208,
   235
vi,1
   1138b21–25: 236
   1138b22–23: 165n43
   1139a4–5: 223
   1139a12: 222n30, 236
vi,2: 176, 191n29, 193, 194n39,
   236
   1139a15–17: 236
   1139a19,31: 192
   1139a20: 206
   1139a21–31: 237n62
   1139a24: 237
   1139a26–29: 169n58
   1139a26–31: 237
   1139a35–36: 236
   1139a35–b4: 193
   1139b1: 193–94, 196
   1139b1–4: 194
   1139b2–3: 194
   1139b3: 195
   1139b4: 198
vi,3
   1139b14–17: 169n58
vi,4: 192, 193n35
   1140a2–6: 192–93
   1140a5: 193–94
   1140a10–12: 194
   1140b2: 192
vi,5: 176, 178, 197, 242
   1140a25–27: 235
   1140a25–28: 197
   1140a28–30: 197n44
   1140b3–4: 177n4
   1140b4–5: 176
   1140b4–7: 176
   1140b5: 197n46
   1140b6–7: 177
   1140b7–10: 197n45
   1140b7–11: 235n60

   1140b11: 197
   1140b11ff: 198
   1140b13: 198
   1140b13–16: 226n39
   1140b16–22: 198n48
   1140b19: 199
   1140b22–24: 219n20
vi,7: 2, 18, 31
   1141a20–33: 243n1
   1141b8: 18
   1141b14–16: 31
   1141b14–23: 221n28
   1141b18–21: 18n36
   1141b20: 19
   1141b21–23: 221n28
vi,8: 5
   1141a25: 5n8
   1141b27–28: 5n8
   1142a23–29: 6n9
   1142a25: 6n10
   1142a26: 6n10
   1142a29: 6n11
   1142a30: 6n9
vi,9: 246
   1142b18: 96n48
   1142b18–20: 246n6
vi,11
   1143b3: 19n39
vi,12
   1143b33–35: 191n32
   1144a27–29: 243
   1144a31–b1: 243n2
   1144a36–37: 207n1
vi,13
   1144b28–30: 218n19
   1145a6: 195n40
   1145a6–11: 191n32
vii: 158n32
vii,1
   1145b12–14: 246n7
vii,2: 220–21
   1145b21–24: 221n26
   1145b31–1146a4: 221
   1146a4–5: 221
   1146a5–7: 221n27
   1146a7–9: 221
   1146a8–9: 207n1, 243n2
   1146a16–21: 157n29
   1146a18–21: 169n58

vii,3: 2, 21, 25, 27, 29–30, 244
   1146b19–24: 244n5
   1146b22–23: 244
   1146b23: 264, 266
   1146b24–35: 21n42
   1146b35–1147a10: 21,
      22nn46–47, 27
   1147a1: 22
   1147a2–3: 21n44
   1147a3: 22n45
   1147a4: 21n44
   1147a4–5: 22n45
   1147a5: 22n45, 24
   1147a6: 21n44
   1147a6–7: 24
   1147a8: 22
   1147a10–24: 21n42, 25
   1147a17–22: 26
   1147a20: 21n42
   1147a24: 21n42, 26
   1147a24–b10: 21n42
   1147a24–b9: 18
   1147a24–b19: 25
   1147a25–26: 30n62
   1147a25–35: 26
   1147a28: 26n56
   1147a29: 27
   1147a32–33: 26n57
   1147a32–34: 28n58
   1147a33: 26n57
   1147a33–34: 26n57
   1147a35: 26n57
   1147b8–9: 21n42
   1147b9: 28, 30
   1147b9–10: 19n39, 22n47,
      30n62
   1147b10–19: 21n42
   1147b12: 21n42
   1147b13–17: 30n63, 221n26
   1147b14: 28, 30
   1147b17: 30
vii,3
   1147a28: 23n50
vii,4: 200
   1148a13–17: 246n7
vii,5: 107, 107n65, 268,
   269n53
   1148b15ff: 107
   1148b18: 269

Index of Aristotelian Passages Cited

1148b20–21: 107n65
1148b25–27: 107n65, 269
1148b27: 269
1148b29: 269
1148b30–31: 269
1148b32–33: 269n53
1149a20: 270
1149a21–22: 270n54
vii,6
  1149a24–1150a8: 106n63
  1149b27–1150a8: 265n44
vii,8
  1150b31–34: 245
  1150b36: 245
  1151a3–5: 246
  1151a11–17: 268
  1151a20–26: 244n5
  1151a23: 265–66
  1151a26–27: 265
vii,9: xxiii, 141, 156, 161–62
  1151a29–b4: 157
  1151a32–33: 157n29
  1151a35–b1: 159n33
  1151a35–b2: 156, 158, 230n51
  1151a35–b3: 159–60, 268n51
  1151a35–b4: 158n32
  1151b2: 157n29
  1151b3–4: 158
  1151b4: 157n29
  1151b17–22: 157n29
vii,11
  1152b13: 205n59
vii,11–13: 200
vii,12
  1152b35: 204n58
  1152b35–1153a2: 204
  1152b36–1153a1: 204n58
  1153a1: 204n58
  1153a7–10: 201
  1153a11: 201n53
  1153a13: 205n59
  1153a29–34: 243
viii,1
  1155b2–4: 163n38
viii,8
  1159a17–21: 156n26
  1159b19–23: 163n38

ix: xxviii
ix,2: xxiv, 141–42, 165–66, 169–71
  1164b23: 170n59
  1164b25–27: 164, 170
  1164b28–29: 170
  1164b30: 170n59
  1164b30–31: 170
  1164b31–32: 170
  1164b34–65a1: 164, 170
  1165a1–2: 170
  1165a7–10: 171
  1165a10–12: 171
  1165a12–13: 165
  1165a12–14: 165n45, 171
  1165a13: 165n48
  1165a33–35: 171n61
ix,4: 242, 259–62, 264
  1166a1–b2: 260n36
  1166a6–8: 260n35
  1166a10–13: 261
  1166a11–12: 260
  1166a12–13: 243n3
  1166a14–19: 225n35
  1166a17–21: 262
  1166a17–23: 262n40
  1166a24–26: 229n49, 260
  1166b2–29: 260n36
  1166b3–4: 260, 261n39
  1166b7–9: 259
  1166b11–13: 259
  1166b13–18: 262
  1166b15–16: 260
  1166b21–22: 264
  1166b22–25: 263
  1166b24–25: 264
ix,8
  1168b28–34: 225n35
x,1
  1172a34: 165n47
  1172a34–35: 165n48
x,1–5: 200
x,4: 201
  1174a20–21: 68n50
  1174b2–9: 69
  1174b23–26: 201
  1174b33: 201

x,5: 200
  1175a22–30: 200
  1175b3–6: 202
  1175b16–17: 202
  1176a15–26: 202n55
x,6
  1176b24–27: 243n3
x,7
  1177a12: 268n50
  1177a21–22: 202
  1178a2–3: 225n35

{*Magna Moralia*} [{*MM*}]:
xxix, 97n50
  i[1],12–16: 72n1
i,15
  1188b19–21: 97
i,33
  1195a16–18: 122n19
ii,6
  1201b11–13: 117n9
  1201b17–19: 117n9
  1201b24–1202a1: 117n9
  1202a1–7: 117n9

Ethica Eudemia [*EE*] 103n57
i,6
  1217a30–35: 197n46
i,7
  1217a35–46: 178n6
ii,1
  1219a38–39: 268n50
ii,3
  1221b18–26: 166n50
ii,4–6: 119
ii,6: xvii, xix, 73, 88–91, 109
  1222b19: 90
  1222b23: 90
  1222b24–25: 90
  1222b24–28: 90n33
  1222b25–28: 280n1
  1222b27–28: 280n1
  1222b29: 75
  1222b30: 106n62
  1222b34–37: 90n34
  1222b40: 106n62
  1223a5: 90
  1223b15–18: 106n62
ii,6–8: 84

Ethica Eudemia [*EE*] 103n57 (cont.)
  ii,6–9: xvii, 72, 74–75, 76n4, 80, 100–101, 103–4, 108, 155, 225, 272, 280
  ii,7: xvii–xix, 72–73, 75–76, 87
    1223a21: 75
    1223a23–28: 88
    1223a29–36: 76, 78, 84
    1223a29–b17: 76, 87–88
    1223a29–b3: 286n6
    1223a33–35: 78
    1223a36–b3: 76–78, 84, 87
    1223a37–38: 92n40
    1223b5–6: 80, 81n17, 82, 93n41
    1223b5–9: 88
    1223b5–10: 76–78, 87, 264n42
    1223b5–17: 286n6
    1223b9–10: 88
    1223b10: 77
    1223b10–17: 76–78, 88
    1223b12–14: 92n40
    1223b17: 77–78, 88, 264n42
    1223b18–19: 78
    1223b18–24: 78
    1223b18–28: 76, 87–88
    1223b19–21: 78
    1223b24–28: 79–80, 283n2
    1223b26–27: 79, 93n41
    1223b28: 79n12
    1223b28–29: 82
    1223b29: 76n5, 79, 81, 93n41
    1223b29–36: 76, 79–82, 89n30
    1223b31: 81n18
    1223b32–36: 93n41
    1223b35–36: 81n18
  ii,7–8: 72n1, 89n30, 108–9
  ii,8: xviii–xix, 72–73, 75–76n4, 80, 82–83, 86, 103–4
    1223b5–6: 95n44
    1223b38–1224a4: 82n19, 284n3
    1223b38–1224a7: 82
    1223b39–1224a2: 82
    1224a1: 82
    1224a2–3: 82
    1224a3–4: 82
    1224a4–7: 75n3
    1224a8–9: 84n22
    1224a8–10: 83n20, 284n4
    1224a8–1224b15: 83
    1224a8–1225a33: 83
    1224a9: 284n4
    1224a9–11: 84n22
    1224a10: 83n20
    1224a13–30: 84n22
    1224a13ff: 94
    1224a15–18: 97
    1224a19: 84
    1224a23–24: 285n5
    1224a23–30: 285n5
    1224a24: 285n5
    1224a24–25: 84, 92n40
    1224a30–36: 85n25
    1224a30–b15: 87
    1224a33–36: 92, 98
    1224a36: 92n40
    1224a36–38: 93
    1224a36–b2: 85n25
    1224a39–b1: 99
    1224b2–5: 85
    1224b2–7: 286n6
    1224b6: 284n4
    1224b7: 85
    1224b7–8: 98
    1224b8: 86n27
    1224b12: 86n27
    1224b13–14: 85, 102, 104
    1224b14–15: 85
    1224b15–17: 77n8
    1224b15–1225a1: 83, 85
    1224b16–21: 255n27
    1224b22: 86
    1224b23–24: 86
    1224b26–29: 86n28, 92
    1224b29–31: 84n21, 86, 93, 99n52
    1224b35–36: 87
    1224b36–1225a1: 87n29, 287n7
    1224b37: 287n7
    1225a2–6: 101
    1225a2–33: 92–94
    1225a2–1225a33: 83
    1225a3: 84
    1225a6: 94
    1225a7: 104
    1225a8–9: 95
    1225a10–11: 95n44
    1225a11: 95, 103
    1225a12: 95–96
    1225a12–13: 95, 103–4
    1225a13–14: 95
    1225a14–17: 96
    1225a14–19: 287n8
    1225a16–17: 97
    1225a17: 287n8
    1225a17–19: 97
    1225a19: 97
    1225a19–22: 97, 107
    1225a21: 106
    1225a22–25: 98
    1225a24–25: 98, 288n9
    1225a25: 98
    1225a26–27: 99
    1225a28: 100
  ii,9: xviii, xx, 73, 76, 100, 106, 111, 113, 115–16, 118–19, 131, 134, 147n11
    1225a36–b1: 284n4
    1225a37: 155n24
    1225b1–6: 122
    1225b1–8: 91
    1225b2: 119, 131–32
    1225b2–3: 135, 154
    1225b4–5: 136
    1225b5: 117, 160n35
    1225b5–6: 148n13
    1225b6: 117, 119, 131
    1225b7: 119, 131
    1225b8–16: 117
    1225b11–16: 91
    1225b14–16: 157n27
    1225b15–16: 106n64
    1225b17: 284n4
  ii,10: xxvii, 75, 210
    1227a18–30: 162n37

Index of Aristotelian Passages Cited

1227a18–31: 231, 232n53
1227a25–35: 202n56
1227a28–30: 162n37
1227a30: 203n57
1227a31–32: 203
ii,11: 75
   1227b19–38: 202n56
iii,2: 243n4
   1230a37: 243n4
   1231a6–17: 245
v: 235
vii,2
   1236a3–6: 235
vii,6: xxviii, 4n5, 247, 249, 254, 259–62, 264, 270
   1240a17: 250
   1240a23–30: 260n36
   1240a24–30: 250
   1240b4–5: 250
   1240b11–21: 251
   1240b11–28: 241, 250–51n17
   1240b13: 251
   1240b13–15: 252
   1240b15–21: 252, 259
   1240b17–18: 261
   1240b17–20: 260
   1240b18: 250n14, 252
   1240b19–20: 250n15, 263n41
   1240b21: 256, 263
   1240b21–28: 77n9, 241, 253
   1240b23–24: 255n28

1240b24–26: 241–42, 253, 256
1240b25–26: 256n30
1240b25–27: 259n33
1240b26–27: 260–62
1240b26–28: 241, 259
viii,1: xxvi, 207–9, 211, 216n14, 217n17, 218–20, 238
   1246a26–b4: 217, 228, 230
   1246a26–b19: 224
   1246a29–31: 146n9
   1246a37: 219n20
   1246a38: 219n22
   1246b2: 219
   1246b4–12: 217, 219, 228
   1246b9: 219, 232n53
   1246b12–19: 217, 220–22n31, 224, 228
   1246b15: 222n31
   1246b15–16: 223
   1246b16–17: 223
   1246b19: 224
   1246b19–20: 223n34
   1246b19–21: 224
   1246b19–22: 225n36
   1246b19–28: 217, 224, 228
   1246b21: 225n36
   1246b21–23: 225
   1246b22: 225n36
   1246b23–25: 224
   1246b24: 226
   1246b24–25: 226
   1246b25: 226n37

1246b25–6: 226n38
1246b25–28: 226
1246b26: 224
1246b28–36: 217, 226–27n42
1246b29: 220n25
1246b32–34: 222n29, 228
1246b32–36: 228
1246b33: 222
1246b36: 220n25
viii,1–3: 207n1

Politica [*Pol.*]
i,13
   1260a12: 20n41
   1260a15–16: 20n41
   1260a39–40: 20n41
iii,4
   1277a14–16: 243n1
iii,11
   1282a3–5: 20n41
iv,11
   1295a36–37: 268n50

Rhetorica [*Rhet.*]
i,9
   1366b7–11: 167n52
   1367b22–23: 243
i,13
   1374b4–10: 105n58
   1374b9–10: 105n58

Constitution of Athens [*Ath.*]
   42.3.3–5: 126n26

INDEX OF SUBJECTS

Note: The terms in this list that appear just in their transliterated Greek form are also typically left untranslated in the book; those English terms that are followed by a transliterated Greek word often appear in the book along with the Greek word.

action [*praxis*], xxvi, 63–69, 121, 130–31, 165–66, 258, 277–79; and making [*poiēsis*], 173–79, 192–97, 205–6; and movement [*kinēsis*], 173–79, 206

actualization [*energeia*], xv, 29–30, 42–52, 61–64, 67–68, 152–53, 184–86, 188–89, 200n52

aiming. *See* archery

akolastos, xxv, xxviii–xxix, 3, 37, 138, 202, 215nn10–11, 240, 242–46, 251n16, 264–70; *akratēs* and 243–47, 264–65, 268; choice [*prohairesis*] and, xxix, 204, 245–46, 264–67; *phronimos* and, 222–23; pleasure and, xxix, 204–5, 244–45, 264–65, 289; suicide and, 264

akratēs, xii, xviii, xxv, xxviii, 77–78, 81, 139, 202, 221, 240–42, 250–52, 254–59, 266–67, 270, 286n6; *akolastos* and, 243–47, 264–65, 268; anomalous, xxiii, 156–60, 162, 195n40; contradiction and, 17; *egkratēs* and, 85–88, 92–94, 98–99, 246–47, 255n27; *phronimos* and, 221–25, 246–47; pleasure and, 156, 244, 255n27, 265–70; practical syllogism and, 3, 21–30, 33–37

apparent good, xxiii, xxvii, 141, 157–63, 195n40, 209–10, 230–34, 274

archery (aiming), xxiv, 142, 163–69, 173–74, 179

choice [*prohairesis*], xviii, 75–76, 82–83, 114, 116, 157, 179, 199, 215, 244, 281–84, 288; *akolastos* and, xxix, 204, 244–46, 264–67; *phronimos* and, 220

circumstances [of human acts], ix, xii, xix–xxi, 1, 71–72, 110–13, 116–21, 129, 137, 272. *See also* constituents

city [*polis*]: xxvii, 170, 192, 206, 234, 243; craft and, xxv, 139–40, 174–76, 179–82; house versus, 252, 261

conscience, 117–18, 255

constituents [of human acts], xix–xxiii, 71–72, 100, 110–138, 140–41, 145, 147–50, 153–54, 160–61, 164, 167–68, 170, 172, 180, 237–38, 272, 288–89. *See also* circumstances

craft [*technē*], xxiv–xxv, 20n41, 67n49, 171n63, 274–75; city [*polis*] and, xxv, 139–40, 174–76, 179–82; *phronēsis* and, 192–93, 235–36

egkratēs, xviii, 78, 240, 246; *akratēs* and, 85–88, 92–94, 98–99, 246–47, 255n27; anomalous, 156–60, 162; pleasure and, 98–99, 159, 255n27, 285–86, 288; *phronimos* and, 246

ekthesis, xiv, 2, 7–15, 20

end, xxiii, 41–42, 63–69, 93, 95, 101–3, 150, 153–63, 172, 175–82, 184–86, 188–89, 201–2, 231–33, 287; as constituent of action, 112–13, 131–36, 141, 147–48, 154–64; of ends [*phronēsis* as], 149–50, 180, 192–97; means and, 158–63, 231–32, 278; per se and, 140–41, 147–48, 154–63; of seeing or thinking, 57, 63

force [*bia*] (as affecting the voluntary), xxvii–xxix, 71–110, 147–48, 172, 272, 282–88

freedom of the will (and universals), 190–91

313

Index of Subjects

Hippias minor (Plato), xxvi, 208–18, 220–22, 225, 227–28, 231, 239, 275

ignorance (as affecting the voluntary): xvii–xxii, 71–72, 91, 96n47, 100, 105–38, 147–48, 155–63, 171n62, 208–9, 211, 219–26, 232, 272, 288–89
involuntary. *See* force; ignorance

making [*poiēsis*], xxiv–xxv, 180–82, 274–75; action [*praxis*] and, 173–79, 192–97, 205–6
movement [*kinēsis*], x, xv–xvii, xxiv–xxv 75, 89n30, 110, 113, 127n27, 139–40, 162–63, 189–91, 271–73, 280–81; accidental quantity as, 257–58; action [*praxis*] and, 173–79, 206; actualization [*energeia*] and, 42–52, 152–53, 184–89; 200n52; conflicting, 202, 264; "physical" structure of, 39–70; self-movement, 182–86, 225; unity of, 132–34, 149–54

object: contrary or conflicting: 202–3, 247–48; of a discipline, 202n56; of a human act, ix, xi, xiv, xvi–xvii, 7, 25, 29, 45, 47n15, 48–52, 55–57, 60–63, 112–13, 121n17, 127–34, 139, 145, 150, 160, 168–69, 173, 176, 272–73; pleasure and, 202–5; of a sense, 6, 40, 61, 186–90, 201

per accidens/per se, xi–xii, xxi–xxiii, xxvi, 115–18, 121–22, 125, 137, 139–72, 195n40, 204, 209–10, 217–20, 230–34, 240, 265, 268, 274–75, 285–86, 288
perception (or the perceptual), ix–x, xiii–xiv, 1–38, 59, 91, 110, 141–44, 146–47, 190–91; of "the auld triangle," 33–34; *ekthesis* and, 2, 7–15, 20; extended experience [*empeiria*] and, 4, 18–19, 20; object of, 6, 40, 61, 186–90, 201; of a particular triangle, 6–7, 33; pleasure and, 201, 205n59; terrain of the mind as, 15–18. *See also* object
per se. *See* per accidens/per se
phronēsis. See craft; *phronimos*

phronimos, 242–43, 275–76; *akolastos* and, 222–23; *akratēs* and, 221–25, 246–47; choice and, 220–221; *egkratēs* and, 246; *Eudemian Ethics viii,1* (as analyzed in), 217–28; human nature and, 229–34; pleasure and, 175, 197–99, 243; practical truth and, 234–38; self-consistent, 37–38; selfishness and, 242–43. *See also phronēsis; spoudaios*
pleasure, xxv–xxvi, 68–69, 94, 117, 164, 200–206, 273–75; *akolastos* and, xxix, 204–5, 244–45, 264–65; *akratēs* and, 156, 244, 255n27, 265–70; *egkratēs* and, 98–99, 159, 255n27, 285–86, 288; good and bad, 200–205; objects and, 202–5; pain and, 199n49; *phronimos* and, 175, 197–99, 243
practical syllogism, xiii–xiv, 1–3, 7, 12, 15, 17–30, 38, 59, 71, 116n5; *akratēs* and, 3, 21–30, 33–37
practical truth, xxvii, 191n31, 208, 229–30, 234–39, 267n48
principle of non-contradiction, xiv, xvi, xxviii, 3, 17–18, 30–38, 40, 55, 57–63, 70, 77–79, 213–24, 240, 247–48, 252, 271, 275, 283n2

seeing, xvi, 40, 57, 60–68, 176, 178, 185–90, 195n41, 279; double, xxvi–xxvii, 216n14, 218–19, 223–24, 227
spoudaios, 161, 240, 251–56, 259, 261, 265–66; near equivalent to *phronimos*, 191n31, 243, 246–47, 265. *See also phronimos*

thinking, xvi, 40, 57, 61–68, 100, 176, 185–91, 193n35, 195, 198, 279; practical, 15–16
Thomistic action theory, ix–xii

voluntary. *See* force; ignorance

will [*boulēsis*], 77–83, 91, 93, 95n44, 147, 158n32, 161, 191, 233, 280n1; the voluntary and, 77–78, 190–91

Action and Character according to Aristotle: The Logic of Moral Life was designed and typeset in Arno by Kachergis Book Design of Pittsboro, North Carolina. It was printed on 55-pound Nature's Natural and bound by Sheridan Books of Ann Arbor, Michigan.

www.ingramcontent.com/pod-product-compliance
Lightning Source LLC
Chambersburg PA
CBHW031405290426
44110CB00011B/266